LEBANON

ARE KNUDSEN
MICHAEL KERR

(*Editors*)

Lebanon

After the Cedar Revolution

OXFORD
UNIVERSITY PRESS

OXFORD
UNIVERSITY PRESS

Oxford University Press, Inc., publishes works that further
Oxford University's objective of excellence
in research, scholarship, and education.

Oxford New York
Auckland   Cape Town   Dar es Salaam   Hong Kong   Karachi
Kuala Lumpur   Madrid   Melbourne   Mexico City   Nairobi
New Delhi   Shanghai   Taipei   Toronto

With offices in
Argentina   Austria   Brazil   Chile   Czech Republic   France   Greece
Guatemala   Hungary   Italy   Japan   Poland   Portugal   Singapore
South Korea   Switzerland   Thailand   Turkey   Ukraine   Vietnam

Copyright © 2013 Are Knudsen and Michael Kerr

Published by Oxford University Press, Inc
198 Madison Avenue, New York, New York 10016

Published in the United Kingdom in 2013 by C. Hurst & Co. (Publishers) Ltd.

www.oup.com

Library of Congress Cataloging-in-Publication Data is available for this title
Knudsen, Are and Kerr, Michael
Lebanon
ISBN 9780199342969 (paperback)

1 3 5 7 9 8 6 4 2

Printed in India
on Acid-Free Paper

CONTENTS

v

CONTENTS

PART III

ENTREPRENEURS, STATESMEN AND MARTYRS

PART IV

TRUTH, COEXISTENCE AND JUSTICE

NOTE ON TRANSLITERATION

This book uses a simplified transliteration of Arabic proper names in accordance with what is commonly used in English literature (e.g. Rafik Hariri, Michel Aoun). The definite article (*al-*) has been omitted where it is not commonly used. All diacritics have been omitted (e.g. Shia instead of Shi'a).

ACKNOWLEDGEMENTS

This volume is the outcome of a research project and an international workshop examining 'Conflict and Coexistence in Lebanon', generously supported by a research grant from the Norwegian Ministry of Foreign Affairs' (MFA) programme on 'Peace and Reconciliation' (LBN-09/003). We would like to thank the participants for their spirited contributions to the workshop (Bergen, 23–4 September 2010) and insightful analyses of the tumultuous post-2005 period that proved crucial to the completion of this book. Please note that the views expressed in this volume are those of the authors and should not be attributed to funding agencies, interviewees or host institutions.

This book has benefitted from the excellent research facilities provided by the Chr. Michelsen Institute (CMI) and we would like to thank CMI for a travel grant that enabled Michael Kerr to come to Bergen as a Visiting Research Fellow. We would also like to thank Magnus Dølerud for coordinating the Bergen workshop and organising the editorial work. We are especially grateful to Professor Augustus R. Norton for contributing a foreword to this volume. Our final words of gratitude go to our families for their support and patience.

Are Knudsen and *Michael Kerr*   Bergen and London, June 2012

AUTHOR BIOGRAPHIES

Fabrice Balanche is a lecturer at the University of Lyon 2 and director of the GREMMO (Groupe de Recherches et d'Etudes sur la Méditerranée et le Moyen-Orient) at the Maison de l'Orient et de la Méditerranée. He holds a PhD and an 'agrégation' in Geography. Since his first fieldwork in the Middle East in 1990, he has spent ten years living in Syria and Lebanon. His books include *La région alaouite et le pouvoir syrien* (Karthala, 2006), analysing the structure and patron-client relations of Syria's Baathist regime and *Atlas du Proche Orient arabe* (Presses de l'Université Paris-Sorbonne, 2011).

Hannes Baumann is a tutorial fellow in the Middle East and Mediterranean Studies Programme at King's College London. He recently completed his PhD, titled 'Citizen Hariri and neoliberal politics in post-war Lebanon' at the School of Oriental and African Studies (SOAS). He is a features editor of the journal *Studies in Ethnicity and Nationalism*.

Amal Hamdan is a PhD candidate at King's College London in the Middle East and Mediterranean Studies programme. Hamdan was a Middle East-based journalist for over a decade, mainly with Al-Jazeera television. She started as a news producer at their headquarters in Doha, Qatar before relocating with Al-Jazeera to Lebanon following the 2005 assassination of former Prime Minister Rafik Hariri. In addition to covering Beirut, she also reported on developments in Iraq, Syria and Egypt.

Sari Hanafi is Professor of Sociology at the American University of Beirut, editor of *Idafat: the Arab Journal of Sociology* (Arabic), and member of the Executive Bureau of the International Association of Sociology and the Arab Sociological Association. He holds a PhD in Sociology from the Ecole des Hautes Etudes en Sciences Sociales-Paris. Hanafi has published extensively on the political and economic sociology of the Palestinian diaspora and refugees, sociology of migration, transnationalism, politics of scientific research, civil society and elite formation. His most recent co-edited books are *The Power of Inclusive Exclusion: Anatomy of Israeli Rule in the Occupied Palestinian Territories* (Zone Books, 2009) and *Palestinian Refugees: Identity, Space and Place in the Levant* (Routledge, 2010).

Sune Haugbolle is Assistant Professor in Arabic and Middle Eastern Studies at the Department for Cross-Cultural and Regional Studies, University of Copenhagen. He holds a DPhil in Modern Middle Eastern Studies from the University of Oxford (2006). His work deals with social memory, media and politics in the modern Middle East. He is the author of *War and Memory in Lebanon* (Cambridge University Press, 2010) and co-editor of *Visual Culture in the Modern Middle East: Rhetoric of the Image* (Indiana University Press, 2012). His articles have appeared in a variety of journals and he is a contributing editor for the journal *Arab Media and Society*.

Michael Kerr is Professor of Conflict Studies and Director of the Centre for the Study of Divided Societies at King's College, London. He holds a PhD in International History from the London School of Economics and specialises in the politics of deeply divided societies. Kerr is author of *Imposing Power-Sharing: Conflict and Coexistence in Northern Ireland and Lebanon* (Irish Academic Press, 2005) and co-editor of *Conflict, Diplomacy and Society in Israeli-Lebanese Relations* (Routledge, 2010). His latest book is *The Destructors: The Story of Northern Ireland's Lost Peace Process* (Irish Academic Press, 2011).

Are Knudsen is Senior Researcher at the Chr. Michelsen Institute (CMI) and holds a PhD in Social Anthropology from the University of Bergen (2001). Knudsen is scientific coordinator for CMI's research collaboration with the Palestinian Institute for the Study of Democracy (*Muwatin*) and co-director of an institute programme on Forced Migration. Knudsen has done fieldwork in Afghanistan, Lebanon, Pakistan and Palestine and specialises on forced migration, transitional justice and political violence. He is the author of *Violence and Belonging: Land, Love and Lethal Conflict in the North-West Frontier Province of Pakistan* (NIAS Press, 2009) and co-editor of *Palestinian Refugees: Identity, Space and Place in the Levant* (Routledge, 2011).

Élizabeth Picard is Senior Researcher in the Institut de Recherches et d'Études sur le Monde Arabe et Musulman (IREMAM), Centre National de la Recherche Scientifique, in Aix-en-Provence, France. She teaches Middle East Politics at the graduate school of politics in the Institut d'Études Politiques in Aix-en-Provence and the Université Saint Joseph in Beirut. She has written extensively about security and identity politics in the Middle East in French and English. Her English language publications include *Lebanon: A Shattered Country* (Holmes and Meier, 1996) and the recent 'Nation-Building and Minority Rights' in *Religious Minorities in the Middle East* (edited by A.N. Longva and A.S. Roald, Brill, 2011).

Ward Vloeberghs is Assistant Professor at the Ecole de Gouvernance et d'Economie de Rabat (Morocco), where he is also deputy director of the Centre for Research on Africa and the Mediterranean (CERAM). Vloeberghs holds a PhD in Political Science from the University of Louvain, Belgium (2010) on the political dimensions of religious architecture in contemporary Beirut. His research interests lie in the politics of architecture, in dynastic power as well as in foreign policy issues, and he has spent several years living in Egypt, Lebanon and Morocco. Vloeberghs is co-author of the Dutch translation of *Halat Hisar*, a poem by Mahmoud Darwish.

Nasser Yassin is Assistant Professor at the American University of Beirut. He holds a PhD in Development Planning from the Bartlett Faculty of Built Environment at University College London. He has advised a number of international organisations (UNDP, UN-ESCWA and UN-HABITAT), governmental and non-governmental organisations on post-conflict rehabilitation, communal conflict and social development. His latest publications include 'City Profile: Beirut' (*Cities*, 2012) and the co-authored 'Evaluating a Community Based Participatory Approach to Research with Disadvantaged Women in the Southern Suburbs of Beirut' (*Journal of Community Health*, 2011).

Marie-Joëlle Zahar is Associate Professor of Political Science and research director at the Francophone research network on peace operations, Université de Montréal, Canada. She holds a PhD in political science from McGill University. She has conducted fieldwork in Lebanon, Bosnia, Angola, Mozambique, the Sudan and South Sudan and she specialises in the study of political violence in conflict and post-conflict societies, the theory and practice of power-sharing, and the politics of post-conflict reconstruction and peace-building. Her publications include the co-edited *Intra-state Conflict, Governments and Security: Dilemmas of Deterrence and Assurance* (Routledge, 2008).

FOREWORD

Lebanon is often depicted as a country on the brink of disorder, yet during 2011—one of the most turbulent years in recent Middle Eastern history—the country proved to be remarkably stable. Dictators were felled in Egypt, Libya, Tunisia and Yemen, and in neighboring Syria even relentless applications of violence by the praetorian guard failed to cow Syrians intent on seeing the back of Bashar al-Assad. Rank-and-file Lebanese citizens have plenty of gripes about corrupt politics, poor public services and a deterioration of the quality of life and environment, but few Lebanese followed the examples of Tunisian or Egyptian contemporises to take to the streets shouting 'irhal' (leave/scram) at their president or prime minister. This is not to say that they have not watched the carnage in Syria without trepidation or worry that instability or civil war next door would inevitably spread to Lebanon. Moreover, people with a living memory of civil war and invasion take stability seriously, even if, as noted in this volume, they have often resisted coming to the terms with the pathologies of past bloodshed.

Moreover, Lebanon's service-oriented economy is keenly dependent on stability. In good years, affluent tourists flood into Lebanon buttressing the economy, filling hotels and restaurants to capacity in summer months, and often leave large deposits in Beirut's banks. If conflict or disorder looms, those same well-heeled guests leave quickly with suitcases and cash in hand. Expatriate Lebanese regularly return large sums of hard currency to their natal villages, towns and cities where nominal state services are typically far from adequate, but these monies only supplement rather than replace salaries.

Lebanon's year of awakening (*sahwa*) was 2005, following the assassination of former Prime Minister Rafik Hariri in February. Giant rival demonstrations, encampments and sit-ins engaged hundreds of thousands of Lebanese, prompting opportunistic western governments, not least France and the United States, to imagine momentarily that friendly pro-western governments might confound Lebanon's oft-demonstrated penchant for inefficient, if not ineffectual governance via consensus rather than domination by a triumphant coalition. In this old land fortunes may be made in politics, but political fortunes are transient. Even firmly declared alliances may evaporate when regional power brokers turn up the heat, or domestic rivalries shift. It would only be a matter of time before the wisdom of "no victor and no vanquished" (*la ghalib wa al-maghlub*) would be revalidated.

If complaints about corruption are ubiquitous, the very essence of rule by consensus is *wasta* (connection) to political players who bestow favours upon supporters, or treat politics as a for-profit business. Citizenship is acknowledged in civil law, but in practice it is sometimes only a cursory dimension of politics. (The Palestinian refugee population, which equals ten percent of Lebanon's population of four million, is accorded no legal standing at all.)

Lebanon is an anomalous state because so much that constitutes politics in Lebanon is conducted on the periphery of the state, if not outside of it. This may seem an odd claim, given the magnificence of the Grand Serail, the Prime Minister's headquarters, and the other architectural accoutrements of state. After all, the head of state is an indirectly elected President, often a respected man of stature, and since the end of the civil war in 1990 regular parliamentary and local elections have been held. The Army and Internal Security Forces are ubiquitous, and senior officers constitute privileged, pampered state elite, but the state does not enjoy a monopoly on coercive power, which is most emphatically demonstrated by Hizbollah's military might. There is a functioning legal system, a viable banking sector and a literate citizenry that is often well informed and productive. Notwithstanding gargantuan public debt stemming largely from post-civil war reconstruction, the debt burden has been restructured and the constitutionally autonomous Central Bank has been a paragon of skilled management, a sturdy mooring for the national economy.

Appearances are deceiving: when Rafik Hariri tackled post-civil war reconstruction he did so through independent institutions well outside of routine government supervision. The two best examples are Council for Development and Reconstruction and Solidere, which were woven more closely to Hariri's personal fortune than to the state treasury.

Equally important, power rests with confessional (sectarian) leaders, both lay and clerical. Some Lebanese disdain their hyphenated citizenship, but it is often difficult to simply be Lebanese. For instance, in order for Lebanese couples to engage in civil marriage they have to travel to Cyprus, since non-confessional marriage ceremonies are not recognised as legal. In the 1990s, President Elias Hrawi attempted to enhance his legacy by legalising civil marriage, but his efforts were quickly drowned in choruses of outrage and dismay from bishops, shaikhs, muftis, imams and patriarchs who warned of moral collapse if the reform was enacted.

Confessional differences have often been mitigated by intra-sect rivalries and inter-sectarian alliances, but the sectarian divide has become enormous in twenty-first-century Lebanon, especially between the Shia and Sunni communities, the two largest in the country. (In contrast, a significant segment of the large Maronite community has, since 2006, aligned under General Michel Aoun with the Shia community, a development which reveals a great deal about the rival worldviews and the failure of the present political system.) In the two major Muslim sects, intra-sect struggles have been largely sublimated to inter-sectarian animosities. Lebanese who lived through the civil war are likely to complain that the sectarian divisions are deeper, more intractable today than during the civil war. Even labour unions and the Labour Confederation, where for years secular left ideologies enjoyed footings, have been reconfessionalised in the last decade.

The Shia community's remarkable solidarity has been an important factor in recent years, but this is a transient political phenomenon. The catalyst for this solidarity was unquestionably the war of 2006. Israel's military campaign largely targeted Shia locales, and the vast majority of the approximately 1,000 civilians killed by Israel were Shia civilians. Prior to the war there were tensions and clashes aplenty within the community, not least between Amal and Hizbollah, but the contradictions dissolved with the existential threat posed by Israel. Hizbollah's security narrative, if not its worldview, suddenly became compelling, not simply for ardent Hizballahis but even for many apolitical and avowedly secular Shia Muslims. The plausibility of Hizbollah's security narrative, that the Shia must protect themselves because the Lebanese Army is incapable of doing so and no one else will, is a crucial explanation for the uncommon unity one finds among many Shia Muslims today. This suggests that outsiders (such as the United States or France) seeking to reduce Hizbollah's influence in Lebanon must redress the security narrative rather than taking steps that validate it. However legitimate Israel's concerns may be about Hizbollah's military capacity and its armory, it is foolhardy to consider Hizbollah's strength without acknowledging how widely and how often the Lebanese and especially Shia Lebanese have suffered from Israel's characteristically disproportionate violence.

If Lebanon's Sunni Muslims see their Shia brethren with visceral distrust, pointing to Hizbollah's provocation of Israel in 2006, its leading role in the 2008 incursion into West Beirut and its alleged involvement in the assassination of Rafik al-Hariri, regional, personal and tactical differences have remained salient. Had Saad al-Din al-Hariri been stronger as Prime Minister then things might have been different, but that was not the case. If Hizbollah has been dependent upon Iranian largesse and materiel, Lebanon's Sunnis have been generously supported by Saudi Arabia, which transparently views Lebanon as its rightful regional domain. Prime Ministers Saad Hariri and Najib Mikati may be far apart on the political spectrum but they both demonstrated their obeisance to Saudi concerns in Lebanon.

Even before the so-called Arab Spring of 2011, Saudi-Iranian jousting was already the main event in Lebanon, but with the developing civil war in neighbouring Syria it has become a blood sport. The fate of the Assad regime will surely reverberate in Lebanon, which is why so many Lebanese watch Syria so nervously. Ties of marriage, commerce and investment link many Lebanese to Syria, and the strategic relationship between Hizbollah and the Assad regime is well known. It is difficult to imagine a conclusion in Syria that does not affect Lebanon dramatically, whether because of large numbers of refugees, violence spilling across the border, or, should the Assad regime be toppled, a messy struggle for power and even a rebalancing of the geopolitical balance to the disadvantage of Hizbollah and its state sponsor, Iran.

If the future preoccupies so many Lebanese, it remains crucial to interrogate the past, to ask fresh questions about sectarianism, conflicts between Lebanese and wars in which Lebanon was a canvas for regional and international warfare. The editors deserve great credit for assembling renowned senior authorities and bright up-and-coming scholars to focus on the recent history of Lebanon, including close examination of the extraordinary if mixed legacy of Rafik Hariri, and the momentous and fast-moving years following the assassination of the former prime minister in February 2005. The often compelling pieces that follow constitute highly original, sometimes path-breaking contributions to the study of Lebanon.

Augustus Richard Norton   Boston, Massachusetts, February 2012

PART I

FOREIGN INTERVENTION, HEGEMONY AND CONSOCIATIONALISM

1

INTRODUCTION

THE CEDAR REVOLUTION AND BEYOND

Are Knudsen and Michael Kerr

This book examines Lebanon's most recent, dramatic, yet least-studied period—namely the years following the 'Cedar Revolution' (2005–2012). From 1992 until his assassination on 14 February 2005, Rafik Hariri was Lebanon's foremost statesman and longest-serving prime minister. He won three consecutive parliamentary elections (1992, 1996 and 2000) and was well placed to win for a fourth time in 2005 when his life was cut short by a massive car bomb in downtown Beirut, the centre of his landmark post-war reconstruction project. Until his death, Hariri's entrepreneurial vision had defined the post-civil war period's extensive renovation and rebuilding of Beirut's Central District. The reconstruction was underwritten by massive public spending financed by costly loans that left the country heavily in debt. While Hariri initially steered a course that found support in Syria, in time he challenged Syrian hegemony in Lebanon, charting an independent course that led to a full confrontation with Syria's President, Bashar al-Assad. The stormy meeting between the two on 26 August 2004, the details of which remain disputed, led to Hariri's resignation as prime minister and to the fateful motorcade tour through central Beirut that was targeted by a massive car bomb killing Hariri, his close aide Basil Fluheian and twenty-one others.[1] The murder of Hariri changed the face of Lebanon and sparked a revolution. This book examines these changes and argues that the Cedar Revolution was a turning point in the contemporary history of Lebanon; one that at least temporarily shattered the *Pax Syriana* that had dominated Lebanon since the signing of the Taif Agreement in 1989.

The Cedar Revolution

Lebanon did experience minor protests in the post-civil war period against Syrian suzerainty, especially after the unilateral Israeli withdrawal of 2000, when several rallies and protests sought to call time on the presence of Syrian troops which had occupied the country since 1976. These protests had little effect, quelled brutally by the army and security forces. In comparison, the mass mobilisation following Hariri's assassination was unprecedented in the country's history and defied a government ban on public demonstrations. The groundswell of grief, disbelief and anger directed at Syria was simply unstoppable and, in the hours following Hariri's murder, thousands converged in the Martyr's Square in Central Beirut in what became known as the Independence Intifada [*intifadat al-istiqlal*], later popularised as the Cedar Revolution.

The Cedar Revolution was seen by many as a new beginning for Lebanon, ending the injustice caused by the civil war and Syria's oppressive control over Lebanon. The three main demands of the revolutionaries were the ending of Syrian hegemony in Lebanon, the withdrawal of all Syrian troops and the establishment of an international investigation into the murder of Hariri. The first and second goals were largely achieved when Syria withdrew its remaining 14,000 soldiers in late April 2005, but the Cedar Revolution lost momentum despite attempts to transform the outpouring of grief into a lasting political platform centred on Hariri's legacy.[2] The third goal turned out to be the most politically divisive issue as the Lebanese split over the question of whether Syria and its allies were responsible for Hariri's murder. This division was evident prior to the Cedar Revolution as the first mass demonstration was organised on 8 March, by Hizbollah, in support of the Syrian regime. This led shortly after to an even larger counter-demonstration on 14 March, which charged Syria with culpability in Hariri's assassination. The Cedar Revolution exposed an existing political fault line between protesters in opposition to Syria's involvement in Lebanon and those who wished to maintain it; divisions which later took the form of two rival coalitions promoting conflicting visions of Lebanon's place in the Middle East.

Coexistence and Consociationalism

The Lebanese system is based on consensus and compromise, and even the most acute crises have eventually been solved by the proverbial 'no victor no vanquished' (la ghalib la maghlub), which is the premise of Lebanon's National Pact. Repeated political conflict in Lebanon has led to violence, stalemate and then a return to the politics of consociational government following painful compromise. When the political system is gridlocked, the streets become the theatre of inter-confessional competition, which is typical of semi-democracies such as Lebanon.[3] The post-2005 period provides several examples of such action: the 'million-man march', the Downtown sit-in and the many strikes that paralysed the Beirut Central District. Prior to the civil war, Lebanon was viewed as a model of peaceful coexistence. However, the National Pact, the power-sharing arrangements that regulate contestation between its Christian and Muslim communities, has broken down several times (e.g., 1958, 1975, 2005, 2006 and 2008). Thus the post-2005 period illustrates the inherent difficulties in maintaining a consociational system in such an unstable region.

Lebanon's rigid power-sharing formula awards recognised religious communities a fixed number of seats in the parliament. The last official census was conducted by the French in 1932 and, since then, all population figures have merely been estimates. The numerical size of Lebanon's confessional groups is linked to the contentious issue of the distribution of power between them, thus the country's demographic makeup remains a hotly contested and politicised issue, especially between its three largest communities, the Maronites, the Sunnis and the Shia.[4] After 2005, Christian-Muslim divisions gave way to the Sunni-Shia split prevalent in the region, the Maronites divided between those whose interests are best served by supporting the Iran-Syria-Hizbollah axis, and those aligned with the US-Saudi alliance. The Sunni-Shia divide has replaced the civil war's Muslim-Christian divide to become the dominant schism in the post-2005 period. This not only causes inter-sectarian conflict but strains a power-sharing system that has created a form of corporate consociational government that favours the Sunnis and disadvantages the Shia, exacerbating existing communal resentment and inter-elite tensions (Amal Hamdan, this volume).

Examining the post-2005 period, it is evident that domestic governance crises are strongly influenced by international relations and the pressure exerted on Syria at any given point. Only when these exogenous pressures are reduced, whether through externally brokered accords (Doha Agreement, 2008), unilateral rapprochement with Syria (Premier Saad Hariri's first visit to Damascus on 23 November 2009), bilateral efforts to end Syria's diplomatic isolation (French Premier Sarkozy welcoming Assad to the Elysée Palace on 9 November 2009) or multilaterally by establishing the Union for the Mediterranean (Paris Summit, 13 July 2008), do political tensions in Lebanon temporarily subside.[5]

From Blocs to Blockage

The Cedar Revolution produced two rival blocs that have since dominated Lebanese politics. With the temporary eviction of Syria in mid-2005, Lebanon experienced a power vacuum that was filled, in part, by new external power brokers, especially the USA and France, aligned with internal actors.[6] Syria's military exit from Lebanon forced Hizbollah to join the government to protect its interests. Despite political differences, Hizbollah collaborated in joint electoral lists with Saad Hariri's Future Movement and, following their electoral victory, joined the new cabinet. Colloquially known as 'unity cabinets' they are neither united nor unitary because they are composed of political adversaries. This explains why unity cabinets have taken such a long time to form, with lengthy bickering between the blocs over their agenda for government and, once approved by the parliament, have been beset by internal divisions. The 'unity' cabinets formed after 2007 were specifically designed to provide the opposition within the cabinet a 'blocking third' of ministerial posts. The 'blocking third' principle can be described as a new power-sharing formula in which consensus, guaranteed by the constitution, is replaced by minority veto.[7] Although cast as a legitimate power-sharing mechanism, it is better understood as power politics, using the threat of force (demonstrations, sit-ins, strikes) to pressure the majority into complying with the minority's demands. This type of non-electoral competition is typical of quasi-democracies such as Lebanon.[8] The multi-party 'unity' cabinets have, since 2005, been gridlocked over the international investigation of Rafik Hariri's assassination and Hizbollah's weapons. These issues have become sectarian emblems that do not lend themselves towards compromise. This has escalated sectarian tensions, predominantly between the Sunni and Shia communities, causing periodic outbursts of street-based violence and paralysis in government. Essentially, this two-bloc system has left Lebanon ungovernable, not simply due to deep-seated political differences, but because of the external linkages which tie the two blocs to their foreign patrons, namely the USA and Iran, which remain at loggerheads over their regional ambitions. Regional conflict reinforces these divisions, as Lebanon remains of strategic importance in the Arab-Israeli conflict bordering both Syria and Israel, putting great strain on the country's impartial protector and guarantor of peace, the Lebanese army. As the Arab Spring develops, it also increases Hizbollah's significance to Iran as the embattled Assad regime struggles to quash a country-wide insurgency.

Weapons of the Weak?

The Lebanese Army has traditionally been a stabilising element and has, since the end of the civil war, taken the utmost care to preserve its neutrality, standing back from internal conflicts and controlling street violence by maintaining a presence in known conflict zones. Despite being bolstered by arms reinforcements from the US and Russia, the Army remains ill-equipped and unable to counteract the military prowess of Hizbollah along Lebanon's border with Israel. Thus, Lebanon is an example of early state-formation where the state has yet to monopolise the use of force.[9] Instead, the country has multiple power bases, in particular armed groups outside state control such as Hizbollah's elite force, the only militia group allowed by Syria to maintain its arsenal after 1990. Although UN Security Council resolution 1559 sought to 'demobilize all Lebanese and non-Lebanese militias', internationalising the arms issue, Hizbollah has repeatedly rebuffed both domestic and international pressures to decommission its weapons and demobilise fighters. Hizbollah claims that its arsenal, which has been greatly enhanced by Iran since its 2006 war with Israel, is integral to its resistance efforts and is only preserved to deter Israeli attacks onto Lebanon. However, in May 2008, Hizbollah deployed its militia on the streets of Beirut following a cabinet decision to uproot its secret communications network, which posed a significant threat to its military capability. Having withdrawn its ministers from the cabinet in November 2006, Hizbollah was unable to veto the decision, responding instead by taking over the part of Beirut that surrounds the prime minister's office. Although Hizbollah scored a tactical victory over the government by demonstrating the superiority of its forces, the veneer of its domestic neutrality vanished, greatly reducing its legitimacy as a popular resistance movement and heightening opposition to its armed status. Israel's unilateral withdrawal from South Lebanon in 2000 saw Hizbollah's popularity soar, but it also raised questions over the continuance of its armed status. Hizbollah has since justified the maintenance of its weapons on the pretext that anything other than the destruction of Israel would represent surrender in the Arab-Israeli conflict, but its political opponents accuse it of using arms to maintain an unfair political advantage in domestic Lebanese politics.[10] Consequently, delegitimising Hizbollah's armed status became a key part of the Future Movement's political programme, despite being approved by Saad Hariri's unity cabinet in 2009 as an integral part of the nation's defence under the trinity formula: 'People, Army and Resistance'. Hizbollah's arms are also implicated in the conflict between the USA and Iran and the proverbial 'Axis of Evil', providing Hizbollah with an added justification for keeping its weapons. Yet, the main reason for not surrendering weapons is that without them, Hizbollah cannot sustain its hard-won position domestically. Disarmament could not only dismantle the movement's political gains but endanger its existence.[11] Thus, Lebanon has a 'credible commitment' problem because the weak state can neither 'assure nor deter', without which Hizbollah cannot and will not consider decommissioning its weapons (Marie-Joëlle Zahar, this volume). Instead, Hizbollah will remain armed to assure its internal protection and deter the threat of an Israeli invasion.

Divine Victory?

The Cedar Revolution upstaged the precarious post-civil war balance by temporarily loosening Syria's control over Lebanon (Michael Kerr, this volume). The 2006 July war between Hizbollah and Israel can be seen as an outcome of this shift in the regional power balance. Hizbollah's cross-border attack on an Israeli patrol led to a massive military retaliation that wrecked much of Lebanon's infrastructure, displaced one million people from the South and killed more than 1,000 civilians before a UN-brokered ceasefire ended the conflict. Despite the devastation of parts of South Lebanon and Hizbollah's headquarters in Haret Hreik in Beirut's southern suburbs, the movement claimed a 'divine victory' that inflated its popularity across the predominantly Sunni Arab world. The seemingly contradictory logic of its claim to victory must be understood from the street-wise perspective that

Hizbollah won because it did not lose, whereas Israel lost because it did not win. In fact, neither side was an unequivocal winner.[12] The war increased domestic tensions over Hizbollah's arms. On the one hand, Hizbollah was charged with devastating Lebanon through its provocative actions against Israel, but on the other hand, Hizbollah charged its internal rivals with conspiring with Israel to bring about its destruction.

In early 2007, a violent conflict broke out in the Nahr al-Bared refugee camp near Tripoli. The Army's siege of the camp led to more than 400 deaths and saw Syria accused of conspiring to undermine the country's stability and unseat the 14 March government headed by Prime Minister Fuad Siniora. The Army was praised for its handling of the conflict, despite the near-complete destruction of the camp and eviction of its 30,000 Palestinian residents. While the Army could claim victory over a militant Islamist group (Fatah al-Islam), soldiers, officers and the general in charge of the operation were later targeted in car bomb attacks. The fifteen-week Nahr al-Bared siege was the country's largest internal post-civil war battle and was framed as an existential crisis between pro-Syrian and pro-government forces. There are high levels of conflict inside some of the Lebanese refugee camps, but this is not caused by support for Islamist militancy, but poor living conditions and militarised governance that spatially enclave refugee camps causing them to become 'fortressed archipelagos' (Sari Hanafi, this volume).

In 2008, Beirut was engulfed by militia warfare that brought the country to the brink of civil war. The crisis was diffused through a surprise breakthrough in Doha, with Qatar brokering an accord between the warring factions. The Doha Agreement brought about the election of Army General Michel Sleiman and the formation of a new cabinet, but it was not a lasting settlement. Subsequent disagreements over the Special Tribunal for Lebanon tasked with prosecuting Hariri's assassins led to a renewed crisis in government. These internal and external conflicts exposed the multi-confessional Lebanese Army's weakness as the nation's impartial arbiter. Moreover, the Army suffers both from inadequate training and imbalanced recruitment, compounding its inability to respond to military crises without a strong political mandate and overwhelming force (Élizabeth Picard, this volume).

Foreign Intervention

During the 1990s, Lebanon was the target for numerous UN Security Council resolutions, most of them related to ending the punitive wars with

Israel in 1993 (Operation Accountability) and 1996 (Operation Grapes of Wrath). This changed on 2 September 2004 when the UN Security Council passed Resolution 1559, following a similar move a year earlier by the US Congress seeking to restrict Syria's influence over Lebanon.[13] Resolution 1559 called for free and fair elections, an immediate end to Syrian troop deployment, the disarmament of all militias and the deployment of the Lebanese Army along the border with Israel. Each of these demands challenged the post-war status quo, which had left Syria responsible for both interpreting and implementing the Taif Agreement. Following Syria's military withdrawal, this raised tensions over whether Lebanon should be governed on the basis of the Taif Agreement, which had not been fully implemented, or UN Security Council Resolution 1559.[14] Those in favour of the first option, rejected Western interference and Resolution 1559, whereas those in opposition to Syria and Iran argued that only the full implementation of Resolution 1559 could bring stability to Lebanon. Regardless of these conflicting interpretations, UN Resolution 1559 introduced a new, externally driven conflict dynamic onto the Lebanese domestic scene. It is widely believed that there is a causal link extending from the demands enshrined in Resolution 1559, the controversial three-year extension of Emile Lahoud's presidential term (confirmed the following day by the Lebanese parliament), the deadly attack on the MP Marwan Hamade who voted against the extension, Hariri's fall-out with Bashar al-Assad and subsequent departure as prime minister in October 2004, and his assassination four months later. This political timeline framed the attack on Hariri and was followed by a series of new UN Security Council decrees and resolutions that began with the establishment of a UN fact-finding mission, followed by an investigative commission and finally the Special Tribunal for Lebanon (STL), which was established to prosecute those charged with complicity in his murder. More UN resolutions were issued later to pressurise Syria into cooperating with the Tribunal, but they were not always unanimous. Ten council members endorsed Security Council Resolution 1757, which ratified the STL, while five states abstained, citing infringement on Lebanon's sovereignty. These divisions mirrored domestic divisions, as the '8 March' opposition group decried the resolution a breach of Lebanon's sovereignty, while the '14 March' coalition took the opposite view, provoking an eighteen-month-long crisis in government.

The Tribunal is a supranational body which Lebanon is obliged to cooperate with and takes precedence over its national courts. Likewise, the criminal investigation into Hariri's murder was tasked to a UN body ('UNIIIC'), reinforced by the UN Charter's strongest sanction (Chapter VII), which demands cooperation from member states and whose authority extends over Lebanon's police, army and military intelligence. Finally, following the 2006 July War, the UN Security Council decided to bolster the UN peacekeeping mission deployed along Lebanon's border with Israel.[15] This made conflict resolution in Lebanon an international matter, which since 1990 had been the prerogative of Damascus. The Tribunal and the many UN Security Council resolutions that underpin it have therefore bureaucratised and internationalised Lebanon's domestic conflicts and made them a matter for international arbitration, diplomacy and decision making.

Redefining the Sunni Community

Historically, the Lebanese Sunnis were ardent supporters of Arabism with Syria as the Sunni Arab homeland. Hariri's assassination and Syria's military departure saw the Sunni community reassess its traditional allegiance, to break with Damascus and favour the strengthening of the Lebanese state. This can, to some degree, be interpreted as a return to the *d'étatisme* of Fuad Chehab's presidency (1958–64). Still, most Sunnis, and Rafik Hariri in particular, saw the state, and especially its bureaucracy, as an obstacle to national reconstruction after the war. Thus, Hariri largely bypassed the state by adding a new tier of institutions under his control, such as the Council for Development and Construction (CDR). Yet from 2005, the state grew in importance as a bulwark against Syrian hegemony, asserting itself in security matters at the expense of Syria's proxy, Hizbollah. It is a measure of this Sunni realignment that from 2005, the Future Movement adopted the Christian slogan 'Lebanon first' which would previously have been unthinkable.[16] To the Future Movement, 'Lebanon first' meant ending the anomaly of allowing armed groups to operate outside the state's control and the honouring of Lebanon's international commitments, in particular those relevant to the Tribunal. The call for a strong state resonated with key demands of the Future Movement for the rule of law, a national defence strategy and justice for Rafik Hariri. The aim of this strategy was to strengthen the state at Hizbollah's expense by delegitimising its outlier status and blame it for exacerbating sectarian tensions. This brought the two movements into conflict with each other, as they mobilised support through their respective religious institutions, the (Sunni) 'Higher Islamic Council' and the 'Higher Shia (Islamic) Council' which provided religious sanction for their political actions.[17] Yet both parties could be termed 'pre-modern', catering mainly to co-religionists on the basis of primordial loyalties.[18] Still, the Future Movement's unique position among the Sunnis allows it to woo non-Sunni groups without alienating its electorate and, to a greater degree than Hizbollah, extend its charitable network outside confessional boundaries.[19] Still, the Future Movement remains a family-based organisation with members controlling key party posts and media outlets such as Future TV, the Orient Radio and the *al-Mustaqbal* newspaper. As a loosely organised movement it draws its strength mainly from Rafik Hariri's political legacy, personal fortune and martyrdom. Hariri's legacy was physically inscribed into Lebanon's most sensitive public space, the Martyr's Square, by the construction of the imposing al-Amin mosque and tomb. This became a central component in the legitimisation of his posthumous role as a 'Martyr of the Nation', creating a crowing epitaph that secured his place in the country's past and a stake in its future (Ward Vloeberghs, this volume). Rafik Hariri's political legacy is closely linked to the monumental post-war reconstruction of Beirut that he oversaw, creating new bureaucratic and corporate institutions, in particular Solidere, a chartered company under contract to renovate Downtown Beirut, of which he was a majority shareholder. Solidere's acquisition of land, the razing of houses, mansions and neighbourhoods have all been criticised, as has Hariri's entrepreneurial vision, which has turned the city centre into a glitzy business metropolis catering for oil-rich elites and international business corporations.[20] His business conglomerate (Oger International) and real estate empire (Solidere) not only renovated the city centre, but took advantage of the local governance system in Greater Beirut to be awarded lucrative real estate contracts under a system of mercantile patronage that merged 'profits and politics' (Fabrice Balanche, this volume). The late premier Hariri was not alone in making such profitable mergers, indeed he was one of a new breed of post-civil war millionaires-turned-politicians who made their fortunes outside Lebanon before reinvesting their capital in political careers in their home country. The careers of Najib Mikati, Issam Fares and Rafik Hariri illustrate how this new 'contractor bourgeoisie' took advantage of the country's neo-liberal economy, bypassing the traditional (pre-civil war) elites to reach the pinnacles of political power, pointing to a class-based rather than confessional route to power in a neo-liberal context (Hannes Baumann, this volume).

INTRODUCTION: THE CEDAR REVOLUTION AND BEYOND

Remembering the War?

The post-2005 period is not only important for the shift it represents in Lebanese-Syrian relations, but also for opening the space for a new social discourse over the civil war which had been stifled under Syrian tutelage. The national reconciliation document, better known as the Taif Agreement, which signalled the end of the war, reconciled Lebanon's traditional elites more so than its people.[21] From 2005, it was possible for the first time to talk publicly about the civil war, a subject hitherto strictly censored by what might be described as an official 'collective amnesia'. New civil society groups, institutions and, most importantly, a new public space were created where multiple histories, rather than a sanctioned official version of the civil war, could exist. Lebanon's sprawling 'memory culture' has drawn mostly on emotional 'memory archives', relying on subjective 'remembrances' of the civil war, thus there remains the need for a more objective and scholarly social history of the conflict (Sune Haugbolle, this volume). Despite a thriving memory culture 'industry', a recent survey indicates that 85 per cent of the respondents (covering all sects) believe that the Lebanese 'have not reconciled with one another'.[22] Post-civil war homogenisation led to major changes in the composition of urban neighbourhoods, yet sectarian tensions sharpened, especially in mixed neighbourhoods situated on the faultline between religious communities in Tripoli and Beirut. In fact, the country remains physically segregated into distinct confessional enclaves, while social interaction among Beiruti youth is highly circumscribed (Nasser Yassin, this volume). Their interaction is symbolically segregated into discrete public and private confessional spheres, creating a 'coexistence without empathy'. In this sense, the Cedar Revolution did not end sectarianism but reinforced it. At the centre of confessional conflict stands the role of the international prosecution of Hariri's murder, an issue that divides the nation.

International Prosecution

Lebanon has a long history of political assassinations dating back to the 1950s. Most of these killings were unexamined and only a few led to credible convictions. The inability to investigate and prosecute assassinations has contributed to widespread impunity. The assassination of Rafik Hariri is the first time a politically motivated murder has come under international investigation, prosecution and, at some point, trial. The formation of an internationalised tribunal, the STL, promises professional investigation, impartial prosecution and credible convictions. The internationalisation of the Hague-based trial meant that prosecution could ideally neither be influenced by local compromise nor external pressure. Unlike domestic prosecution which has failed due to lack of evidence, political meddling or third-party pressure, the Tribunal is expected to prosecute offenders to the full extent of its mandate. Despite trenchant criticism of the Tribunal's lack of legitimacy, the UN Security Council, the EU and the Quartet (UN, USA, EU and Russia) have pledged support for the Tribunal and for the prosecution to proceed. This means that the judicial process cannot be substituted for a local compromise, even though this has been advocated as the only feasible solution to avoid a domestic security crisis.[23] The Tribunal has made criminal liability a legal question to be decided by the court and not, as usual in Lebanon, a question to be settled politically out-of-court. This makes the Tribunal a threat and prone to allegations of being a political tool and not a legal body (Are Knudsen, this volume). The Tribunal has divided the population between those who perceive it as seeking the truth and those believing it seeks to distort it. The Tribunal has charged four Hizbollah members with responsibility for Hariri's murder, but none of the accused has been detained. Hizbollah has dismissed the Tribunal's charges, and sought to end Lebanon's collaboration with it, and especially to stop paying Lebanon's share of the Tribunal's budget. However, non-compliance with the country's international obligations has become increasingly difficult. Ending Syria's hegemony opened the way for new, mostly Western, states to assume this role, especially the USA and France,[24] working together with Germany and the UK bilaterally and multilaterally as permanent members of the UN Security Council and as key member states of the EU. Established in 2003 and taking effect from 2007, the EU's European Neighbourhood Policy (ENP) and accompanying accession mechanisms promote economic integration, public policy and security sector reform in the southern Mediterranean. Lebanon's dire economic situation and crushing debt has made it a main beneficiary of ENP-funds and the EU has committed EUR 150 million to Lebanon during 2011–13. The ENP's budget and project support gives the EU considerable leverage with Lebanon's government, although democracy promotion is limited by the country's 'dual power' situation.[25] The importance of economic measures is demonstrated by the UN using the threat of economic sanctions should Lebanon default on its obligation to pay its share (49 per cent) of the Tribunal's huge annual operating costs. The threat of sanctions made Prime

Minister Najib Mikati bypass the cabinet and transfer USD 32.6 million from the prime minister's office to the Tribunal, not only preventing sanctions but averting a governmental crisis. Despite opposing the transfer, Hizbollah grudgingly let it pass. The deal was supported by Syria which, reeling under intense internal protests in the wake of the Arab Spring, needed to prevent a collapse of the Hizbollah-backed cabinet.

Arab Spring

In retrospect, the Cedar Revolution can be seen as a precursor to the wave of popular uprisings sweeping the Middle East from late 2010 (Michael Kerr, this volume). In Tunisia, the self-immolation of a young street vendor abused by corrupt government officials sparked a public outcry over heavy-handed political oppression. The 'Jasmine Revolution' overwhelmed the regime and later spread to neighbouring countries, principally Egypt, Libya, Yemen and Bahrain and, most recently, to Syria. The unrelenting civil unrest and brutal government crackdown in Syria has seen the country descend into a civil war that will most likely engulf Lebanon. The Arab Spring and the Cedar Revolution were both sparked by the death of one person. These revolutionary movements converged on the nations' centres and morphed rapidly into largely peaceful protests against long-term oppression fuelled by a youthful desire for freedom and dignity. In addition, both led to the rapid dismantling of the regimes, autocratic in the case of the Arab Spring, hegemonic in the case of the Cedar Revolution. The Cedar Revolution brought protesters onto the streets in two consecutive mass demonstrations that later solidified as rival political blocs that have continued to divide the country. The euphoria of the Cedar Revolution was dashed in the years that followed and saw a reversal of Syria's political exit from Lebanon, violent confrontations, political gridlock, war with Israel, and serious internal conflicts. The Syrian debacle has the greatest potential impact on Lebanon and has raised fears that the Assad regime will attempt to displace conflict to Lebanon, which could end up bearing the brunt of the regime's downfall.

The Book

This volume situates post-2005 developments in Lebanese politics and society within a regional and international framework. Taking an interdisciplinary approach, new and established Lebanon scholars offer fresh analyses of the changes within Lebanon's consociational system of government, the security challenges facing the Lebanese Army and Hizbollah and the political legacy of former Lebanese Prime Minister Rafik Hariri, before addressing prescient questions of memory and public discourse over the civil war, urban segregation and sectarianism, issues of Palestinian governance and the STL.

The book is divided into four sections and following this introduction, the first part ('Foreign Intervention, Hegemony and Consociationalism') features Michael Kerr's scene-setting chapter which analyses the developments in international politics that handed Lebanon to Syria under the tutelage of President Hafez al-Assad. Kerr argues that while 2005 marks a turning point in Lebanese domestic and regional politics, it should be viewed as part of the cycle of conflict that Lebanon has been embroiled in for decades. Lebanon has yet to resolve the internal issues that left it particularly vulnerable to influence from states seeking to advance their foreign policy objectives in the region through this divided society, or regain the sovereignty it began to lose after 1967. As such, he argues that Lebanon remains trapped within the cycle of conflict that led to civil war in 1975–6, which saw Syria consolidate its hegemonic control over the country through the dereliction of the Taif Agreement after 1990. This scenario changed after 2003, when the USA sought to effect regime change in countries where it saw a threat to its interests, bringing the USA, UK and France together in a transatlantic alliance to end Syrian hegemony in Lebanon, later enshrined in the UN Security Council Resolution 1559. Still, Syria and Iran were subsequently able to regain their political hegemony over Lebanon despite the reversal of fortunes that Hariri's assassination spelt for the anti-US alliance in the Middle East from 2005. The 'Arab Spring' in Syria could have a detrimental impact on Lebanon's fragile power-sharing system and spell yet further conflict.

Amal Hamdan argues that the political crises in Lebanon since 2005 are rooted within 'corporate consociationalism', a flawed system of power-sharing which exacerbates communal grievances of unequal political participation. Extended to Lebanon, the Taif Agreement's corporate consociational framework has exacerbated existing inter-communal grievances over the distribution of executive authority. This flawed form of consociationalism continues to cultivate communal resentment and instability, as well as tensions between the main political representatives of the Sunni and Shia communities. Thus Hizbollah and Amal seek to modify the Taif power-sharing formula, while the Sunni Future Movement dismisses Shia communal grievances of unequal power-sharing and insist on maintaining the stipulations of Taif, which elevated the Sunni community. Hamdan concludes that unless corporate consociationalism is replaced with a more stable form of consociational democracy, the resumption of conflict in Lebanon is likely.

The recurring security breaches raised by Hamdan is the topic of the next section ('Sovereignty, Security and Violence'), where the authors grapple with the challenges of political instability, the role of the armed forces in protecting the country's sovereignty and its multiple power bases. In her contribution, Marie-Joëlle Zahar argues that the roots of political instability in Lebanon can be found in the entanglement of domestic and regional issues. In this respect, the 'Cedar Revolution' did not really constitute a break with the past as Lebanon remains permeable and vulnerable to external influences. Zahar argues that foreign intervention in Lebanese politics is, to a great extent, a consequence of Lebanese factions seeking to gain the upper hand and take advantage of each other. Based on primary sources, Zahar's chapter uncovers the ways in which communities fearful for their political survival manoeuvre to shield themselves from political marginalisation and exclusion. Considering the impact of foreign interventions on the dynamics of conflict and coexistence, the chapter argues that foreign intervention has a lasting and detrimental impact on the rules of the game and the pervasiveness of confessionalism. The resulting explosive mix of 'made-to-fit rules' and 'acute confessional threat perception' accounts for the permeability of Lebanese politics.

Following on from Zahar, the post-Cedar security dilemmas are treated in Élizabeth Picard's analysis of the restructuring of the Lebanese Armed Forces (LAF) and the security forces which were intended as the main pillar of post-civil war reconstruction. Picard argues that, from 2005, the armed forces remained prone to fragmentation and were often privatised, while authoritarianism loomed as the ultimate recourse against state dissolution and societal strife. This compromised the LAF's military capability and its ability to guarantee state sovereignty. The 'national dialogues' sought to resolve the army's role and delimit Hizbollah's military capability by addressing the question of 'non state arms'. This meant that the army's political mandate remained contested. Additionally, a shortage of equipment and inadequate training has prevented the LAF from becoming a credible alternative to Hizbollah's 'Islamic resistance'. This has forced successive post-2005 governments to pay tribute to, and legitimate, the rival defence force. While the LAF has improved its military performance, it paid a heavy price in defeating the Islamic militants who were taking control of the Nahr al-Bared refugee camp in 2007. After universal conscription was abolished by the parliament in 2005, the security forces were prone to unbalanced sectarian recruitment and sensitive to private interests. This change compromised the army's ability to resist competing political agendas and is one reason for its increasing intervention on the intra-state arena and inability to engage militarily in inter-state conflicts.

The issue of internal strife is the topic of the next chapter where Sari Hanafi examines the problem of violence and governance in Palestinian refugee camps, colloquially referred to as 'islands of (in-)security'. Based on focus group interviews in three refugee camps, two of them regarded as the country's most violent, as well as personal interviews and survey data, Hanafi debunks the myths of Palestinian 'exceptionalism', in particular the notion that internal violence is the result of Islamist sympathies or 'militancy'. Instead, his analysis shows that the refugee camps suffer from militarised governance which produces specific forms of disciplinary violence. Coercive (state) and political (factional) violence are the predominant violations inside camps. Hence, Hanafi contends that violence in the the camps is a result of twin governance failures: first, externally by successive government policies of exclusion and marginalisation and secondly, the lack of legitimate, democratic governance structures inside camps that hold camp dwellers hostage to factional in-fighting. Taken together, these prevent meaningful improvement of the socioeconomic living conditions for the residents and lead to widespread disillusionment, apathy and powerlessness, especially among the youth. Long-term deprivation, exclusion and marginalisation are the results of state policies towards refugees that have generated specific forms of systemic violence inside refugee camps that continue to jeopardise the security of the Palestinians and the Lebanese alike.

The third section ('Entrepreneurs, Statesmen and Martyrs'), deals with the late Rafik Hariri's legacy as entrepreneur, statesman and martyr of the nation and especially the amalgamation of these roles in his political career and posthumously, as the country's guardian spirit. Hannes Baumann, in his contribution, argues that several of the most prominent Lebanese politicians of the post-civil war era hail from the new contractor bourgeoisie. This class emerged in the 1970s due to changes in the country's role in the capitalist world economy and consists mainly of Lebanese *émigrés* to the Gulf who accumulated great wealth as private contractors. The chapter compares the careers of three most prominent contractors-turned-politicians; Rafik Hariri (Sunni), Najib Mikati (Sunni) and Issam Fares (Greek Orthodox), across three dimensions—obtaining political office, furthering their personal economic agenda and popular mobilisation. Their class position and wealth are comparable, meaning that differences in their careers must be explained with reference to other variables such as their international alliances and sectarian affiliation. Lebanon's new contractors provide an interesting case study of neoliberal politics in the specific context of Lebanon's sectarian state.

Baumanns' chapter is followed by an in-depth analysis of the implications of neo-liberal policies in the career of the late Rafik Hariri. Fabrice Balanche examines Hariri's role in the convergence of politics and property development in Greater Beirut following the globalisation of the post-civil war economy. Paradoxically, the end of the civil war and return to peace impoverished the urban masses as real estate prices skyrocketed. This helped revive the urban bourgeoisie since they possess the social skills, financial capital and political clout needed to succeed in the new liberalist economy. Yet, this globalised context also makes Beirut's urban space a new battlefield, pitting the liberalist 'law of the market' against the traditionalist protection of 'sectarian territory'. The urban bourgeoisie with the Hariri family at its apex extend their property development to low-income areas, in the process seeking to expel those who cannot afford the new and costly urbanity. In order to prevent eviction, low-income families threatened by demolition of their homes have no other option than to seek recourse to tribal solidarity and accept communitarian protection. In order to illustrate this issue, Balanche shows how the residents in Ouzai, a popular low-income coastal zone, resisted plans to raze their neighbourhood by seeking protection from their Hizbollah patron.

Ward Vloeberghs' analysis of the hagiography of the late Rafik Hariri shows that it was forged gradually, especially after his violent death, through a number of discursive and propagandistic acts and artefacts. The chapter analyses the political ramifications of Hariri's carefully crafted 'martyrdom', the main aim of which was to keep Hariri's symbolic legacy at the heart of Lebanese political life. The dynamics that contribute to establishing Hariri's symbolic legacy as a martyr are four-fold and entail processes of appropriation, instances of negotiation, practices of contestation and instruments of confirmation. While exploring these dynamics, the chapter emphasises the links between politics and the built environment in order to illustrate how

19

these visual and verbal references are related to Hariri's political programme, and how they link up with the predicament of his heirs. It concludes that Hariri's heritage is neither stable nor clear-cut, but rather a malleable narrative that could be mobilised depending on contextual imperatives, be it on the local or the regional level.

The book's fourth section ('Truth, Coexistence and Justice'), is concerned with the impact of the late Rafik Hariri's assassination and the subsequent Cedar Revolution on the post-2005 period's memory production, urban sociality and criminal justice. In his chapter, Sune Haugbolle argues that political changes in Lebanon since 2005 have altered the conditions for cultural production and public debates about the legacy of the Lebanese civil war, a topic that prior to 2005 was subject to a state-sponsored amnesia. The sensitivity of the civil war has led to a focus on the subjective experiences of the war, thus dealing mainly with 'memories' of the war. This has, Haugbolle argues, made 'memories of the war' displace a more objective, but also much more divisive, historiographic analysis of the events of the war. Based on the analysis of a series of significant memory productions since 2005, including plays, films and public commemorations, Haugbolle proposes a way to overcome the division between history and memory. He argues that academics and memory-activists alike have become preoccupied with 'memory culture' as the primary object of engagement with the country's civil war heritage. By contrast, scholarly work on the social history of the war is poorly developed and mostly lacking. Haugbolle argues that despite war-memories' limitations as 'objective' historical sources, the country's memory culture provides 'emotional archives' of everyday war experiences for constituting a social history of the civil war. These representations can be systematised and become the object of historical work. Conversely, debates among professional historians about particular events during the civil war, the interpretations of which continue to divide social and political groups today, can and should form the basis for discussions in Lebanon about the war and its meaning today.

Nasser Yassin's contribution explores the social implications of political sectarianism in post-Cedar Lebanon and unpacks the complex mixture of socio-spatial perceptions and practices. Based on focus group interviews with one hundred Lebanese youth aged between eighteen and twenty-five, from various sectarian communities living and studying in the Greater Beirut area, he examines how young women and men construct symbolic boundaries between themselves and others, leading to highly compartmentalised forms of social relations. The young men and women distinguish between many different types of public, private and intimate spaces depending on the utilisation of these spaces and places and the meaning they ascribe to them. Private spaces and intimate relations are mostly reserved for same-sect members while public spheres in the city or workplace allows for a more inclusive, yet impersonal inter-sectarian mingling. The chapter shows the young Beirutis' subtle navigation of the sectarian terrain enabling them to coexist within the confessionally enclaved spaces of their 'contested' city. This has given rise to an impersonalised, urban sociality characterised by 'coexistence without empathy'.

Finally Are Knudsen examines the impact of international prosecution by the Special Tribunal for Lebanon, set up under UN auspices to prosecute the murder of Rafik Hariri. The Tribunal has emerged as the single most divisive issue in Lebanon, drumming up Sunni-Shia sectarian tensions. Since its inception in 2009 the Tribunal's legitimacy, objectivity and independence have been challenged. The Tribunal, it is claimed, has become politicised and its ultimate purpose is not judicial but political and seeks to impose a Western agenda on Lebanon. This was inevitable as the Tribunal is seeking justice for one victim who was close to Western allies. To the Tribunal's critics, politicisation means that its ultimate purpose is not to prosecute Hariri's assassins but to pressure Hizbollah, blackmail Syria and weaken Israel's enemies. The claim of politicisation brings the Tribunal into conflict with Lebanon's foremost politico-military movement, Hizbollah. Hizbollah and its allies insist on ending Lebanon's cooperation with the Tribunal. The pro-Hariri coalition insists on full cooperation with the Tribunal and refuses to take part in any government not fully committed towards this goal. Neither side is likely to compromise on this issue in the short term and it heralds a period of political instability, sectarian tensions and international mediation with the Tribunal in the shadow of Syria's internal revolt.

2

BEFORE THE REVOLUTION

Michael Kerr

Introduction

Conflicts in societies experiencing division over identity—be it religious, ethnic, nationalist or a mixture of these characteristics—inevitability become most pronounced, exaggerated and difficult to regulate during times of insecurity and crisis. Delicate governmental compromises designed to facilitate inter-ethnic coexistence in divided societies are often reliant upon regional and international stability for their longevity. An irredentist claim to all or a part of a state's territory, the presence of weak or permeable borders, or the inability of a government to maintain a monopoly of violence across all parts of its territory may detrimentally affect its capacity to manage or regulate ethnic, religious or cultural heterogeneity. Destabilising variables such as these may even provoke security dilemmas that are well beyond the means of the state to control or alleviate, which draw state and non-state third-party actors into its domestic politics and, in turn, exacerbate weaknesses inherent to its system of government. At different turning points in Lebanon's contemporary history, such factors significantly undermined the fragile power-sharing system of government that has managed conflict between its various Christian and Muslim communities since 1943. Focusing on these historical 'moments' and how they challenged and

23

reshaped Lebanon's governmental system, its political culture and urban landscape, informs us about the changing nature of the state and society, about the different communities that comprise it and about how they each react to change.

Offering an interdisciplinary perspective, this book's purpose is to analyse political, cultural and socioeconomic developments in Lebanon since the assassination of former Prime Minister Rafik Hariri and the withdrawal of Syrian forces that had occupied the country since 1976, the most recent turning point in the history of this most deeply divided society. This opening chapter sets the volume in its appropriate historical context and, in doing so, considers Lebanon's place within a Middle East state system in transition. Anti-authoritarian revolts, internationally backed armed insurgencies and popular democratic protest movements have overthrown military Arab nationalist regimes across North Africa and threatened oil-rich monarchies in the Gulf. It is far too early to judge the outcome of these revolutionary movements, but if Lebanon's recent history is anything to go by, then the flotsam and jetsam from the dramatic sea change that is underway within the Arab world will surely wash upon its troubled shores—its porous borders retain their magnetism for the troubles of this contested region.

In theory, Lebanon is governed through the distribution of political power between its Christian and Muslim communities, a corporate consociational form of government under which voters are obliged to vote for candidates from electoral lists of religiously defined candidates.[1] Since gaining independence, the Lebanese have failed to consolidate their state through this weak form of government, yet its power-sharing system has proved to be one of the most resilient and enduring forms of government the region has known since the collapse of the Ottoman Empire. More than that, it is one that is accepted and supported by all of Lebanon's political communities and their representatives, which is not something many of its neighbours could claim. Traditionally, the Lebanese do not govern without consent. Nevertheless, during the second half of the twentieth century, Lebanon 'won and lost' its sovereignty, the freedom and independence it gained from the French in 1943, along with the sort of pluralist and democratic institutions of government that Arab populations from the Maghreb to the Arabian peninsula are now demanding for the first time.

The primary objective of this chapter is not to determine whether Lebanon is on the cusp of breaking its cycle of political violence and instability. It is far too early to tell. Neither is it an attempt to predict how Lebanon will emerge from the transition that has been taking place in the Middle East since the September 11 attacks on the US World Trade Center in 2001, nor whether it can avoid civil war during this transition, or ever act as a model for democratisation in the region. Rather, it offers a reflective view of Lebanon as it sits uncomfortably at the centre of what is undoubtedly the most significant period of change in the Middle East since the 1979 Iranian Revolution, and one which holds as much uncertainty for the people of Lebanon, most of whom wish to return to their pre-1975 system of government, as it does for the peoples across the Arab world who are demanding radical constitutional reforms from regimes that seem incapable of reform.

This chapter does assert that the post-2005 period invokes a new scenario for Lebanon, making it relevant to consider this nodal point as an epoch in this divided society's modern history. In analysing the period in question, its main contribution to the scholarly debate over Lebanon is to reflect on some of the changes that it brought about, be they lasting or ephemeral, and the challenges they represent for a state which, despite the resilience of its power-sharing system of government, remains hotly contested and unconsolidated in the first decades of the twenty-first century.

Hizbollah Rising

The assassination of Hariri on 14 February 2005 led to the withdrawal of Syrian forces. Lebanon's Arab Spring provoked a new cycle of domestic conflict as the USA and Iran competed to fill the political vacuum and consolidate their interests in the Levant. In Lebanon, this took the form of a struggle for power between those who sought to salvage what they could from the old National Pact at a moment of Syrian weakness and international isolation (and while a US government that had ended Baath Party rule in Iraq in 2003 appeared determined to break the mould of a Middle East state system which had endured since the end of the mandate period), and those resolved to maintain the country's stature as a vanguard state at the frontline of an Arab-Israeli conflict in which the Iran-Syria-Hizbollah axis challenged US hegemony in the region.

The US-led invasion of Iraq was the driver of a catalytic cycle in the Middle East. In Lebanon, it sparked a reactionary process in which secondary catalysts such as Hariri's killing broke the post-civil war status quo. From this emerged the rival protest movements 8 March and 14 March, provoking the 2006 Israeli-Hizbollah war in Lebanon,[2] the 2007 Nahr al-Bared conflict,[3] the clashes between Hizbollah and Lebanese government forces in 2008,[4] the Doha Agreement which sought to resolve this internal conflict[5] and finally the collapse of the national unity government in 2011,[6] which saw Syria and Iran restore their influence through Hizbollah, albeit at a time of great crisis for the Assad regime in Damascus. In fact, it may be taken as a sign of Lebanon's continued importance to Iran and its centrality to the international relations of the Middle East that Syrian President, Bashar al-Assad, was able to secure a government in Beirut that was firmly in-tune with the Damascus-Tehran alliance at the very moment his regime faced its greatest threat since the bloody Hama uprising of 1982.

In 2005, many viewed Syria's military exit as the beginning of 'a new chapter' in Lebanon's history—the post-civil war 'moment' when Lebanon would at last begin to reclaim its independence and sovereignty after decades of Syrian domination.[7] Lebanon's latest political contortions were dubbed the 'Independence intifada' or the 'Cedar Revolution' by optimistic commentators and activists,[8] as US support appeared to present an opportunity for Syria's opponents in Lebanon to snatch victory from both the tragedy of Hariri's murder and the defeat that Syria's dereliction of the Taif Agreement had been for them.[9] In no sense of the term 'revolution', however, did the protests in Beirut, which were the first popular Arab uprisings since the second Palestinian *intifada* of 2000, (albeit organised and manipulated by political leaders to a far greater extent than in Tunisia, Egypt or Libya in 2010–11) manifest into the sort of constitutional changes that might be described as revolutionary. So much so that in the space of six years Lebanon had come full circle. At the beginning of 2011 Syria was again in the political ascendancy, only this time around with the military prowess of the Damascus-Tehran alliance—forged after the 1979 revolution between Syrian President Hafez al-Assad and Iranian revolutionary leader Ayatollah Khomeini—reinforced in government by Hizbollah rather than Syrian troops on the streets of Beirut.

It is perhaps unsurprising then that Lebanon, given its pluralism, freedoms, culture of power-sharing, and its propensity to act as a barometer of tension and a harbinger of 'things to come' in an increasingly volatile region, was the place which reacted first and most loudly to the impact of Western intervention in Iraq. After Hariri's murder, the Lebanese government willingly took the bait, buying into the notion that the US government's break with realism in the Middle East might mark the beginning of the end of Lebanon's lengthy troubles and its inability to insulate the state from the gravity of its more powerful neighbours. If Lebanon could detach itself from its centrality to Iranian and Syrian foreign policy objectives—the quest to achieve strategic parity with Israel and Iran's determination to ensure that Bashar al-Assad maintained his father's pragmatic alliance—then this might represent the first step in Lebanon regaining its sovereignty and entering the first world on the wave of US power. So the argument went. On 12 July 2006, however, Lebanon was plunged into an international conflict that was beyond its government's control, hostilities erupting after Hizbollah captured two Israeli soldiers during a surprise cross-border attack by the Islamist militants.[10] War continued for thirty-three days before a ceasefire was agreed on 14 August, with the Lebanese Army and UNFIL deployed in the south.

The crisis in Lebanon's government sharpened after Syria's withdrawal when the Lebanese government unsuccessfully attempted to resolve Hizbollah's outlier position within the state—that of a political party with a militia more powerful than the Lebanese Army, or a 'resistance force' operating without the consent of its partners in government after 2005. The Taif Agreement had provided for the disarmament of all Lebanese and Palestinian militias with one exception—Hizbollah.[11] Syria and Iran maintained the Islamic group in order to make Israel's occupation of southern Lebanon uncomfortable and as a bargaining chip in any future negotiations towards a regional settlement. When Israel ended its occupation of southern Lebanon in May 2000, low-level conflict continued between Hizbollah and Israel over the contested Shebaa Farms.[12] The farms were captured by Israel from Syria during the Six Day War of 1967, but Lebanon claimed them as part of its sovereign territory, thus granting Hizbollah a pretext for its continued military presence in the Shia-dominated south.

The Lebanese government attempted to avoid civil war over the double life of Hizbollah—the Islamist militia's political and paramilitary duality. An extra-governmental National Dialogue Committee was established, made up of representatives from the different Lebanese factions. Although this met regularly in 2006 and prevented the outbreak of internal conflict, the authority of Prime Minister Fuad Siniora's technocratic government dwindled in the months prior to the Israeli invasion. The National Dialogue Committee mirrored the division between the two Lebanese camps—the 8 March pro-Syrian alliance of Hizbollah and Christian leader General Michel Aoun and the anti-Syrian 14 March coalition of Sunnis, Christians and Druze. The anti-Syrian coalition sought strong Western support to assist Lebanon's democratically elected government to survive the crisis and fill the political void created by Syria's departure. The USA attempted to redress the regional power balance by further isolating Syria and weakening Iran's position in Lebanon. The outcome of Israel's invasion had the opposite effect, diminishing what little authority Prime Minister Fuad Siniora's government still enjoyed and exacerbating tensions between the country's pro- and anti-Syrian camps.

The Israeli invasion backfired—Hizbollah held out longer than Israel could withstand international calls for a ceasefire. The conflict ended with the Israeli government and its Western backers accepting a humiliating climbdown and Hizbollah was seen to be a military force capable of withstanding a sustained Israeli ground and air assault in Lebanon. The failure of the US-backed Israeli war enabled Hizbollah to consolidate its domestic position and significantly shift the centre of gravity in Lebanon's inter-confessional system towards Tehran. In fact, Hizbollah's ascendancy in Lebanon was apparent before the war even ended. Siniora publicly backed Hizbollah leader Hassan Nasrallah after the 'Qana massacre',[13] distanced his government from the USA by cancelling talks with US Secretary of State Condoleezza Rice in Beirut[14] and described the victims of Israeli attacks as 'martyrs'. He then denounced the Israeli government as 'war criminals',[15] declaring that Lebanon would be the 'last Arab country to make peace with Israel'.[16]

The war between Israel and Hizbollah came about for a number of reasons. Following Syria's military withdrawal, Lebanon's government was deadlocked over the unwillingness of Syria's opponents to accept Hizbollah in government without movement on the decommissioning of its weaponry. At the same time, Israel was keen to remove Hizbollah's forces from its Lebanon border, weaken its political support base and reduce Iran's influence in the Israeli-Palestinian conflict. In order to advance these objectives, the Israeli government took the Shia Arab Islamists by surprise while a hawkish administration resided in Washington and tensions between the USA and Iran over the latter's nuclear development programme and regional challenge to Israeli military hegemony were at the forefront of Middle East politics. Likewise, the Bush administration also wanted to weaken Hizbollah, further isolate Syria and limit the role Iran played in Arab politics through its support for the Palestinian Islamic Resistance Movement Hamas controlling Gaza. The Lebanese government and the

14 March alliance had a clear interest in the USA advancing these objectives. Through increasing attacks on Israel, Hizbollah sought to support Hamas, consolidate its political-military position in Lebanon and enhance its regional status as the only non-Palestinian Arab force willing to challenge the Israelis. Therefore, there was a convergence of US, Israeli and anti-Syrian Lebanese interests in delivering a knockout blow to Hizbollah, at a moment of Syrian weakness after it raised tensions on Lebanon's border with Israel in 2006. Nevertheless, while Hizbollah operates under orders from Syria and Iran, it was most likely trying to displace conflict from its domestic arena onto the international stage.

The 2006 conflict in Lebanon should be seen in the context of the break with realism that Bush's interventionist agenda represented for parts of the Middle East. Moreover, President Barack Obama's unconvincing efforts to retreat from his predecessor's foreign policy underscores just how far Lebanon is from realising its independence, finally consolidating the state and healing the multifaceted divisions of the civil war period. Nevertheless, there was a deceptive appearance of stability about Lebanon in 2010, as the old survivors of pan-Arab nationalism's heyday and the oil-rich monarchs of the Gulf struggled to contain and meet calls for widespread political reform from the Arab street in societies that have never experienced the freedoms, pluralism and independence that Lebanon enjoyed until 1975, and set out to regain in 2005 by loosening the grip of Damascus over its internal political process. This is the Lebanon that some view as a model for democratisation in the Levant. That may sound unduly optimistic to seasoned Lebanon watchers, but the country became democratic rather than authoritarian after 1943 due to a pre-existing balance of power between its communities. As such, some might argue that it is 'revolution proof'. These are defining features of the state.

Lebanon is a weak hybrid state in a system dominated by strong centralised governments, yet the culture of power-sharing that exists between its different ethnic communities has endured. This is true for Lebanon in the post-2005 period under consideration. Some of the actors have changed and significant shifts have occurred with respect to the external linkage politics that bind Lebanon's communities to regional and international patrons, but still, no one community can win out over all the others and, in the long term, no single external power can shape Lebanon's political course solely in its own interests. Lebanon's weakness remains its strength. Regardless of what changes the Arab Spring brings to the Levant, the chances of the establishment of authoritarian rule in Lebanon are limited to the imposition of hegemonic control by a third party such as Syria or Iran, as was the case in the 1990–2005 period. Lebanon's diversity may again lend itself towards democratic pluralism at some point in the future. This is the lesson that must be learnt from the civil war period if Lebanon is to one day become a liberal consociation, as opposed to a corporate consociation in which power is divided unevenly rather than shared equally among its different communities.

On the other hand, it is more likely that Lebanon's recent conflicts are a portent of what lies ahead in this part of the Middle East. Iraq, Syria, Israel and the Palestinian Territories are all part of the same neighbourhood as Lebanon. They share similar patterns of religious and ethnic heterogeneity, while states such as Bahrain, Saudi Arabia and Yemen govern in the absence of the sort of national consensus that has, in the past, been brokered between Lebanon's elites on the premise of recognising ethno-national or inter-communal diversity, using power-sharing as a means of managing divisive social, cultural, political and religious variables. For over half a century Israel and Lebanon were the only countries in the region to have adopted democratic institutions which, however imperfect, attempt to reflect the diversity of their societies in efforts to govern with a considerable degree of inter-communal consent. The Palestinian Territories and Iraq followed suit in 2005 with rather mixed results, as a culture of power-sharing takes a long time to gestate. As with the trajectory of political developments in Lebanon since independence, its pluralism means that it will only be able to influence the Middle East state system in a normative sense, and the knock-on effects of regional change will continue to shape and reshape its politics, such is the fate of a weak divided society in a region that remains an epicentre of the global economic and geo-strategic interests of great powers and aspiring powers.

On the surface, the 8 March and 14 March movements represent a different regrouping of Lebanon's communities. The Christians strategically split between those who are more afraid of the Sunnis and those who are more afraid of the Shia. The Shia are in conflict with Sunnis and this split, both in Lebanon and across the region, on the surface at least, mirrors US-Iranian competition for influence in the Arab world. Beneath the surface of these two new Lebanese alliances, the political groups that comprise them are the participants of old communal factions from the civil war period, communal monocultures such as the Lebanese Forces which is Maronite,

Hizbollah which is Shia, and while Michel Aoun and AMAL have a few Shia and Christian supporters respectively, the bulk of their constituents adhere tightly to Lebanon's communal cleavages. So while everything appeared to have changed in 2005, very little had changed, except perhaps that before the clashes between state forces and Hizbollah militiamen in May 2008, there were communal vetoes in Lebanon's power-sharing system, whereas after this incident there appeared to be a party veto which no other group could challenge—that of Hizbollah. If we discount the Palestine Liberation Organisation's (PLO) influence in the early 1970s, as they were not a Lebanese faction, then this is a new and unwelcome development in Lebanon's power-sharing system, although the PLO were not dissimilar. Moreover, the Special Tribunal for Lebanon is also a new development and may be viewed as a temporary external veto in the international struggle for Lebanon that occurred after Hariri's murder.

A New Phase in an Old War

In the post-2005 period, one interesting development that is worth noting is the absence of any deep division over whether the state of Lebanon in its current form should actually exist, which is one of the central theses of Theodor Hanf's seminal work on the civil war.[17] The civil war resolved that particular issue and Lebanon certainly became more 'Lebanese' after the war, and as a consequence of it. Yet Syria's military withdrawal from Lebanon cast up two competing and contradictory 'Lebanons' in the post-2005 period, conflicting alternative images of a state drawn from antagonistic Lebanese identities, which offer radically contrasting visions of its people, the state and its place within the Middle East. These visions predate 2005, and they have tested the National Pact,[18] broken it in 2006 and 2008, and stalled the project of fully implementing the Taif Agreement, with its new electoral recommendations and provisions for decentralisation, both of which hold the potential to shift Lebanon away from what is an externally managed consociational system to a more liberal democratic polity.[19] Like the pre-war conflict over the state that the National Pact momentarily papered over, one is an image of Lebanon that is Western-orientated, while the other is that of a country tailored to the East, harnessed to Persian nationalism in its post-revolutionary Islamist form and Syria's refusal to give up the ghost of the Arab-Israeli conflict. One lesson of the civil war period that must be learnt here, is to accept the different identity-forming narratives of the Lebanese, albeit endeavouring to find commonalities between them, and abandon the 'one nation fits all' Jacobin nationalist idealism that in the past sought to negate the legitimacy of old ethnic communities and their identities, for this only serves to fracture Lebanon further and make peaceful coexistence more problematic.

It is here that Lebanon is stuck. It remains a deeply divided society which has neither recovered from nor resolved the many internal and external problems that led to the collapse of the state in 1975, many of which have now taken on new dynamics in the post-Cold War world. And if we reflect on Lebanon's contemporary past, while it is clear that 2005 does mark a significant turning point in Lebanese history, given the regional transition that it is an integral part of, it is unclear whether Lebanon can take a positive step forward towards consolidating a plural democratic state, with a power-sharing system that evolves from what is a corporate power-sharing system towards a more modern liberal consociational form of government, in the political vacuum that persists.

At a number of turning points in Lebanon's contemporary history both the state and its peoples have been tested to their limits, and these moments provide ample evidence for us to be certain that what lies ahead for Lebanon remains inextricably linked to the US-Iranian conflict and the Arab Spring. These points have occasionally yielded positive results for Lebanon. Anglo-Franco rivalry in the Middle East during the Second World War led Lebanon to its independence in 1943 when a Maronite-Sunni/Christian-Muslim elite forged the National Pact. In 1958 pan-Arab nationalism exacerbated Lebanon's inter-communal tensions and while President Camille Chamoun's efforts to extend his presidential term under cover of the Eisenhower Doctrine led to US and Egyptian intervention, this reset the balance at the heart of Lebanon's power-sharing system and marked the beginning of a period of stability and prosperity under Fuad Chehab's presidency.[20] In more recent times however, these 'moments' of crisis have resulted in lengthy civil war, loss of sovereignty and long-term political instability for Lebanon. The influx of PLO guerrillas to Lebanon following the 1967 Arab-Israeli War led to the incremental erosion of Lebanon's sovereignty, and exacerbated existing internal divisions over the National Pact to breaking point in 1975.[21] The following year, the failure of US-sponsored Syrian intervention to prevent the collapse of the state accentuated the rapid internationalisation of what became the war for Lebanon.[22]

In 1989, with the Soviet Union on the brink of collapse, an internationally brokered agreement at Taif, Saudi Arabia, marked the beginning of the end to a civil war which had divided and engulfed the Lebanese state for fifteen years. Amending the National Pact, Lebanon's Christian and Muslim parliamentarians reconciled their differences and agreed upon a return to power-sharing. The agreement contained a number of proposals which dated back to the 1976 Constitutional Document, which was a failed attempt to reformulate the National Pact shortly after the war began. So the end of the war for Lebanon represented a return to the status quo regarding what form of government Lebanon would have. But there was a price to be paid for ending its conflicts—what Lebanon gained in terms of security and stability after 1990 it lost in terms of sovereignty and independence. How the Taif Agreement was to be interpreted and whether it would in fact be implemented at all, largely depended on what pressure the USA was prepared to put Syria under in the years that followed, pressure that might have ensured that a return to power-sharing in Beirut heralded a new beginning for Lebanon. In the event, the USA accepted a Syrian solution to Lebanon's turmoil, and Taif led to a period of unfettered Syrian hegemonic control through undemocratic power-sharing institutions. During the period of 1990–2005, Lebanon experienced a form of corporate consociation that amounted to little more than direct rule by proxy from Damascus. Understanding the reasons why this happened and why Lebanon's civil war ended when it did are central to any analysis of what the Arab Spring might hold for Lebanon and whether its break with Syria in 2005 was a step forward in its journey towards state consolidation and the implementation of Taif, a step sideways or a step backwards.

Had the Gulf War—which was only possible due to the disintegration of the Soviet Union—not drawn Syrian President Hafez al-Assad into the US coalition against his most deadly rival, Saddam Hussein, then Syrian domination in Lebanon might not have been so complete quite so quickly. More than that, a return to power-sharing at the end of the Cold War reinforces the widely held view that violence in Lebanon could only be regulated, and a start to the country's reconstruction made, when there was some realignment in, or readjustment of, the political forces struggling for control over the Middle East. The same argument can be made for the post-2005 period in Lebanon.

In much the same way that the prevention of Lebanon's civil war was beyond its political leaders, exogenous forces largely determined when and how the conflicts taking place within its borders would end. In fact, the settlement agreed by the Lebanese at Taif had been accepted by the majority of its political factions the year after hostilities broke out, when US Secretary of State Henry Kissinger brought Assad into his government's sphere of influence in 1976. Kissinger was quick to grasp an opportunity from the tragedy of Lebanon's disintegration.[23] Viewing its conflict through the prism of the Cold War, he sought to provoke a split between Moscow and Damascus whilst the Soviet Union's main allies in the region, Syria and the PLO, were at odds in Lebanon. So Kissinger used Lebanon as a bargaining chip with which to detach Assad from his alliance with Moscow. Assad and Soviet leader Leonid Brezhnev clashed when Kissinger facilitated Syria's military occupation of Lebanon, as US, Israeli and Syrian interests converged against the PLO.[24] This occurred when the PLO and its revolutionary allies, the Lebanese National Movement who operated from Beirut and controlled two-thirds of the country, attempted to assert their control over the remainder of the disintegrating state. Kissinger then facilitated a limited Syrian military intervention with Israeli consent, as a means of imposing a political settlement on its warring factions and reducing Fatah leader Yasser Arafat's powerbase. All three parties wanted to curtail the PLO's freedom of movement in Lebanon and prevent Arafat from emerging as the main beneficiary of a Christian defeat in the civil war. Kissinger's worst-case Cold War scenario envisaged Arafat consolidating the PLO's control over most of the country and establishing a radical pro-Soviet state on Israel's northern border.

The opportunity to weaken Syrian-Soviet ties by bringing Assad in from the cold made this policy doubly attractive to Kissinger in his struggle for mastery of the Middle East. But by the end of 1976 Kissinger was out of office, his plans for a comprehensive Middle East settlement lay unfulfilled and 12,000 Syrian forces occupied Lebanon. Assad had acted in Lebanon to extend his influence in the Arab world as Egyptian Prime Minister Anwar Sadat made peace with Israel. Assad's Lebanon policy was quite simple—there would be no solution to the civil war which did not first and foremost suit Syria's interests in the Arab-Israeli conflict and further its irredentist claim to its smaller neighbour. This was a policy which Assad sustained for the remainder of his life and the Taif Agreement represented the high watermark of his intervention, as it internationally legitimised Syria's role in Lebanon's political and military affairs. There were other regional and international interests played out during these negotiations, but everyone present knew the solution would be a Syrian one, and that Assad would be the final arbitrator of any agreement reached. As the force on the ground in Lebanon, the USA and the Arab League needed Syria to implement and police any agreement reached at Taif. Nevertheless, almost all the participants wanted to dilute Syria's influence and Arabise Lebanon's rehabilitation as far as possible. During the negotiations, Assad distanced himself from the proposed accord and flexed his muscles in Lebanon, until any linkage between Syrian troop withdrawal and political reform was dropped from the text.

The USA wanted to clear up the Lebanese crisis at the end of the Cold War. It had become a running sore, spreading tension throughout the region. Israeli security concerns vis-à-vis Hizbollah and the export of the Iranian revolution to Lebanon deeply worried Washington.[25] Before the emergence of Hizbollah, Lebanon could have been excluded from a regional peace deal, thus the USA and Israel wanted Lebanon and the Islamic militia firmly under Syrian control. Through Saudi diplomacy, the USA sought to impose an agreement on Lebanon that limited Assad's control over the country. The Saudis also wanted to limit Syria's political dominance in Lebanon, position themselves as the second Arab power vis-à-vis Syria, enhance their role as a Middle Eastern peace broker and reinstate Lebanon's traditional elites, particularly the Sunni community whose position had been hijacked by Syria during the war. Rafik Hariri and Saudi foreign minister Saud al-Faisal were the men at the centre of this petro-diplomacy. Although it lacked the military might of Syria, Saudi Arabia's strength lay in its financial power and close ties with the USA. At Taif, the Saudis promised massive monetary aid to rehabilitate the country, through Hariri, if not for the Lebanese, then certainly to limit Syria's influence.

Having occupied the country since 1976, Assad succeeded in blocking any overtly pro-Western settlement to the long-running Lebanon crisis. Thus Taif ushered in a new era of internationally legitimised and politicised Syrian control over Lebanon. When the USA set out to end the war in the late 1980s, once again it accepted that this could only be achieved through 'a Syrian solution', which amounted to a degree of political and military rule from Damascus. Enjoying Arab league support, Syria did reinstate power-sharing in Lebanon but it was not a democratic form of consociational government. The fact that Hizbollah, the party in Lebanon with the largest degree of freedom, remained outside of the state and acted to the tune of the Syrian-Iranian alliance, above the authority of any Lebanese government, reinforces this view.

So the global transformation that occurred in the late 1980s and early 1990s had a great impact on Lebanon, as the USA again tried to bring

Assad in from his Cold War bunker. Ever elusive, historians will remember the Machiavellian Baath Party leader as the man who ultimately won this post-Cold War tussle, for after Taif he consolidated the political and military dominance that he set out to achieve through his 1976 détente with Kissinger. For the USA, however, Lebanon was a price that it was willing to pay to have Assad realign his state by joining the US-led coalition against Saddam Hussein. To a large extent, the Gulf War sealed Lebanon's fate and determined the outcome of the political process that ended its civil war. Iraq's invasion of Kuwait in August 1990 provided the opportunity for Assad to contribute to the defeat of his competitor under the guise of supporting a US-led coalition. In turn, it offered the USA much-needed Arab legitimacy for its anti-Saddam front. Syria was too important in the regional scene to be ignored and the USA used the Taif Agreement to improve its relations with Damascus.

The USA, the Israelis and the Syrians shared an interest in regulating Lebanon's conflicts at the end of the Cold War. Many of Lebanon's political divisions remained unresolved, as did the problems posed by its centrality to the Arab-Israeli conflict and post-Cold War geo-strategic rivalries in the Middle East. Hizbollah replaced the PLO, becoming a far more reliable proxy for Assad and a more enduring and troublesome adversary for Israel to contend with on its northern border. More than that, the financial, military and ideological support Hizbollah received from its Iranian sponsors greatly exceeded the support the PLO received from Arab states and its Cold War backers in Moscow.

The Taif Agreement released Lebanon from the cycle of regional and internationally driven violent conflict that was played out between its multifaceted rival ethno-national alliances, and the internal territorial conflicts taking place between and within its different communities. But at the same time it entrusted Syria with the restoration of its political institutions. Lebanese nationalists subsequently argued that the USA and Saudi Arabia had sold Lebanon's soul to the devil at Taif and, in fact, many prominent Lebanese politicians and commentators were murdered after having made such remarks, such as *al-Nahar* editor and member of parliament Gibran Tueni and prominent Lebanese academic Samir Kassir.[26] Given the collapse of the National Pact in 1975 and the consumptive civil war that followed, realists in Washington accepted the view that only a firm hand from Damascus could truly end the war and regulate conflict on Israel's northern border.

The Gulf War was the first major challenge the USA faced to its post-Cold War dominance in the Middle East, marking a realignment of regional and global alliances after the Soviet Union had left the stage. However, while the lack of bipolar rivalry in the region boded well for the initiation of an Arab-Israeli peace process, it also gave Syria the push it needed to play the lead role in ending Lebanon's war. By invading Kuwait, Saddam Hussein undermined the Saudi reconstruction plan, upsetting the regional equilibrium that was crucial for the resuscitation of consociational government in Lebanon.[27] For the Syrians, joining the US-led alliance against Iraq was about consolidating its position in Lebanon. Just as the outbreak of war in Lebanon brought Kissinger and al-Assad together, the end of the Cold War marked another high point in US-Syrian relations. Lebanon was expedient to the wider regional interests of the USA, as was the case in the post-2005 period, a deal-maker on which agreement may be reached, a bargaining chip with which external actors were prepared to gamble in efforts to consolidate their regional positions.

With the world's attention firmly focused on the crisis in the Gulf, rebuilding Lebanon was no longer of pressing concern. Some might say that Kuwait was saved at Lebanon's expense, as the Arab world's pledges of investment and support vanished. Whether the USA intended to pressure Syria to implement Taif and set a timescale for military withdrawal is difficult to judge, but if Kissinger's détente with al-Assad is anything to go by then Syrian domination was a price that the USA was willing to pay to end the war and reduce political violence on Israel's northern border. And given Assad's track record of intransigence and intractability in defending Syrian interests in Lebanon, the road to reconfiguring democratic pluralism between its different communities was never likely to have been smooth after 1990. As such, any hope that Taif would lead to the reconstitution of Lebanese sovereignty evaporated. Officially, the USA supported the full implementation of Taif, but prior to 11 September 2001 Washington did not push Syria to implement its provisions in the letter and spirit of the accord.[28] And it was Assad's ability to successfully implement this policy that was the defining variable in US-Lebanese Cold War and post-Cold war relations.

Conclusion

The struggle for Lebanon again took on new dimensions as old Cold War battlelines were redrawn following al-Qaida's attacks on the Pentagon and World Trade Center on 11 September 2001. These terrorist attacks were a catalyst for US intervention in the Middle East, military engagement which represented a significant break with the *realpolitik* that marked US policy towards the region during the Cold War, as Bush sought to curtail Iran in its ambition to attain strategic parity with Israel and be the dominant regional power in the Middle East. Lebanon, Syria and Hizbollah remain central to this conflict. Lebanon's political future is at the mercy of changing regional geopolitics in the Levant, international and regional conflicts that the Arab Spring has sharply exacerbated. The USA suffered a setback as a consequence of the civil war that erupted in Iraq following its invasion, with both Iran and Turkey considerably enhancing their influence in this fledgling consociational state. What the USA is now prepared or able to do to prevent Iran further extending its influence in Iraq, or maintaining it in Syria, is unclear at the time of writing. What is certain is that it will have an enormous impact on Lebanon's fragile political process and the post-2005 period is unlikely to be the final chapter in either the struggle for Lebanon or Lebanon's quest to consolidate the state.

The search for peace and stability in Lebanon has consistently been hampered by a lack of positive external support for the implementation of the sort of power-sharing framework which regulates conflict between its different ethnic communities and prevents them from exploiting external support to the detriment of those that they share power with. Until Lebanon experiences a 'unity of purpose' between those intervening in its political process—acting with the intent to implement its power-sharing arrangements and establish lasting peaceful coexistence amongst its communities *as an interest in and of itself*—this deeply divided society will remain trapped in the same cycle of violence that led it to civil war in 1975–6. The state of Lebanon remains unconsolidated and Lebanon remains no closer to breaking the cycle of externally driven conflict that has plagued it since the late 1960s. Regardless of the fact that all of Lebanon's factions accept and support the idea of power-sharing, collectively, they lack the power or the will to implement a power-sharing accord. And they lack the support of states that hold an interest in positively implementing and policing a Lebanese peace agreement, rather than manipulating it for their own selfish strategic interests.

3

THE LIMITS OF CORPORATE CONSOCIATION

TAIF AND THE CRISIS OF POWER-SHARING IN LEBANON SINCE 2005

Amal Hamdan

Introduction

Although academic critics of consociational democracy frame this form of power-sharing as the cause of political instability and conflict in Lebanon,[1] its opponents concede that consociational democracy provides 'sound engineering' for states that cannot hope just yet for 'beautiful architecture'.[2] It was this sound engineering in the form of the 1989 Taif Agreement which ended the 1975–89 Lebanese civil war that claimed an estimated 100,000 lives.[3] Taif was also a milestone in the country's constitutional reforms as it formally re-established consociational democracy as the foundation for power-sharing among Lebanon's eighteen confessional communities.[4] However, the consociational principles and spirit of Taif were sacrificed shortly after the agreement was brokered when Lebanon came under Syria's hegemonic control in 1990[5] and consequently the implementation and interpretation of Taif was left to Damascus.[6] Not surprisingly, Syria 'made a mockery' of its power-sharing principles.[7]

The failure to fully implement Taif meant that consociationalism in Lebanon was pending[8] from 1990 until 2005. Then in 2005 former Prime Minister Rafik Hariri was assassinated, forcing Damascus to loosen its hegemonic grip on Lebanon. Since Hariri's death, the country has been politically polarised into two camps, the 14 March coalition, which includes the anti-Syrian Future Movement (Future) and the 8 March bloc, which is led by pro-Syria parties Hizbollah and Amal. Since 2005 these parties have been central in the divisive struggle and as the primary political representatives of the Sunni and Shia communities,[9] the political confrontation has taken on a sectarian dimension. While both camps concur that restoring consociationalism by fully implementing Taif[10] could resolve the political crisis, Taif has yet to be implemented. If political rivals agree that Taif in practice could resolve the crisis, why has it yet to be implemented?[11] Underlying the crisis is a longstanding predicament in Lebanese politics—political factions disagree on the interpretation of Taif's text and practice. Although such differences have long been typical of Lebanese politics,[12] disparities over the text and practice of Taif alone do not account for the failure to implement it.

This chapter argues that rifts over Taif's text and practice mask a deeper political conflict resulting from communal grievances of unequal power-sharing, as a consequence of the corporate consociational framework of Taif. Corporate consociationalism predetermines state positions based on ethnic, cultural or confessional group identities. Extended to Lebanon, this form of power-sharing has meant that the posts of the president, prime minister and house speaker are reserved exclusively for the Maronite, Sunni and Shia communities respectively. Corporate consociationalism is accurately criticised for creating communal grievances of unequal power-sharing and in the past, has facilitated the eruption of internal conflict. Arguably, Taif's corporate consociational features are potentially setting the stage for a resumption of conflict between the political leadership of the Shia and Sunni confessional groups, Hizbollah, Amal and Future. Examining their perceptions of power-sharing will show that the current crisis is a struggle over the distribution of power between the Sunni and Shia communities as a result of Taif's corporate consociational framework, which has resulted in Shia grievances that power-sharing is unequal with the Sunni. To what extent are deep political divisions since 2005 related to aspirations of the Shia political leadership to revise Taif's distribution of power and increase the Shia stake within the corporate consociational formula? Hizbollah and

Amal harbour ambitions to modify the current consociational formula to redistribute power and increase the Shia community's authority, while Future insists on preserving Taif, since its formula provided Lebanon's Sunnis with a preeminent political position, a powerful motivation for Future to maintain this agreement. The scope of this chapter does not overlook historic Druze resentment of corporate consociational practices[13] and Maronite misgivings with Taif[14] but focuses on the positions of the Sunni and Shia political leaderships.

It is necessary to briefly elaborate on the theory of consociational democracy and its different forms. It is important to note that this study does not suggest replacing consociationalism in Lebanon with an alternative system but seeks to highlight the limits of corporate consociational democracy.

Re-Assessing Consociational Democracy

Advancements in Lijphart's classic consociational theory emphasise the necessity for broad representation of significant communities in executive authority.[15] However, the critical advancement O'Leary introduced to Lijphart's theory has bridged a gap between consociationalism in theory and practice.[16] O'Leary challenges Lijphart's view that representation of segmental communities alone within executive government is sufficient for consociational democracy[17] and instead emphasises the necessity for meaningful participation, along with representation, of significant segmental communities in executive power.[18] Thus O'Leary provides a monumental distinction in the practice of consociational democracy, the mere allocation of seats along ethnic lines to reinforce representation of segmental communities does not sufficiently denote power-sharing. What is necessary for democratic and stable power-sharing is the genuine participation of significant ethno-confessional groups within executive power.[19]

Consociations are distinguished as corporate and liberal, based on the criteria of defining group identities. Questioning whether consociations are based on predetermined or self-determined group identities[20] addresses a widely-held criticism of consociationalism—that corporate systems 'further entrench and institutionalise pre-existing and often conflict-hardened ethnic identities'.[21] Thus corporate consociations are defined as accommodating groups according to ascriptive criteria, such as ethnicity or religion, on the assumption that such identities are both fixed and internally homogeneous.[22] Extended to Lebanon, implementing corporate consociationalism has meant accommodating the Sunni, Shia and Maronite communities by allocating the state's top three posts to these communities. This flawed model of consociationalism is accurately criticised for providing privileges to groups exclusively accommodated within a fixed formula and bars individuals from outside ascriptive groups. It is this far-less democratic model of consociationalism that continues to be reinvented and implemented in Lebanon.[23] As a corporate consociational agreement, Taif cemented the confessional allocation of the state's highest offices by reserving them to the Sunni, Shia and Maronite communities alone.[24] It is this model of consociationalism that continues to exclude other communities from top posts and consequently cultivates communal resentment and political instability.[25]

Thus Taif has been criticised for upholding corporate consociational features.[26] The corporate consociational distribution of powers fuelled grievances of unequal political participation among the Sunni, Shia and Maronite segments. Shia political factions particularly emphasise that their community's participation in executive government is insufficient.[27] As Taif's corporate consociational formula bars the Shia from ever holding a top position of executive authority, the presidency or premiership, arguably Shia grievances stem from corporate consociationalism.

The 1975–89 war provides evidence that corporate consociationalism could facilitate the eruption of internal conflict in Lebanon. Consequently, the resumption of violence as a result of Taif's corporate consociational formula is not unlikely. The following is a brief account of the corporate consociational implementation of the National Pact and resulting communal tensions which preceded the prolonged conflict.

Corporate Consociationalism and Conflict

The domestic dimension of the 1975–89 war[28] was partially premised within Sunni-Shia resentment of Maronite political hegemony,[29] stemming from the corporate consociational implementation of the 1943 National Pact. The National Pact was an arrangement between Sunni and Maronite leaders in order to gain independence for Lebanon from the French mandate.[30] It allocated the highest offices to the largest confessional communities at the time—consequently, the president would be Maronite, and the prime minster Sunni,[31] leaving the Shia excluded from any top executive government position. However, the fathers of the Pact did not intend for corporate consociationalism to permanently determine the distribution of executive offices as indicated by one of the Pact's architects: 'the Pact has been interpreted too rigidly... the confessional distribution of offices of state... was not intended to last forever. It was thought of as provisional. It was not an essential element of the Pact'.[32] Yet this formula lasted until 1975, only to be reinvented and reinforced in Taif in 1989.

Further, it is worth noting that despite the seeming 'Maronite-Sunni'[33] pact, the Sunni community complained of unequal political participation. Sunni resentment was rooted in the considerable discrepancy of power between the prime minister and president—executive authority was concentrated in the presidency,[34] making it in principle the most powerful post, while the prime minister's position was far less influential.[35] The exclusion of the Sunni and Shia communities from genuine participation in executive power fuelled resentment towards the Maronite political leadership. Communal friction mounted as the Sunni and Shia groups increasingly questioned the division of power between the state's highest offices[36] and heightening perceptions of Maronite hegemony.[37] Thus, Sunni-Shia aspirations to reform power-sharing based on corporate consociation practices fuelled, if not directly facilitated, the outbreak of conflict. This is corroborated by the Sunni community's political and military alliance with armed Palestinians, premised upon calculations to weaken the Maronite community and secure gains within the consociational system.[38] Previous research notes that the 'PLO... became an extension of the Sunni community in the absence of a Lebanese Sunni militia that could match the Christian forces'.[39] A Future Movement politician acknowledges that the Sunni community used the threat of Palestinian weapons to undermine Maronite control and elevate the Sunni position within the political system.[40] Further, after Taif politically elevated the Sunni community by empowering the prime minister's office,[41] Sunni rhetoric of Arab nationalism and Palestinian statehood diminished considerably.[42]

The Shia community also made the issue of 'excessive' presidential powers a 'political rallying point'[43] during the first two years of fighting, further corroborating the case that grievances of unequal power-sharing as a result of corporate consociational practices facilitated the outbreak of conflict. It should not be overlooked that the corporate consociational application of the National Pact corroborates O'Leary's theory.

Thus, the implementation of the National Pact within a corporate consociational framework created and fuelled communal grievances that culminated in conflict that lasted until a new power-sharing arrangement was brokered, an arrangement that reduced the powers of the Maronite office and elevated the Sunni and Shia positions.[44] This was the Taif Agreement.

Taif

While power-sharing in the form of the 1989 Taif Agreement may be hailed for ending the prolonged conflict,[45] it failed to remedy deep-rooted grievances of unequal participation among the Shia.[46] Instead of correcting the criteria for allocating positions, Taif reinforced corporate consociationalism by reinstating the confessional allocation of offices. Taif cemented what the founding fathers of Lebanon did not mean to do—it restored corporate consociational practices, thereby firmly establishing a source of communal friction and instability and failing to resolve one of the most significant weaknesses of power-sharing in Lebanon.

It is necessary to provide an account of Taif's redistribution of power to illustrate that corporate consociationalism shifted communal grievances that are resurfacing today. Taif significantly modified the distribution of power among the Sunni, Shia and Maronite communities: 'the highest political representatives of the Shia and Sunnis became more influential than that of the Maronites'.[47] Taif reduced the authority of the president, previously the most powerful position, while the prime minister's position was significantly empowered.[48] Viewed through a confessional and consociational prism, Taif politically elevated the Sunni community as the prime minister 'inherited the president's dominant position in the executive'.[49]

The most significant modification of power was made in the council of ministers.[50] Taif transferred executive authority from the president to the cabinet as a collective body.[51] The text leaves no room for interpretation: 'executive power is given to the Council of Ministers'.[52] Theoretically, this redistribution of executive authority could have satisfied a crucial parameter stipulated by O'Leary that all significant communities should participate in executive government, as Taif shifted executive power from a position reserved for a single confessional community to a collective body where all communities participate.[53]

A final reform regarding the redistribution of power is whether or not the finance ministry post was reserved exclusively for the Shia community, a hotly contested issue between Hizbollah, Amal and Future. Although it is not written in the accord, its proponents (Hizbollah and Amal) maintain that it was verbally agreed to during the proceedings. Future argues that this was never agreed on at Taif.

It is necessary to reiterate that prior to Taif, the Sunni and Shia communities maintained grievances of unequal participation in power-sharing and the reinforcement of corporate consociational features in Taif shifted these grievances to the Maronite and Shia communities. While Taif remedied Sunni objections of unequal participation,[54] it failed to comprehensively resolve Shia grievances[55] and created resentment among the Maronite community. In the final outcome, the Sunni community emerged with the most gains from Taif: 'They [the Sunni] have emerged as the principal sectarian winners in the constitutional "fine-tuning": their leader, the prime minister, is now primus inter pares in the troika'.[56]

It should be noted that Hizbollah was not present at Taif and were strongly critical of the accord in the first two years after the war,[57] particularly the corporate consociational allocation of offices.[58] Hassan Nasrallah stated in 1997 that Taif cannot be 'accepted as a conclusive formula',[59] providing an early warning that a conflict over power-sharing was bound to resurface. Amal's assessment of Taif is slightly less critical. In theory, the agreement provided a balanced formula of participation among the Sunni and Shia, but left to the late Hariri's specific interpretation and implementation of power-sharing, it undermined Shia participation within executive authority[60] and consequently failed to balance power. While both parties allege that Taif failed to balance power by overly empowering the post of the prime minister,[61] arguably their criticism is rooted within the accord's corporate consociational formula which bars the Shia community from ever holding a top executive government position. Hizbollah Member of Parliament Ali Fayyad, who is also the party's chief constitutional architect, is clear: 'There is no doubt that Taif gave a central position to the Sunni confessional community through the position of the prime minister'.[62] Further indications that Shia grievances are rooted within Taif's corporate consociational distribution of power is Hizbollah's suggestion to re-assess the 'constitutional prerogatives allotted to the three heads of the country's constitutional institutions',[63] to resolve the political crisis.

Although divisive disputes such as the disarmament of Hizbollah and the United Nations-backed Special Tribunal for Lebanon formed to investigate Hariri's assassination are widely believed to be the root of political polarisation since 2005, rival factions concur that these disputes are symptoms of a deeper conflict.[64] 'To varying degrees, *all* the leaders know they need to find a mechanism for coexistence—but the problem is that the three main sects have become hostages... The Sunnis are hostages to the Hariri assassination and the implementation of Taif... The Shia are hostages to Hizbollah's arms... The Maronites are mainly hostages to the... nostalgia of the president's past'.[65]

Not unlike simmering Sunni and Shia grievances before the 1975 conflict, underlying the current crisis are Shia grievances that they are excluded from equal participation in executive government. Incidentally, the resurfacing of Shia resentment and the struggle over power-sharing was inevitable.[66] Hizbollah, Amal and Future's interpretation of Taif's text and practices highlights the disparities between the rival camps.

Taif and the Dispute between Representation and Participation

Although Taif 'balanced confessional representation',[67] Hizbollah and Amal allege it failed to balance confessional participation,[68] raising O'Leary's distinction between representation and participation in executive government.[69] These factions maintain that the Shia community's participation in executive government is insufficient. 'Consociationalism is not only representation, for example, the distribution of seats in parliament based on proportional representation and cabinet—what is needed is actual participation in executive decision-making'.[70] Fayyad is clear: Hizbollah believe that Taif failed to establish 'a complete consociational democracy'.[71]

So would a 'complete consociational democracy' entail reassigning the post of the prime minister, reserved for the Sunni community, to the Shia community?[72] When this question was put to Hizbollah, the response was swift and icy: 'This is not proposed'.[73] When pressed, the Hizbollah MP was resolute: 'No. Never has this been suggested and never has anyone considered it... The Shia objective is not for domination or to take the position of any of the confessions'.[74]

While they refused to stipulate what constitutes a fair power-sharing formula, Hizbollah and Amal were consistent that Taif failed to provide equal participation within executive government, indicating that these factions maintain aspirations to revise the power-sharing formula. Future insists that Taif's power-sharing formula represents balanced communal participation[75] which has yet to be truly tested as it was left to Syria's interpretation and implementation, and insist that any amendment to Taif will only be considered after it has been put into practice.

Thus Shia communal grievances of unequal power-sharing undermine not only the survival of Taif,[76] but also potentially set the stage for internal violence. The potential for a resumption of conflict is compounded by the heightening of sectarian identities since 2005.[77] The Sunni community's attitude underwent a 'striking transformation' of exacerbated sectarianism and hostility towards the Shia.[78] Within this context, Future perceive Hizbollah and Amal's distinction between participation and representation through a sectarian Sunni prism.[79]

While Hizbollah, Amal and Future concur that Taif has yet to be fully implemented,[80] this section will specifically examine the following points of contention highlighted by both sides: did Taif in practice transfer executive authority to the council of ministers or not; and was there an agreement at Taif to exclusively reserve the post of the finance ministry to the Shia community or not? Elaborating on the perceptions of both sides illustrates that these disputes are actually symptoms of corporate consociationalism.

Hizbollah and Amal argue that, in practice, Taif has not distributed executive authority to the council of ministers and contend that executive power was monopolised by the prime minister, beginning with the late Hariri.[81] Transferring executive power to the cabinet was intended to balance communal participation in executive government. Hizbollah and Amal maintain that failure to implement this reform has created unequal participation in executive government between the Sunni and Shia and the root of the ongoing crisis is a 'crisis of perception'[82] over where executive authority lies. This allows us to infer that the political struggle since 2005 is rooted within the aspirations of both Hizbollah and Amal to amend Taif's power-sharing formula in order to increase the Shia community's authority within the Lebanese system. This is corroborated by Hamdan's assessment that modifying power-sharing will solve the ongoing crisis by 'ninety per cent'.[83] Future dismisses this assessment and insists that executive power has been distributed to the cabinet and consequently, Taif balanced communal political participation. Is this rift genuinely grounded within a dispute over practice or is it a symptom of Shia communal grievances, rooted in Taif's corporate consociational framework? Although Hizbollah and Amal blame Hariri for mismanaging the distribution of power, the following provides evidence that these objections are grounded in corporate consociationalism.

As stated, Hariri is perceived as primarily responsible for engineering and hijacking supreme executive authority.[84] 'Taif gave power to the council of ministers—Hariri took the power for the prime minister'.[85] Hariri is further accused of implementing the power-sharing arrangement based on his own interpretation: 'Hariri... took Taif and said "*I* am Taif now"... and he held the power in the council of ministers. He took from all the communities their rights to participate and kept it for himself'.[86]

Yet is the contention of Hizbollah and Amal that Taif failed to transfer executive authority to the cabinet and balance executive power-sharing entirely due to Hariri's implementation? Or are such arguments essentially predicated within grievances stemming from the corporate consociational nature of Taif? A Hizbollah assessment that the Shia community's participation within the council of ministers would not sufficiently denote equal participation in executive government—although they are allocated the same seats as the Sunni—suggests the latter: 'There is participation but it is not at the level of participation that is allocated to the Sunni confession and the Maronite confession'.[87] This clearly indicates that Hizbollah's objections are predicated in Taif's corporate consociational features which bar the Shia community from a top executive government position—and not merely a dispute over practice.

Future insists that Taif in practice distributed executive power to the council of ministers.[88] Future Movement Member of Parliament Nohad al-Machnouk assesses allegations that Hariri usurped executive authority as 'an over-exaggeration… due to the character of Rafik Hariri… he was a huge character and prominent and that is why it seemed that the authority was installed in one position'.[89] He further dismissed allegations that Taif's power-sharing formula failed to equally distribute power between the Sunni, Shia and Maronite communities.[90]

While Hizbollah and Amal emphasise that their parties have never explicitly recommended amending Taif, Future Movement political actors point to criticism of the distribution of power as evidence of implicit aspirations to modify the consociational agreement. 'Hizbollah maintains a desire to amend Taif without explicitly stating that it wants to amend Taif—but it is clear from their stances that they want to undermine the prime minister's position and the privileges of this position. This position appeared from the very signing of Taif because from the very first day there were debates between Hussein el-Husseini and Salim al-Hoss—between the Sunni and Shia—about *how* to implement Taif'.[91]

Are the objections of Hizbollah and Amal that Taif overly empowered the position of the prime minister justified? The reforms in Taif created a very powerful prime ministerial position: 'The constitutional reforms in Taif… were a zero-sum game whereby the prerogatives of one authority are removed and vested in the hands of another… The president of the council does not directly benefit from the loss of the powers of the presidency, but rather from the fact that he is the head of the authority which has inherited executive power, i.e. the Council of Ministers'.[92] Lebanese academic Paul Salem is blunter: 'The prime minister indeed is the strongest executive branch office—obviously stronger than the president, obviously stronger than anybody... It is a problem that no high official in the executive branch is a Shia or ever will be under the Taif agreement'.[93]

Former Prime Minister Fuad Siniora's political advisor believes that all three major confessional communities have objections to Taif's distribution of power: 'We have three positions that are all clashing: the Christian point of view is that the president's power was removed and should be restored... Amal and Hizbollah or the Shia general point of view is that the prime minister's privileges exceeds the authority of the speaker of parliament and this should also be modified; and then there are law and constitutional experts, Christians and Sunni, who view the position of the parliament speaker as unshakeable and contains unlimited authority in parliament... So every faction takes the view that the other side has power that needs to be amended. As soon as we enter a phase to try to make amendments, there will be a conflict between these three factions [Sunni, Shia, Maronite]'.[94] Thus the dispute over whether or not Taif transferred executive power to the council of ministers is indicative of a deeper dispute stemming from the agreement's corporate consociational formula.

Another dispute over Taif in practice is whether there was an agreement to reserve the finance ministry position exclusively for the Shia community. Hizbollah and Amal contend that it was verbally agreed on at Taif;[95] while Future refuses to acknowledge that it was even suggested.[96] It is worth reiterating here that Hizbollah were not present at Taif's proceedings. Viewed through a corporate consociational prism, the post of the finance ministry could symbolically elevate a confessional community's participation in executive government because the finance minister co-signs executive decrees which also require the signatures of the Maronite president and the Sunni prime minister.[97] Consequently, for Hizbollah and Amal, reserving the post of finance minister for the Shia community could have elevated the Shia community's participation in executive power. 'When there were discussions about the finance ministry for the Shia [community], the discussion was aimed at elevating the participation of the Shia within political decision-making', explains Hizbollah MP Fayyad.[98] Hizbollah's assessment indicates the significance of symbolic gestures in power-sharing: signatures in consociational systems in post-conflict, divided societies are not simply ink on paper—but rather symbolise a community's political participation: 'the prime minister is a Sunni and he issues and signs decrees and therefore every decision or decree issued from the council of ministers or legislative draft law needs the signature of the Sunni prime minister. It also needs the signature of the Maronite president. But it does not condition for the Shia signatory for these decisions'.[99]

But would allocating this post to the Shia community really provide a panacea for deep-rooted grievances of unequal political participation or is this dispute simply another symptom resulting from corporate consociationalism? Future's refusal to acknowledge there was any such agreement at Taif is upheld by Hizbollah and Amal as evidence that the Shia community has been deliberately barred from the echelons of executive power within the Taif regime. Further, Hizbollah and Amal blame the late Hariri for restricting access for the Shia community to the finance ministry post.[100] Yet the debate over the finance ministry post is arguably a symptom of Shia communal grievances stemming from Taif's corporate consociational formula and not merely a dispute over implementation.

Implementing Taif: The Conflict over its Preservation or Revision

Although rival factions concur that implementing Taif's consociational principles could provide a prescription to the ongoing political crisis,[101] Hizbollah, Amal and Future disagree on how to put Taif into practice. It is necessary to emphasise that diverging perceptions of how to implement this consociational agreement do not indicate the inability of Lebanese leaders to manage power-sharing in the absence of Syrian or external domination.[102] Future insist that they do not oppose a reassessment of Taif, but that this must occur only after the agreement's gradual implementation. Hizbollah and Amal dismiss Future's condition to gradually implement reforms and insist that all of Taif be put into practice, including the controversial principle to abolish political confessionalism. Any objections to Taif's reforms are grounds to reassess the entire consociational agreement, according to Hizbollah and Amal. The following illustrates that these disparities over how to put Taif's reforms into practice mask an underlying struggle between rival factions over the preservation or revision of Taif's distribution of power. Future favours preserving Taif because it elevated the Sunni community's position while Hizbollah and Amal are fighting for its reassessment in order to increase the Shia community's authority in executive government. The perceptions of both sides support this assessment.

Future acknowledge that Taif is not flawless and, in principle, do not oppose its reassessment but insist that this must happen only after implementing the agreement's electoral reforms.[103] Their condition to gradually implement Taif is attributed to placating Christian fears regarding the provision to abolish political confessionalism.[104] Since the Sunni emerged with the most gains at Taif,[105] to what extent is this condition grounded within fears of losing their preeminent position within a non-confessional political system? It is not controversial to propose that Future's motivations are premised on fears that revising Taif may not guarantee the Sunni the same privileged position. The electoral consequences of abolishing political confessionalism for Future indicate that this condition is a pretence to avoid a revision of Taif within concerns that Hizbollah and Amal could demand a redistribution of power.

Political confessionalism under Taif equally distributed parliamentary seats between Muslims and Christians,[106] even though the total of Lebanon's Christians comprise less than 50 per cent of the population. Hence, sixty-four seats in parliament, or half the legislature, are allocated to Christian confessional groups, a clear demographic over-representation of Christians.[107] Abolishing political confessionalism would make it highly improbable for the Christian electorate to secure 50 per cent of parliamentary seats. It is within this context that Future says it is upholding the rights of 'Christian partners' by not fully implementing Taif and this contentious article.[108]

But is Future's condition to delay the implementation of this provision entirely based on concerns for the Christian community? Since political confessionalism guarantees an equal number of parliamentary seats to the Sunni and Shia communities, could Future also harbour fears of losing Sunni seats?[109] Arguably, Future's vested interest—and share in parliament—is also at stake if political confessionalism is abolished: 'It's... harder for Future to monopolise the Sunni political community than it is for Hizbollah and Amal... it's probably easier for them to, not to monopolise the Shia political groups, but to overwhelm and dominate', explains Richard Chambers.[110] Consequently, there are no guarantees that the Sunni will be able to maintain their current proportion of parliamentary seats. Arguably, it serves the interests of both the Sunni and Christian communities to maintain political confessionalism and based on these calculations Future insists on the gradual implementation of Taif.

Future prioritises the implementation of Taif's electoral districting system, before any possible modifying of the power-sharing agreement. Large multi-confessional districts known as the *muhafaza*[111] were endorsed to replace the *qada*, small districts with minimal cross-cutting confessional cleavages. The impact of electoral districting on mitigating or exacerbating communal friction should not be underestimated: rival political factions say *qada* districting fuelled sectarianism and communal tensions prior to Taif.[112] Within this context, Taif's constitutional designers recommended the *muhafaza* system to establish cross-confessional voting,[113] reduce sectarianism and, most significantly, create a legislative electoral system based on proportional representation (PR). 'Taif did not specify that the electoral system was to be proportional representation but this is what was implied in the text... When Taif states that the electoral system should achieve an accurate representation for all the powers and factions within Lebanon, how can all the factions... and all the political powers be represented except by the proportional system?... There is no way for there to be fair representation as stipulated... by Taif except through the proportional system'.[114] The intention of Taif to establish a PR electoral system should not be underestimated within the context of efforts to engineer a stable consociation. For post-conflict divided societies like Lebanon, the election of a broadly representative legislature is deemed crucial[115] in ensuring the widest representation of communal groups[116] and reducing communal tensions. Some scholars advocate PR electoral systems as optimal to achieving this.[117] Furthermore, as the size of electoral districts directly influences the extent of proportionality,[118] Taif's recommendation to enlarge districts should not be underestimated within the context of broad communal representation. However, since 2005, electoral laws have consistently violated Taif and reinstated the detrimental *qada*, thereby failing to produce legislators widely representative of communal groups and factions.[119] The head of an electoral system-monitoring organisation acknowledges that this has fuelled communal tensions.[120] It is within this context that Future prioritises electoral reform based on Taif—al-Machnouk described it as no less than 'a matter of life and death'.[121]

Yet is Future's condition to reform the electoral system before amending Taif entirely premised upon calculations that electoral districting could provide a panacea to the country's ongoing predicaments? Without a doubt Future is serious about electoral reforms. However, it is more plausible that Future's unrelenting stance not to amend Taif before the implementation of electoral reforms is premised on the movement's unwillingness to repeat what it perceives as Sunni political concessions under the gunpoint of Hizbollah. Any amendment to Taif prior to electoral reforms may signal to Future forced political concessions under the pressure of Hizbollah's military might. Future is unequivocal: power-sharing will not be amended under the threat of Hizbollah's arms. 'We need to create a logical electoral law, implement it—and then we will discuss everything. But to be forced to compromise under pressure, in the presence of weapons, it will not provide a peaceful result'.[122] Future's heightened level of hostility and suspicion towards Hizbollah's weapons further reinforces its unwillingness to be making political compromises, such as revising Taif. Future accurately interpreted Hassan Nasrallah's suggestion in 2011 to 'develop the political system'[123] as Hizbollah covertly stating ambitions to revise Taif's power-sharing formula. 'He [Nasrallah] tried to prettify the meaning… but it is not going to work. They are looking for war! Nobody will sign peacefully for any major changes in the constitution. They will find no Sunni to sign. No way'.[124]

Future's hostility stems from Hizbollah's military takeover of Beirut and parts of Mount Lebanon in May 2008[125]—despite Nasrallah's vow that their weapons would never turn inward. When Siniora's government attempted to challenge Hizbollah's *de facto* security apparatus by announcing it would take measures to dismantle Hizbollah's private telecommunications network,[126] deemed vital to their military operations, the party's response was a swift military takeover of Beirut.[127] Consequently, for the Sunni community which had largely favoured Hizbollah's possession of arms within the context of deterrence against Israel,[128] Hizbollah lost its previous legitimacy of resistance. 'These arms… are no longer related to the cause of fighting Israel'[129] says Siniora. Importantly, such grievances are not confined to Future—the severe loss of trust towards Hizbollah within the Sunni community is evident. Mohammad Safadi says for the Sunni it was 'as an unexpected jolt' when Hizbollah turned their weapons inwards: 'You could say safely that 80–90 per cent of the Sunnis do not support Hizbollah anymore'.[130] The swiftness of the takeover was perceived as a humiliating[131] defeat for the Sunnis[132] and Hizbollah had demonstrated it held the military and political balance of power in Lebanon.

The prospect of resumed conflict in Lebanon with a Sunni-Shia dimension prompted Qatar,[133] backed by Saudi Arabia, Syria, Iran and the USA,[134] to initiate a resolution. Lebanese leaders were flown to Qatar where a conflict regulation mechanism in the form of a consociational agreement known as the Doha Accord[135] was brokered. For Future, the Doha agreement indicated that Hizbollah and Amal were not unwilling to use force to secure revisions in power-sharing. Future's grievances are rooted in this agreement as they maintain political concessions were secured at the gunpoint of Hizbollah.[136] It is this precedent that has become part of the Sunni consciousness and Future's narrative that Hizbollah is willing to employ military force to secure political gains; a precedent Future is adamant they will not allow to be repeated. 'Someone pointed their guns at [us]... I cannot ignore the existence of these arms and open discussions',[137] says Siniora. Further: 'I must keep my faith in Taif because it is not acceptable to modify agreements... based on a change within the balance of power... When the situation is calmer and people are no longer tense... then we can discuss Taif—any part of it—none of it is sacred'.[138]

Hizbollah's response to this severe loss of trust within the Sunni community is that their use of arms internally was an 'exceptional' reaction.[139] Fayyad provides a tacit and unprecedented[140] acknowledgement that Hizbollah's actions were a mistake. While the Siniora government crossed a political 'red-line' when it announced intentions to dismantle the telecommunication network,[141] Fayyad admits that Hizbollah's response also crossed a 'red-line'.[142] A crucial departure in Hizbollah and Future's perceptions is found regarding the Doha agreement, indicating the depth of polarisation. Future bitterly recalls the accord within the context of forced concessions.[143] Hizbollah perceives it within a positive context, as ending an eighteen-month political deadlock and paving the way for a new conflict regulation agreement that 'created a sort of coexistence for two years'.[144]

Yet is this the only attainable goal for Lebanon—periods of coexistence lasting for two years before the eruption of another political crisis, leaving the country teetering on the precipice of conflict? This is the ominous assessment of Hizbollah—unless genuine participation within executive power-sharing is achieved, Lebanese politics will be stuck in an endless cycle of violence followed by conflict regulation in the form of consociational agreements.[145]

For Future, the disarmament of Hizbollah is interconnected with any potential renegotiation of power-sharing. Indicative of Future's severe loss of trust with Hizbollah is the movement's refusal to even participate in dialogue regarding power-sharing. 'After the armed takeover of Beirut, I no longer have the willingness to sit down with Hizbollah for any dialogue before they are disarmed... I lost all trust because they wanted dialogue and said they would be willing to discuss… when we disagreed with them… they used their arms against us… They have other plans and agendas for dominance and it's through their arms'.[146] Consequently, Future stipulates the disarmament of Hizbollah as a key condition before re-evaluating the distribution of power,[147] a term Hizbollah has no intention of meeting within the context of power-sharing.[148]

Hizbollah and Amal oppose a gradual implementation of Taif and insist on the comprehensive application of all of its principles, including the abolishment of political confessionalism.[149] Any objections to putting this provision into practice justify re-negotiating Taif 'to increase participation',[150] providing evidence that the dispute over practice covers Hizbollah-Amal ambitions to revise the power-sharing formula.

Amal dismisses Future's proposals to begin implementing Taif by tackling electoral reforms first. 'We don't believe in selectivity. This is Taif—let's implement it, *fully* implement it',[151] says a senior Amal politician. Amal and Hizbollah argue that demands for Taif's gradual implementation correctly indicate concerns regarding parts of Taif, which consequently justifies revising this power-sharing arrangement or creating a 'new social contract'.[152] Amal and Hizbollah acknowledge that creating a non-confessional political system could potentially take at least ten years[153] and yet they insist that this contentious provision be put into practice—what are the incentives of Hizbollah and Amal to abolish political confessionalism?

Under political confessionalism, the Shia—and by extension Hizbollah and Amal—are allocated only twenty-seven seats in parliament from a total of 128.[154] Abolishing political confessionalism would eliminate the fixed quota of seats and, according to neutral electoral monitors, it is highly probable that Hizbollah and Amal could secure more than twenty-seven seats,[155] thereby increasing their legislative power. While they may not like Taif's corporate consociational framework, fully implementing the agreement may increase the Shia community's share in power.

Thus the dispute over Taif's gradual or full implementation belies a deeper struggle as Future is fighting to preserve Taif's power-sharing formula while Hizbollah and Amal are seeking to revise it.

'Shia Silence', Maronite Protests

While Hizbollah and Amal are emphatic that they have never explicitly called for a revision of Taif,[156] what they implicitly state speaks volumes. Their suggestions for a new 'social contract'[157] to resolve political imbalances are veiled calls to modify or even replace Taif. Fayyad's definition of this seemingly liberal notion substantiates this view: 'When we discuss a new social contract it means we are discussing a new national pact... Or at the least a new constitution'.[158] It should not be overlooked that Hizbollah and Amal's main Christian ally, Michel Aoun, has been vocal in explicitly demanding Taif's amendment.[159] Future believes that Hizbollah and Amal deliberately avoid making such calls to avert a possible confrontation with the Sunni community:[160] 'They don't want to create the crisis within the Muslim [communities] so they have left it to the Christians... to Aoun... to announce and repeat this all the time'.[161]

Finally, Hizbollah's clarification of Nasrallah's proposal to 'develop the political system' further corroborates the case that these parties are looking to modify the power-sharing formula. Fayyad says the political system refers to 'the current formula based on Taif that distributes the top positions between the three sects and distributes power based on a certain balance'.[162] This clearly suggests revising Taif's corporate consociational distribution of power, an implication not lost on Future: 'It is clear that Hizbollah wants to amend Taif. Hassan Nasrallah expressed this... when he said ... "let's discuss developing the constitution or the system"'.[163]

Finally, corporate consociationalism is not the sole cause for Hizbollah and Amal to increase the Shia community's political participation. The collective desire of a new generation of Shia to compensate for their community's past political marginalisation[164] compounded by frustration that their role in Lebanon is strictly limited to military activities against Israel also fuels motivations to amend Taif. Since Israel's 2000 withdrawal from South Lebanon, the Syrian-backed Shia political leadership has sought a greater role in domestic politics.[165] Syria's 2005 withdrawal from Lebanon further prompted Shia factions to participate in domestic politics, leading Hizbollah to join the government for the first time.

Clearly Amal and Hizbollah want to be counted as major political forces[166] and not merely military powers (particularly in the case of Hizbollah). A senior Amal figure expressed the Shia community's frustration: 'Lebanon was liberated in 2000—and what was the role of this group [the Shia] within Lebanese society—only when Israel occupies Lebanon should they become involved to liberate it and until then, "please sit aside and you are not equal citizens"? It's not fair. It's not fair', says Hamdan, adding that if political rivals are unable to implement Taif and balance political participation, it is necessary to broker a new power-sharing agreement.[167] Clearly the increased domestic participation of the Shia political leadership is undermining Taif's consociational formula and the communal balance of power. Yet internal variables alone are not responsible for the undermining of Taif. The following section examines exogenous variables to illustrate that power-sharing in Lebanon cannot be separated from regional dynamics and the new political landscape emerging in the Middle East.

Regional Dynamics: Shaping Lebanese Consociation

Since 2005 the corporate consociational balance of power in Lebanon has become tightly intertwined with regional dynamics, including the rise of Iran's influence in the Arab world, Saudi-Iranian rivalry and the potential ousting of Bashar al-Assad amidst unprecedented anti-regime protests in Syria.[168] Hizbollah, Amal and Future agree that these regional dynamics cannot be separated from power-sharing in Lebanon. Thus, a senior political actor in the Hizbollah-Amal alliance analyses Future's unwillingness to amend Taif as Sunni insecurities, as a result of turmoil in the predominantly Sunni Middle East since 2003. The removal of Saddam Hussein in Iraq, the consequent rise of Iran's influence in the Arab world, the assassination of Hariri and the toppling of Egypt's Hosni Mubarak has left Lebanon's Sunnis insecure regarding their previously dominant position.[169] 'The Sunni sect in Lebanon considers itself to be the "Arab" sect in Lebanon—and the Arab world and the Arab political system is crumbling'.[170] Similarly, Future assesses Hizbollah-Amal motivations to increase Shia participation in executive government within the context of uprisings against Assad's regime which could potentially topple their vital regional ally: 'The Shia are now feeling seriously threatened because of the magnitude of the crisis in Syria'.[171] It is worth noting that fear clearly is a powerful force shaping the attitudes of the Sunni and Shia political leadership.[172] Shia fears are still rooted within grievances of political marginalisation, while the root of Sunni fears is unchanged since Hanf's monumental work—it still 'derives from a gradual, seemingly inexorable loss of power'.[173]

Future opposes any reassessment of Taif within the current regional climate in order to thwart Iranian ambitions for greater influence in Lebanon vis-à-vis Hizbollah. The 2003 ousting of Saddam Hussein allowed Tehran to secure its foothold in Lebanon through its ally Hizbollah. Under Hussein, Iraq had played a key role in containing Iran's interference in the Arab world and the toppling of Hussein's regime allowed Tehran to become the most influential power in Baghdad and beyond: 'The occupation of Iraq... paved the way for Iran to expand in Iraq, in Syria, in Lebanon',[174] notes a Future politician. Furthermore, expanded Iranian influence in Iraq—the heartland of the Arab world—gave rise to a political confrontation with Saudi Arabia[175] which traditionally played the role of prime guardian for Arab and Sunni interests. This political struggle took on a sectarian Sunni-Shia dimension and these political and confessional confrontations spilled over into Lebanon.

Incidentally, Future does not underestimate the interference of regional powers in the brokering of a new formula. 'We must take into consideration the balance of power between external actors. There will be a conflict between Saudi Arabia, Syria and Iran and they will *all* interfere and apply pressure regarding Taif so the amendments will be to their benefit or to the benefit of their internal ally'.[176] Thus Future's unwillingness to re-address power-sharing is also premised upon fears that consociational deals in Lebanon could serve as another frontline for the Saudi-Iran confrontation which could trigger an internal conflict: 'If we enter a phase to amend Taif, we will be opening the door to conflicts that will have no end in sight'.[177]

The uprising in Syria against Assad has meant that 'the connection between what happens in Syria and Lebanon seldom has been so stark and so perilous'.[178] Future perceive Hizbollah-Amal ambitions to reassess power-sharing within the context of these protests—the demise of Assad potentially poses a threat to Hizbollah and Amal's[179] regional guarantor in power-sharing,[180] since the Syrian regime secured the Shia community's political gains at Taif.[181] Within this context, the prospective ousting of Assad signals to Hizbollah and Amal a potential threat to the Shia community's political participation. Thus, the timing of Nasrallah's statement to 'develop the political system' should not be overlooked. The prospect of the house of Assad collapsing has prompted Hizbollah to fortify its own house within the Lebanese mansion[182] by seeking to elevate the Shia stake in a revised consociational agreement.

However, Future does not underestimate the consequences for Lebanon should Assad fall. 'There is danger if Syria enters a civil war, it will have direct consequences in Lebanon'.[183] While Future emphasise that the Shia community are anxiously monitoring developments in Syria, clearly the Sunni political leadership is equally apprehensive. Future believes that uprisings in Damascus and the fate of Assad will determine the final outcome of the shape of the Middle East and the future of Lebanon. 'Everyone… is waiting for what will happen in Syria. That's it. And based on the outcome, we will move forward'.[184]

Conclusion

Corporate consociationalism has fuelled communal tensions between the Sunni, Shia and Maronite communities since independence, as they each harbour perceptions of political exclusion and unfair participation. Under the National Pact's corporate consociational application, the Sunni and Shia communities resented Maronite political hegemony. While Taif elevated the Sunni community's participation in power-sharing, the corporate consociational framework heightened Shia grievances of unequal participation and created Maronite resentment. Underlying political polarisation since 2005 is a struggle between the Sunni and Shia political leaderships over power-sharing, as a result of Shia communal grievances of unequal participation in executive power with the Sunni community.

Taif and the Doha Accord support Hanf's assessment that 'conflict can bring forth coexistence'.[185] In fact, the Lebanese are historically wily bargainers, reflected in their past replete with communal power-sharing deals and shifting alliances.[186] Yet is this the definitive, unfortunate fate of Lebanon—a pentathlon of conflicts, shifting communal grievances and revised power-sharing agreements? Unless corporate consociationalism, which orchestrates shifting communal grievances of unequal power-sharing, is replaced with a more stable consociational system, endless cycles of internal conflict are not unforeseeable in the future of Lebanon.

PART II

SOVEREIGNTY, SECURITY AND VIOLENCE

4

FOREIGN INTERVENTIONS, POWER SHARING AND THE DYNAMICS OF CONFLICT AND COEXISTENCE IN LEBANON

Marie-Joëlle Zahar

Before the country descended into civil war, Lebanon's power-sharing regime was hailed by experts as a successful experiment in consociational democracy.[1] It has since become commonplace to describe Lebanon as particularly vulnerable and permeable to regional and international conflicts. Some have even gone so far as to describe conflicts in Lebanon as 'wars of others'.[2]

Two important dimensions of statehood are evoked to understand the fragility of present-day Middle Eastern politics. The first, strength/weakness reflects the balance of power between state and society; the second, 'hardness'/'softness', refers to 'the extent to which state-society relations also exhibit extensive transnational characteristics'.[3] On this account, Lebanon is both weak and soft.

Lebanon is weak by design as from its inception, the state has been penetrated by society and it has forsaken the regulation of social relationships. Lebanon's consociational system provides for proportional representation of all major Lebanese confessions in state institutions. Socially, the Personal

Status Regime (*nizham al-ahwal al-shakhsiyya*) grants religious tribunals legislative and executive authority over the personal status of their flock. Lebanon is also soft—competing transnational ideologies, communalism and socio-political identification resonate on the Lebanese political scene. Some analysts blame the country's ills on the destabilising impact of such transnational ideologies—Nasserism in the 1950s, the Palestinian cause in the 1970s, Shia Islamism in the 2000s.[4] Most suggest that Lebanon's weakness and softness are related, with the first described as a facilitating condition for the emergence of the other.

Lebanon's weak economic and military capabilities are sometimes used to explain the country's vulnerability. But 'local actors deploy transnational ideologies or bandwagon with external actors to strengthen their positions in domestic struggles'.[5] In spite of rich empirical accounts,[6] to date, there are few theoretical accounts of the dynamics of conflict and coexistence in Lebanon. The theoretical accounts that exist also tend to focus on the impact of outsiders on power-sharing rather than probe the manner in which insiders draw outside powers into their games.[7]

This is the intended contribution of this chapter. I argue that, as far as the entanglement of domestic and regional issues are concerned, the 'Cedar Revolution' did not really constitute a break with the past. To understand this continuity requires that we ask why Lebanon is so permeable and vulnerable to external influences. What are the mechanisms involved in the linkages between the domestic and international arenas?

The chapter traces the causes of permeability and vulnerability in the post-civil war era. It argues that foreign intervention in Lebanese politics is, in great part, a function of Lebanese factions seeking to gain advantage over each other. It also identifies specific institutions and rules in the Lebanese power-sharing formula that facilitate such patron-seeking behaviour. Based on primary sources, the chapter uses the period between 2004 and 2010 to uncover the ways in which communities that fear for their political survival manoeuvre to shield themselves from political marginalisation and exclusion.

The chapter then proceeds to analyse the impact of foreign interventions on the dynamics of conflict and coexistence in Lebanon. Comparing US and French intervention to Syria's meddling in Lebanese politics, the chapter assesses their impact.[8] While others have tended to highlight the security implications of such practices, I argue that foreign intervention has a lasting and detrimental impact on the 'rules of the game' and the pervasiveness of confessionalism. The resulting explosive mix of 'made to fit rules' and 'acute confessional threat perception' accounts for the permeability of Lebanese politics.

A Brief Exposition of the Lebanese Political System

Lebanon has often been described as a mosaic, an extremely plural society lacking consensus on fundamentals, including the identity of the country and the fairness of representation and distribution.[9] Lebanon's diversity is not only religious. Deep class divisions overlay the religious map of Lebanese society. There are also strong regional and clan allegiances. These cleavages tend to reinforce one another, contributing to the environment of protracted social conflict.[10]

Although analysts disagree as to the weight of various factors in the outbreak of civil war, first in 1958, then in 1975, they tend to agree on the elements of the explosive mix. Analyses of the onset of violence in 1958 stress the political and social marginalisation experienced by Muslim communities.[11] They also highlight the manner in which disagreements over the identity of the country and its foreign policy orientation[12] increased its vulnerability to regional and international conflicts. Thus, at the time of the outbreak of violence in 1958, the Lebanese were deeply divided between supporters and opponents of Nasserism and in 1975, they fundamentally disagreed about the Palestinian presence in Lebanon.[13]

The Taif Agreement brought Lebanon's second post-independence civil war to an end—it built upon a long tradition of consociational power-sharing.[14] Whereas the National Pact of 1943 had put extensive powers in the hands of the Maronite Christian president, Taif recalibrated the pre-war allocation of powers, curtailing these wide prerogatives and vesting most executive powers in the council of ministers, customarily led by a Sunni. It also changed the allocation of parliamentary seats from 6:5 in favour of Christians to fifty-fifty.

In its attempt to address Lebanon's permeability,[15] Taif established a number of 'rules of the game' intended to prevent any community from prevailing over others. These could be summarised as: ensuring mutual peaceful coexistence between the different confessional groups in the country (*al-'aysh al-mushtarak*) and guaranteeing that each group be properly represented politically (*sihhat al-thamthil al-siyasi*).[16] While Taif did not specify the mechanisms intended to implement these principles, their inclusion clearly acknowledged that, in spite of claims to proportional representation, the pre-war political system was flawed and that these flaws contributed to the outbreak of civil war. It also provided safeguards to prevent any community from establishing *de facto* control of the executive branch. The Taif Agreement stipulated that a majority of two-thirds of government was needed to vote on major issues including '… war and peace, [and] international treaties…'[17] This reflected the perceived limits of the National Pact which had simply sought to ensure that Lebanon would maintain neutrality on foreign policy issues. It is worth noting here that the first post-independence civil war was triggered by a decision by then-President Camille Chamoun to side with the US-led Baghdad Pact, a decision strongly contested by other communities and made possible in part by the wide prerogatives enjoyed by the Maronite president under the 1943 National Pact.

Probing the Causes of Lebanon's Permeability and Vulnerability

Lebanon's conflicts have often been described as wars of others on Lebanese soil.[18] Such a picture portrays the Lebanese as victims, a people caught between a rock and a hard place, located at the heart of a conflict zone and who cannot but deeply feel the reverberations of regional shockwaves, be they related to the Arab-Israeli conflict, to the struggle for power between conservative and radical Arab states in the 1950s, or in more recent times, to the war on terror and the regional power struggle between Sunnis and Shias.

This is a truncated perspective. The Lebanese do not only suffer the reverberations of regional events, they sometimes provoke and invite foreign intervention into their domestic affairs. During the 1975–90 civil war, Syrian and Israeli troops were invited in by Lebanese politicians. Syrian troops were acclaimed by (ironically) Christians when they responded favourably to the request of then-President of the Republic Suleiman Frangieh to assist the pro-status quo forces which were facing the prospect of defeat at the hands of anti-status quo forces (mostly Muslims).[19] In the late 1970s, Christian politicians looked to Israel for military assistance and political support.[20] After the signing of Taif, observers argued, Syria did not want to be the arbiter of every decision in Lebanon. Rather, incapable of prevailing upon one another, Lebanese leaders called upon Damascus to help them settle their internal disputes. Numerous analyses document Syria's post-Taif influence on, indeed manipulation of, Lebanese elections, judicial procedures and security forces.[21] 'There is less by way of analysing the manner in which Syrian officials were drawn into the morass of Lebanese confessional politics'.[22] Yet, Lebanese politicians drew Syria further into Lebanese politics, using Syrian interests in stability to gain relative advantage over one another.

Whenever the ruling troika failed to reach an agreement, they would tread the road to Damascus in search of a way out of their deadlock. Syrian authorities thus became intimately involved in such delicate processes as the formation of electoral alliances. Syria's intelligence chiefs in Lebanon, Ghazi Kanaan and Rustum Ghazaleh, Vice-President Abd al-Halim Khaddam and former Chief of Staff Hikmat al-Shihabi, vetoed the inclusion of anti-Syrian candidates on certain lists, forced the leaders of some lists to take in pro-Syrian candidates, balanced religious candidates with secular ones in some districts and balanced among their own allies in others.[23]

Similar trends can be observed in the period between 2004 and 2010. In the next section, I expound the logic that drives Lebanese communities to search for outside patrons. I argue that Lebanese communities face a credible commitment problem deepened by the nature of the Lebanese state. Under such conditions, the search for, and the reliance on, external allies to maintain the balance of power between communities is a political survival strategy. Second, I document the manner in which alliances with outsiders have been established by framing domestic adversaries as 'common enemies', thus entangling Lebanese political conflicts with broader regional and international struggles.

Marginalisation and Exclusion: Lebanon's Politics as a 'Credible Commitment' Problem

The primacy of Lebanon's sectarian system need not be restated.[24] It contributes to making Lebanon a weak state. State weakness prevents the state from fulfilling its dual role to deter and assure. Weak states have no credible deterrent. They do not have the wherewithal to prevent sub-state groups from using violence. Neither can a weak state credibly assure those groups that comply with the rules of the game that no other group will take advantage of them nor, in instances where state weakness results in its capture by private interests, can it assure aggrieved groups that it does not constitute a threat to them.[25] Empirical evidence suggests that such is the fate of states whose institutions are established as part of a negotiated settlement to end civil wars.[26] Negotiated settlements often follow military stalemates whereby neither side is capable of prevailing. Subsequent agreements follow the rule of the 'lowest common denominator' as factions agree on political rules that guarantee them maximum autonomy and minimum interdependence. State institutions are weakened while sub-national institutions are strengthened. Though not purely a post-war phenomenon, this pattern has been further deepened in recent years.

These conditions contain the seeds of a 'credible commitment' problem. When the state fails to deter and assure, it cannot credibly commit to protect sub-national communities. In such circumstances, sub-national groups have one of two options open to them as they seek to acquire the means to defend themselves against perceived threats: build up their military strength or enter into alliances with stronger powers that can protect them.[27] Therein lies the explanation for the behaviour of the main Lebanese protagonists before and after Lebanon's civil war.

In the next section, I present evidence to the effect that the Lebanese state was seriously weakened following the withdrawal of Syrian forces from Lebanon. I describe the reasons why communities belonging to the two main political coalitions of the time, 14 March (Hariri-led, pro-Western) and 8 March (Hizbollah-led, supported by Syria and Iran), felt threatened and feared marginalisation. These feelings, combined with the weakness of the Lebanese state, prompted protagonists to look beyond Lebanon's borders for patrons and allies. I then document the manner in which communities framed their adversaries to draw outsiders into Lebanese politics.

Lebanon's Failure to Deter and Assure

When Syria's military was forced to withdraw from Lebanon in April 2005, following the 'Cedar revolution' and the assassination of former Lebanese Prime Minister Rafik Hariri, the Lebanese state could neither be said to have the ability to deter nor assure.

On the deterrence front, the Lebanese state does not have a monopoly over the use of legitimate violence. Although the Taif Agreement provided for the demobilisation of all non-state armed groups, Hizbollah was granted an exception by the government of the day because, it was argued, its weapons were intended to fight Israeli occupation of Lebanon.[28] When, following Israel's decision to withdraw its troops in May 2000, the state failed to deploy the army beyond the Litani River, questions arose as to the ability and willingness of the military establishment to fulfil its role as sole defender of the country. While the army ultimately deployed to South Lebanon following the summer 2006 Israel-Hizbollah war, its limited deterrence capability would soon be further highlighted.

When violent Islamist contestation rose in the Palestinian camp of Nahr al-Bared in 2007, the army's response revealed structural challenges including 'poor managerial and strategic skills at the top, inadequate equipment and training, poor coordination among security agencies and perennial concerns about force cohesion'.[29] Concern about force cohesion reflected the extent to which Lebanon's sectarian logic still permeates the military establishment. Although 'post-war reconstruction of the Lebanese military focused on making it more representative of Lebanon's socio-political and sectarian make-up',[30] the force remains risk-averse and seeks to preserve cross-sectarian unity among its ranks.

Reflecting such concerns, the army's decision to remain on the sidelines during the May 2008 armed confrontation between supporters of 8 March and 14 March would drive the final nail in the coffin of the Lebanese state's deterrence capability. Sparked by the government's decision to dismantle Hizbollah's telecommunications network and to dismiss Lebanese Armed Forces (LAF) General Shoukeir, the airport security chief, because of his ties to the party, the confrontation was the first time that Hizbollah used its weapons against another Lebanese faction in the post-civil war period, in violation of its commitment never to do so. The military's decision to overturn both ministerial decisions underscored the ambiguity of the relationship between the LAF and Hizbollah. Whereas both the government of the day and its foreign allies had been trying to re-establish the LAF as the only armed institution in the country,[31] it was the army leadership which bestowed Hizbollah with the means to sustain its military activities. While the army argued that this was intended to defuse the crisis by taking steps 'that would not harm public interest and the security of the resistance',[32] on that fateful day, both government and opposition understood that no credible deterrent could be deployed to ward off the use of violence by potential challengers to the state in Lebanon.

The Lebanese state could no more assure than it could deter. The state's ability to act as an impartial arbiter of the political game was seriously harmed by the practice of politics under Syria's custodianship. Not only did the Syrian authorities reinterpret provisions of the Taif Agreement as it suited them, notably concerning the withdrawal of Syrian troops from Lebanon,[33] they also transformed implementation of the agreement into a menu for choice, selecting those items that suited their strategic objectives and discarding items for which they had little use.[34] Several analyses document the manner in which Syria influenced, and indeed manipulated, Lebanese elections, judicial procedures and security forces.[35] Whoever disagreed with Syria's implementation style or objectives in Lebanon was swiftly and severely reprimanded.

Faced with a state which was incapable or unwilling to defend them against violence by one another and unable to provide them with guarantees that it would not pose a threat to them, various Lebanese communities felt severely threatened. Christians were the first to experience such an existential threat. Under Syria's yoke, they had been the main target of repression. Their main wartime political parties were undermined from within or outlawed and their most recognisable wartime political leaders forced into exile or thrown in prison. Members of the Christian Lebanese Forces and supporters of General Michel Aoun were variously arrested, detained, imprisoned, tried and sentenced. The heavy-handed treatment of political opponents at the hands of the security forces and the judiciary, including arbitrary arrests, torture during detention and highly controversial trials in front of military courts, came under the scrutiny of local and foreign human rights organisations. This became known as *al-ihbat al-massihi* (Christian hopelessness and discontent). Christian communities feared total political marginalisation and many Christians came to regret the loss of the strong executive prerogatives of the Maronite presidency which had historically served as security guarantees, guarantees without which Christians would not be able to defend their 'vision of Lebanon' or secure a place in the country's political landscape.[36]

The Christians were not alone in fearing political marginalisation and exclusion. In 2004–5, a number of events stirred similar fears among the Shia. Among others, these included the forced Syrian withdrawal from Lebanon and the summer 2004 vote at the UN Security Council of a resolution calling for the disarmament and demobilisation of all factions in Lebanon. UNSC Resolution 1559 is perceived by the Shia, particularly by Hizbollah, as proof that they are the target of a concerted campaign for political marginalisation and even physical elimination. When politicians belonging to the 8 March movement resigned from government in December 2006, they were expressing concerns that Hizbollah and the broader Shia community were not being given a fair hearing by the 14 March-led government of Prime Minister Fuad Siniora. In the ensuing political deadlock,[37] the government of Siniora would staunchly refuse to give in to the demands of Hizbollah and its allies that they be given an effective minority of one-third plus one, so as to give the opposition veto power on matters of national interest. This, a central provision of executive power-sharing as per the terms of Taif, had incidentally been the request of Christian political forces in 1992, when pro-Syrian groups forced the holding of the first post-war parliamentary elections against the objections of Christian political forces. Christian political leaders argued at the time that the government could not go on with its decision to hold elections because one of the communities was not represented in government and that any decision taken in such circumstances would be a violation of the principles of the Taif Agreement regarding the need to uphold mutual coexistence and to take decisions of national interest by consensus. Their objections were brushed aside and elections were held which, because the main wartime Christian political factions boycotted them, paved the way for their political marginalisation.

Framing Adversaries as 'Common Enemies'

This was the context in which the two main political blocs of the day, the 14 March and 8 March coalitions, turned to outsiders for support. To secure support, both used framing to highlight 'common threats' that their Lebanese opponents posed not only to them but to their allies. To illustrate this, I discuss the activities of Christian Lebanese lobbies in the USA. While this should not be taken so far as to argue that Lebanese political forces compelled outside powers to intervene in Lebanese politics, the ability of Lebanese factions to frame their domestic opponents in terms of broader international struggles created a convergence of interests with foreign powers and contributed to the latter's intervention in Lebanese politics.[38]

Three goals summarise the programmatic objectives of Lebanese-American lobbies: secure the withdrawal of Syrian forces from Lebanon; ensure continued relevance of Christian forces in the Lebanese political equation; and prevent Iran from gaining a foothold in the country through its alliance with—and the growing domestic importance of—Hizbollah. The United States Committee for a Free Lebanon (USCFL),[39] believes 'that the USA has vital interests in the Middle East. [It] sees the region, with its profusion of dictatorships, radical ideologies, existential conflicts, border disagreements and political violence, as a major source of problems for the Free World'.[40] A strong proponent of peace and free trade as well as democracy in the Middle East, the American Lebanese Coalition[41] also asserts that 'a free and democratic Lebanon serves the national interest of the United States'.[42] Still, in the 1990s, Lebanese-American lobbies failed to convince Washington of the importance of a free and democratic Lebanon. When Taif was signed, the USA hailed it as 'the first step toward restoration of a sovereign, unified and independent Lebanon, free of all foreign forces'.[43] The first Bush administration openly condemned then interim prime minister, General Michel Aoun, for rejecting the agreement.[44] However, Washington expressed little concern when Syria failed to redeploy its troops in accordance with Taif or when the first post-war elections went ahead in 1992 in spite of a Christian boycott. Instead, in 1997, the US administration 'deliberately obstructed the appearance of someone invited to testify before congress'[45] when, mindful of Syrian sensitivities,[46] Washington refused to issue General Aoun a visa to appear before a congressional hearing on US policy towards Lebanon as requested by Rep. Benjamin A. Gilman, chairman of the House International Relations Committee. In February 2001, Secretary of State Colin Powell abruptly cancelled a stopover in Beirut after discussing tensions in South Lebanon with Syrian officials in Damascus. This prompted an angry Rafik Hariri, then prime minister, to declare that 'it is not enough for him to visit Damascus... Lebanon is Lebanon and Syria is Syria'.[47] Reflecting the general sentiment of Lebanese-American lobbies, a May 2000 report strongly criticised the Clinton administration for soft-pedalling 'Syria's record on terrorism and its acquisition of weapons of mass destruction'. The report bemoaned the fact that the USA 'possesses enormous leverage over Syria that it does not seem willing to use'. It advocated that the Executive Branch openly call on Damascus to end its occupation of Lebanon.[48]

The post-9/11 political and cultural environment in the USA created opportunities for the Lebanese-American lobbies to 'frame' their concerns about Syria's presence in Lebanon and about the growth of Hizbollah in terms increasingly germane to worries on the Hill. Lebanese-American lobbies used a language consonant with US national security concerns. USFCL, for example, advocated a change in Lebanon's alliances in order to rid the country of the 'rogue regimes of Iran, Syria and Hezbollah'. The American Lebanese Coordination Council stressed its role as a think-tank committed to fighting terrorism and exposing oppressive regimes suspected of sponsoring terrorism, and/or violating international laws and human rights. It saw itself as:

Helping US public officials and security agencies better understand the mentality and convictions of terrorists in order to apply the proper methods necessary to win the war on terrorism [and] providing policy-makers of various government agencies and international organizations with thorough research and studies on Lebanon and the greater Middle East region.[49]

Allying themselves to conservative think-tanks such as the Middle East Forum, Lebanese-American lobbyists approached members of Congress to win them over to their perspectives. Writing in *Foreign Policy in Focus*, a critic of the USCFL described the group's neoconservative alliances as follows:

USCFL's core supporters, which it calls its 'Golden Circle', include several members of the Bush administration: Elliott Abrams, Richard Perle, Paula Dobriansky, Michael Rubin and David Wurmser. Other prominent neo-cons in the Golden Circle include Daniel Pipes (Middle East Forum and US Institute for Peace), Frank Gaffney (Center for Security Policy), Jeane Kirkpatrick (American Enterprise Institute or AEI), Michael Ledeen (AEI), David Steinmann (Jewish Institute for National Security Affairs) and Eleana Benador (Middle East Forum). Also included in this circle of those who have donated US$1,000 or more to USCFL is Republican Eliot Engel, the congressional representative who was the main sponsor of the Syria Accountability and Lebanese Sovereignty Restoration Act of 2003.[50]

And the author of the article concludes: 'USCFL may be "non-sectarian", but its list of core supporters and the "pro-Lebanon" groups listed on its website signal its neo-conservative and pro-Likud sympathies'.[51] Though this may have only played an indirect role in the US decision, nevertheless, in their attempts to convince the US administration to side with them against domestic political opponents, Christian Lebanese political forces successfully framed Hizbollah as part of a broader regional, indeed international, geopolitical game—the war against terror.

A similar dynamic can be traced in the manner in which pro-Syrian politicians associated dissent of Syrian-style implementation of Taif with collusion with Israel. Under Syria's watch, the mostly-Christian political opposition was accused of threatening national concord, a crime punished with removal of the immunity that Taif's amnesty provisions granted to all wartime leaders. Following Syria's withdrawal from Lebanon, 14 March politicians framed Shia discontent with the power-sharing formula as no more than Syrian/Iranian machinations to destabilise Lebanon and strengthen the hand of a terrorist organisation. Hizbollah and other 8 March political forces, on the other hand, attempted to force the resignation of Siniora in 2006 by claiming that he and his government had col-luded with Israel in the summer 2006 conflict to rid Lebanon of Hizbollah, thus putting narrow political interests ahead of the national interest in preserving the 'national resistance'.[52] Based on the preceding analysis, one might argue that the Lebanese might be better off if left to address their political problems in isolation from broader forces. This is easier said than done. Structural forces related to the nature of the Leba-nese state drive communities to seek the support of foreign allies and prevail upon their domestic opponents. Compounding the problem is the fact that foreign interventions contribute to the creation of a vicious circle. This vicious circle has two elements: first, foreign intervention affects the rules of the game thus contributing to state weakness; and second, it impacts the perception of existential threat which underpins the com-munities' search for allies.

Weakening Institutions: Rules of the Game Made to Fit[53]

Foreign intervention in the domestic affairs of the Lebanese has led to the constant adaptation and re-adaptation of the rules of the game to fit the taste of the day's local strongmen and the concurrent strategic interest of dominant foreign powers. This has hampered the institutionalisation of politics and contributed to state weakness, the very weakness that prompts communities to question the state's ability to deter and assure.

Under Syria's custodianship of Taif, electoral contests were tailored to fit. The electoral law and the design of electoral circumscriptions changed in 1992, 1996, 2000 and 2004 to secure the victory of Syria's local allies. Little changed when the USA and France, working in part through the UN Secu-rity Council, replaced Syria as the major outside interveners in Lebanese politics. Although they did not directly interfere in crafting the rules of the game, Paris and Washington supported the outcome of the summer 2005 parliamentary elections which brought the 14 March coalition to power, in spite of serious flaws that marred the electoral campaign.

The parliamentary elections in mid-2005 (and again in 2009) did not depart from the norm of post-war Lebanese elections that, 'far from expand-ing the parameters of accountability, representation, and contestation, have instead restricted citizens' electoral and hence political choices'.[54] The prob-lems stemmed both from the electoral system[55] and from aberrant electoral practices. Under the Lebanese electoral system, voters cast votes for predetermined party lists with the winner taking all seats in the district. While results confirmed the depth of cleavages in Lebanese society, they also underscored the unrepresentative nature of a system that allowed entire party lists to be voted in with the narrowest of margins.[56] The 2005 contest was held under the 2000 Election Law which drew constituency boundaries to weaken Christian representation, thus contravening the principle of proper political representation (*sihat al-tamthil al-siyasi*) enshrined at Taif. Most of the sixty-four Christian seats were in Muslim majority areas and strong Christian leaders were hamstrung in their efforts to get elected.[57] Furthermore, the campaign of Future Movement leader and head of the 14 March coalition, Saad Hariri, was accused of vote buying. Although the European Union Observer Mission 'directly observed some instances of vote buying, where fuel coupons or cash were given to voters in exchange of their vote, and was aware of other similar practices involving provision of free medical services [and the] payment of university tuition costs,[58] Western powers ultimately chose to describe the election process and outcome as 'free and fair'. The West thus acted much as Syria had done before—it turned a blind eye to the malpractice and labelled a flawed electoral process 'free and fair' because it had brought Western allies to power.

Washington, Paris and the UN further sowed the seeds of the crisis of power-sharing which paralysed Lebanon from November 2006 until May 2008 only to re-emerge at the end of 2010. This it did in two ways. First, the US administration insisted on the disarmament of Hizbollah and refused to engage with the party which it dubbed a 'foreign terrorist organisation', even though Hizbollah had done quite well in elections that the USA described as free and fair, and in spite of the fact that the party was in government for the first time in its history. Second, Western involvement in setting up the Special Tribunal for Lebanon (STL) would also deeply weaken the Lebanese state's capacity to assure Hizbollah that it was not bent on destroying the party and marginalising the Shia. Indeed, and while the Tribunal did not initially seem to target Hizbollah, the investigation ultimately resulted in the issuance of arrest warrants against four party members and contributed to the polarisation of domestic politics. Much as Syria and its allies had labelled critics as Israeli agents of destabilisation, accusing them of attempting to torpedo national coexistence and harm the implementation of Taif, Western powers and the 14 March coalition labelled Hizbollah a terrorist organisation, refusing to grant a fair hearing to Shia demands for a revision of the old sectarian power-sharing formula in ways that would acknowledge the growing demographic and political weight of the Shia. After the 2006 summer war between Hizbollah and Israel, the Party of God accused its partners in government of colluding with the enemy, while US support for the Siniora government strengthened the uncompromising attitude of the 14 March coalition, which accused Hizbollah of building a state-within-the-state and of standing as the major obstacle to the reinforcement of state institutions. US backing also influenced the steadfastness with which the Siniora government refused to give in to the demands of the 8 March coalition for a blocking minority in government of one-third plus one. Neither the resignation of Shia cabinet members on 11 November 2006 nor the siege of government organised under the auspices of the movement of civil disobedience launched by 8 March coalition members weakened the resolve of Siniora and his allies. In a context where their main community organisation was coming under Western attack as a 'terrorist organisation', Lebanon's Shia pressed hard to ensure that the rules of the political game would secure their effective inclusion. To be able to exercise veto powers, the 8 March opposition required an effective blocking minority. Only then would it be able to ensure compliance with Taif's provision that decisions on matters of national interest could not be taken by majority but required a national consensus. This rule was one of the instruments designed at Taif to ensure effective power-sharing within the executive. Ironically, Christian political forces had first raised this issue back in 1992 when the first post-war government went ahead with the organisation of elections that summer in spite of the resignation of Christian ministers. The USA, which had exhorted the parties to respect the Taif Agreement, did not acknowledge that this could be construed as a breach of Taif. Instead, it chose to accuse the 8 March forces of fomenting a coup against the government with the support of Iran.

The establishment of the STL would provide another occasion for conflict among the Lebanese. The politics behind the STL clearly contravened, if not the letter, then at least the spirit of Taif, which required national consensus on issues of national interest. That this consensus was not obtained continued to wreak havoc in the fabric of Lebanese politics, as the announcement in late 2010 that the STL was about to issue indictments triggered a political crisis that in early 2011 lead to the fall of the government of Prime Minister Saad Hariri.

Following the resignation of Shia ministers in November 2006, the government went ahead and approved documents concerning the statutes of the STL. This could be construed as a violation of the two-third majority rule. Of the original twenty-four-member government, only seventeen ministers were still in post, barely more than the legal two-thirds, while the government also lacked any representation from one of the three major communities. In January 2007, opposition parliamentarians drafted a petition calling for charges to be laid against Prime Minister Siniora for violating the Lebanese Constitution.[59] House Speaker Nabih Berri, himself a Shia, argued that by so doing, the prime minister was preparing the ground for adoption of the STL statutes under Chapter VII of the UN Charter, a process that would remove the tribunal from the orbit of Lebanese law and only increase 8 March concerns regarding its impartiality and credibility.[60] For opposition members, this was a 'highly political' project 'tailored to implement verdicts that have already been reached'.[61] When, on 30 May 2007, the UN Security Council voted for Resolution 1757, paving the way for the establishment of the STL, five UNSC members abstained and denounced an unacceptable intervention in the domestic affairs of Lebanon. This was an omen of things to come. The STL has become another occasion for deep political disagreement in Lebanon, with Hizbollah construing it as an 'Israeli project' and warning of dire consequences if party members were named in the indictments that were issued in mid-January 2011. For the BBC's Middle East editor, Jeremy Bowen, 'the tribunal's work has a much wider impact than finding out who assassinated Hariri. It is part of the big confrontation in the region between the US and its allies on one side; and Syria, Iran and their allies on the other'.[62] The subsequent announcement of the indictments led to the fall of the government of Saad Hariri and could later spark sectarian violence.

Heightening Confessionalism: Framing and Fear in the Lebanese Context

The intervention of outsiders has rendered the deconfessionalisation of Lebanon's political system as elusive as ever. It has also contributed to reawakening sectarian feelings and stoking up sectarian tensions in society. Under Syria's watch, from 1990 until 2005, confessional politics had been the norm in Lebanon.[63] Although Taif sought to restore balance to what had been a highly skewed system favouring the Maronite community,[64] Syria's custodianship of the agreement resulted in 'al-ihbat al-massihi'. For their part, politicians reverted to behaving as protectors and promoters of their communal interests, as illustrated by what became known as the politics of the troika, or the tendency of the Maronite president, Sunni prime minister and Shia speaker of parliament to invoke customary practice in jockeying for communal predominance and stepping beyond the bounds that the Lebanese constitution had set for each of their offices.[65]

This situation only worsened after 2004 as both political coalitions, 14 March and 8 March, feared marginalisation by the other. As protagonists jockeyed for dominance on the Lebanese political scene, their foreign allies were only too willing to either stand by or lend a hand as the rules of the political game were interpreted and reinterpreted to fit the political imperatives of the day. This not did not only exacerbate political confessionalism, it increased confessional expressions in society.

Increasing confessionalism results from perceived feelings of threat and/ or political marginalisation. Among Christians, these fears can be traced to a number of decisions taken during Syria's custodianship of the Taif Agreement: the electoral laws of 1992 and their impact on the effectiveness of Christian political participation; the naturalisation decree of 1994 which affected the demographic equilibrium between communities as it resulted in the naturalisation of an 80 per cent majority of Muslims; and the stark failure to rehabilitate internally displaced persons, the majority of whom were Christians.[66] This 'retribalisation' of communities reaches into all walks of society. In 2010, it expressed itself in the controversy over a draft bill preventing the sale of land across confessions. Prompted by a reported rise in the sale of land belonging to Christian owners to Iranian interests, often through Lebanese Shia third parties, bill-drafter and Labour Minister Boutros Harb argued that: 'There are suspicious sale operations of Christian territories happening as if there is a trend of expelling Christians from their land', adding that 'Christian presence in Lebanon allows cultural and religious diversity'.[67] Drawing inspiration from a 1984 *fatwa* (religious decree) by the then vice president of the Higher Shia Council, Sheikh Mohammad Mahdi Chamseddine, preventing the sale of Muslim land to non-Muslims in mixed areas in order to preserve religious diversity, Harb argued that this proposal was intended to preserve national coexistence.

While Christian fears are stoked by perceptions of Iran's hidden hand working through the Lebanese Shia, Shia, similar fears exist among Sunnis. The reawakened Sunni-Shia rivalry is inscribed in a larger rivalry between Iran and Saudi Arabia to don the mantle of regional leadership. Tensions began surfacing during the 2006 summer war when, as already discussed,

Shia leaders accused Siniora and 14 March of having tacitly supported the American-backed Israeli assault on Hizbollah in an attempt to eliminate the Party of God from the Lebanese political map. In May 2008, tensions culminated in two days of open armed confrontation between supporters of both sides. Sunni fears of the Shia ascendancy in Lebanon have developed in the context of what has been termed a larger regional Shia awakening. 'These fears revolve around a perception that events in the region are united by a common logic that would, in time, establish a "Shia crescent" uniting Iran, Alawite-controlled Syria and the Lebanese Hizbollah. Such an axis, were it to become reality, could compete for political predominance with Sunnis, thus not only threatening Saudi Arabia but all Sunni leaderships in countries with sizeable Shi'a populations'.[68]

The Shia community has also experienced retribalisation. Illustrative of the hardening of sectarian identity was the decision of the minister of state, Adnan Sayyed Hussein, to resign from government on 12 January 2011 only minutes after ministers representing the 8 March coalition resigned *en masse* following the collapse of a Saudi-Syrian initiative to resolve serious political tensions over the STL. Hussein, a Shia, was supposed to be the independent minister named by the president under the provisions of the Doha agreement, which brought the armed confrontations of May 2008 to an end. At the time, the 8 March coalition wanted a blocking minority of one-third plus one in government to be able to veto decisions that, it felt, went against the national interest—14 March was opposed to this demand. The solution came in the form of a compromise whereby the president would name an independent minister of state to prevent either side from automatically being able to either pass resolutions by virtue of its numerical majority or block resolutions because it had a one-third plus one minority. That Hussein would side with his community, thus ensuring the fall of the government, is but an indication of the depth of communal solidarity borne out of fears of marginalisation. These fears were initially prompted by Western attitudes towards Hizbollah, expressed in UNSC Resolution 1559, as well as by American official statements during the summer 2006 conflict with Israel. Views of Hizbollah as a mere extension of Iranian and Syrian interests have fed the perception that the Lebanese Shia are under threat and that their perceived legitimate demands for a greater share of power were being brushed away. 'At a time when they are designated terrorists and denied legitimacy, the Shi'a of Lebanon, once labelled Lebanon's only truly national community, are now embracing the country's confessional system, seeking to assert their role and protect themselves against elimination by carving out a place for themselves in this system'.[69]

'Plus ça change'

… more and more Lebanese are today brandishing their confessionalism, …, as both emblem and armour. Emblem, because confessional identity has become the most viable medium for asserting presence and securing vital needs and benefits… Confessionalism is also being used as armour, because it has become a shield against real or imagined threats.[70]

This chapter has traced the tendency of Lebanese communities to rely on foreign powers to the twin impact of fears that they will be politically marginalised or even liquidated, and concerns that the Lebanese state is incapable of credibly committing to either deter or assure communities in its midst. To secure the support of foreign powers, the various communities resort to framing their adversaries in terms that play on the security concerns of the specific power that they target. Thus, Christians have often been labelled as Israeli or Western agents, whereas Shia have been associated with rogue states and international terrorism. The chapter further established that international interventions in Lebanese domestic politics have created a vicious cycle in as much as their intended or unintended consequences have actually worsened communal fears and politicised the Lebanese state, thus further eroding its capability to deter and assure.

While there is little new to these dynamics, as compared with the era of Syrian dominance in Lebanon, or even with pre-war dynamics, a few changes are still worth noting. Lebanese communities complained about political marginalisation before the war. Their threat perceptions now revolve around attempts at full exclusion, even physical elimination. This reflects, first and foremost, deterioration in their relationship to the state. Before the 1975 civil war, the Lebanese state was perceived as unable to deter and now it is increasingly perceived as unable or unwilling to assure. The difference is significant in that the state is now seen as a direct threat to some of its citizens. The state's captivity by communal interests reflects the failure to institutionalise the rules promoting fair participation and preventing exclusion that were set at Taif. Between 2004 and 2010, this was aided and abetted by foreign powers, particularly the USA, who, in the context of the 'war on terror', did not only seek to bring Lebanon into their orbit, but took the opportunity to attempt to rid themselves of the perceived terrorist threat posed by Hizbollah.

That the USA did not intervene in May 2008, that Hizbollah did not use its military victory as a prelude to a full takeover and that the 2011 resignation of the Shia ministers ushered in a 'non-violent coup' that replaced pro-Western Prime Minister Saad Hariri with pro-Syrian Najib Mikati suggest that Lebanon has come full circle. As far as the entanglement of domestic and regional issues is concerned, the 'Cedar Revolution' did not really constitute a break with the past. Instead, politics in Lebanon continue to revolve around communal perceptions of insecurity and efforts to address this insecurity by drawing outsiders into Lebanese politics. Developments surrounding the issue of the STL are the latest illustrations of this dynamic. At a time when the rest of the Arab world seems to be undergoing major transformations, the inability of the Lebanese to overcome their communal identities and join together in a common state and nation-building project does not bode well for either stability or democracy.

5

LEBANON IN SEARCH OF SOVEREIGNTY

POST-2005 SECURITY DILEMMAS

Élizabeth Picard

This chapter explores a main hypothesis—short of regaining its status of sovereign nation-state in the international arena, post-2005 Lebanon might be considered a state with limited sovereignty, where citizenship remained dubious and national interest controversial. In a state of this kind, armed forces are prone to fragmentation along primordial identities and are often privatised, while authoritarianism looms as the ultimate recourse against state dissolution and societal strife. The chapter is organised in two sections.

The first section looks into the role, capabilities and interventions of national armed forces on the domestic and regional scenes. It stresses the limits of the military leadership's efforts to make Lebanon's national forces a powerful agent of national defence due to structural weaknesses and the transformation of war. It examines the political obstacles that prevented the state from acquiring a monopoly of legitimate force by contrasting the Lebanese Armed Forces (LAF) with the 'national resistance' led by Hizbollah. It shows how new international security threats shifted security policies from the national to the global arena. It concludes that the Lebanese security sector might be characterised as domestically 'bifurcated' and internationally subordinate.

The second section examines the image of the new army, police and intelligence institutions and the state's efforts to instil an ethos of patriotism among draftees and enhance pluralism within military units. It argues that despite such intentions and tangible improvements, the armed forces were not immune to the segmentation of society exacerbated by the 14 March/8 March division, which undermined cooperation between security institutions. In the meantime, in a context of privatisation and outsourcing of security missions, security institutions became prone to selective military-civilian cooperation within confessional networks.

Research on Lebanon's exceptionality rightly stresses the pluralism of its society following the adoption of 'consensus democracy' in the 1926 Constitution and the 1943 National Pact. A logical corollary is its 'weak state' status (illustrated in the slogan 'Lebanon's strength lies in its weakness'), its limited sovereignty, its sectarian communal groups maintaining autonomous links with regional states and international powers, and armed forces which are limited in their scope and unequipped to cope with external challenges. Traditionally, Lebanon's external defence was neglected and, with the exception of the first Palestine War (1948–9), the state remained neutral in international and regional conflicts. The relationship between militarisation and state-building, presumed self-evident among nations arising from de-colonisation[1] was deliberately distended. On the one hand, the military and senior officers ostensibly remained aloof from political conflicts. The political elite, on the other hand, kept them at a distance, even as they tried to manipulate them. With few exceptions, the Lebanese regime could be described as civil.

Lebanon's exceptionality was challenged by a traumatic experience. It was victim to one of the earliest 'new wars' of the twentieth century (1975–90), the country torn from within by sectarian militias, prompting intense diplomatic and military intervention by regional states and major powers, including the UN. In the wake of the civil war, it became necessary to rebuild the country's devastated infrastructure and adapt it to the globalisation of trade and finance. As implied in the Taif Agreement,[2] priority should be given to military and police institutions, normatively erected as the 'central pillar' of the new state. From 1990 to 2005, reconstruction of the security sector remained strongly impeded and dangerously lopsided, at odds with both the official discourse and public opinion. The reformed Lebanese armed forces remained unable to establish state authority over national territory and become a melting-pot for citizenship as had been expected after implementation of general drafting. Three contextual elements help explain this failure: (a) the enduring segmentation of Lebanese society along primordial (family, clan and sect) faultlines; (b) the steady percolation of Syrian Baathist political culture into the Lebanese polity during nearly thirty years (1976–2005) of military presence and arbitrary rule; and (c) Lebanon's security remained threatened by regional and international tensions that related to the Arab-Israeli conflict.

The year 2005 was a landmark in the history of post-war Lebanon, its significance epitomised by ex-Prime Minister Rafik Hariri's assassination in February, not long after he had promoted the adoption of UNSC Resolution 1559. The three contextual elements presented above were overturned, raising a new set of problems. First, the reconfiguration of the national scene split the political arena into two coalitions aligned along pro-Western ('14 March') and pro-Syria and pro-Iran ('8 March') stances. This ideological division reinforced Lebanon's confessional segmentation, especially between Sunnis and Shia, while the Christians split into two adverse forces. How would this affect civilian and political confidence in, and support for, Lebanon's armed forces? Second, while Syrian military and intelligence left Lebanon within a few weeks of Hariri's assassination and Damascus pretended not to be concerned with Lebanon anymore, changes in bilateral relations were slow due to the strength of the strategic alliance between Hizbollah and Syria, and because the Syrian regime had woven dense and complex networks of trans-boundary collaborators, especially within the Lebanese military and intelligence. Would Lebanon be able to conceive and lead a national defence of its own, free from regional priorities? Third, the 14 March coalition which led the government from June 2005 until January 2011 committed itself to close security cooperation with the West. UNIFIL's role in the South was upgraded after the 2006 war[3] and Lebanon received new armaments for the struggle against trans-national terrorist networks. Could this strategic turn lead to a detachment from Syrian influence and Iran's agenda and reinforce domestic security without raising the prospect of domestic conflict?

Military Reconstruction and National Sovereignty

In the wake of the civil war, rebuilding Lebanon's armed forces in order to restore the sovereignty of the state required the adoption of a series of institutional and technical reforms. It also meant giving the military access to financial resources, new equipment and ammunition, and revising the government's national defence strategy. However, Syrian withdrawal and the growing involvement of Western powers in Eastern Mediterranean security issues did not result in a U-turn in Lebanese defence strategy and security policy. Rather, regionally and internationally, Lebanon's army and security forces remained caught in a double bind. On the one hand, they became a Western proxy in the fight against *jihadist* networks. On the other hand, they proved unable to recapture the monopoly on national defence from Hizbollah. Thus Lebanon remained hostage to regional conflict as well as to international tensions, most notably growing animosity between the USA and Iran.

The rehabilitation of Lebanon's armed forces after the civil war, and their rebirth as the cornerstone of the new state, was intended to mark a radical departure in terms of state-military relations. Before the civil war, the Lebanese confessional elites considered the state inherently civilian and non-belligerent. Army recruitment was kept low, as was the budget, and the military was distanced from political affairs. In this respect, General Fuad Chehab's ascension to the presidency in the wake of the 1958 crisis constituted an exception. President Chehab devoted himself to social and political reform from 1958 to 1964, and his regime projected an image of efficiency and honesty. At the same time, he let the *Deuxième Bureau* (B2)—the military intelligence—meddle in the electoral process and administrative affairs.

Memory of *Chehabism* as a patriotic and development-oriented doctrine explains why so many Lebanese put their trust in the military after the civil war, even more so when the Syrians withdrew in 2005. The population longed for order and was willing to see the military play a central role in Lebanon's political reconstruction. In return, the new military command, first under Emile Lahoud (1990–8), then Michel Sleiman (1998–2008), was made out of officers who were nurtured by *Chehabism*, having begun their careers in the 1970s. Its Orientation Directorate publicised a document describing the military as defenders of societal values—patriotism and solidarity.[4]

Syria, for its part, targeted security requirements as a tool of control over the society and polity in accordance with the Baathist model. Part IV of the Taif Agreement and the bilateral Treaty of Brotherhood imposed on Lebanon in May 1991 organised unequal cooperation in every domain, between a dominant power and the state. A defence and security agreement made official the presence of some 15,000 to 25,000 Syrian military personnel and the subordination of the Lebanese army and police to their Syrian counterparts. The head of Syrian intelligence in Lebanon (General Ghazi Kanaan and, after 2002, General Rustom Ghazaleh) imposed the Assad regime's will on the Lebanese presidents. A 'common destiny' (*talazum al-masarayn*) in the face of Israel and other external dangers was the ideological rationale for this domination, which was condemned by the UN in September 2004[5] and lasted until the forced withdrawal of the Syrian armed forces in April 2005.

Syria encouraged the building of a large army based on conscription and trained for traditional twentieth century warfare—a model already obsolete in Syria and the Middle East.[6] Syrian hegemony was exercised at all levels, from the frequent convocation of Lebanese senior officers at Syrian military intelligence headquarters in Anjar to the presence in every military base of a Syrian liaison officer whose authority was paramount. Syrian control was so complete that the minister of defence, Mustafa Tlass, declared: 'Thanks to the Lebanese army, Syria is at peace on its western flank'.[7]

Reform, Conscription and Armament

In a context of international lack of concern and domestic despondency, the military command under General Lahoud and their Syrian patrons rapidly gained control. A stream of reforms shook the Lebanese military in anticipation of state reform. The new army underwent several important changes, including the placement of dozens of officers on early retirement. This was used to get rid of insubordinate elements and provide intensive training for new recruits and old cadres at the Fayadiyeh military academy as well as at 'friendly' military schools (IMET programs in the USA, the École de Guerre in Paris, and staff schools in Damascus and Aleppo). Army command imposed discipline and the (re)-training of men who had previously been confined to barracks, as well as selective recruitment and new assignments. All in all, rapid promotion resulted in an officer corps of some 3,000 men. Expertise, responsibility and corporatism appeared to be the watchwords for this post-civil war army.

LAF and security institutions were subject to organisational reform which was neither discussed in nor voted for by parliament. A Central Council for Security (*Majlis al-amn al-markazi*) was formed in 1990[8] and the Supreme Defence and Security Council (*Majlis al-a'la lil-difa' wal-amn*)

87

re-established in 1991,[9] thus formalising the centralisation of competing information networks under Syrian tutelage. Army intelligence and the General Security Directorate were reorganised in 1990 and 1998, and entrusted to the same pro-Syrian officer, Jamil al-Sayyed.[10] On the whole, the military was reshuffled into twelve brigades and as many specialised units (marine, airborne regiment, republican guard, special forces, etc.) under five regional commands.

Syria worked to domesticate the Lebanese army, police and security services through the allocation of significant budgetary resources and economic privileges, and by upgrading the social status of the officers. Officers received supplementary pay for cooperation with Syria in the form of a training allowance while attending a Syrian military academy, or an invitation to officers' clubs. Some officers were provided with new vehicles and SUVs for personal use and granted housing credits by *Iskan askari* (Military housing), a foundation created in 1994 on the Syrian model.

Another novelty was the implementation of general conscription.[11] The military was expected to become a tool of social integration, but conscription raised recurrent protests among all sectors of society, as most conscripts remained idle after six months' training. Several surveys illustrated the project's flaws, revealing resistance and failures, and even its perverse effects, yet compulsory army service was abrogated by a non-controversial parliamentary vote, thanks to a convergence of interests between a majority of MPs and the Syrian command in January 2005. Three years later, armed forces were made up of career and contracting personnel only.

Lebanon's budget deficit had resulted in the abrogation of conscription, and as early as 1997, Rafik Hariri was complaining of the excessive cost of military service.[12] Military expenses became a burden for the government as police and army numbers increased four-fold from 1991 to 2002, employing almost one-tenth of the country's wage earners and supporting half a million people out of a population of 3.5 million. Eighty per cent of the army, police and general security budgets were spent on wages, training and benefits for personnel, officers and enlisted corps. Between 1992 and 2008, defence spending remained Lebanon's largest budgetary item at over 10 per cent, after debt service and education. Retired military and police personnel received a total of USD 2.4 billion in end-of-service indemnities and pension payments between 1993 and 2002—an exorbitant figure with regard to the state budget and its deficit.[13]

Paltry amounts were left for equipment and armaments. The army was plagued by a 'structural deficit in terms of material' which was never made up for during two decades.[14] Most of its systems consisted of worn equipment transferred at no or low cost from other states.[15] Still, levels of foreign support remained minimal from 1990 to 2006 and purchases and gifts were made up essentially of equipment of a defensive nature.[16]

While never officially acknowledged, the reason for this deficit was that the Western powers which traditionally supported Lebanon were reluctant to help rebuild Lebanon's security sector while it remained tightly interconnected with and dependent upon the powerful Syrian forces stationed within the country's borders. Syria was no more willing to rearm the Lebanese military, fearing a resumption of the civil war and worrying about the effect a Lebanese military empowerment might have on the Eastern Arab-Israeli front. As a testimony to LAF impotence, governments refrained from acting to reclaim state sovereignty over the occupied South and, following Israeli withdrawal in 2000, only a limited ISF-army force of one thousand men crossed the Litani. Fear of controversy within the armed forces that might lead to resignations and even secession accounted for such paralysis.[17]

A few years later, when Lebanon was confronted with two major military aggressions—an insurgency in Nahr al-Bared in 2007 and the massive 2006 Israeli attack—its armed forces not only lacked adequate equipment and training, they remained plagued by inefficient organisation, management difficulties and lack of strategic direction. These dysfunctions and the government's lack of a security policy were crudely exposed.

A Lebanese Proxy in the 'Global Fight Against Terrorism'

Lebanon has long been a case study for Western intervention in the Middle East. Its state institutions were largely shaped by the *Règlement organique*, a system imposed by European powers on the Sublime Porte in 1864, and through the French mandate from 1920 to 1943. After independence, Western intervention in Lebanon was frequent, from the US landings during the civil war in 1958 to the creation of UNIFIL in 1978 and the failed mission of the Multilateral Force in 1982–3.

Ending the civil war did not secure state sovereignty. Israel's twenty-two-year occupation of South Lebanon lasted until May 2000. Only then was a limited contingent of national military and police dispatched south of the Litani to cooperate with UNIFIL.[18] Still, several contested areas (Shebaa, Ghajar, Kfar Shuba) remained under Israeli control, occasioning skirmishes over the 'Blue Line' between Israeli Defence Forces (IDF) and Lebanese irregulars organised by Hizbollah and backed by Syria. In the meantime, Islamist mobilisation in Palestine (*Intifada al-Aqsa* in 2000) and then in Iraq echoed among Lebanese Sunnis and Palestinian refugees. *Jihadist* militants who had mobilised in the Ayn al-Hilweh (Sidon) refugee camp and fought the Lebanese army in the highlands of Denniyeh in January 2000 were arming, training, and travelling back and forth to Iraq with the support of Syrian intelligence.[19]

Before 9/11 and the designation of al-Qaida as the global enemy, the USA and its NATO allies had led the Lebanese security services into the fight against international drug trafficking, illegal immigration, human trafficking and terrorist networks. Cooperation remained limited until the US-led invasion of Iraq in 2003, which gave rise to a local and transregional Islamic insurgency that spilled over into neighbouring countries, and even Lebanon.[20] Following the 'Cedar Revolution' and the withdrawal of Syrian military and intelligence, Western military cooperation increased as the Lebanese army became gradually involved in the fight against *jihadist* local cells and guerrillas.[21] The globalised 'war against terror' bound Lebanon in 'strategic partnership' with its Western allies.[22]

Western powers were willing to reform and train the LAF, on their own terms and in relation to their strategic priorities. The US Congress, which had kept military cooperation at a low level since the US retreat from Beirut in 1983, approved an aid budget in February 2007 that included USD 280 million for security.[23] In May, when an Islamic insurgency moved from Tripoli to the camp of Nahr al-Bared, Western governments labelled Fatah al-Islam[24] a 'danger to international security'. On the whole, between 2005 and 2010, Lebanon was promised nearly USD 720 million worth of military material from Washington and the LAF were advised to 'prioritize a domestic counterterrorism mission'.[25] More specifically, top-brass US officers stressed the 'necessity to counterbalance the influence of Syria and Hizbollah'.[26]

The LAF's war against Fatah al-Islam in Nahr al-Bared illustrated the conflation of domestic Lebanese security issues with the regional and international agendas of third parties interfering in Lebanon. Moreover, it shed light on the dilemma plaguing Lebanon's defence strategy. Should the LAF have given priority to an international conflict and the defence of its national borders, or to the fight against local insurgents—a large number of whom were Lebanese citizens? The battle against a few hundred *jihadist* insurgents entrenched in the Palestinian camp north of Tripoli lasted for over three months (24 May to 5 September 2007), causing a high level of destruction and human loss.[27] It was finally won when LAF special forces flattened the insurgents' stronghold with emergency supplies of armed helicopters and missiles.[28]

Fighting Sunni Muslims, a majority of whom were Arabs, and even Lebanese, with the logistical support of Western powers, was not met with universal domestic approval. Beyond the problem of the army's operational capability lay divisions within Lebanon's political leadership. Who should make national security decisions—the Maronite president, the Sunni prime minister or the sectarian majority in parliament? Furthermore, the lack of consensus regarding security priorities resulted in confusion amongst Lebanon's elites. In the 8 March camp, Hizbollah warned that it would 'not accept or provide cover or be partner in [the military assault]',[29] while in contrast, its Syrian patron kept a low profile and even offered technical assistance.[30] In the Free Patriotic Movement, Hizbollah's main Christian ally, solidarity with LAF prevailed because General Michel Aoun, who had been commander-in-chief between 1983 and 1988, retained support within the army. In the 14 March camp, cooperation with the West barely masked internal discord as Defence Minister Elias Murr described the refugee camp of Ayn al-Hilweh as the utmost danger to Lebanon, while Sunni leaders maintained ambivalent relations with extremist groups within their electoral constituencies.[31]

In order to bypass the political stalemate, the LAF's decision making had to bypass the civilian leadership and Commander-in-Chief Michel Sleiman took the responsibility for seeking further Western support, engaging special units in the battle and launching the deadly air assault. The final victory in Nahr al-Bared contributed to enhancing the image of the military nationally and paved the way for Sleiman's accession to the presidency in 2008. It prompted a reappraisal of LAF structures in order to upgrade the special forces and give them a central mission,[32] and it underlined the crucial issue of Western arms supplies—an issue which remained prescient.[33] The victory was nevertheless considered unjust among Islamist segments of society and extremely costly in terms of military losses. Three months later, François el-Hajj, the brilliant general who led the battle of Nahr al-Bared, lost his life in his booby-trapped car and in the year that followed the LAF were targeted several times in the Sunni areas of Tripoli.[34]

A 'Bifurcated' National Defence

Since 1985, when Hizbollah began marginalising and eliminating rival groups, it had become *the* military actor confronting Israel in Lebanon. Born under the auspices of the Islamic Republic of Iran, it was legitimised by Syria as the main national resistance group and therefore exempted from the post-war demobilisation that occurred in 1991 on the pretext that the South remained occupied. Until the Israeli withdrawal of 2000, Hizbollah substituted for the LAF in South Lebanon, organising and leading a successful guerrilla resistance against the IDF and their local proxies. After the Israeli withdrawal, the *Muqawama al-Islamiyya* (Islamic resistance) now renamed *Muqawama al-Wataniyya* (national resistance) took exclusive military control of the 'liberated' areas down to the international border, heralding a globalised trend towards privatisation and trans-nationalisation of the security sector. Thanks to family and sectarian connections, and to the skilful blurring of boundaries between military structures, party organisation and Shia society, Hizbollah enjoyed great support. Narrow localism and regional strategy, clerical domination and the cult of armed sacrifice, contributed to eroding the weak territorial nation-state of Lebanon, while Hizbollah benefited from powerful transnational networks centred on Tehran, which provided financial resources, armaments, and political and religious support.[35]

Hizbollah could be considered a paragon of the new military structures fighting asymmetric wars in the wake of the 'revolution in military affairs'. A unified, strictly hierarchical military institution of a few thousand combatants, with a command structure inspired by the PLO, it was organised in small, mobile, extremely well trained, decentralised autonomous cells which combined sophisticated intelligence technology, high-tech arms and audacious improvisation. These characteristics accounted for its success in its war of attrition against the Israeli occupying forces prior to 2000, as well as for its remarkable resistance against Israel's attack in the summer of 2006.

As suggested by Emile Hokayem, 'In the best of all worlds, [Lebanon] would have a serious defence review that would conclude that [it] needs a military fashioned *à la* Hizbollah—special forces, light infantry, officers and NCOs that have a sense of initiative, good communication, anti-tank weaponry, good intelligence and reconnaissance assets, some helicopters, coastal radars, even air defence at some point [...] Such a force would do a far better job at protecting Lebanon at a much cheaper cost, and the Israeli

Qualitative Military Edge would not be an insurmountable problem'.[36] In stark contrast, the LAF was a bystander in the thirty-three-day war between Israel and Hizbollah, merely coordinating relief efforts for the population and ensuring order following the hostilities. Neither equipped nor deployed to play a meaningful role, the LAF suffered losses with little response, scrambling to protect their men and firing anti-aircraft weapons to no avail.[37] On the civilian side, Siniora proved unable to obtain even defensive arms or civil protection equipment from his Western allies, who did not want him to engage the national army on the side of Hizbollah. Only at the end of the war, and after the passage of UNSC Resolution 1701 increased UNIFIL's mission in terms of manpower, scope and resources, did the government send 15,000 military south of the Litani in close cooperation with the international force.

Since 2005, questions over the future of Hizbollah's militia have proved a stumbling-block in Lebanon's quest for state sovereignty and a monopoly on legitimate violence within its borders—the main point of contention between 14 March and 8 March within and outside the 'consensus' government. It featured at the top of the agenda of the National Dialogue conference, and even more so after a provisional compromise was signed in Doha in May 2008 between the majority and the opposition which stressed the necessity to 'promote Lebanon's state authority all over the Lebanese territory'. Inside the LAF, Hizbollah's public stance remained a bone of contention among officers divided between the two camps. While intelligence units were prone to share information with Hizbollah during the 2006 war, observers noticed sectarian resentment and distrust towards fellow Shia.[38] Disarming the 'national resistance' by force would have been far beyond the LAF's military capabilities and the authority of the government. Its integration into the Lebanese army seemed improbable in the short term.[39] First, because coordination would have to be negotiated between radically antagonistic political camps, and second, because this would have required a radical change in the regional balance of power. Syria would not relinquish its political and logistic support to Hizbollah and its other Lebanese and Palestinian allies in Lebanon as long as the regime did not strike a satisfying deal with Israel and the USA over the Golan Heights. For Iran's part, its leadership highly valued their local Near Eastern allies either as proxies or as a safety valve for regional tension.

While Lebanon remained on the faultline between the 'moderate axis' and the 'resistance front', Lebanon's defence strategy remained caught in this double bind. On the one hand, a covert strategic relationship between the 'national resistance' and the LAF was fostered under Syrian tutelage. This involved intelligence sharing, a tolerant approach to Hizbollah training and the trafficking of arms between the Syrian border, the Beqaa and the South. Hizbollah's leadership referred to this as 'conceptual continuity'[40] as illustrated in the 1998 and 2004 jointly organised prisoner exchanges with Israel.[41] Implicitly, this strategic relationship extended to Syria as overtly acknowledged by President Michel Sleiman during his visits to Damascus (August 2008, June 2010), and to Iran as suggested at the time of his visit to Tehran (November 2008).[42]

On the other hand, coordination between UNIFIL II and the Lebanese brigades deployed in South Lebanon steadily improved as the UN force succeeded in involving Lebanese officers in tripartite security meetings with IDF representatives. In return, Lebanese officers mediated between UNIFIL and Hizbollah in the new security zone.[43] Western military cooperation extended to include the surveillance of Lebanese territorial waters, the national airport and land border control between Syria and Lebanon in conformity with UNSC Resolution 1701. Through Lebanese cooperation with several members of NATO, members of UNIFIL II and through the military and police operations against *jihadist* militants, Lebanon was experiencing a kind of integration of its security sector into the 'war on terror'—an integration paralleled by the financial and political support the international community granted to Lebanon's bankrupted economy and polity.[44]

Identity Controversy and its Effect on National Security

Throughout Lebanon's history, sectarian constituencies expressed varying degrees of confidence in the national army and security forces, while military recruitment followed the informal rules of political patronage along religious and family networks. The LAF and police forces reflected the sectarian segmentation of government rather than its demographic balance—Christians dominated the officer corps until 1975 and the commander-in-chief remained a Maronite by tradition. Shia from poor peripheral regions made up the bulk of the LAF's troops while Sunnis, especially from the cities, were under-represented.[45] During the civil war, the military institutions split along sectarian lines with officers and soldiers joining different militias on the basis of confession. When the war finally ended, the 'Eastern' (Christian) branch of the LAF remained under the command of Aoun while the other branch, under Lahoud and his Syrian patrons, garrisoned the rest of the country.[46]

Although the idea of reunifying and rehabilitating Lebanon's security sector met with general consensus, the way the war ended precluded any 'secularised' vision of national security. Peace was imposed from outside and the domestic balance of power ignored. Against such a background, the military remained enmeshed in the primordial ties and sectarian dynamics of Lebanon's different confessions and sensitive to inherited tensions and solidarity networks. What could be observed beyond the display of military ethos was that civilians and military of the same kin adopted similar sectarian patterns in their social behaviour and political commitment.[47]

To begin with, the demobilisation of their militias left a whole sector of Christian society outside of the reintegration process. The result of this ostracism was the disaffection of the Christian youth towards advancing in a military career and a division within the Christian community on the issues of national defence and state sovereignty. Then, in a context of economic ultra-liberalisation, post-war civilian elites involved officers in financial and political deals under Syrian patronage. Last but not least, the national legitimacy of the army and the police as institutions was eroded among a population gripped by sectarian loyalties. With regard to these negative trends, the dramatic events of 2005, rather than being a turning point, had a revealing and accelerating effect.

Demobilisation, Disarmament and Reintegration, and the Confessional Rebalancing of the Military

One of the key concepts behind the push to rehabilitate Lebanon's armed forces was blending the rank-and-file, thereby enhancing a shared national identity. As early as 1991, Emile Lahoud undertook a reshuffling of the army corps with a view to making it more pluralistic. For half a decade he imposed a rotating system among the twelve brigades deployed in the five main regions as a means of severing local sectarian connections. This measure was costly, however, and proved unpopular with the officers until it was scaled down in the 2000s.

In June 1991, Lebanon's parliament passed a law imposing the demobilisation, disarmament and reintegration of some 40,000 former militiamen into civilian or military service.[48] Conceived by Syria, the operation was hastily implemented and incomplete, with several militias hiding their heavy weaponry and selling other weapons to groups in the Balkans and the Caucasus. Moreover, hundreds of militiamen involved in war crimes were smuggled to Europe, the Americas and Australia. Only around 4,000 ex-militiamen (of whom 85 per cent were Muslim) and a few dozen officers joined the regular armed forces. The main Christian militia group, the Lebanese Forces (LF), was excluded from state institutions in retaliation for its opposition to Syrian rule, thus causing a deficit in Christian representation within the military. Furthermore, nearly 69 per cent of the 253 (out of some 2,000) army officers forcibly retired were Christians. The percentage of Christians in the officer corps declined to 47.1.[49] Among the rank-and-file it was even lower, as the army encountered great difficulty in attracting Christian youths, because they became increasingly reluctant to serve under Syrian rule and prone to emigration. This was true even for remote provinces like Akkar, a traditional reservoir of poor Maronite recruits. It kept declining, down to 41 per cent in 2000—an accurate reflection of Lebanon's overall sectarian composition.[50] It was similarly reported that the percentage of Christians among the draftees dropped down to 25 per cent.[51] Although difficult to corroborate, reports on a new recruitment policy sponsored by the ministry of defence after 2005 underlined the confessional balance conundrum, as it was said that Minister Murr wanted to increase the number of Christians in the army by recruiting them for special forces units. As a result, Christian under-representation in LAF and intelligence appeared a major concern for the ministry of defence.[52]

The year 2005 saw a major rift within the Christian community over the army. While supporters of the Free Patriotic Movement (FPM) highly valued the figure of the military leader and men in uniform, many top-brass officers in return remained sympathetic to Aoun, their ex-commander-in-chief. The memorandum of cooperation signed between FPM and Hizbollah in February 2006 has to be interpreted against this background,[53] as well as the alignment of Aoun and his FPM on strong anti-Israeli lines together with Hizbollah, Syria, and even Iran and Hamas, especially during the 2006 war. For their part, Samir Geagea and his LF adopted the opposite position, as the 14 March/8 March divide reactivated the intra-Maronite splits of the late 1980s. While LF milieus tended to distrust the military institution and favour self-defence, their leader blamed Hizbollah's provocative strategy and persistent security cooperation with Syria, criticising the army command for being soft on the Shia party.[54]

It was sometimes argued that after the Christians lost their dominant position within Lebanon, they became a middle force able to balance between two agonistic Muslim communities. But the Taif Agreement marked a considerable defeat for the Christian community and a reduction in national defence involvement, despite the traditional designation of a Maronite as commander-in-chief of the army. After 2005, the polarisation between the 14 and 8 March camps was not simply a reflection of demographic change in Lebanon, but also a testimony to the Christian community's reluctance to adapt to new domestic realities and new regional trends. A large majority of Christians, even among FPM supporters, felt at odds with the party's official stance on national defence, its solidarity with the 'national resistance' and wished for peace with Israel more than reconciliation with Syria.[55] While this explained their reluctance to enlist in the armed forces, it exposed the divided loyalties of the army's Christian officers when they were confronted with warfare or domestic strife.

Corruption and Repression: Dealing with the Syrian Legacy

In a context of structural incapacity of the judiciary, discrepancies between the image that the army and police intended to project and their actual behaviour on the ground raised doubts with respect to their nature and mission. They contributed to undermining public confidence until 2005, when a crucial question arose—would the withdrawal of Syrian forces help Lebanon return to the rule of law and escape the Middle East authoritarian pattern?

The Baathist regime had aptly distilled its authoritarian mode of accumulation into Lebanon—clientelist redistribution combined with predatory practices. Taking advantage of Lebanon's ultra-liberal post-war economy, the Syrian leaders had secured the lion's share of the huge benefits from financial and real-estate investments of the privatised reconstruction and established fruitful networks of trans-boundary trade. Far from diminishing after 2005, this Syrian-Lebanese collusion remained an enormous source of profit for corrupt entrepreneurs in both countries. The difference was that now it required bigger bribes and opened the door to more direct military involvement as the Lebanese army and security forces had recovered part of their autonomy.

During fifteen years (1990–2005) the Lebanese army and police had been subordinate, sometimes forced partners in the trans-boundary trafficking of primary goods such as oil products and cement, in the exploitation of Syrian manpower in Lebanon and, in some occasions, in channelling arms to Hizbollah. Officers were considered desirable partners by civilian entrepreneurs because of their supposed proximity to lawmakers and the Syrian leadership, who chose its agents in dealing and trafficking among state personnel through a mix of reward and threat.[56] Some entered the unruly economy under the pretext of implementing security missions such as closing illegal quarries, enforcing construction legislation and repressing infiltrated Syrian workers. The police, because of their daily interaction with the society on the ground, were even more affected, although petty corruption did not match the great stakes involving the hierarchy. Along with political leaders and senior civil servants, senior officers have been cited in corruption scandals alleged to cost the Lebanese state more than USD 1.5 billion per year.[57] Rumours persisted of senior Lebanese officers being partners to Syrian leaders in extortion from companies and banks. Between the end of the 1990s and early 2003 (the date of its collapse), Bank al-Madina seemed to have been involved in a kickback scheme that supplied Syrian and Lebanese civilian and military officials with cash, real estate, cars and jewellery, in exchange for protecting and facilitating a multi-billion dollar money laundering operation. 'While lower people like generals and officers would get cash, the big shots would get cheques'.[58]

There was no indication that the Syrian withdrawal in 2005 and the forced retirement of higher officers surrounding president Lahoud— Mustafa Hamdan, commander of the presidential guard; Jamil al-Sayyed, director of Sûreté Générale; domestic security head Ali Hajj, and the commander of army intelligence, Raymond Azar; four overtly pro-Syrian higher officers, who were imprisoned in Beirut in August 2005 on suspicion of complicity to murder and terrorist acts—was enough to put an end to the stream of loyalties, goods and funds circulating over the Syrian-Lebanese border with the complicity of security personnel.

Such collusion belied the apparent opposition between those who wished to 'privatise' the state for the sake of globalised capitalism (epitomised by Rafik Hariri) and those who depicted the state as the protector of citizens' security, promoter of full employment and fight against corruption—the 'strong state' promised by Lahoud upon his accession to the presidency.[59] Rather, the balance between business and military interests implied a sharing of power and profits between merchants and men in arms in a common 'network of privileges'[60] exerting arbitrary domination over the society.

Although far from the *mukhabarat* state, the post-Taif state had become more coercive than the consensus state of the 1960s and 1970s. Importation of the Baathist model and translation of Syrian stakes into the Lebanese political arena brought long-lasting changes in the culture of the military institutions and in civilian-military relations. This authoritarian turn was praised by president Lahoud on Army day (1 June 2001) when he declared that 'officers should employ an iron fist in commanding respect for a state of law and for national security. Security officers are a key element of the state'. Confronted with extra-parliamentary opposition and street demonstrations, the political leadership routinely resorted to police and even army intervention, extra-judicial procedures and illegal imprisonment. Arbitrary use of force by state institutions targeted advocacy associations and demonstrations against Syrian occupation. A military ethos characterised by the use of all necessary force presided over the repression of supposed *jihadist* groups rather than the police ethos of use of minimum force. Together, the new military and police participated in the diffusion of authoritarian patterns and the trivialisation of the domination of the men in arms.

Political Strife and Fragmentation of the Security Order

During the *Intifadat al-istiqlal* [Independence uprising] of Spring 2005, several signals raised great but fragile expectations of a return to a legal and fair national security under civilian rule, in a clear breach with Syrian practices. The army commander-in-chief Michel Sleiman provided some insight into this change while commenting on LAF's dealing with the huge civilian demonstration which took place on 14 March 2005: 'We execute the political will which emanates from a generalised national consensus... I approached this question from the point of view of the will of the nation, which is to say, the wish to live in peace. As a result I applied the popular political wish and not the official decision'.[61]

Still, withdrawing Syrian forces had left Lebanese security institutions unprepared and hardly adequately equipped in view of their new autonomy and responsibilities. Moreover, they had set up a number of separate and competing services, each accustomed to refer to their Syrian patrons while transversal cooperation had been kept at minimum. Post-Syria security services remained attached to specific political leaderships and tended to act as autonomous forces. The republican guard, an elite corps assigned to the presidency had been reinforced, equipped with modern weapons, and was commanded by officers trained in Homs and Damascus. Major General Ashraf Rifi was promoted to the head of ISF by 14 March Minister of Interior General Hassan Saba in April 2005. At the *Sûreté Générale*, Major General Wafiq Jezzini, an officer known for his Amal sympathies, replaced Jamil al-Sayyed in September 2006. Since Hariri's assassination and the subsequent withdrawal of the Syrian military, at least five rival intelligence units, each attached to a different confessional leader, overlapped and obstructed information exchange while the ministry of interior proved incapable of staffing a joint-operations room as agreed in August 2005.[62] A dozen booby-trapped cars took the lives of anti-Syrian political and intellectual figures in the following months, and the work of the UN International Independent Investigation Commission on Hariri's assassination remained continuously obstructed by conflict between intelligence services and paralysis in the judiciary.[63]

Fragmentation of the legal security forces prompted the re-militarisation of the society. Once the Syrian lid lifted, every sectarian and political group scrambled to rearm and train their militants. Private security companies, and even foreign operators, offered their services to every local *zaim*.[64] Among the Christians, 14 March LF and 8 March FPM launched mutual accusations of secret training and breaches of the demobilisation law. Pro-Syrian militias such as Baathists in the Beqaa, the Syrian Social National Party in Beirut, Alawite gangs in Tripoli and even Amal, prepared intensively for urban fighting. Hizbollah took a decisive step in paralleling state security services by organising a sophisticated communication network whose discovery ignited relations between majority and opposition in May 2008.[65] Even Hariri's Future Movement[66] began hastily recruiting *shabab* from deprived northern mountain areas and organising them into private companies, such as *Future Security Plus*, in order to prepare the defence of Beirut's Sunnis.

Instead of smoothening national reconciliation, the 2005 revolutionary turn paved the way for domestic strife, leading to intense polarisation between 14 March and 8 March embodying the famous 'Riviera vs Citadel' model[67] and a chasm between Sunnis attached to the legacy of the Hariris and Shia federated by Hizbollah, reverberating the Middle Eastern division exacerbated by the Iraqi crisis and the growing fear of Iran's regional status.[68] Extreme political tension prevailed from December 2006 to May 2008, and again after Prime Minister Saad Hariri's forced resignation in

January 2011. The government was paralysed and the struggle shifted from the realm of elite politics to that of street politics. 8 March parties organised rallies and sit-ins in downtown Beirut close to the *Grand Sérail*, the government headquarters. Clashes erupted during the general strike of January 2007 and acts of 'civil disobedience' and 'popular rage' became more and more frequent, until Hizbollah's takeover of Beirut in May 2008, which left eighty dead and two hundred wounded in one week.

The challenge posed by mounting sectarian strife had a direct effect on security forces, especially on ISF. It underlined the distinction between ISF and LAF when dealing with social and sectarian unrest, although both institutions acted as police forces. After the 2005 legislative election granted 14 March a government majority, Prime Minister Fuad Siniora endeavoured to strengthen the ISF, now released from Syrian control and directly under the responsibility of a loyal minister of interior. Within a few months, the forces grew from 14,000 to 20,000 with a view to recruit 6,000 more in 2011.[69] Their training and equipment received special attention from the USA and France, whose governments considered their role 'crucial for the independence, sovereignty and security of Lebanon'.[70] An elite guard of some 1,000 men meant to ensure the Sunni prime minister's personal security was recruited among Sunnis, and an independent intelligence service, the *Far' al-ma'lumat* (intelligence branch) was created in 2006.

Although ISF included a high proportion of Christians, and even Shia, they were considered by 8 March opposition as the armed wing of 14 March, more specifically of the Sunni leadership. They were accused of pursuing a sectarian agenda in their handling of demonstrations and local strife and became increasingly exposed to confrontation with better armed and trained 8 March militia groups and special units, namely Hizbollah and SSNP militants, during the crisis of May 2008. Not only did they lose these battles, but they also suffered a setback in their perceived national legitimacy.

The army, rather than ISF, was sent in January 2007 and 2008, and again in May 2008 and September 2010, to contain Sunni-Shia and Druze-Shia fighting. With rare exceptions,[71] LAF coordinated with Hizbollah forces when the former took over security in city areas. This coordination echoed their successful cooperation in southern areas between the Litani and the Blue Line after 2006. At the same time it contrasted with episodes of dysfunctional communication with ISF, namely when ISF stormed Islamist militants' quarters in Tripoli on 20 May 2007 without notifying the army and provoked a deadly retaliation from Fatah al-Islam against twenty-seven soldiers. This raised questions about the political neutrality of LAF in a period when the commander-in-chief became the new president.[72] Some suspected them of pro-14 March sympathies as a result of Minister of Defence Murr's alignment. Others suspected them of proximity with the Syrian regime when Sleiman, then his successor as head of LAF Jean Kahwaji, visited Damascus. In the end, the military failed to consolidate a third force loyal to the president within the 'consensus' government. This failure underlined the limits to the 'patriotic mission' they were allegedly trusted with.

Conclusion

At the time the civil war ended, the Lebanese shared a common vision. Their national army and security forces would be rebuilt as united and efficient institutions and become the main pillars of state reconstruction. This conviction was relayed and reinforced by public commitments of political leaders and Western allies. Among all constituencies, the military enjoyed a most positive image and became the symbol and model for national reconciliation. Still, the reality of such a positive image could not be tested as long as Israeli occupation lasted, and while Syria dominated the country militarily and politically. The passage of UNSC Resolution 1559 in 2004 and the new division of the political arena following Hariri's and others' assassinations in 2005 raised new challenges and brought new liabilities for state security institutions.

A first question was whether the LAF had the capability to guarantee state sovereignty and contribute efficiently to national defence. Yet, shortage of military equipment and inadequate training prevented them from substituting for Hizbollah's 'Islamic resistance' as blatantly demonstrated during the 2006 Israeli war in Lebanon. Moreover, the impossibility for the Lebanese state to recover a monopoly on the use of force as prescribed by UNSC Resolution 1701 was acknowledged successively by prime ministers Fuad Siniora and Saad Hariri, who both had to pay tribute to, and legitimate, the rival defence force. Although the LAF did improve its military performance thanks to friendly cooperation with UNIFIL II south of the Litani, it paid a heavy human price in suppressing the Islamist stronghold of Nahr al-Bared in 2007. The LAF was only able to overcome the latter once their Western allies delivered lethal armaments. In view of the persistence of Arab-Israeli hostility, access to offensive military material remained scarce, in spite of US and French pledges of support.

The second issue concerned the capacity of security forces (LAF, police and intelligence) to resist social dynamics of fragmentation and competing political agendas—an issue which became crucial following leaks from the UNIIIC that revealed bitter competition between security institutions as well as their susceptibility to foreign influence. After universal conscription had been abolished, both the military and the police, but also various intelligence units, were characterised by unbalanced sectarian recruitment, and became more sensitive to political and economic interests. Because the ISF were accused of partiality in dealing with social unrest and confessional strife, the LAF had to assume responsibility on several occasions. Although successful at temporary appeasement, the LAF's intervention in the domestic arena merely reflected its paralysis in the international arena. In a country where the two most recent presidents came from the military, the obedience or autonomy of the security forces with regard to national and foreign powers remained an irresolute issue.

6

ENCLAVES AND FORTRESSED ARCHIPELAGO

VIOLENCE AND GOVERNANCE IN LEBANON'S PALESTINIAN REFUGEE CAMPS

Sari Hanafi

Introduction

'No doubt, this development [of violence] has a logic of its own, but it is a logic that springs from experience and not from a development of ideas'.[1]

This chapter investigates the governance and violence affecting camp-based Palestinian refugees in Lebanon. It focuses on twin governance failures that make them objects of state governance and subjects of interpersonal and factional violence. It contends first that the violence is not the result of an Islamist (or *jihadist*) militant ideology for a specific political or social cause, but rather of the dismal living conditions that give rise to that cause; and second that the lack of legitimate governance structures in the refugee camps has prevented any improvement in living conditions. This has generated specific forms of violence that jeopardise security for Palestinians and Lebanese alike. Long-term deprivation, exclusion and marginalisation are the result of state policies towards refugees that have generated specific forms of systemic violence inside the refugee camps.

LEBANON AFTER THE CEDAR REVOLUTION

Post-Taif Lebanon is an acutely sectarian country in which the Palestinians constitute a minority 'sect', but without a recognised place in the sectarian system. This renders them politically, economically and socially marginalised. However, the main problem for this group of refugees is that they are spatially 'enclaved'. The right-wing Lebanese political party leaders and Lebanese security and military agencies enclave undesirable groups and confine them in what, following Agamben, can be termed 'spaces of exception'.[2] This applies not only to refugee camps but also to violence-prone, popular quarters such as Tripoli's Bab al-Tabaneh and Jabal Mohsen, and is considered a necessary measure for ensuring Lebanon's security. This policy has parallels with the global paradigm of the 'war on terror', which enclaves detention centres such as the US Guantanamo base in Cuba and Brazil's favelas in order to facilitate the 'free' circulation of 'civilised' people in what Petti has described as 'fortressed archipelagos'.[3] Building on the insights of Agamben and Petti, this chapter seeks to deconstruct and debunk the myths circulated through the Lebanese media about the forms and magnitude of 'Islamist violence' in Palestinian refugee camps and especially in the Ayn al-Hilweh refugee camp in southern Lebanon.

In *Homo Sacer: Sovereign Power and Bare Life*, Agamben labelled this kind of condition as living under a 'state of exception'. The paradox of the camp-based Palestinians in Lebanon today is that they are 'excluded from rights while being included in law-making'.[4] They enjoy neither the civil rights of Lebanese, upon whose territory they reside, nor those of foreigners living in Lebanon. Excluded from the 1951 UN Convention on Refugees, which stipulates that refugees have the right to work without a specific work permit, Palestinians in Lebanon are obliged not only to secure such a permit, but even to pay an exorbitant fee for one. By virtue of their statelessness, as Agamben and Arendt have argued, refugees represent a disquieting element in the ordering of the modern nation-state. For all practical purposes, in that it is only rarely and arbitrarily enforced, Lebanese law has been suspended within the confines of the refugee camps. In this sense, the camps have become Agambian 'spaces of exception'. The residents live in a 'zone of indistinction between outside and inside, exception and rule, licit and illicit, in which the very concepts of subjective right and juridical protection no longer make any sense'.[5]

This chapter is based on primary sources that include interviews with five focus groups and community leaders on violence and governance, mainly in the most violence-prone refugee camps: Nahr al-Bared, Beddawi (north-

106

ern Lebanon) and Ayn al-Hilweh (southern Lebanon).[6] Additionally, the chapter makes use of secondary sources, in particular the findings of the International Information Survey in 2009.[7]

By recording the positions of a wide range of community members on questions of governance, rather than simply restating the refugees' dire socio-economic conditions as other studies have done, I seek in part to relocate the focus group participants from conventional misery discourse ('bare life') on refugees to the 'political life' of their actual experiences.[8] To this end, I first discuss briefly the history of Palestinian camp governance in Lebanon and the securitisation of the camps, and then examine three types of violence: the Lebanese authorities' violence, attacks on individuals and property and finally, violence between political factions.

The Palestinian body politic in the camps[9]

The creation of 'popular committees' in the Palestinian refugee camps in Lebanon was based on the Cairo Agreement (1969).[10] Before the agreement, the camps in Lebanon were governed by a state of emergency and under Lebanese security agencies' control (*gendarmes* and *Deuxième Bureau*). Between 1970 and 1982, the Cairo Agreement meant that the police had to negotiate access to the camps through powerful popular committees, which granted or refused entry on a case-by-case basis. Julie Peteet has analysed the different conflict resolution methods during this period.[11] At the time, the traditional authority structures remained in place, as did customary forms of dispute settlement. However, the camps thereafter witnessed the emergence of a new elite, whose legitimacy was based on the Palestinian national struggle. This situation changed after 1982, when participation in the national struggle was no longer sufficient for someone to become a powerbroker.

After the forced departure of the PLO leadership from Lebanon in 1982, the PLO's popular committees and security committees were dismantled (except in the camps in the south), and were replaced by committees that were weaker and significantly pro-Syrian. The new committees lacked legitimacy because they were not made up of elected members (as before), nor were they recognised by the Lebanese authorities. The camp residents instead resorted to traditional power brokers such as *imams*, local notables [*wujaha*] and local security leaders to resolve quarrels and disagreements before turning to the police. While such informal conflict resolution methods were mostly successful in the past, the refugee camps are no longer harmonious, communitarian and headed by local notables. This is due to many factors, but mainly to urbanisation and migration. The continual transformation and transgression of power-sharing within the camps is critical, especially when compared to the situation after the PLO was evicted in 1982.

Recent research in the refugee camps in Lebanon has demonstrated a fundamental crisis of governance in the camps,[12] which suffer from the presence of dozens of competing factions vying for power and influence. In theory, one or two popular committees and their associated security committees govern individual camps and do so under the supervision of the PLO or a coalition of camp-based factions. The committees are comprised of representatives from each faction—who are appointed, not elected—yet are expected to keep the peace, solve internal disputes, provide security, interact with the Lebanese government and aid agencies, and administer the camp in coordination with UNRWA.[13] In some camps, such as Ayn al-Hilweh, an additional education council was established, composed of representatives from all factions as well as local religious authorities. However, despite the thin veneer of cooperation and coordination between the many popular committees, some focus group participants complained that these committees rarely agreed on important issues, failed to coordinate their activities, did not enjoy popular legitimacy, and were not recognised by the Lebanese government. The committees are neither able to protect their constituents from harassment by the Lebanese security forces controlling the camp perimeters, nor hold UNRWA accountable for its shortcomings. In short, the committees promote factional infighting and bolster patron-client politics, causing Palestinian disunity. As Knudsen observed during his 2003 fieldwork in the camps:

Both among the secular and Islamist lobbies we find a plethora of smaller and larger groups, often with conflicting views and sometimes involved in fratricidal battles that weaken the refugee community and ultimately undermine their quest for political hegemony. None of them are able to speak on behalf of the whole refugee community and this serves to 'compartmentalise' and therefore weaken the Palestinian nationalist struggle to regain their homeland.[14]

In this regard, little has changed in recent years. Today, Ayn al-Hilweh has two popular committees and two security committees, which purport to represent the camp's roughly 70,000 actual residents (47,500 officially, according to the UNRWA website). Recently, a new layer of governance was added: a 'follow-up committee' composed of representatives from all the camp factions, both secular and Islamist. Yet, many interlocutors still lamented the 'lack of a political reference, the absence of a unified Palestinian position'.

In 2007 the Nahr al-Bared refugee camp was destroyed in a 15-week battle between a militant Islamist group (Fatah al-Islam) and the Lebanese Army. The focus group participants warned that unless Palestinians in Lebanon are permitted to strengthen their own political and security authorities, they will not be able to prevent a similar outbreak of violence. In the words of one Nahr al-Bared resident: 'There has to be a higher council … to represent the Palestinian people as a whole, especially in the diaspora camps in Lebanon such as Nahr al-Bared, Ayn al-Hilweh, and Beddawi, because we are no longer sure that the events of Nahr al-Bared could not happen elsewhere'. A neighbour agreed: 'If the Lebanese state had permitted politicians or the PLO leadership to form a [Palestinian] security force, Fatah al-Islam would never have gained a foothold in the camp'.

Indeed, in the months leading up to the conflict in Nahr al-Bared (December 2006 to March 2007), the residents of the camp tried repeatedly to remove Fatah al-Islam members from their midst. To this end, the PLO engaged in armed clashes with the militants throughout the month of March.[15] The outcome of these clashes, however, was inconclusive and was dismissed by the Lebanese authorities as merely 'routine' Palestinian infighting, in spite of the fact that Fatah al-Islam was made up largely of non-Palestinians.[16] The security committee of Nahr al-Bared and the PLO lacked both the resources and the mandate to deal with Fatah al-Islam on their own. The popular committees lacked resources, which prevented them from fulfilling their municipal functions. Moreover, the committees lacked skilled technicians with expertise on urban regulations (zoning and construction codes), water, sanitation and electricity.

There is a tapestry of multiple, partial sovereignties, which include 'real sovereigns', such as the Lebanese government, but also 'phantom sovereigns', such as the PLO and other factions, as well as UNRWA and other humanitarian agencies, which also contribute to the state of exception and participate in the suspension of the law through various emergency measures. These measures are contradictory. Rather than creating order in the camp, they leave it in a state of chaos and anomie. Each actor—government, faction or agency—must compete, not for the allegiance of each Palestinian resident, but instead for control over each refugee. 'Contrary to our modern habit of representing the political realm in terms of citizens' rights, free will, and social contracts, from the point of view of sovereignty, only bare life is authentically political', suggests Agamben.[17]

There is agreement among refugees interviewed for this chapter, that the popular committees and the factions, in their present form, do not represent the best interests of Palestinians in Lebanon. As will be shown, this situation is made worse by the mobilisation of the political factions, which causes disillusionment among the majority and radicalises a minority of the refugees.

Political disillusionment

Disillusionment can be understood as the disenchantment that follows from the loss of hope and belief in the future. The different focus groups, especially the youth group, testified to a low degree of political activity among the youth in the camps. Out of eighteen people interviewed in this group, only three had engaged in political activities in the year preceding the interview. This differs significantly from the situation in the past, when most people participated in a variety of political activities, including commemorations. Among those in the youth focus group, some were absorbed with securing life's necessities, while others appeared weary of politics and disinclined to join political factions. The one notable exception is the Hamas supporters, who were quite active both in the Nahr al-Bared and Beddawi camps. One of the indicators of the strength of each faction can be inferred from the results of the election of the UNRWA Staff Union. In the election of April 2009, Hamas won the majority of the seats in the north of the country, while Fatah prevailed in Beirut and in the south.

The consequences of the disillusionment are very important for the long-term relationship between the youth and their community and society, as well as for social cohesion within the community. The tendency to favour migration is another indicator of this political disillusionment. According to the International Information survey, if a Palestinian state were declared without acknowledging the right of the Palestinian refugees to return to their homeland, 36 per cent of respondents would prefer resettling in a Western country, about 11 per cent moving to an Arab country, whereas about 32 per cent would prefer to remain in Lebanon.

Typically, young people expressed anger, outrage, pessimism and apathy toward the Lebanese and Palestinian polities. Politicians were seen as inefficient, untrustworthy,[18] useless and corrupt, 'looking out for themselves' and not placing the Palestinian cause first. They considered the popular committee lacking in relevant experience to manage the camp, and felt that the committee members had 'lost touch' with their constituency. Many of the interviewees felt that the dwindling Palestinian political authority reflected a crisis of substantive moral purpose. Others asserted that it demonstrated the ways in which the Lebanese authorities undermined the popular committees. Yet others believed that Islamic conceptions of good governance and righteousness were not being followed. Many felt unrepresented by the political factions. One youth in Ayn al-Hilweh reported that 'my brother was arrested at a check point. My dad went to an old friend from Hamas seeking his help. Effectively, the representative of Hamas in the Ayn al-Hilweh camp intervened and he was released after one week'.

When the International Information survey asked respondents which 'Palestinian factions live up to their expectations', 37.4 per cent of surveyed youth named Fatah.[19] This figure dropped to 25.5 per cent for Hamas and the more marginal secular and Islamist factions got only 18 per cent. The remaining 19.1 per cent of the respondents stated that none of the factions were performing according to their expectations. Young people are not necessarily 'depoliticised', but rather disillusioned with the fragmented and factional political structure (except for Hamas, which is considered an alternative to the traditional Palestinian factions). They feel isolated from the political process, as expressed in both the focus group interviews and in the results from a similar focus group survey carried out more than a decade ago by the Civitas project.[20] They express the need to have more channels of communication to connect them with the various governing bodies that serve them.

In the following section I will show that in spite of being a mostly non-violent society, feelings of powerlessness can lead to the eruption of violence. In fact, Palestinian society in the three camps under study (Beddawi, Nahr al-Bared and Ayn al-Hilweh) is on the verge of falling into a deep malaise.

Violence in the camps

Studying social and political violence in the camps is not an easy task, and there are hardly any statistics on the subject. The only statistics found were in a report on violence, monitored by the Palestinian Human Rights

Organisation (PHRO).[21] In addition, some reports provide indicators of violence, such as the annual reports from PHRO[22] and the Najdeh Association[23] which include information on domestic violence. Additional data can be found in my own interviews with community leaders and individuals in the camps and in Lebanese newspaper reports on violence.[24]

The PHRO report for the first five months of 2010 shows three types of violence: the Lebanese authorities' violence, attacks on individuals and property and violence between factions (Table 1).[25] The large majority of the incidents, about 84 per cent (62 out of 74 incidents), were in the Nahr al-Bared camp in the north.

Militarised violence

As the table indicates, thirty out of seventy-four incidents of violence (40 per cent of the total violence surveyed in the refugee camps) were perpetrated by the police and army intelligence. This violence is under-reported by the media. Interviewees reported many arbitrary arrests and the obstruction of freedom of movement for the refugee population. This is corroborated by another PHRO report[27] that shows a systematic pattern of violating Palestinians' right to unrestricted movement, especially in camps such as Ayn al-Hilweh and Nahr al-Bared. This not only hinders individual mobility but also hurts business. According to a recent Fafo survey,[28] the checkpoints at the camp perimeters hamper business activity and prevent customers and suppliers from entering and add to the daily suffering of the resident refugees.[29]

In the absence of a formal mode of law enforcement and camp policing, different Lebanese security agencies are intervening. One UNRWA area officer reported that historically 'I used to receive calls from one or two agencies of the camp's security administration in case there was a problem. Now there are at least four such agencies. This shows how far the Lebanese security agencies have infiltrated the camp and appointed collaborators'. One member of the popular committee in the Beddawi camp confirmed this account, stating that 'a few years ago, we used to denounce and isolate the collaborators—now who is not a collaborator?' Instead of bringing attention to the asymmetrical power structures and collusion between the popular committees and military intelligence, the media, particularly newspapers, emphasise a mode of cooperation between them.[30]

Table 1: Violation by type and region January-May 2010.

Type of violation	North	South	Beirut	Total
Attack on individuals	2	5	2	9
Arbitrary arrests, torture and humiliation	16	–	1	17
Hindering mobility	11	–	–	11
Violation due to discrimination against refugee status	1	1	–	2
Violation of the right to decent housing	11	–	–	11
Violation of the right to education and social care	2	2	1	5
Violation of the right to health[26]	19	–	–	19
Total	62	8	4	74

Source: PHRO 2010.

There is a near total discrepancy between rhetoric and practice. Former Prime Minister Fuad Siniora has referred to Nahr al-Bared as a model of camp governance, to be implemented in other camps. The Vienna document issued in 2008 by the Lebanese government for the donors' conference to rebuild the ruined Nahr al-Bared camp uses the term 'community policing'. In practice, however, the Lebanese authorities have opted for a militarised governmental regime in the form of counter-insurgency policing. Some refugee camps, such as Ayn al-Hilweh, are under siege by the army, which monitors entry and exit points, but the Nahr al-Bared camp and its surrounding area are a military zone and governed by the Internal Security Forces (ISF) through the semblance of a police station.[31] However, the camp dwellers seek to resist such militarised governance and a few resort to violence. This echoes Susan Buck-Morss' claim concerning the 'dialectic of power'.[32] In the new governance plan, a division of labour emerges through which the army ensures a regime of separation and control, while the ISF controls the economic and political status of the camp, facilitating economic extraction and exploitation. State governmental control is characterised not by the enforcement of well-defined rules and laws, but by the suspension of these rules through a skewed bureaucratic apparatus that impose different modes of intervention and whose very unpredictability is the key to its effectiveness. The intervention takes the form of real or suspended violence: some researchers and human rights activists were arrested in 2010 because of their criticism of LAF's role in governing the Nahr al-Bared camp,[33] and another activist reported staying away from his home in the Nahr al-Bared camp for more than three months because he was afraid of being arrested by the LAF.

Militarised camp governance is based on two principles: nominal inclusion of the camp under Lebanese sovereignty, with simultaneous geographic exclusion. The inclusion is institutionalised by discrimination, especially through the 2010 law on 'the right to work' for Palestinian refugees and the 2001 ruling that curtailed their access to 'property ownership'. The material outcome of separation and its twin pillars of legal persecution and enclaved geography create a deep sense of spatial exclusion and endemic disorientation for Lebanese and Palestinians alike.

The inclusion and the separation of the camps both presuppose the exclusion of their dwellers from the pale of law and the normalisation of a 'state of exception' in which the Palestinians collectively as well as individually, are subject to arbitrary violence and coercive regulation of daily life. Hence, Nahr al-Bared becomes in effect an experimental 'laboratory' for control and surveillance by the LAF and ISF.

Attacks on individuals and property

According to a PHRO report, minor offences against individuals and property represent a miniscule part of the violence in the camps (only nine out of 74 offences during the first five months of 2010).[34] Social constructionist theorists caution us about statistics that do not take into account what some categories of the population would perceive as offences to be reported and others not. This means that violence tends to be both underrated and underreported. In 2007 a local NGO undertook a study of domestic violence based on data from counselling centres that worked with 209 female victims, the majority of them single women (52 per cent). Some 89 per cent of this violence was of a psychological nature. Young girls between 15 and 19 years were the main sufferers of domestic violence (38 per cent of the victims).[35] This illustrates the problem of gender-based violence in Palestinian society inside the camps.

Some of the above-mentioned violent incidents are localised, familial disputes which escalate into problems between political factions. An example from the Ayn al-Hilweh refugee camp began as a quarrel between two youngsters over the outcome of a game of pinball, which sparked a clash between Fatah and a local Islamic group.[36] In the same vein, vandalism targeting schools reveals communitarian tension and a problematic relationship between this camp and its non-Palestinian neighbours. In mid-July 2010, a Christian school in the Burj al-Shemali camp near Tyre was vandalised by graffiti praising Imam Ali. The culprits were a group of young men from adjoining neighbourhoods.

Some violence is related to drug dealers in the camps. On 14 September 2010, a clash erupted between armed men in a street in the Ayn al-Hilweh camp, wounding one bystander. Reports attributed the scuffle to a crackdown on drug dealing after the head of the PLO's armed militia had promised that drugs would be eradicated from the camp and drug dealers handed over to the Lebanese judiciary.[37]

Violence between factions

In 2009, about 700 homicides (some of them politically motivated) were reported in Lebanon, but only a few of them took place in refugee camps.[38] Thus refugee camps are not the major sites of violence in the country, nor are refugees the only agents of violence. Still, factional in-fighting remains a major source of violence inside the camps.[39] However, political factions can be either sources of disorder in the camp or conversely guardians of order.

In recent years political violence in the refugee camps has increased, owing in part to heightened tensions between different factions, but there has been no such increase in the Ayn al-Hilweh camp. This is due to a certain political rapprochement between the political factions and the establishment of a 'follow-up committee' composed of all political factions, including the Islamists. In the 2009 International Information survey,[40] some 89 per cent of the camp dwellers found that the security situation was 'bad or very bad'. The deteriorating security situation came as the second most pressing problem (37.4 per cent of the respondents), followed by the lack of jobs and the deteriorating economic situation. The Pursue survey, conducted in 2010 in the Ayn al-Hilweh camp, showed a significant reduction in the camp's perceived security situation.[41]

When clashes erupt in the Ayn al-Hilweh refugee camp employees stay away from work and checkpoints, schools and shops are closed and medical services are disrupted.[42] The following examples illustrate the nature of violent encounters, particularly concerning 'strategic' areas inside the camps, such as mosques. In September 2010, three people were wounded in the al-Buss refugee camp near Tyre, after a dispute between clerics loyal to either Fatah or Hamas resulted in armed clashes. The clerics disagreed on who would lead prayers at the camp's mosque.[43] Another clash over the control of a mosque happened in 2008 in the Burj al-Barajneh camp between Islamic Jihad and Fatah and resulted in the death of one person.

Some incidents involve violence by Palestinian political factions directed against the camp residents. The murder of Reem, a 17 year old female living in the Shatila refugee camp (Beirut), is revealing.[44] As a Palestinian from Syria residing in Lebanon, she was reportedly afflicted by psychological problems and drug addiction. At around 4:15 am on 1 July 2008, at the western entrance of the Shatila camp, Reem was stopped at the gate and asked by the head of the security committee in the camp why she was entering at night with her boyfriend. When she replied that it was none of his business, she was shot by the personal bodyguard of the head of the local security committee. The security committee came to the scene to review the incident but left her bleeding for 45 minutes before an ambulance arrived and took her to the hospital. A coroner came to the hospital to investigate the murder, but quickly closed the file. Soon afterwards, her family was authorised to pick up her body and she was buried later the same day. The PHRO fieldworker asked the security committee whether the murderer would be handed over to the Lebanese security forces. They replied that they were waiting for a response from Reem's family whether they would file a formal complaint or accept financial compensation [*fidyya*]. What is particularly significant in this story is the complicity between the Palestinian security committee and the Lebanese police, both treating Reem as a *homo sacer*,[45] a person who can be 'eliminated' by anyone without punishment.

Still, political factions can and occasionally do play a positive role by mediating between parties in conflict and in enforcing certain community norms and customs. A psychologist working for a Palestinian NGO acknowledged this role, praising the work of the factions in resolving all types of health-related problems and coordinating efforts to help and assist patients inside the camps. Indeed, some focus group participants, the members of security committees in particular, insisted that the security situation in the camps would be worse without the political factions: 'The factions have their advantages. They serve the people in the camps and act as a buffer. Without them, the camps would a mess. The factions stand in the way of those who want to create havoc'.

Ayn al-Hilweh: The myth of global jihadi violence

Over the past decade, the refugee camps have been the scene of a religious revival, influenced by the growth of a conservative Sunni Islam in urban areas such as Tripoli and Sidon, where Lebanese Islamist groups such as *al-Jamaa al-Islamiyya*, the Muslim Brotherhood and various Salafist preachers have been competing for new bases of support. This conservative Islamic ideology has also been aided by the growth of satellite television, especially Saudi media (Iqra, al-Majd, Annaas, etc.). This religious transformation has at times also featured elements of sectarian rhetoric, which take aim at Hizbollah (Shia) in order to foster a sense of unity within the Sunni community. Additionally, the Lebanese authorities' discrimination against refugees and the lack of a coherent refugee policy have left the camp dwellers in a state of impoverishment and legal purgatory. Finally, there is a growing bitterness at the retreat from, for some even the defeat of, the Palestinian national project because of the infighting between Hamas and Fatah in the Occupied Palestinian Territories, as well as the American occupation in Iraq and their military and political intervention in the region.

The work of Laleh Khalili concerning Palestinian commemorative practices vividly illustrates these changes.[46] According to her work, in the 1970s these practices were related to transnational ideologies and world events. At that time, the PLO was a liberation movement connected to other liberation organisations around the world. However, from the 1990s onwards, the collapse of the communist bloc and the concomitant rise of Islamism interacted with the fragmentation of the Palestinian national movement to modify commemorative themes. The guerrilla hero melted into the image of the martyr, and heroic battles were replaced by massacres, which demonstrated a lack of hope and a prevailing retreat from the development of the national project.

In an attempt to understand to what degree Islamic movements are supported by young Palestinians in the camps, the International Information survey asked them 'which of the main Islamic movements' projects performed up to their expectations'. The majority of the youth (74.7 per cent) responded that no one group lived up to their expectations, while a tiny percentage opted for the smaller, 'fringe' Islamist groups.

In contrast to the picture transmitted by the media, the vast majority of the youth do not endorse violence against civilians as being 'always justified'. However, about 70 per cent maintain that what is referred to as Palestinian suicide bombings they consider to be martyrdom operations against their Israeli enemy, and thus always justified. A smaller number (about 20 per cent) find martyrdom operations to be 'sometimes justified'. Based on the latter two findings, it is obvious that the youth distinguish between resistance and terrorism. While the majority rejects indiscriminate violence, they consider martyrdom operations legitimate.[47]

The focus group interviews with members of two of the 'fringe' Islamist movements, Usbat al-Ansar[48] and the Islamic Jihadist Movement,[49] demonstrated that these groups are playing a major role in curtailing camp-based violence and not, as the Lebanese media would have it, simply in generating it. Moreover, there is no evidence that camp-based Islamist groups are connected to al-Qaida, as stated by many Lebanese politicians and the media. Some of the Islamist groups inside the camps, while unaffiliated with al-Qaida, may nevertheless espouse a rhetoric of 'global *jihad*' similar to that of al-Qaida, and some groups have even sent men to Iraq to fight against the coalition forces. My fieldwork in July 2009 showed a tremendous change in the organisation and outlook of these fringe Islamist groups: the dissolution of Jund al-Sham,[50] the near-elimination of Fatah al-Islam and the political transformation of Usbat al-Ansar into a more mainstream Islamist group with a local social agenda rather than a global *jihadist* one.[51] Thus, my fieldwork data debunks the sweeping image of Ayn al-Hilweh as a stronghold of al-Qaida,[52] and the claim that there is a significant shift in the identity of camp dwellers from national identity towards a broader Islamic identity.[53] Even if there is an unresolved problem of 'fugitive' Palestinians inside the camp, their purported contribution to a 'global *jihad*' is no different from that of any Sunni locality in the region. Recently, the PLO, Hamas and other political groups sought to consolidate the camp's many factions and organised a follow-up security committee composed of all the secular and Islamist parties. In December 2011 the PLO established a new police force in the camp that included most, but not all factions, yet the internal divisions within Fatah remain the main impediment to this effort. The case of Ayn al-Hilweh is therefore different from that of Nahr al-Bared, where the presence of Fatah al-Islam was primarily a phenomenon *in the camp* and not *of the camp*, that is, the militants used the camps for 'strategic localisation'[54] in order to wage guerrilla warfare. Thus, Fatah al-Islam's presence in Nahr al-Bared was an exceptional rather than a typical case. There is thus no al-Qaida phenomenon among the Palestinians in Lebanon.

The Islamists in Ayn al-Hilweh do not have a military agenda in Lebanon. Instead, interviews conducted in mid-2009 found that they were staying operational, waiting for the day to fight for Palestine. A leader of Usbat al-Ansar argued that the Ayn al-Hilweh camp was being targeted by the media and Lebanese politicians in order to destabilise Lebanon and create sectarian tensions (Sunni versus Shia). A leader of the Islamic Jihadist Movement seconded this analysis, claiming: 'The objective of some Lebanese authorities is to make Ayn al-Hilweh become like Nahr al-Bared in order to destroy it'. However, Islamist actors recognise the specificity of Ayn al-Hilweh, arguing that unlike the other camps, 'the presence of Islamists in Ayn al-Hilweh is an integral part of camp life. We have been here since the 1970s. We are not foreigners. Our main objective is to help people to abide by Islamic values. Historically, our social environment is plagued by alcoholism, delinquency and drugs'.

The Islamist Party of Liberation [*Hizb al-Tahrir*] is also active in the Ayn al-Hilweh camp. A local party member employed by UNRWA stated: 'Since its establishment, *Hizb al-Tahrir* has denounced any participation in the political system, such as joining committees or other elected councils. Hamas has given up the Palestinian land. We cannot; it is an Islamic endowment [*waqf*]. Waiting for the Caliph, we don't need to impose anything on any one. We should keep our faith until this moment. We have some obligations, but the importance is later on. *Hizb al-Tahrir* thus does not have any political agenda here in Lebanon. We are a party that preaches the good of Islam and is interested in a social agenda. We do not have even light arms'.

On behalf of Islamic Jihad, which is a nationalist Islamist group, the group's leader in Ayn al-Hilweh declared: 'Yes, we are supported by Iran but we have an independent position. Our agenda is exclusively Palestine. We don't even wish to operate from Lebanon. We are here to support our brothers in Palestine. We only have light individual arms'.

In spite of the fragmentation of the Islamic scene in Ayn al-Hilweh, there is one figure who is very influential and respected by the majority of the camp dwellers and political factions: Sheikh Jamal Khattab, the leader of the Islamic Jihadist Movement and imam of the camp's al-Noor Mosque. For the past twenty years he has intervened in all sorts of family, neighbourhood and social problems.

Although a calm person, during the interview Sheikh Khattab suddenly changed his tone, becoming bolder as he talked about the security of the camp: 'We cannot afford to threaten the security of the camp or its residents in order to protect one or more people. Safety of the camp is the most important consideration'. He was aware that some Lebanese authorities wanted to use Ayn al-Hilweh as a stronghold against Hizbollah and emphasised the good relationship with this party: 'We have held several meetings with Hizbollah and we supported them [in the 2006 war] by welcoming those displaced [from the south] to Ayn al-Hilweh. People here gave them blankets and food. We even sent blankets to Sidon. We did not participate with Hizbollah in the war because it was fought with rockets and not fighters. We only have light arms which would have been useless anyway. We have a very good relationship with some Lebanese Islamist groups'.

Ayn al-Hilweh cannot be considered a hideout for al-Qaida fighters, nor does al-Qaida's 'global *jihad*' find support among the camp population. Its influence among the population is also insignificant, as the findings from the International Information survey demonstrate. They asked respondents (youth from the four camps) whether murdering civilians was justified in order to solve grievances with their government. The large majority, about 73 per cent, answered that such actions were 'never justified' and only about 5 per cent answered that they were 'always justified'.[55]

Conclusion

This chapter has aimed to challenge the misperception, common among the Lebanese, that the Palestinian refugee camps are 'islands of insecurity'. The everyday violence prevalent in the camps is not the result of a militant ideology, but rather of discrimination, urban segregation and state violence. Both political and everyday violence are found in the camps, yet neither is particularly prevalent.

This chapter has demonstrated that internal camp governance is in a state of crisis. The popular committees have been delegitimised by both the Lebanese authorities and the camp dwellers. This governance crisis may be aggravated in the near future. The recent uprising in Syria has resulted in refugees flowing across the border into Lebanon, and these new regional developments threaten the uneasy truce between the PLO and the many pro-regime factions in the camps. Weakened Syrian influence in Lebanon (a likely result of the Arab uprisings) could provoke conflict over power and authority within the camps, as opposing factions, including the PLO, seek greater influence at Syria's expense.

Islamism has emerged during the past decade and, for better or for worse, has become a new and powerful force in the refugee camps. For some, it has brought out the best in people, compelling them to behave in 'sound' and 'Islamic' ways, abating violence, delinquency and moral degeneration while simultaneously encouraging increased cooperation among neighbours, improved health and social services. On the other hand, the Islamist factions have brought with them new problems, especially the inability to engage with existing or historical modes of governance, both Lebanese and Palestinian. These developments have divided the Palestinian community, exacerbating political discontent among the majority (especially the youth), while radicalising a tiny minority.

PART III

ENTREPRENEURS, STATESMEN
AND MARTYRS

7

THE 'NEW CONTRACTOR BOURGEOISIE' IN LEBANESE POLITICS

HARIRI, MIKATI AND FARES

Hannes Baumann

The change of government from Saad Hariri to Najib Mikati in January 2011 was surrounded by frantic media analysis.[2] Did the backing Mikati received from Hizbollah mean that the Shia movement had taken over the government? Could Mikati's protestations of independence be taken seriously? Much of the analysis skirted over one of the most interesting aspects of this changeover—how important was the fact that both prime ministers were billionaire businessmen? This chapter explores the interplay of their economic interests with the politics of sectarianism and foreign alliances.[1] Hariri and Mikati are part of a 'new contractor bourgeoisie', consisting of Lebanese *émigrés* who had become wealthy contractors in the Gulf in the 1970s. Several of them returned to Lebanon as investors and politicians in the 1980s and 1990s. The most prominent examples are Rafik Hariri, Najib Mikati, Issam Fares and Muhammad Safadi. What explains the rise of these new contractors? What explains variations in their relative success as politicians and investors in Lebanon? This latter question will be measured along three dimensions: success in reaching political office; in gaining control of institutions to further their economic agenda; and in gathering a popular following. In order to address these questions, the careers of four new contractors will be examined—Rafik and Saad Hariri, Najib Mikati, and Issam Fares.

The Sunni businessman-politician Rafik Hariri and his son Saad remain the benchmark of success for this new class. The elder Hariri served as prime minister (1992–8, 2000–4). After Rafik Hariri's assassination, Haririally Fuad Siniora (2005–9) and then his son Saad (2009–11) assumed the position of prime minister. The Hariri business empire has a large stake in Lebanese banking, construction and the media. Rafik Hariri started building up a popular following from the mid-1990s onwards and his son shaped this 'movement' into a coherent organisation. Sunni businessman Najib Mikati acted as minister of public works and transport from 1998 to 2004, headed a caretaker government in 2005, and was appointed prime minister again in January 2011. His company Cellis held a mobile phone operating licence from 1994 to 2002. He has also built up a popular following through clientelism, but he cannot nearly match Hariri's ability to mobilise. Finally, the Greek Orthodox businessman Issam Fares served as deputy prime minister from 2000 to 2005. He has business interests in the media and used to own a Lebanese bank. He also engages in philanthropy but has been unable to mobilise a significant popular following.

In order to address the question, three dimensions of similarities and differences between the businessmen-politicians will be examined. The first is their pursuit of collective economic and individual business interests. All members of the new contractor bourgeoisie support a neoliberal transformation of the economy and the state in order to create investment opportunities for the private sector. Such market reforms are not politically neutral but strengthen the power of the capitalist classes.[3] Furthermore, neoliberal reforms are often accompanied by cronyism and rent-seeking through privatised monopolies, where 'networks of privilege' shape markets to their own advantage.[4] The new contractors therefore also compete among each other for contracts and the chance to snatch up privatised state enterprises and to control market-regulating agencies. The second dimension is international politics. Due to the 'softness' of the Lebanese state, Lebanese politicians seek foreign alliances in order to bolster their domestic standing.[5] The new contractors are no exception. The choice of foreign allies and the strength of support the businessman-politician receives is a major determinant of political success. Rafik Hariri's relatively greater success is best explained with reference to the strong backing he received from the Saudi monarchy. The third dimension is sectarianism and the mobilisation of popular support through clientelism. The sectarianism of the new contractors is not expressed with the militancy displayed by movements such as the Lebanese Forces or Hizbollah. Yet the new contractors cannot remain outside the confessional system. The power-sharing formula that allocates political office according to sect shapes the horizon of political ambition for new contractors and forces them to act as representatives of 'their' sect, even when they pursue a wider economic agenda. Electoral success is premised, first of all, on mobilising voters from the businessman's own community. An important determinant of the success of a new contractor is also the 'space' for new leaders in the politics of the confessional community. The Shia, Maronite and Druze communities emerged with sectarian leaderships who had achieved a virtual monopoly on the 'representation' of their own community in Lebanon's confessional game. The same was not true for the highly fragmented politics of the Sunni community, which made it easier for new contractors to rise to the top. The chapter is divided into three sections. The first one explains the rise of the new contractors during the civil war from 1975 to 1990. The second section looks at the Hariri governments between 1992 and 2004, contrasting the overwhelming success of Rafik Hariri with the less successful strategies of Najib Mikati and Issam Fares. The third section examines dynamics since 2005. Saad Hariri monopolised Sunni politics to an unprecedented degree. This is a considerable problem for the Mikati government. However, the power struggle between the two billionaires obscures the significant interests they share. A final section concludes.

Explaining the Rise of the New Contractors

The predominance of businessmen in Lebanese politics is not new. The commercial-financial bourgeoisie of the pre-war era was central to the formation of the country's state and economy. The National Pact of 1943, which formalised confessional power-sharing, can be seen as a compromise between the Maronite and Sunni bourgeoisie.[6] The former dominated trade with Europe and the USA, while the latter had strong relations with the Arab Gulf. Despite opposing nationalist ideas among the two communities, their bourgeois families reached a confessional compromise which made the Lebanese state a vehicle for the appropriation of rent from financial intermediation between Arab East and Western financial markets and from entrepot trade entering the Arab market via Lebanon. The economic and political elites of the country remained so closely intertwined as to be virtually congruent as most *zuama*—the political leaders of the pre-war era—hailed from a few dozen bourgeois families.[7] This web of families maintained Lebanon's *laissez-faire* economic system. The increasingly illiberal economic environment in 'revolutionary' Arab states and the underdeveloped banking systems in the Gulf allowed Lebanese bankers and traders to act as vital intermediaries between the Arab world and the global economy. The dominance of Lebanon's bourgeois families came under attack in the 1960s and 1970s. President Fuad Chehab expanded the developmental role of the state and undermined the bourgeoisie's economic power and their political power, based largely on maintaining a sectarian clientele. Furthermore, the social crisis arising from Lebanon's barely restrained economic liberalism led to the rise of predominantly Muslim popular leftist movements.[8] Together with the Palestine Liberation Organisation (PLO), they eventually challenged the power of the Maronite-dominated state in the civil war of 1975. On the other side of the ideological divide, popular Maronite movements such as Kataeb and later the Lebanese Forces undermined the ability of Christian *zuama* to compromise with their Muslim counterparts.

During the civil war, the bourgeois families lost their role as the dominant capitalist class to the new contractors. This was due to domestic developments and wider changes in the world economy. With the demise of the Bretton Woods system and the rise of Wall Street-centred global finance, the Gulf countries started recycling their oil income directly into US banks. Within Lebanon, the civil war led to the dominance of militias in the economy, affecting trade and finance.[9] These internal and external developments did not completely destroy the pre-war bourgeoisie but broke its economic and political dominance. The stage was set for the rise of the new contractor bourgeoisie. The oil boom in the Gulf had led to large-scale migration of Lebanese to the area. The continued oil boom increased the number of Lebanese workers in the Gulf from 50,000 in 1970 to 210,000 in 1979–80, representing slightly more than a third of the nation's workforce.[10] A small but not insignificant number of Lebanese *émigrés* managed to accumulate great wealth as contractors in the Gulf. Their success was due to a mixture of personal entrepreneurial flair and connections to key individuals with access to royal contracts. In the late 1970s and early 1980s this new contractor bourgeoisie returned to Lebanon to invest and to seek political influence. As the heads of transnational enterprises, the new contractors belong to a faction of the 'transnational capitalist class' that promote neoliberal globalisation.[11]

Class analysis is thus a crucial and neglected element in understanding post-civil war Lebanese politics. However, its exclusive focus on actors' relationship to the means of production tends to be too crude an instrument to understand the behaviour of business elites in specific domestic contexts.[12] It is therefore necessary to adopt a more 'sociological' perspective, focusing on the role of 'elites' and how the elites that belong to the capitalist class promote their interests and how state elites relate to capitalists.[13] In other words, the question is how classes organise and how they are politically represented in pursuit of their interest. 'Elite' is a more open category than class. It allows for a richer account of individuals and groups beyond their economic position and including such identity categories as sect. Elites are conventionally defined as 'decision-makers', while Bourdieu defines them as those with a high degree of social, symbolic, economic and cultural capital.[14] The two definitions are not mutually exclusive as decision-makers are likely to also possess great 'capital'. These different ways of thinking about elites are both important for the study of the new contractors: while Hariri's network gained control of centres of decision-making, other contractors were forced to focus more on building up a network that is strong in 'cultural capital'. Bourdieu also provides a framework to think about the way in which economic power—the power to shape systems of accumulation—can be used to obtain symbolic power—the power to confirm or transform the social order.[15]

Rafik Hariri had left Lebanon for Saudi Arabia in 1964, unable to pay for his studies and in search of employment. His first attempts at contracting ended in bankruptcy due to highly volatile oil prices, and the attendant volatility in input prices for construction.[16] Having experienced more than one cycle of boom-and-bust, Hariri struck gold in 1976 by teaming up with Nasr al-Rashid, a Saudi engineer from a prominent family who had access to royal contracts. Al-Rashid increasingly came to rely on Hariri's ingenuity for the fulfilment of highly complex contracts. Hariri's success is therefore due both to his own personal qualities and the patronage politics of the Saudi 'rentier state'. Hariri had no direct access to the Saudi King, but this changed in 1982. In the wake of the Israeli invasion of Lebanon, Hariri demonstrated his political usefulness to King Fahd of Saudi Arabia by initiating the clean-up of Beirut. The King was pleased and took over the funding for the project.[17] From then on, Hariri acted as a 'Saudi mediator' between the different factions of the civil war. As 'the real voice of King Fahd'[18] and through the use of chequebook diplomacy, Hariri was able to participate in civil war diplomacy—negotiations to end the Shouf war in 1983, the Geneva and Lausanne meetings in 1983 and 1984, the militia agreement in 1985 and the Taif Agreement in 1989.[19] In the early 1980s Hariri acquired Banque Mediterranée, established a second bank and started three major urban development projects that only came to fruition in the post-war period. These development projects included the seeds of Solidere, the reconstruction project for central Beirut.[20] A student loan programme supported almost 32,000 students between 1983 and 1996 but, importantly, Hariri had not yet used it to build up a consistent grass-roots following.

The wealth of Najib Mikati derives from the Arabian Construction Company, founded by his brother Taha in Abu Dhabi in 1967. It enjoyed great success in the Gulf. At one point Taha Mikati also took some subcontracts from Rafik Hariri.[21] In 1982, Najib and Taha Mikati founded telecommunications company Investcom, which penetrated markets such as Sudan, Liberia and Yemen.[22] It also ran an analogue mobile phone network in civil war Lebanon. In 1983, the Mikatis bought the licence for the British Bank of Lebanon from the British Bank of the Middle East.[23] The Mikatis are understood to have maintained good relations with the Syrian regime. In 1988 Taha and Najib Mikati founded the Azm wa Saade foundation, which provides health and social services.[24]

Issam Fares is a Greek Orthodox from Akkar in North Lebanon. He first cut his teeth as a merchant in Abela Group, one of Beirut's traditional trading houses owned by a prominent Greek Orthodox family.[25] He then became a hugely successful contractor by owning a controlling interest in Netherlands-based Ballast Nedam. Through good contacts within Saudi Arabia, he secured highly lucrative contracts, most famously for the bridge linking Saudi Arabia to Bahrain. He later sold the group and invested in a variety of oil, real-estate and media interests through a holding company called Wedge Group. In 1983 Fares opened Wedge Bank in Lebanon, employing former President Elias Sarkis as its chairman.[26] Fares supported Bashir Gemayel's bid for the presidency in 1982, but thereafter built close ties to the Syrian regime via Ghazi Kanaan, the Syrian head of intelligence in Lebanon. This was partly because Fares' home region of Akkar was under close Syrian control. In 1987 he started the Issam Fares Foundation, which established health centres in Akkar and pursued other projects in the cultural and social sphere.[27]

The Hariri Governments 1992–8 and 2000–4

Of the three new contractors described here, Rafik Hariri was in the best position to take over a political role because Saudi support had given him access to civil war diplomacy. Hariri became prime minister in 1992. He remained in office until 1998 and then returned from 2000 to 2004. Together with a network of technocratic experts, Hariri promoted a neoliberal reconstruction programme. The underlying logic was to make Lebanon 'competitive' in a 'new Middle East', in which there would be no Arab-Israeli conflict and in which liberalising Arab economies would integrate fully into the world market. The way to achieve competitiveness was to build 'world class' infrastructure and to avoid the currency crises that had wrecked the Lebanese economy in the 1980s. The central projects of the Hariri cabinets were the rehabilitation of infrastructure and especially the reconstruction of central Beirut, as well as the stabilisation of the Lebanese pound through government over-borrowing. The primary function of the state was to make the economy 'competitive' through the provision of infrastructure and a good business environment, but it was to play only a minimal role in income redistribution and welfare provision.[28] While often presented as a purely technical and 'common sense' project, neo-liberalism is also highly political. Firstly, neo-liberalism involves the reassertion of the power of capitalist classes.[29] Secondly, the restructuring of the state, markets and privatisation provide scope for cronyism and rent-seeking.[30] Hariri's reconstruction programme was neoliberal in both these senses. He sought to open up investment opportunities for foreign investors and for the new contractor bourgeoisie, while also seeking to ensure that he and his business allies obtained the largest slice of the pie. The politics of reconstruction in central Beirut and the effects of 'anchoring' the exchange rate through government borrowing at high interest rates have been described in great detail elsewhere.[31] The important point here is that Hariri applied a neoliberal logic determined by his class position. In order to realise the two policies, Hariri placed former employees and associates at the head of the institutions in charge of reconstruction and finance: the Council for Development and Reconstruction (CDR) and Solidere, the central bank and the finance ministry.[32] Hariri was not in complete control of economic policy. When he was out of office from 1998 to 2000, President Emile Lahoud and Prime Minister Salim al-Hoss obstructed the Solidere project and changed the *modus operandi* of government debt-management. Hariri's efforts at privatising state-controlled entities such as the electricity company, telecommunications and the national carrier Middle East Airlines were countered by former militia leaders and the military establishment, all allied to Syria. Hariri's rivals feared a curtailment of their patronage power or they sought to prevent Hariri from acquiring even more economic power.

The alliance with Saudi Arabia had been the basis for Hariri's ascent to power. Saudi Arabia brokered the US-Syrian concord which facilitated the Taif Agreement of 1989 and enabled Syrian troops to dislodge its greatest opponent, General Michel Aoun, from the presidential palace in 1990.[33] In return for Saudi acceptance of Syrian dominance in Lebanon, the Assad regime tolerated Saudi-ally Hariri as prime minister. Hariri's 'reconstruction' was running alongside the 'resistance' by Hizbollah. In the 1990s, Rafik Hariri defended Syrian dominance in Lebanon and supported the marginalisation of any opposition to Syria. However, this was an alliance of convenience and tensions between Hariri and Damascus were coming to the fore from the mid-1990s onwards. The breakdown of the Syrian-Israeli peace negotiations in 2000, the Israeli withdrawal from Lebanon and regional tension in the wake of the Iraq invasion then led to deteriorating relations between Hariri and the new President Bashar al-Assad.

An important factor in the ability of different contractors to rise to high political office was their position in Lebanon's sectarian politics. The prevalence of Sunni politicians among the new contractor bourgeoisie is striking. Emigration patterns played a role because it is possible that Sunni Muslims were more drawn to the Gulf, while Shia would be more likely to migrate to West Africa or the Americas, and Christians were drawn to Europe. However, a more important factor is the state of the civil war-era leaderships among different sects. The Kataeb party, the Lebanese Forces and Aoun monopolised leadership among Maronites. There was limited space for a Maronite businessman to become a political leader. Some Shia contractors had become wealthy in the Gulf or in West Africa but they tended to support established political movements such as Hizbollah or Amal, which had virtually monopolised leadership within their community. Among the Druze, Walid Jumblatt's PSP was the dominant force. The situation of the Sunni leadership was very different. The pre-war Sunni *zuama* had been marginalised by popular Nasserite movements and their militias during the civil war, helped by their alliance with the PLO. The militias lost much of their power after the expulsion of the PLO from Beirut in 1982 and military action by Syrian-allied Shia and Druze militias in 1983 and 1984.[34] Sunni Islamists never achieved the same prominence, coherence and influence within their own community as Hizbollah did within the Shia community. The assassination of Sunni Mufti Hassan Khalid in 1989 further fragmented the sect's leadership. This fragmentation allowed for the rise of Hariri and other Sunni contractors to high political office. No pre-war *zuama* or civil war militias could automatically lay claim to the role of prime minister, the highest position reserved for Sunnis in Lebanon's power-sharing formula.

When Hariri became head of government in 1992, he still styled himself primarily as a 'national' leader rather than someone with a narrow sectarian agenda. He contrasted his reconstruction programme with the sectarian violence of the militias. His student loan programme was already winding down and Hariri refused to engage in the kind of large-scale grassroots clientelism usually associated with sectarian leadership. Hariri's main interest was his neoliberal reconstruction programme. He also sought to shape public opinion through his TV channel Future TV, a stake in the *al-Nahar* newspaper, fostering close relations with a large number of journalists and eventually opening his own paper called *al-Mustaqbal*. In the 1990s Hariri sought positive coverage of his reconstruction programme rather than sectarian agitation. Hariri's neglect of his own sect led to some disappointment among the grassroots within his community. Sunni *zuama* maintained electoral independence from Hariri in the 1992 and 1996 parliamentary elections. Sunni Islamist movements such as *al-Ahbash* and *al-Jamaa al-Islamiyya* experienced a brief flowering and some limited electoral success. However, all this changed when Hariri imposed himself as the prime leader of his community from the mid-1990s onwards.[35] In 1996 Hariri had his favoured candidate elected mufti, a position that had remained vacant since Mufti Hassan Khalid's assassination.[36] From 1999 onwards, the Hariri Foundation also started engaging in grassroots clientelism, building health centres and schools in predominantly Sunni neighbourhoods. Although the health centres are open to patients from any confession, the location and the association with Hariri work as signifiers that these are 'Sunni' institutions.[37] In preparation for the 2000 parliamentary elections, Hariri politically neutralised the Maqasid association, which had traditionally been

Beirut's premier Sunni philanthropic association and a patronage instrument of the Salam family.[38] Hariri's transformation from a 'national' to a specifically 'Sunni' leader in the mid-1990s was an electoral strategy. The businessman-politician was coming under increasing political pressure from rival politicians allied to Syria, especially when army commander and Hariri-nemesis Emile Lahoud was elected president in 1998. Hariri resigned as prime minister. In order to return as the head of government, Hariri sought electoral success, which in Lebanon is best achieved through sectarian mobilisation. There can be little doubt that Hariri would have been able to build a grassroots base beyond his Sunni community, but this would be viewed as an encroachment by rival leaders. Means of curtailing such encroachment included blocking accreditation by the health ministry, rejection of a health centre by municipal authorities or—in times of heightened sectarian tension—the threat of physical attacks on Hariri institutions.[39] The confessional system had disciplined the new contractor.

Hariri had become more like the *zuama* of the pre-war era, using sectarian clientelism to win elections.[40] However, there are also differences between the clientelism of the pre-war *zuama* and the new contractor Hariri. One difference is scale. The *zuama* tended to dominate particular locations, for instance the Salams in Beirut or the Karamis in Tripoli. Hariri managed to build up a truly national presence by spending amounts that were beyond the financial capability of the *zuama*. In the late 1970s he started charitable works in his home town of Sidon but then quickly moved to provide services across the whole country through his student-loan programme from 1983 to 1996. In the parliamentary elections of 2000, Hariri became the foremost Sunni politician in Beirut, winning all the seats in the capital for his list and relegating traditional Sunni Beiruti leaders to the second rank. Such complete domination in a locale other than the region of origin would have been inconceivable for a pre-war *zaim*. Secondly, Hariri relied primarily on his own wealth and funding from the Gulf to pay for his philanthropic ventures. In contrast, the philanthropic associations controlled by pre-war *zuama* were often financed collectively through donations by bourgeois families or the middle class. The *zuama* therefore had to be much more responsive to the interests and ideologies of these constituencies while the new 'super-*zaim*' Hariri was financially independent from domestic Lebanese groups.[41]

The contrast between Hariri on the one hand, and Mikati and Fares on the other, is instructive. It illustrates the conditions for success and failure of new contractors. As a Sunni Muslim, Mikati also had ambitions to become prime minister. However, he lacked the powerful foreign sponsor that Hariri had in the shape of Saudi Arabia. The warm relations that Mikati had fostered with the Syrian regime could not make up for this shortcoming. The Syrians relied much more on other types of elites—on former militia leaders such as Nabih Berri or Walid Jumblatt, on the military and intelligence establishment around Lahoud, and on loyal allies such as Michel Murr. Mikati did enjoy some political success. He became minister for transport and public works under the Hoss government in 1998, when Hariri was out of office. He retained his ministerial position until 2004. Despite the grand title, these ministries were of little use to Mikati. They had been marginalised in the reconstruction effort by the CDR, headed by a Hariri loyalist for most of the time between 1991 and 2005. Mikati's main interest was in telecommunications. In 1994 Cellis had won a 'build-operate-transfer' (BOT) project. One-third of the company was owned by Najib and Taha Mikati, France Telecom owned the rest.[42] However, Mikati had no direct control of the institutions in charge of telecommunications. The second mobile phone operator was Libancell. Their relationship with the government was fraught. Both the Hariri and Hoss governments imposed various charges on the mobile phone companies and turned down offers to convert the ten-year BOT contracts into twenty-year operating licences.[43] At stake were the large profits of the duopoly. In 1998, revenue from mobile phone operations reached USD 440 million.[44] The sector's future was held up by a squabble between Hariri, who sought to privatise the sector, and Lahoud, who sought to appropriate as much of the mobile phone profits for the state as possible. In the end, Lahoud managed to control the telecommunications ministry from 2000 to 2004 and to impose his favoured solution. Mikati sold his stake in Cellis to France Telecom, and in December 2002 both mobile phone companies formally transferred their assets to the state.[45] Mikati is not completely reliant on income from within Lebanon, however. His investment company M1 Group owns New York and London real estate, French fashion company Façonnable and interests in oil exploration in Colombia.[46] Hariri also eclipsed Mikati in the size of his popular following. Mikati had built up a philanthropic association that could act as a patronage instrument at election time. He first entered parliament as a deputy for Tripoli in 2000 on the list of Maronite *zaim* Suleiman Frangieh, while Hariri refrained from fielding his own candidates in the constituency, probably following pressure from Syria.[47] While Mikati managed to build up a following in Tripoli, he never managed to create the national reach that Hariri and especially his son Saad achieved. Furthermore, while Hariri had managed to gain control of a major economic and symbolic space in Beirut—the Solidere area—Mikati never achieved the same economic success in the capital.

Issam Fares was less successful than either Hariri or Mikati. As a Greek Orthodox, his advance to the highest state position was blocked by Michel Murr, who had supported Syria's policy in Lebanon since the mid-1980s and was one of Assad's closest allies in the country. From 1992 to 2000, he was deputy prime minister, the highest position a Greek Orthodox can occupy. Fares only managed to obtain the post from 2000 to 2004. The post provides the holder with little power and Murr's influence stemmed more from his control of the interior ministry (1994–2000), a position later held by his son Elias (2000–4). Fares, meanwhile, was stuck with a largely ceremonial role as deputy prime minister without any control over institutions that shaped economic policy. Fares had allied himself with Lahoud, who sought to draw a wealthy businessman into his network to counter Hariri's influence in Lebanon. Like Hariri and Mikati, Fares built up a philanthropic association but it fell far short of the size and scope of the Hariri Foundation. It runs health centres and supports schools in Fares' home region of Akkar and supports a number of social and cultural projects in the north.[48] Fares first entered parliament in 1996 on a joint list with Omar Karami and Suleiman Frangieh. However, the peripheral location of Fares' home region and the spread of the Greek Orthodox throughout Lebanon made the kind of sectarian rallying that Hariri achieved among Sunni Muslims impossible.

The limitations Fares faced in terms of his position in the confessional system and popular mobilisation led him to adopt alternative strategies along two lines.[49] First, he spent a lot of time and money in cultivating ties to American politicians. Fares was already involved in brokering closer relations between Syria and the USA in the 1980s, a rapprochement which eventually facilitated the Taif Agreement and the ousting of Aoun. Fares became a master at playing the game of informal financial contributions and cultivating 'friendships' with leading American politicians among both major parties. The most visible such initiative is a lecture series at Tufts University, for which speakers receive generous remuneration and which has featured former President George Bush Sr., former Secretary of State James Baker, former President Bill Clinton, former Senate Majority Leader George

Mitchell and Colin Powell shortly before he was called upon to serve as secretary of state for George W. Bush Jr. Fares used his influence on US politics in the 1990s to maintain American tolerance for Syria's role in Lebanon.[50] The second pillar of Fares' influence is public opinion. His media empire is of a different nature and smaller than Hariri's. After the arrest of Lebanese Forces leader Samir Geagea in 1994, Fares took a 10 per cent stake in the ownership of the Forces' TV station LBC.[51] Damascus regarded Fares as a 'safe pair of hands' to curtail the station's habitual criticism of Syria. Fares also created public policy think-tanks. He funded the Issam Fares Institute for Public Policy and International Affairs at the American University of Beirut (AUB) and a domestic public policy institute staffed with intellectuals and former government officials sympathetic to Fares. The point is not that all researchers at the AUB institute are beholden to Fares, but the institute increases his visibility in the public sphere and invitations to 'eminent' Arab and international personalities such as Lakhdar Brahimi, Amr Moussa or Aaron David Miller raise Fares' profile. As mentioned, elites are conventionally defined as 'decision-makers', while Bourdieu regards them as those rich in cultural, financial or social capital. Fares managed to gather a network of elites endowed with great 'cultural' capital who wield symbolic power—the power to confirm or transform the social order. This was partly to make up for the failure to gain control of institutional centres of decision-making.

The New Contractors Since 2005: The Siniora, Hariri and Mikati Governments

On 14 February 2005 Rafik Hariri was assassinated. The immediate question from the perspective of the Hariri network was about the future of the 'movement'. One can only speculate why Saad was chosen to succeed his father rather than his brother Baha or his aunt Bahia. In any case, the heir had to come from the family's inner circle. Saad Hariri became the knot that held together all the strings of power of the Hariri network—personal wealth, the Saudi alliance and 'Sunni leadership'. Saad Hariri had previously been in charge of parts of the Hariri business empire and nothing in his professional experience marked him out for political leadership. This is further evidence that the neoliberal project of the new contractor bourgeoisie was being mediated by the familiar sectarian, clientelist and dynastic dynamics of Lebanese politics.

Saad Hariri put himself at the head of the coalition that was striving to get Syria out of Lebanon and which had received a fillip by Rafik Hariri's assassination. Saad's father had been reluctant to join the opposition against Syria, which included the many traditionally anti-Syrian Christians, Jumblatt's Druze as well as a growing secular 'Democratic Left', which was fed up with Syrian authoritarianism. Within the sectarian logic of Lebanese politics, the fact that Hariri brought 'the Sunnis' into the opposition camp was highly significant. The anti-Syrian opposition formed the 14 March coalition, named after the rally staged on that day in 2005. The 8 March coalition brought together the Shia movements Hizbollah and Amal and, eventually, the predominantly Christian supporters of Aoun, who had opposed Syrian influence during the 1990s but did not trust Hariri, Jumblatt or the 14 March Christian factions who all tried to marginalise him. Under the leadership of Saad Hariri, the 14 March coalition achieved the resignation of pro-Syrian Prime Minister Omar Karami, leading to the appointment of Mikati as an interim head of government to oversee elections in May 2005. More importantly, 14 March achieved the withdrawal of Syrian troops in April.

The internal factionalism linked up with the wider agendas of regional and global powers. The USA and France came together to pressure Syria over the Hariri assassination. The two countries had fallen out over the Iraq War in 2003 but there had been a rapprochement when French President Jacques Chirac led the way in putting together UN Security Council Resolution 1559 in September 2004.[52] The resolution called for Syrian non-interference in Lebanon's presidential elections and the disarmament of Hizbollah. Saudi Arabia also joined the international coalition on Lebanon. On the initiative of these major states, the UN International Independent Investigation Commission (UNIIIC) was established by the UN Security Council on 7 April 2005 to investigate the crime. Later, the STL was set up in May 2006. Its mandate was to prosecute the perpetrators of the Hariri assassination as well as later political assassinations. The investigation and the tribunal are instruments of the USA, France and Saudi Arabia as well as 14 March to pressure Syria and Hizbollah. However, defenders of the court argue that the investigation is independent of any governments.[53]

Sectarian solidarity was a major factor in rallying popular support behind Saad Hariri after his father's assassination.[54] The success and the limits of this strategy arose from Hariri's position in the Sunni community. Rafik

Hariri had built some of his own institutions, especially the Hariri Foundation and a political organisation called 'Future Movement'. However, more often than not Hariri was not so much displacing existing Sunni structures but using patronage resources and a highly flexible 'ideology' to draw existing Sunni social, religious and political organisations into his network. The Future Movement could be all things to all people, claiming to pursue a range of contradictory goals such as a champion of neo-liberalism, defender of the Sunni community, ally of Saudi Arabia and the West, opponent of Syria and Iran, and patron of the poor. The backdrop to this strategy of sectarian mobilisation was the emerging Sunni-Shia rift in Lebanon. Within the confessional logic of Lebanese politics, the assassination of the most prominent Sunni leader was perceived as an attack on the whole community. 14 March immediately blamed Syria, achieving the withdrawal of al-Assad's troops. This, in turn, increased the insecurity of Hizbollah, which had relied on Syria to protect its status as a legitimate resistance movement. The domestic rift was exacerbated by sectarian violence in Iraq and the development of a regional 'Sunni-Shia split', which also involved a deepening of Saudi-Iranian conflict, regarded as 'Sunni' and 'Shia' powers respectively. The 2006 war between Israel and Lebanon exacerbated the sectarian divide. While Hizbollah considered it a vindication of the need for 'resistance' as deterrence, 14 March denounced the 'recklessness' the militia had displayed in drawing Lebanon into a war. Hizbollah ministers and their allies had participated in the government of Fuad Siniora after the May 2005 elections but in December 2006, five Shia ministers and one Christian associated with 8 March withdrew from the cabinet. 8 March organised a protest camp in central Beirut, demanding that Siniora step down. Given Lebanon's power-sharing formula, the protest was interpreted as a Hizbollah attack on the Sunni prime ministership and hence on the Sunni community as a whole. The Sunni-Shia split thus led to a closing of ranks within the Sunni community and provided the rationale for an alliance with Western powers and Saudi Arabia to oppose the Shia movement, which was supported by Iran and Syria. This closing of ranks meant that Saad Hariri achieved virtually unrivalled leadership of the Sunni community.

The near-absolute hegemony of Hariri in the Sunni community led to incongruous alliances. In defence of what was still a neoliberal economic programme, the billionaire mobilised Sunni followers from the most deprived areas of Lebanon, such as Akkar in the north. The Future Movement relied heavily on patronage and the ever-expanding health and social service provisions of the Hariri Foundation.[55] Saudi Arabia allegedly spent 'hundreds of millions' of dollars to ensure the electoral success of the Future Movement and its allies in the 2009 parliamentary elections.[56] The mobilisation of Sunni Muslims was primarily political but inevitably included a religious element, stoked by the political mobilisation of the Sunni Mufti and religious shaykhs on behalf of the Future Movement.[57] The Hariri camp courted Islamists, especially in Tripoli and the Akkar region. It entered into an alliance with the Lebanese branch of the Muslim Brotherhood, pressed for an amnesty for militants arrested over Islamist violence in Denniyeh in 2000 and recruited former salafist Khalid Dahir as a parliamentary deputy.[58] At one point, the Hariri movement started arming its supporters via a private security company.[59] The strategy of armed confrontation with Hizbollah failed when the Shia militia and its allies took control of much of the capital in May 2008, surrounding Hariri's residence. The Future Movement functionary in charge of arming Sunni youths was thereafter demoted.[60] The clashes led to the Doha Agreement that brought together 14 March and 8 March leaders. The subsequent rapprochement between Saudi Arabia and Syria led to a Hariri visit to Damascus. However, Hariri's swift readiness to compromise after an extended period of communal mobilisation—which even included arming his supporters—resulted in disillusionment with the billionaire's leadership. Some Sunni allies of the Future Movement distanced themselves from it.[61] Hariri was learning a lesson that the pre-war Sunni *zuama* had had to learn as well—sectarian mobilisation makes elite compromise more difficult.

The governments of Fuad Siniora and Saad Hariri between 2005 and 2011 focused on the struggle against Syria and Hizbollah, but also sought to deepen neoliberal economic reforms. The finance ministry, the CDR and the central bank remained in the hands of people closely associated with the Hariri camp. The Hariri network thus controlled the most important economic institutions of the country. The commitments of the Siniora government at the 'Paris III' donor conference in 2007 reiterated the neoliberal programme of the previous Hariri governments, including privatisation of state-controlled entities and welfare reform aimed at curtailing patronage opportunities of political rivals.[62] However, this agenda was almost impossible to realise against the interests of rival elites. When the Siniora government mooted the abolition of the Council of the South and the Central Fund for the Displaced it met determined opposition from Speaker Berri and Jumblatt who use these institutions as patronage instruments.[63]

Saad Hariri's government was brought down by the veto of 8 March ministers in January 2011 over his refusal to renounce the STL that was to indict and try Rafik Hariri's assassins. Mikati assumed the post of prime minister with the backing of 8 March, in what the Hariri-owned newspaper *Mustaqbal* (Future) called a 'constitutional coup' by Hizbollah.[64] 14 March refused to participate in the government. Appropriating the language of popular protests in Tunisia and Egypt, the Future Movement declared a 'day of anger'. The protesters complained that the Shia group Hizbollah had taken over the decision of who should be prime minister, a position reserved for Sunnis. As one Sunni cleric put it at a Tripoli rally: 'Saad Hariri is the only man who represents the Sunni faith [...] We will not accept [Hezbollah leader] Hassan Nasrallah choosing our Prime Minister'.[65] The protesters argued that Hariri was the only true representative of the Sunnis and that Mikati therefore lacked legitimacy—hence the talk of a 'constitutional coup'. This sense of ownership of the prime minister's post is unprecedented in Lebanese history. Rivalries between different Sunni politicians were common in the pre-war and civil-war eras and only since 2005 has the Hariri camp managed to lay exclusive claim to the post. The choice of protest site was also highly symbolic and protests were concentrated in Tripoli, Mikati's home town. In response, Mikati showed that he could also speak in a sectarian language. On Lebanon's premier political talk-show, called Kalam al-Nas, Mikati responded to suggestions he did not represent 'the Sunnis' by saying: 'I don't accept anyone to question my Sunnism. If there's a Sunni in Lebanon, it's me. I won't accept it! And those who want to hand out certificates [of Sunnism] can go do it on their own. I'm Sunni in belief, Sunni in practice, Sunni in politics and I'm the number one defender of the Sunnis in Lebanon [...] So [whoever is questioning my Sunnism] can get lost, with all my respect for the muftis and who else is concerned with this issue. I'm the number one Sunni in Lebanon!'[66]

Despite the display of popular anger by Future Movement activists, it would be simplistic to label the Mikati administration a 'Hizbollah government'. It is true that Mikati would not have become prime minister without the backing of Hizbollah and the other 8 March members, but he also had some leeway. Hizbollah only held two minor ministries and Mikati immediately assured the USA that he would steer an independent path.[67] There were important continuities between the governments headed by the Hariri camp and the Mikati administration. The most crucial one was the continuation of Hariri's policy of government debt management. Muhammad

Safadi took over the finance ministry under Mikati. Safadi, too, is a new contractor from Tripoli.[68] Mikati fended off demands by Aoun to hand the finance ministry to his Free Patriotic Movement (FPM).[69] Given the 'anti-corruption' stance adopted by the FPM, such a move would have led to great unease among investors. Hailing from an established trading family, he migrated to Saudi Arabia in 1975, where he became rich by building residential compounds. Safadi had close relations with the head of the Saudi air force, Prince Turki al-Nasr. In 2000 he founded the Safadi Foundation, which offers health, educational and social services.[70] He first entered parliament in 2000 and became minister of public works under Siniora in 2005 and minister of economy and trade in 2008 until Mikati appointed him finance minister in 2011. Although previously allied to 14 March, he is clearly trying to steer an independent course and keep his options open.

Together with the central bank governor and the prime minister, the finance minister is a central player in the management of government debt. Previously, the Hariri camp had fought hard to maintain control of the finance ministry. From 1992 onwards, the Hariri camp was in control of the finance ministry, the post of prime minister and the central bank. The policy adopted in 1993 eventually pegged the currency to the US dollar by, at times, borrowing more on behalf of the government than was needed to finance the government deficit. This scheme drove up the demand for Lebanese pounds, but also raised interest rates on government debt, leading the country into a debt trap.[71] The main beneficiaries were Lebanese commercial banks and their depositors. Lebanese pound deposits are highly concentrated because only the country's financial and economic elites had the necessary savings to invest in government debt instruments in this way.[72] The government therefore needs to maintain the confidence of the country's financial elites and one way of doing so is to appoint one of the new contractors as finance minister. A second political aspect of debt management is mentioned in an IMF working paper from 2008, which shows that the continuous rollover of Lebanese government debt depends on an 'implicit guarantee' from donors and international financial institutions.[73] On closer inspection, the main guarantor is Saudi Arabia. The kingdom bought up government bonds when investors refused to take them anymore, it provided the largest chunk of concessionary loans at the 'Paris II' donor conference that prevented financial crisis in Lebanon in 2002 and it transferred USD 1 billion to the Lebanese central bank during Israel's war with Lebanon in 2006.[74] The government therefore needed someone who could manage relations with the Saudi monarchy. Safadi ticked both boxes. As a new contractor, Safadi reassured Lebanon's financial elites—the owners of banks and holders of deposits—and his close relations with the Saudi royals meant that the 'implicit guarantee' would be maintained.

The most crucial instance of continuity between Hariri and Mikati was over the issue of funding for the STL. As the court is a hybrid containing international jurists and Lebanese judges, the Lebanese government is obliged to cover 49 per cent of the STL budget. Hizbollah sought to undermine the international tribunal by forcing Mikati's government to withhold its share of the funding. Mikati would not budge, threatened to resign over the issue and eventually paid the government's dues in December 2011. The reasons are numerous. Mikati himself said that he wanted to fund the tribunal in order to avoid possible international sanctions against Lebanon.[75] There are also other factors coming into play. Mikati could not be seen to go against his own community, where most felt strongly about the STL and regarded the assassination of Rafik Hariri as an attack on the community itself. The STL was thus a sectarian issue, too. Secondly, Saudi Arabia was pressing for the STL and very few Sunni politicians in Lebanon can defy the region's premier Sunni power. After the failure of Nasserism in the late 1960s and the defeat of the PLO in the early 1980s, Saudi Arabia emerged as the primary ally of the Sunni community. Saudi Arabia also exerts great economic power in Lebanon and its role as guarantor of Lebanon's government debt has already been mentioned. Mikati had previously relied on good relations with Riyadh to mediate with Hariri. Prior to the 2009 parliamentary elections, Saudi Arabia had reportedly engineered an electoral alliance between Hariri, Safadi and Mikati in Tripoli in order to avoid a deep division within the Sunni community.[76] As a businessman who had accumulated his wealth in the Gulf, Mikati, too, had close links to Saudi Arabia. Upon taking up the position as prime minister, he stressed the importance of close ties to the kingdom.[77] Saudi support for the tribunal is therefore likely to have played a large role in Mikati's decision to provide the STL funding, as was also reported in the Lebanese press.[78]

Conclusions

The rise and the success of the new contractor bourgeoisie confirms the importance of class in analysing Lebanese politics. The emergence of the new contractors was due to changes in Lebanon's role in the capitalist world economy and the oil boom in the Gulf. They replaced the commercial-financial bourgeoisie that had dominated the pre-war economy and politics. Rafik Hariri's neoliberal reconstruction programme has to be understood with reference to his class interest. The businessman-politician and the neo-liberal technocrats in his network were a formidable force for neoliberal reform. Their ability to realise this project was circumscribed by rival elites—especially former militia leaders—and by Syria. While Hariri was able to shape reconstruction and finance, he was prevented from privatising state-controlled enterprises. Analyses of Lebanese politics often neglect class and political economy in favour of sectarian dynamics and international factors. The argument here is not that class trumps other forms of politics or determines them. Rather, the challenge is to bring the three levels of analysis together. The comparison of Rafik and Saad Hariri, Najib Mikati and Issam Fares illustrates the importance of sectarian position and international alliances in explaining the different strategies of new contractors and their relative success.

The civil war had left the Sunni community with a leadership vacuum that was filled by Rafik Hariri. From the mid-1990s onwards, Hariri transformed himself from a 'national' leader to a specifically 'Sunni' leader. He did so for electoral reasons and used philanthropy to build up a clientelist network. This strategy of sectarian leadership became even more intense under his son Saad, who effectively monopolised Sunni political leadership in Lebanon. This was partly a function of the increasing rift between Sunni and Shia Muslims, which was driven by domestic and international politics. Hariri's monopoly curtails the ability of politicians such as Mikati or Safadi to lay claim to the post of prime minister. Fares, meanwhile, is held back by his status as Christian Orthodox. He therefore focuses his efforts on public policy think-tanks. International alliances are also crucial to understanding the relative success of different new contractors. Hariri enjoyed strong support from Saudi Arabia. Mikati and Fares were allied to Syria, although they also maintained ties to the kingdom. Despite the obvious differences in alliances between Hariri and Mikati, the willingness and the ability of Prime Minister Mikati to chart an independent path from Hizbollah over the STL funding issue shows that the similarities between new contractors can be as important as the differences.

8

THE RECONSTRUCTION OF LEBANON
OR THE RACKETEERING RULE

Fabrice Balanche

The socio-economic dimensions of the Lebanese conflict have often been overlooked in favour of political and geopolitical readings since the Syrian withdrawal in 2005.[1] The same is true of the Arab Spring of 2011. Granted, the search for freedom and democracy are universal aspirations. But the deterioration of real or perceived living conditions and a frustration born of unequal economic growth also generates political contestation.[2] The endemic conflicts in Lebanon are thus not a simple effect of regional geopolitics, even if they accentuate the internal problems. Based on my experience living in Lebanon (2003–7) and research in political geography in this country conducted over the past decade, this chapter argues that the policy of reconstruction[3] followed by Prime Minister Rafik Hariri and his successors in this post[4] is largely responsible for the current crisis, because it was unable to solve any of the pre-1975 problems. As George Corm writes: 'It is either wilful blindness or a dangerous illusion to think that trade and some luxury tourist services will solve the grave structural, political, economic and financial crisis with which the country has been struggling since the end of the war'.[5]

145

From the end of the civil war in 1990 until the Syrian withdrawal in 2005, political tensions existed but were mostly silenced by the presence of the Syrian army. Following the Syrian army's departure, these conflicts could no longer be suppressed. After the civil war, the reconstruction of the Lebanese state was confronted with many difficulties such as foreign occupation (by Syria and Israel), former militia control of various parts of the territory, widespread corruption and, moreover, an international process that can best be described as 'a steady decline of state institutions' with globalisation. Moreover, Hariri tried to place Lebanon on the path of economic liberalisation, a political position whose declared aim was to restore Beirut's pre-war position as an international financial centre and a tourist destination for wealthy Arabs from the Gulf.

This chapter proposes a political geography reading of the conflict in Lebanon since 2005. For this, we need to go back to Lebanon's reconstruction policy since 1990, and particularly its impact in Beirut, where it appears to have been a mere continuation of the civil war by other means.[6] The proposed approach consists of a reading of space to understand the dialectical relationship of power struggles.[7] The study of public policy and the different actors is thus an essential first step, before subsequently considering the interplay of various spatial scales. Since Lebanon is an arena for regional and international conflicts, geopolitics are inescapable. However, although spatial processes in Lebanon are strongly connected with regional policy, the latter should not be a prerequisite for analysing Lebanon. In fact, social and therefore territorial fragmentation in Lebanon, mostly due to civil war, is responsible for weak state sovereignty, not the other way around.[8]

Hariri's Lebanon: An 'Under-Developed' Country

After fifteen years of civil war (1975–90), Lebanon embarked on a policy of national reconstruction under the leadership of Rafik Hariri, a Lebanese businessman of humble origins who made his fortunes in Saudi Arabia and was appointed prime minister in 1992 as the result of a Syrian-Saudi agreement. The combination of profit and politics has been a constant feature of Lebanese political life, even at the height of the civil war. Indeed, the country witnessed its only truly independent executive policy during the term of President Fuad Chehab from 1958 to 1964. However, this brief attempt to build a strong and modern state ran up against coalitions of notables from all the major Lebanese confessional communities, as well as the intervention of major powers. Hariri was the perfect inheritor of this Lebanese political class—'*fromagistes*', in the words of Fuad Chehab—which sought to take economic advantage of political power instead of implementing a public policy benefitting the people.[9] Hariri regarded the reconstruction of Lebanon as a means of bringing Beirut back to the position it enjoyed before the civil war.[10] He sought to re-establish the city as the interface between the East and West, as a hub for commercial traffic, as a tax haven that would attract capital from the Gulf and as the favourite destination for tourists from the petrodollar monarchies. It has succeeded on the latter two points, becoming a tax haven and attracting Arab tourists but, as we shall see, it has lost its importance as a port and a hub.

Hariri's policy was part and parcel of a very ambitious economic project. It sought to establish Beirut as a metropolis capable of integrating Lebanon into the new global economy, a policy that was certainly optimistic in its evaluation of a prompt resolution of the Arab-Israeli conflict and reconciliation between all the Lebanese factions. To the discharge of Hariri, after the end of the Cold War, many businessmen, politicians and people in the Near East were optimists too, but it seems that Hariri ignored the economic changes that were taking place in the Middle East during the time when Lebanon was torn apart by civil war. In fact, since 1975, the countries of the Gulf had begun developing their own transport infrastructures and investing their financial resources. The city of Dubai had established itself as the main economic centre in the Middle East.[11] But still Hariri based his post-war reconstruction of Lebanon on the myth that Lebanon would, once again, be the 'Switzerland of the Middle East'.

Tourism and finance were promoted at the expense of manufacturing and agricultural activities. Hariri signed an association agreement with the European Union, which included a free-trade agreement, as well as various free-trade agreements with other Arab countries, notably Syria. In this respect, he joined the Arab common market (GAFTA).[12] Faced with brutal competition from the whole world a few years after the end of the civil war, and without any government backing, Lebanon's industrial sector, which at the time was still important,[13] was quickly shattered by foreign competition. In 2009, the industry's contribution to GDP was 6.1 per cent, against 13.7 per cent in 1997[14] and 15.9 per cent in 1970.[15]

Some dissenting voices complained that this policy was Hariri's way (and more generally the Sunnis' way) of weakening the Christians, since most industrialists belonged to the Christian communities, while the Sunnis controlled Lebanon's trade and the import and export markets.[16] In Lebanon, any political decision is interpreted in sectarian terms. Of course, one cannot exclude the communitarian aspect of any economic decision taken in Lebanon, as communities and politics are linked, hence the constitution of a Christian opposition to Hariri's policies. Nevertheless, in this case, we have at hand a more traditional opposition between production and trade interests in the Middle East,[17] an opposition that is itself based upon two different conceptions of the role of the state. Producers want protectionism and merchants an open market. In the first case, the state is a protector, while in the second it is an obstacle to private business interests.

Economic liberalisation ruined many professions in the manufacturing sector, especially ones that required certain skills that were not offset, either in quantity or in quality, by the reinforcement of the tourism sector and the development of finance. The resumption of youth emigration, especially of Lebanese graduates, was a direct consequence of this policy. Between 1996 and 2001, emigration percentages, in both absolute and relative terms, rose to levels even higher than those during the civil war.[18] This was a cruel awakening to those who had hoped to return to Lebanon after their forced exile. The middle classes that had resisted the conflict were becoming more and more impoverished, whereas political patronage (clientelism), mostly established on confessional grounds, resumed its role, undermining the fragile return to democracy.

Indifferent to the deterioration of the standard of living of the majority of Lebanese, Hariri, like the Lebanese oligarchy in general, was preoccupied with the reconstruction of Beirut. The ruins of the city centre were put under the control of a private company named 'Solidere'.[19] Most of the damaged buildings were demolished by the company, except those with patrimonial significance, such as the Beirut Synagogue. Those who sold properties were given shares from the company, but Hariri was the major shareholder.

The creation of Solidere necessitated a vast campaign of corruption and bribery by Hariri that targeted all the main decision-makers of the country.[20] Solidere has been in charge of the reconstruction of downtown Beirut ever since, and this area became the symbol of the 'new Lebanon'. The Hariri government therefore concentrated investments on Beirut and its communication infrastructure, to the detriment of the rest of the country. The financial power of prime minister and businessman Hariri and his control of the Beirut municipality allowed him to draw huge profits from the reconstruction of the downtown area.

Controlling the Beirut Municipality

Lebanon's municipal officials are elected democratically, without any obligation to comply with confessional quotas.[21] This is contrary to the legislative elections where a fixed number of deputies by religious confession are elected and the nominations for the key posts as (Maronite) president, (Sunni) prime minister and the (Shia) speaker of parliament. Despite their non-confessional nature, the lists for municipal elections try to respect the communitarian distribution of the population. Politicians justify this principle by reference to the National Pact of 1943, which defines Lebanon as a consensual democracy where no major confession (Sunni, Shia, Maronite, Druze, Greek Orthodox, Greek Catholic and Armenian) should be excluded from power.[22] More practically, this system helps garner the largest number of votes by incorporating representatives of each community.

However, the representation of the population within the municipality is based on registered voters and not actual residents. Indeed, the Lebanese do not vote where they reside but in their village of origin, where their ancestors lived in 1932, the year when the first and only population census was completed in modern Lebanon.[23] The transfer of legal domicile is possible in theory but very difficult in practice. Officially, the electoral lists were not changed after the civil war, to avoid regularising the displacement of population after the war.[24] Examples include the expulsion of Christians from the Shouf and West Beirut, or Muslims from East Beirut.[25] Unofficially, politicians have an interest in freezing the electoral lists in order to control the voting process through traditional middlemen who negotiate the purchase of votes for MPs and municipalities. It is not uncommon on election day to see buses chartered by officials and political parties filled with registered voters in their community of origin with which they have not had any physical link for the past half-century. They come to vote for the list of the highest bidder. These practices often change the outcome of the polls and augment the disillusionment of the Lebanese about their political institutions.[26]

Often enough, the elected mayors and members of the municipal councils are, like the voters, fictitious residents. They present themselves for elections to defend the interests of their family or to become the natural successors of a relative who is also the head of the municipality. Nepotism is a very vivid Lebanese political tradition. In addition, municipal management can be very lucrative through the control of real estate since the mayors are empowered to issue building permits.[27] In Beirut, businessman

Hariri evoked communitarian sensibilities[28] and deployed his enormous financial assets[29] in order to control the municipality. Nobody could succeed against Hariri's fortune in Beirut. As prime minister, he also controlled the nomination of the *muhafez* [governor] of the city, who is appointed by the cabinet, the council of ministers. The mayor is traditionally from the Greek Orthodox community, since it is one of the two original Beirut communities (the second one is the Sunni community). On the other hand, the Maronite, Shia, Armenian and Druze populations consist of communities who have recently moved to the city. They are still mostly on the margins of the urban space, even if they will eventually be integrated into the city's urban fabric.

The political conflict between President Emile Lahoud (in office from 1998 to 2007) and Prime Minister Hariri had repercussions for the municipality of Beirut. Between 2000 and 2005, the *muhafez* was a man close to Lahoud, while the municipal council was supporters of Hariri. During this period, the *muhafez* consistently opposed the construction projects of Hariri. After the Syrian withdrawal in mid-2005,[30] Hariri's successor, Prime Minister Fuad Siniora,[31] managed to appoint a new governor (the former governor became a minister in Siniora's cabinet on behalf of the opposition) who was more sympathetic to the business interests of the Hariri family. His appointment allowed Hariri's business ventures to resume construction projects despite the political turmoil afflicting the country. Indeed, the growth of property investment after 2005 is more likely to be linked to the total control of the municipal executive power by the Hariri family than to any confidence in the Lebanese economy.[32] This control provides the Hariri family with a steady income from the urban services that are delegated by the municipality to private companies. For example, Sukleen, a company owned by the Hariri family through a figurehead, obtained the contract for rubbish collection in Beirut and the Greater Beirut Area with an inflated fee of USD 100 per ton, while it only earns USD 25 per ton in the municipality of Zahleh, another major city of the country.[33] To avoid a default from the cash-strapped municipalities, Sukleen obtained, by virtue of a decision of the council of ministers, the right to be refunded directly by the Autonomous Municipal Fund (*La caisse autonome des municipalités*). This fund is, in theory only, under the control of the ministry of interior but is, in fact, controlled by the ministry of finance and, therefore, by Hariri partisans. From 1992 to 2004, except during the short-lived Salim al-Hoss government (1998–2000), Siniora, Hariri's childhood friend, was finance minister.

THE RECONSTRUCTION OF LEBANON

After the Syrian withdrawal in 2005, Siniora became prime minister (2005–9) but maintained control over the ministry of finance through his collaborators.[34] The last finance minister in the (Saad) Hariri government (2009–11) was Raya Haffar al-Hassan, a member of the board of the Future Movement. Recently, Alain Bifani, general director of finance, denounced the Hariri and Siniora governments for their lack of transparency and accountability in the ministry of finance.[35]

It is generally acknowledged that the profits generated by Sukleen, amounting to about USD 60 million per year, are used to finance the electoral campaigns of the Future Movement which is controlled by the Hariri family.[36] The new government, formed in June 2011 under the premiership of Najib Mikati, tried to cancel the Sukleen privileges and refused to pay the company until a new agreement was reached.[37]

In 2010, more than 1.5 million inhabitants lived in Greater Beirut, or about 35 per cent of Lebanon's total population. Despite its size, Greater Beirut has no executive institution or even an umbrella coordination entity. The *muhafez* of Beirut does not have this prerogative, since he only governs the municipality of Beirut with its 400,000 inhabitants and 20 square kilometres (which is less than 23 per cent of the Greater Beirut population and 8 per cent of the urbanised area).[38] The bulk of the urban area is located in the *muhafaza* of Mount Lebanon (an autonomous *Mutassarifat* during the Ottoman era)[39] because administrative divisions did not change after the French mandate, and most of the urban growth takes place outside the Beirut *muhafaza*. There has been no attempt to create a 'metropolitan council' to govern Greater Beirut. This is due to irreconcilable differences between the Shias living in the southern suburbs, headed by Hizbollah and Amal, the Sunnis who form the majority within the capital and who are led by the Future Movement of the Hariri family, and the Christians, who are powerful in the eastern suburbs of the city. The southern suburbs, *Dahiyeh*, have an informal management unit created and directed by Hizbollah and in charge of the suburb's municipalities.[40] However, this unit cannot serve as a substitute for the state in large-scale infrastructure projects other than in emergency cases. During the Israeli blitz in the summer of 2006, large sections of the southern suburbs were devastated by Israeli warplanes. To reconstruct them, Hizbollah's development wing, *Jihad al-Binaa*, conceived a reconstruction project tasked to rebuild the *Dahiyeh*, called *Waad* (promise), after the 'promise' given by Hassan Nasrallah.[41] The southern suburbs constitute a single Shia urban entity, while the eastern suburbs are torn

151

between the various Christian political parties—the Lebanese Forces,[42] the Free Patriotic Movement,[43] the Kataeb[44] and local leaders like Michel Murr.[45] There is no overall management of the metropolitan area, which partially explains the difficulties in establishing viable systems for transportation, water and electricity. But above all, this institutional blur benefits the property developers by offering them investment opportunities they would not have obtained through an agglomeration council representing the entire Greater Beirut area. Even if such a council, like the municipalities, had little concern for urban planning, all political parties would be represented in it and could therefore oppose, or at least denounce, the excesses regarding the management of real estate. The Hariri family is the main beneficiary of the weakness of local governance in Greater Beirut, which has ensured that there is minimal legal impediment to its many real estate projects.

The Privatisation of Beirut's Reconstruction under Hariri

The city of Beirut is run in accordance with the financial interests of the Hariri family.[46] Building permits in the most lucrative areas are routinely blocked by the municipality if the projects are not led by a member of the Hariri clientele. Conversely, when partisans of the Hariri clan want to sidestep the regulations on urban development, such as building height etc., they receive exemptions.[47] This can be substantiated with reference to the Lebanese chapter of Transparency International, which claims that: 'As a result of this arrangement, the late Prime Minister Hariri became the sole decision-maker on matters related to the economy and most importantly the reconstruction process, whereas the speaker of parliament, Nabih Berri, was in charge of the reconstruction and relief program for the south of Lebanon and the president of the republic, Elias Hrawi,[48] had special interests in the oil and gas sector'.[49] Yet, the main symbol of the Hariri family's grip on the city of Beirut is Solidere,[50] a chartered company in charge of reconstructing and managing the city centre, which was ravaged during the war.

Solidere was created in 1992, and initially won the concession for renovating the city centre for twenty-five years, which later was extended to seventy-five years in November 2005 by the council of ministers.[51] Through several figureheads,[52] Hariri gathered the majority of the shares.[53] The destroyed buildings and damaged properties were expropriated from the original owners under dubious circumstances.[54] As compensation, they received shares in Solidere, but the stock prices were manipulated so that small shareholders panicked and sold their shares when they were at their lowest, only to be purchased by Hariri.[55] This strategy strengthened his financial assets and secured his grip on Solidere.

Selling as well as renting apartments and offices in properties rebuilt by Solidere guaranteed huge profits for several reasons. First, construction costs were low due to cheap Syrian labour. Second, the land on which buildings were built had been acquired virtually for free. Third, huge investments in infrastructure served to encourage companies and traders to relocate to the city centre. Indeed, downtown Beirut is served by a formidable network of urban highways that were either superimposed on the existing urban fabric or were made to cross the city through tunnels. Moreover, the city centre is only fifteen minutes away from the airport and only five minutes away from the sea and seafront promenade, the *Corniche*. It is also located in the centre of the main axes that permit citizens to leave Beirut without spending hours in traffic jams. The traditional shopping areas, like Hamra Street and Ashrafieh, were deliberately neglected in order to encourage the owners to relocate to the downtown area. Foreign companies quickly realised that it was better to have their offices in downtown Beirut in order to benefit from proximity and ease of interaction with the Lebanese administration.[56] Finally, the location in downtown Beirut allowed foreign companies to divert a portion of their profits. Financial transfers officially intended to support commercial facilities in downtown Beirut were in fact recycled in Lebanese banks that invest in the profitable Lebanese treasury bonds.[57]

The Lebanese state under Hariri financed a great deal of infrastructure development with public funds. Highways, power plants, public schools and an oversized airport (renamed 'Rafic Hariri Airport' after his murder)— all of them paid many times their real construction costs as a method of financing the political allegiance of rival politicians through their clientele of contractors. In part, some infrastructure works were implemented by Hariri's own contracting companies. The use of political power and state money for private purposes is not limited to the reconstruction of downtown Beirut. This strategy was used in the municipality of Beirut too, which is under the control of the Hariri family thanks to the municipal council and the many administrations in charge of the urban development of the city, such as the department of urban development and the CDR. Building permits were issued to Hariri partisans only, and the prime minister had an informal right of refusal over plots that interested him, especially along the seafront where luxurious high-rise buildings catering for rich Saudi customers or Lebanese emigrants are constructed. The residential model of Solidere and the public services it provides attract many Lebanese, as the urban services in the remainder of the city are deficient.

A new residential area was to be erected in the southern area of Beirut between the golf course and the sea: 'the Elyssar project'.[58] The land is occupied by illegal residents, mostly Shia who fled southern Lebanon after the Israeli occupation.[59] To force the departure of these residents, Hariri began by separating the district located near the sea, Ouzai, from the rest of the suburbs by means of the Beirut-airport-Sidon highway. Then a second highway, parallel to the first, was set to destroy the commercial centre of the district. The residents refused to be moved and have their properties expropriated, and rallied behind Hizbollah to stop the bulldozers. The highway to the south and the north of the Ouzai district was completed in 2000.[60] The prime minister was waiting for a more favourable political situation in order to complete the remainder of the project. While the first highway was partly motivated by public interest, the goal of the second one was the expulsion of the residents of Ouzai in order to claim the seafront and construct luxurious buildings, which would become the extension of the ones facing the sea in downtown Beirut. Had this highway been indispensable for reducing traffic in this region, it could have been built as a flyover, as was the case for the express highway crossing the Armenian district of Burj Hammoud in East Beirut. The prime minister did not want to lose the votes of the Armenians, who were defending the unity of their neighbourhood.[61] Additionally, the poor, popular neighbourhood of Burj Hammoud did not hold the same potential for property development as Ouzai, hence Hariri had no problem in getting the Lebanese government to finance the additional cost of the work, especially since the job was done by companies he owned.

The territory of Beirut is coveted by property developers eager to attract the investment potential of the affluent Lebanese diaspora and wealthy Arabs of the Gulf. It is true that Beirut is a unique city in the Middle East thanks to its relative moral freedom and festive atmosphere. Moreover, Lebanese emigrants seek to acquire plots and properties in order to stay connected with their country and strengthen the Lebanese identity of their children. In comparison, the majority of the Lebanese were impoverished by the civil war and the country's brutal entry in the global market. The war had more or less protected the population of Beirut from real estate speculation and structural adjustment. The return of peace was, paradoxically, an economic disaster for many people, given the characteristics of the political reconstruction that followed.[62] Lebanon is facing a social housing problem of great magnitude, but the contestation quickly becomes communitarian because of the Lebanese political system and the territorial struggle for urban space, both of which are organised along confessional lines.

Social Crises, Communalism and Territorial Fragmentation

Income differences are substantial and growing between the lower class, working in the local sector (agriculture, industry, domestics services, etc.), and the upper class, attached to the global sector (international finance, import/export, luxury retail, real estate, etc.). The increases in real estate prices are the clearest expressions of globalisation in Beirut. The downtown area has become a gated community for the global class, while the rest are excluded from this part of the city. The occupation of downtown Beirut, between September 2006 and May 2008, by the opposition to the Siniora government, was not only a political campaign targeting the government's support of the STL, it was also a fight against the urban exclusion of the hundreds of thousands who invaded downtown Beirut—opposition supporters also claimed 'the right to the city'.[63]

During the decade 2000–10, the real estate prices in Beirut increased by about 400 per cent.[64] Additionally, in many places illegal settlements in the vicinity of the downtown area are under pressure from property barons. In places such as Bachoura and Ayn al-Mreisseh, poor Shia settlers have pleaded with Hizbollah and Amal for protection against eviction.[65] The Sunni urban class is also impoverished by the effects of globalisation but, unlike the Shia opposition led by Hizbollah, does not complain about Hariri policies because the Sunnis do not protest against their own government out of confessional solidarity. Although betrayed by the economic system, it supports the system's masters. In this confessional society, vertical links are more powerful than horizontal links. For instance, in Tarik al-Jdideh, a lower middle-class Sunni quarter of Beirut, the population adamantly supports the Hariri family. People are frightened by poverty and unemployment, but they consider that the danger comes from the Shia-dominated southern suburb, the *Dahiyeh*. There were many riots at the Dahiyeh-Tarik al-Jdideh border, pitting young people from both sides against each other. *Shabab* (young men) from Tarik al-Jdideh want to protect their quarter from 'invasion', like the militias did during the civil war. In January 2006, four people were killed in Tarik al-Jdideh, and the army declared a curfew to protect Beirut from sectarian violence between the Shia and Sunni.

The fear of dropping down the social ladder is creating a neighbourhood-level unity against *Dahiyeh*, which is perceived by the Sunni of Tarik al-Jdideh as being rural and Shia in nature. The same situation prevails in Tripoli between Jabal Mohsen (pro-Syrian Alawi quarter) and Bab al-Tabaneh (pro-Hariri Sunni quarter).[66] Most of the Sunnis are clients of Hariri's Future Movement, and Muslim associations, such as al-Ahbash, received money from the Hariri family, yet ended up turning against it. In these places Hariri can recruit guards for private security companies such as 'Future Secure Plus'.[67] Hariri realised that he needed his own militia for protection against the Hizbollah threat. The Lebanese army would never fight against Hizbollah due to either political sympathy or weakness. In May 2008, Hizbollah overran the Sunni neighbourhoods of West Beirut in a few hours, following a government crackdown on the group's secret telecommunications network.[68] In this case, Hariri's private security company was unable to prevent his mansion from being surrounded by opposition militia.

Clashes can occur at any time in Beirut. In August 2010, the al-Ahbash group clashed with Hizbollah, its political ally, in a mixed Sunni and Shia quarter of Beirut, leaving three people dead.[69] This was the most severe security incident since May 2008. Beirut's mixed neighbourhoods have become urban conflict zones due to the high concentration of socio-economic problems along confessional boundaries. Since the end of the civil war and departure of the Maronite Christians, these Muslim-majority neighbourhoods remain the prime sites of communitarian confrontation. The confrontation between them cannot simply be reduced to a dichotomy of 'pro-Syrian' and 'anti-Syrian' groups.

Partisans of the State against Entrepreneurs and Militias

'Pro-Syrians' versus 'anti-Syrians': this is how most Western media caricature the current political conflict in Lebanon.[70] According to this stereotype, the Syrians want to re-establish their hegemony over Lebanon and, in order to do so, they use the Lebanese people and more particularly their long-time ally, Hizbollah. Western media and television portrays a stand-off between, on the one hand, the bearded Islamist rambling in Arabic, and on the other, respectable politicians who speak French and English fluently and who are presented as the ramparts of democracy and modernity. While it is difficult to understand Lebanon—hence the dictum: if you think you understand Lebanon, you have not studied it long enough—it seems that Manichaeism plays an important role in this country. The ruling coalition holding power from May 2005[71] until January 2011[72] consisted of three major parties—the Future Movement of Saad Hariri, the Progressive Socialist Party (PSP) of Druze leader Walid Jumblatt[73] (the Druze form about 5 per cent of the Lebanese population) and the Lebanese Forces (LF), formerly a Christian militia lead by Samir Geagea. The essential element in this coalition is the Future Movement, composed mainly of Sunnis (25–30 per cent of the Lebanese population), while the other two parties (PSP and LF) represent smaller portions of the Lebanese population. The coalition is called '14 March', in reference to the giant gathering dubbed the 'Cedar Revolution', which took place in 2005, demanding the withdrawal of Syrian troops from Lebanon following Hariri's murder. But what did these leaders do before becoming the champions of Western chancelleries?

Walid Jumblatt was one of Syria's most faithful allies during the Lebanese civil war and until the autumn of 2004, when he suddenly switched sides and decided to join the anti-Syrian opposition. Following the parliamentary elections in August 2009, Jumblatt left the 14 March coalition and, two years later, formally joined the Hizbollah-led opposition (8 March). In January 2011, the Saad Hariri cabinet collapsed, and Jumblatt supported Najib Mikati as new prime minister.[74] The LF leader Samir Geagea was tried and imprisoned in 1994 on multiple murder and terrorism charges, but informally because of his opposition to the Syrian stranglehold. As for Saad Hariri, who presents himself as the successor to his father's legacy, we tend to forget that Rafik Hariri as the prime minister of Lebanon was brought to power by Syria and ruled Lebanon with its support, until he decided to challenge his erstwhile protector.

On the other hand, the 'pro-Syrian' coalition (if we borrow the terminology used by official news channels) is formed by Hizbollah and its allies—the Amal Movement (Shia), the Free Patriotic Movement (FPM) of former General Michel Aoun (a secular group mainly composed of Christians), the Nasserists, the Communists, and people of all communities who are opposed to both parties and the families who back the Future Movement of Saad Hariri. Hizbollah did not participate in any Lebanese government up until 2005. Throughout the post-civil war period of Syrian occupation, Hizbollah was part of the parliamentary opposition to the governments headed by Rafik Hariri. The FPM represents the majority[75] of Christians[76] in Lebanon. Before joining hands with Hizbollah, Aoun was decidedly anti-Syrian, but has since the 2006 'memorandum of understanding' with Hizbollah moderated his stance for electoral reasons.[77]

In Lebanon, the electoral alliances are strategic and not ideological. The personal interests of ruling families, as well as greed and presidential ambitions, are the elements that help compose and recompose coalitions. However, since the withdrawal of Syrian troops from Lebanon, politics are timidly regaining some ground. What we see during 'pro-Syrian' opposition demonstrations is a gathering of people from all communities and from rather modest backgrounds, who are asking for a just and lawful government. This situation generates political conflicts that are grafted onto communitarian ones. Those instabilities are thereafter recovered by regional geopolitics with Syria, Iran and Israel at one side, Saudi Arabia and the USA on the other. Each community in Lebanon is trying to get help from an external power in order to impose itself on the national scene. Money and weapons are flowing into Lebanon, as tensions rise.

Beirut Urban Conflict and the Regional Cold War

The massive sit-in in downtown Beirut between October 2006 and May 2008 (coming to an end after the Doha Agreement) demanding the resignation of the government, symbolises the excluded people's 're-appropriation' of the city centre, which was traditionally a place of communitarian and social mixing before it was appropriated by Solidere and offered to wealthy Arab tourists and to the Lebanese upper classes.[78] By installing a protest camp[79] in downtown Beirut over the concessions of Solidere, the Lebanese opposition not only protested against the creation of the STL,[80] but also against the massive acquisition of the public domain by the businessman Rafik Hariri, and after 2005 by his son Saad: 'In September 2010, a year after taking office, Saad Hariri took possession of 29,486 square metres of downtown Beirut, under payment of Solidere, in the work of clearing the ruins of the capital. Since the beginning of urban renewal in Beirut (1992), the Hariri family has acquired one-third of the project's available land (107,102 square metres of 291,800 square metres)'.[81] At the same time, it discourages investments in the city centre by impairing the economic activity. Indeed, the military deployment in the city centre as well as the transport restrictions and the mere sight of the camp discourage most regulars and tourists from going there. Shops and restaurants closed their doors and moved their activities to other parts of the city—Hamra,[82] Gemmayzeh[83] and Sassine.[84] Faced with this local economic crisis, the government of Siniora declared a tax exemption for those who maintained their activities in the city centre.

The attack in Beirut by Hizbollah in May 2008 showed the extreme fragility of the politico-economic system of the Hariri family. Young Sunnis recruited in security companies to protect West Beirut quickly disbanded when faced with the Hizbollah and Amal militias, demonstrating that mercantile patronage within the Sunni community has its limits.[85] Certainly it helps to buy votes during elections or to mobilise the population for demonstrations, but in case of armed conflict it is ineffective. Hizbollah's ideological hegemony of the Shia community, coupled with Iranian financial support, has been much more successful.

The Hariri coalition of 14 March managed to win parliamentary elections in 2009 thanks to its huge financial resources, its ability to bring in voters from abroad in strategic areas like Zahleh[86] and the fact that Aoun's party lost 10 per cent of its votes because of its agreement with Hizbollah. Nevertheless, Saad Hariri was unable to keep his majority in the parliament because most of the PSP group of Jumblatt left the 14 March coalition majority in January 2011 to join 8 March.

In Greater Beirut, a real struggle for territory has begun. Globalisation reinforces land speculation, which leads to the expulsion of the poor and middle classes from downtown Beirut. It threatens their very existence in the suburbs, where geographical amenities, the coastline and hills, are very attractive for luxury-orientated property developers. While expulsion measures mostly target illegal settlements, the very concept of legality remains questionable in the Lebanese context, especially in the south. The 'crony capitalism' that is developing in Lebanon produces a legality of two sorts, which works like a spider's web, allowing influential people to pass while stopping the insignificant.

The territorial disputes are reflected in the political opposition between, on the one hand, the supporters of Hizbollah, Amal and the FPM of Aoun, and on the other, those of the Future Movement of Saad Hariri, the LF of Geagea, as well as the PSP of Jumblatt until the latter switched sides in January 2011. It sheds light on the opposition between supporters of a strong state that provides protection against the consequences of a global economy, and supporters of a weak state run by feudal forces and businessmen: 'What's more, Hariri at present seems less state-builder than potential state-profiteer, holding the country hostage to a huge public debt accumulated by his capital spending programme that exceeds forty-fold the debt the country was labouring under during the civil war'.[87] Of course, Hariri did not keep this money for himself, but shared it with Amal leader Berri, Jumblatt and Syria, his allies until 2004.

At the regional level, these conflicting points of view fall into a larger and more dangerous opposition between the USA and Iran, an opposition which can also be analysed in reference to the globalisation of the economy today that has been instigated by the USA. The political, economic and social system developed by Iran and Syria is not compatible with the liberalism movement conveyed by globalisation.

Lebanese political parties are well integrated into the regional geopolitical system, as the Future Movement is funded by Saudi Arabia, Hizbollah by Iran, while Christian and Druze parties are divided between both sides. That is why the social conflict disappears, obscured by geopolitics and communalism. People believe they are better protected by their community than by state or social class unions. In the Middle East, social class unions are rare but powerful. In the 1950s, a small rural bourgeoisie union obtained power in Egypt, Syria and Iraq, forgetting religious cleavages, but soon broke down with tribalism and communalism again taking centre stage. In Syria, after the Baath Party revolution, the Alawites excluded the Sunnis, the Ismailis and the Druze from power. In Lebanon, Chehab's presidency represented a period when middle-class interests converged to create a state, but it was too short-lived to modify the existing social structure.[88]

Conclusion: The Failure of National Reconstruction with a Liberal Policy

According to Jacques Levy, 'The object of political geography is to study the relationship between geographic and political space in the widest sense of the word politics, that is to say, covering all the phenomena governing the organisation of the management and regulation of a collective society'.[89] In the Middle East, the relationship between political regimes and space is mainly based on political patronage. The quality of the relationship between local social groups and the central government influences the national integration of the different territories and their regional organisation. A city is a place of power, and consequently a place that power seeks, as a matter of priority, to control—*a fortiori* in the case of a capital like Beirut. After twenty years of reconstruction, the spatial organisation of Greater Beirut is a direct expression of the political and economic strategies of those elites in Lebanon who have endured. It is an undeniable economic success for the elite, but a failure in terms of a resolution of the Lebanon conflict.[90]

The post-war reconstruction of downtown Beirut by Solidere, and more generally the real estate projects launched in Greater Beirut (residential, commercial and entertainment sites), were sold as investment opportunities for Arab capital and for the Lebanese diaspora. This urban planning, that was inherited from the Gulf and was imposed on a Mediterranean city struggling to recover from the devastation of a dreadful war, is the reflection of Hariri's political governance—an executive supported by foreign capital that was essential for a population impoverished by the war, but also by the effects of 'Dutch disease'.[91] Today, there is a blatant difference between those who benefit from huge profits from a global market and those who subsist on on meagre incomes from the local market.

The liberal economic policy followed by successive Hariri governments increased the divisions within Lebanese society. This situation is most acute in Beirut, where the wealthy of the diaspora as well as the rich dealers related to the Hariri family live alongside the poverty-stricken Palestinian refugees and the impoverished Lebanese social classes. It is this politics of reconstruction in Lebanon that led to the extremely tense political situation that we know today. It has considerably increased the social gaps in the country, especially in Beirut. But is it really a characteristic of Lebanon only? Or is it a feature that accompanies the model of governance in a global world, where the liberal management of urban spaces and the co-optation of local institutions by developers and property speculators, like Rafik Hariri, are the main strategists? In this context, the collapse of Saad Hariri's government in January 2011 should have limited impact on Lebanon's socio-economic outlook. This is because it will be difficult for another government, even if it enjoys several years of stability—which is quite unlikely in Lebanon—to modify Hariri's economic system and go against the forces of globalisation.[92] However, with the new government, dominated by Hizbollah and Aoun's party, businessmen are partly kept out of public affairs and this could potentially allow for a reconstruction of the state. After two decades of systematic predation, the internal political situation is now more favourable to the return of *Chehabism*. Unfortunately, in a corrupt environment like Lebanon,[93] it is impossible to eradicate 'abuse of entrusted power for personal gain'.[94] Rafik Hariri was not the only corrupt politician in Lebanon, but he contributed to the system on a scale according to his massive wealth. That is why the Hizbollah 'counter-society' is as successful in Lebanon as the Communist counter-society was in France after the Second World War,[95] if we want to do a heuristic parallelism.

9

THE MAKING OF A MARTYR

FORGING RAFIK HARIRI'S SYMBOLIC LEGACY

Ward Vloeberghs

Introduction

In the late 1970s, at the age of thirty-five, Rafik Hariri acquired his first private aeroplane.[1] Twenty years later, he owned a Boeing fleet that inspired awe in wealth watchers, plane spotters, and beyond. Whether as a business-man or a politician, extraordinary accomplishments were a recurrent feature of Hariri's remarkable life. Even his death and the period following it are beset by spectacular events, some of which make up Hariri's legacy and form the starting point for this chapter, which will analyse how Hariri's legacy as a statesman and as an entrepreneur has been magnified after his death. It explores the various techniques, strategies and instruments deployed in the myth-making process that surrounded the commemoration of Hariri during the months following his assassination by a massive car bomb on 14 February 2005.

With hindsight, Hariri's dramatic death heralded a new chapter in Leba-non's history. The political turbulence triggered by his abrupt disappearance contributed to the eruption of a devastating war between Hizbollah and Israel on 12 July 2006. It would be a mistake, however, to assume that the glorification of Hariri started only in 2005. Though that date marks the beginning of a transformative period in Lebanese political history, the starting point of the idolisation of Hariri goes back much further, since his reputation had been firmly established by the time he first became prime minister in 1992.

This chapter examines the local political context of Hariri's nascent 'martyrdom' as well as the international ramifications of his assassination before arguing that significant efforts have been made to keep Hariri's legacy at the heart of Lebanese political life. The dynamics that contribute to establishing Hariri's symbolic legacy as a martyr are fourfold and entail processes of appropriation, negotiation, contestation and confirmation. Finally, this chapter will illustrate how these efforts related to Hariri's political programme and link up with the predicament of his successors.

The Birth of a Martyr

One of the key components of Hariri's legacy is his proclaimed 'martyrdom'. While martyrs, especially politically styled martyrs, are not uncommon in Lebanon, their appearance in the public realm is nonetheless a complex phenomenon. Indeed, the concept of martyrdom is recurrent and well established in Lebanese politics, either through political assassination (very few of which have, in fact, been successfully investigated) or through the religious concept of martyrdom that is deeply embedded, and indeed cultivated, by Christian and Muslim Lebanese alike.[2] Yet, in spite of the ubiquity of martyrs, the political use of martyrs in public discourse is far from uniform or straightforward.

As far as Hariri is concerned, his political commemoration was established gradually, through a combination of remarkable societal change, political manoeuvring and historic events. As Volk has suggested, 'martyrs live on in the memory of subsequent generations not only as a "lesson" but also as a profound reassurance of group survival against the odds. It is the specific circumstances that led up to the martyrs' death, the tragedy preceding the dying, that make for a narrative worth (re)telling'.[3]

In Hariri's case, his legacy was given a decisive orientation by the events that dominated the Lebanese political scene immediately after his assassination. The month that followed his untimely death became a constitutive element in Hariri's 'martyrdom' and it marks the public birth and consecration of Hariri as a 'national hero' on Martyrs' Square, between 14 February and 14 March 2005.[4] This succession of unprecedented events in which Lebanese of various confessional backgrounds converged on the central squares of the capital, has been labelled the 'Cedar Revolution', 'Beirut spring' or 'independence Intifada' and represents a critical juncture in Lebanese political history.[5]

According to Volk, 'martyrs became national symbols because they *did not* give up their ethno-religious affiliation; instead, they died and were commemorated as members of their communities who gave the ultimate sacrifice together with members from others'.[6] The explosion that cost Hariri his life also killed more than twenty other Muslims and Christian citizens, some of whom were accompanying his motorcade (such as his bodyguards and his close aide Basil Fuleihan, the former minister of economy) and others who were just bystanders.

Hariri's 'martyrdom' was reinforced by three events that had far-reaching consequences for Lebanon—Hariri's funeral, the resignation of Prime Minister Omar Karami and the withdrawal of Syrian troops from Lebanon. Hariri's funeral on 16 February in which hundreds of thousands participated, produced sensational scenes of popular grief as well as anger at the regime of Lebanese President Emile Lahoud (1998–2007) whom the Hariri family declared *persona non grata* at the ceremony. By contrast, French President Jacques Chirac (1995–2007) and his wife flew in later that day and appeared with Hariri's widow at the freshly arranged gravesite.

Riding on the momentum this created, considerable numbers of young Beirutis launched a sit-in in front of the Martyrs' Statue on 18 February, both in homage to Hariri and in defiance of the government's orders banning demonstrations. Day after day, the protests grew more politicised and anti-Syrian slogans proliferated. It became clear that Hariri's assassination was being exploited by several political actors, including members of the so-called Bristol Gathering.[7]

On 21 February 2005, US President George W. Bush and Chirac released a joint declaration calling on Syria to leave Lebanon and two days later Druze leader Walid Jumblatt revealed details of threatening remarks apparently made by Syrian President Bashar al-Assad to Hariri prior to his death.[8] It is in this context that, on 24 February, the Irish policeman Peter FitzGerald arrived in Beirut to head a preliminary UN investigation which was then followed by the United Nations Independent International Investigation Commission (UNIIIC) and, in turn, the establishment of the STL.

Meanwhile, the opposition called for a general strike and on 28 February 2005 thousands of protesters ignored government instructions prohibiting popular meetings by flocking onto the Martyrs' Square, which they renamed *sahat al-hurriya* (Freedom Square). This culminated into a second apex and the biggest victory so far for the demonstrators when Prime Minister Karami, who had succeeded Hariri as premier in October 2004, was forced to resign. The third defining historic moment came only a few days later, on 5 March, when President Bashar al-Assad announced a two-phased withdrawal of Syrian troops.

In response to the political escalation at the Martyrs' Square and to clarify its own stance, Hizbollah called for a demonstration to be held on 8 March, the anniversary of the Baath Party's coming to power in Syria in 1963. The demonstration sported no party imagery, carrying only national Lebanese flags. Half a million people gathered on Riad al-Solh Square, next to the Martyrs' Square, carrying portraits of Assad to express their gratitude for helping to bring stability to Lebanon during the past twenty-nine years.[9] Participants heard Hizbollah Secretary-General Hassan Nasrallah denounce American interference and criticise Resolution 1559 as Israeli-inspired.[10] It was the first important and most visible testimony since Hariri's death that the Lebanese were not uniformly supportive of the anti-Syrian discourse.

In response, the Bristol Gathering staged a trans-communitarian mobilisation in reply to Hizbollah's demonstration of popular, mainly Shia support. On Monday 14 March 2005, Lebanon witnessed the largest public rally in its history. It has been claimed that one out of every four Lebanese answered the appeal to participate in a gathering that left a profound impression on millions of people's collective memory.[11] Cheering crowds chanted *hurriya-siyada-istiqlal* (Liberty, Sovereignty, Independence) or *haqiqa, hurriya, wihda wataniya* (Truth, Liberty, National Unity), thus contributing to startling scenes of euphoric nationalism. It is worth recalling, however, that although it has been portrayed as the expression of accumulated anger, the 14 March demonstrations were first and foremost a reaction to what had happened a week earlier for without 8 March there would have been no 14 March.

National or International Martyr?

As shown, Hariri's assassination generated an unprecedented outcry among Lebanese Sunnis who rallied against Syria. Thus, the maelstrom of events had transformed Rafik Hariri—who was increasingly being referred to as *ar-ra'is ash-shahid*, the martyr president—from a moderate Sunni politician into a Lebanese 'martyr', celebrated for his contribution to the liberation from Syrian occupation. For most of his career, however, Hariri had been a pragmatic Lebanese politician who understood the strategic importance of compromise with Syria, as his numerous friendships in and visits to Damascus illustrate. However, Hariri's assassination was soon to generate a feeling of communitarian solidarity among Lebanese Sunnis who felt collectively threatened. This 'deepened sense of sectarian persecution' led to a reconfiguration of the local as well as the regional political landscape.[12]

Secondly, if Hariri's career was marked by a sense of the spectacular, his fondness of the big, bigger, biggest is apparent even in the way he died and the repercussions his death triggered. In effect, an international enquiry and subsequently a special tribunal were set up under the aegis of the UN to investigate the circumstances and perpetrators of the crime, thereby setting a controversial legal precedent.[13] In a sense, the historic campaign unleashed by Hariri's assassination bears witness to Hariri's pervasive posthumous power. Nonetheless, while every community in Lebanon has its martyr(s), Rafik Hariri's international stature was too big to be ignored.

The weeks of initial euphoria in early 2005 were soon eviscerated by a series of political assassinations that spread fear among the 14 March parliamentarians, who eventually took refuge in the Phoenicia Intercontinental Hotel, ironically just opposite the site where Rafik Hariri was assassinated.[14] Hariri's death also provoked a new struggle for power in Lebanon among regional and international actors.

The political vacuum created by Syria's withdrawal from Lebanon was matched by an increasingly acrimonious conflict between two geopolitical axes pitted once more against each other on Lebanese territory.[15] On the one hand, Chirac's diplomats saw Hariri's assassination as an opportunity to reconcile with the US administration following a row over military intervention in Iraq in 2003. The shared resentment towards the Syrian regime aligned both of these Western powers with major Sunni regimes such as Saudi Arabia, Jordan and Egypt—all of whom joined and supported the 14 March politicians in their battle against the 8 March camp. That coalition itself was, on the other hand, being viewed as a proxy for the ever more assertive Damascus-Tehran axis that featured extensions from Iraq (Muqtada al-Sadr) to Lebanon (Hizbollah) and Palestine (Hamas).

Forging a Martyr's Legacy

These national and international shifts are insufficient, however, to fully explain the significance of Hariri's symbolic legacy as a martyr because they do not inform us about how Hariri's hagiography, carefully crafted around the notion of his 'martyrdom', unfolded. In order to fully illustrate this we must look at various means (understood as resources) and various locations or scenes that participate in moulding and nurturing the exceptional status of Hariri as a modern-day martyr.

The presence of visual, rhetorical and financial means which often hold political and/or religious connotations is a recurrent characteristic in the development of Hariri's symbolic legacy and can be understood by analysing four aspects of his political person: processes of appropriation; instances of negotiation; practices of contestation; and instruments of confirmation.

Processes of Appropriation

One of the key components that fostered these dynamics consisted of physical transformations of the built environment. Some of these spatial modifications contributed to develop what Volk calls a 'memorial'. In Lebanon, Volk contends, 'memorials of Muslim and Christian martyrs successfully, if temporarily, generate attachments to a national community, which is why political elites continued to build them'.[16]

The most obvious memorial to honour Rafik Hariri is his commemorative tomb, known as *darih*, which has been gradually developed into a shrine.[17] Immediately after the assassination of Hariri, his family acquired a plot of land to provide a site for Hariri's final resting place. To accommodate the funerary complex, a spacious white shelter was erected next to the Muhammad al-Amin mosque which Hariri himself had commissioned on Martyrs' Square.

The choice to erect the burial site on this particular location and not, as many expected, in his native town of Sidon, where Hariri had already commissioned two commemorative mosques (one for each of his parents), was part of the family's political strategy to emphasise his sultanesque stature. Crucially, the positioning of Hariri's tomb, which stands on its own, and the graves of his bodyguards, which are lined-up in a separate chamber, was by no means coincidental. Its location complies with aesthetical (in the visual axis of the Martyr's Statue), political (next to the mosque, with access to the square) as well as religious (aligned to Mecca) guidelines. The importance of intervention by the family and the appropriative dimension of its decision can hardly be ignored or overstated and may indeed be an early expression of a will to reconfigure Beirut's emblematic square and the whole of downtown Beirut as a neo-Ottoman assertion of Sunni power through Hariri-related edifices:

One noteworthy evolution has been the steady development of the tomb into an ever more elaborate shrine where activities of remembrance exhibit both political and religious dimensions. It is important to bear in mind that the physical appearance of the *darih* mirrored the prevailing political climate through constant shifts in the political ornamentation surrounding the tomb.

Thus, one could argue that the 'martyr Hariri' underwent a metamorphosis. During the first weeks and months the trans-confessional dimension of Hariri's martyrdom was being stressed and most slogans and images sported visual and verbal references to various religious traditions and the strong Druze and Christian partisanship was illustrated by the participation of Walid Jumblatt, Amine Gemayel and other politicians allied to Hariri. So much so, that Hariri almost became a national hero and a trans-confessional saint, conceptualised here as *Mar Rafiq* (Saint Rafik).[18]

However, as sectarian tensions in Lebanon increased from 2006 onwards, the 'martyr president', as well as his gravesite, rapidly lost their national character and gained distinctive Sunni references and thus became symbols of confessional belonging and partisan power.

The transformation of the gravesite has been operated through numerous and on-going (re)arrangements of ornamentation and glorification items on display around Hariri's tomb. Frequent visits by dignitaries that established the tomb as an important platform from where political speech was launched or through the use of religious paraphernalia (prayer booklets, framed verses, Quranic recitations), the shift clearly went from an inclusive attitude towards a more exclusively Sunni one.

Perhaps the most interesting characteristic in this evolution of the tomb was how it became part of a process of appropriation—defined here as the process of gradually taking possession of something that initially does not formally belong to the actor but who eventually comes to be seen as its owner. This process of making something (material or immaterial) one's own may be accomplished in various ways—physically, legally, symbolically, violently or peacefully.

In the case of Hariri's tomb, this process was quite obvious. Although the plot initially belonged to Solidere[19] and came into the possession of the

Hariri family only after his assassination, the site was transformed almost overnight into a memorial with an international radiance that has, ever since, been developed into a major component of Hariri's martyrdom.[20] It is essential, however, to note that the *darih* does not fulfil this task on its own. In fact, both the tomb and the mosque play that role, which is why they should be understood as jointly constituting Hariri's mausoleum. Both locations are not only being paired visually, the tomb has also been organically connected to the mosque via a direct passage.

The elaborate gravesite is an eloquent illustration of the practices of appropriation that contribute to the shaping of Hariri's symbolic posthumous legacy. The choice of location plays an essential role in strengthening Hariri's dominance over the Beirut city centre. It is no coincidence therefore that, at the ambitious two-day inauguration ceremony of the Muhammad al-Amin mosque in October 2008, his son Saad declared the mosque to be the coronation (*tatwijan*) of his father's reconstruction efforts in Beirut.[21]

Hariri's involvement in the construction of the Muhammad al-Amin mosque can indeed be seen as another process of appropriation, albeit one operated by himself during his lifetime. Plans to construct a major place of worship had been simmering for almost a century and a half. In 1853, the Sunni establishment developed a plot of land offered by the Ottoman sultan into a small prayer hall referred to as *zawiyat Abi Nasr*.[22] Although early plans for a prestigious mosque were cherished by the local community, throughout the decades the project remained a collective dream due to lack of means, competing actors and internal bickering over the tutelage of the *zawiya*. In spite of far-reaching fundraising efforts including Saudi King Faisal and Egyptian President Nasser (then rivals), a decisive commitment and the indispensable finances failed to materialise.

It was only around the turn of the millennium, after decades of delay, that Hariri became publicly involved in the project—reluctantly at first, later as its main protagonist. A convergence of interests with the Mufti of Lebanon produced the breakthrough when Hariri made the construction of the Muhammad al-Amin mosque in *his* reconstructed city centre a priority. Triggered by political competitors in the context of the 2000 elections, Hariri sought to overcome all technical, legal and financial obstacles in his determination to attach his name to the project and to erect the long-awaited place of worship which, at the same time, would increase his religious credentials as a devout, powerful and generous Sunni leader (*zaim*).[23]

Following discussions at his residence in Qoraytem, Hariri secured an agreement with members of the Muhammad al-Amin Association in order to resolve its legal dispute with *Dar al-Fatwa* (the main Sunni authority in Lebanon regarding matters of Islamic law, including properties) and pledged to cover the full costs of the construction.[24] The mosque was completed in 2006. Although Hariri did not live to see its completion, the Muhammad al-Amin mosque became a majestic place of worship, boasting a distinctive silhouette that established the building as an intended benchmark of Islamic architecture in the most symbolically valuable part of Beirut. Because of its longstanding history, its prominent location (on the corner of Martyrs' Square and Emir Bashir Street) and because of the prestige involved the mosque also became a building of (communal as well as personalised) power.

It is possible, therefore, to look at the mosque as an instance of patronage by Hariri to his constituency and as a manoeuvre to sideline Sunni rivals. Not only did Hariri succeed where many others had failed but, by turning the plans for the mosque into a tangible reality, he made a longstanding communal aspiration bear fruit through an act of personal appropriation. With his decisive intervention, Hariri—who had long before started to look for a location in Beirut to erect a monumental mosque—took over the project and transformed the urban environment in a pervasive way that crowned his rise to power in Beirut and in Lebanon as a whole.

Instances of Negotiation

It took four years (2002–6) to construct the Muhammad al-Amin mosque, and this process contributed significantly to the enhancement of Hariri's symbolic legacy in Beirut. These examples have to do with what could be termed 'instances of negotiation'. Negotiation can be understood here as a practice which occurs when actors with different aims, interests or views engage in a formal discussion, or any other form of communication, in their attempts to settle an issue. While negotiations occur in various situations and can take a variety of forms (verbal or not, material or not), this chapter will look at two particular instances of negotiation. The first is architectural with political ramifications, whereas the second pertains to a political ideology which affected the project for the construction of the 'Hariri' mosque, as the Muhammad al-Amin mosque has occasionally (erroneously but tellingly) been named.

First we will consider the complex relationship between the Muhammad al-Amin mosque and the Maronite cathedral of St George, which stands adjacent to the mosque's western facade.[25] Although the mosque has been presented as the symbol of exemplary interfaith coexistence at the time of its inauguration, it is hard to ignore the visual dominance of the mosque over the cathedral. Indeed it seems difficult to deny a confessional connotation to the mosque, since the project originated to counterbalance a gift of land to the Lazarist sisters and since the mosque largely took shape in coordination (or lack thereof, according to some)[26] with the Maronite cathedral.

The mosque's strategic location does not only translate into physical prominence of the Sunni community within the Lebanese capital, it also operates on the symbolic level since the mosque has been said to 'dwarf the cathedral'.[27] So evident has this dominance been that some Christian Lebanese view it as a humiliation, which triggered architectural retaliation by the Maronite clergy in the form of adding a campanile to the St George cathedral that will match the height of the mosque's minarets.

Besides being a prism to analyse inter-communal relations, the construction of the Muhammad al-Amin mosque also represents an important expression of Hariri's religious identity and, thus, a key component of the memorial that enshrines his martyrdom. The very fact that Hariri succeeded in erecting the mosque at that specific location, and to have it built according to this particular scheme with its four minarets and its distinctive neo-Ottoman style, says a great deal about the power he wielded at the time. If this first instance of negotiation highlights a dynamic which intervened partly before and partly after Hariri's death, the second example relates exclusively to Hariri's lifetime.

In as far as architecture can be said to be a concrete expression of a society's opinions and preferences, the construction of the Muhammad al-Amin mosque and the subsequent installation of Hariri's tomb is the most tangible evidence of the defeat of alternative narratives and competing visions of society.

The construction of the mosque with Hariri (and, to a lesser extent the Mufti) as its main commissioners also represents a symbolic victory of Hariri over his opponents at the time. Although at first it may seem somewhat irrelevant for the mosque project, the animosity between Hariri and President Lahoud must be recalled here. In fact, Lahoud encouraged potential opponents of Hariri, such as Salim al-Hoss (a leading Sunni politician, prime minister between December 1998 and October 2000) and Prince al-Walid bin Talal (an influential Saudi-Lebanese entrepreneur), to get involved in the Muhammad al-Amin project. This contributed to Hariri's decision to take possession of the project according to his own preferences.[28]

Underneath Lahoud's attempts to counter Hariri in his own backyard—the Solidere perimeter—lay deepened antagonisms between two diametrically opposed political projects. The political discourse deployed by Lahoud, a former army chief of staff who had overseen the reconstitution of the Lebanese Armed Forces (LAF), evolved around the necessity to strengthen state institutions. Over time, this insistence on regulation by the Lebanese Republic translated into a systematic beefing-up of the security apparatus, which hampered Hariri and his political allies, as well as his business partners who had set up new or parallel administrative bodies while championing liberalism and mercantile policies in their more lenient approach to bureaucratic rules. Though enforced with Syrian backing, this opposition between Hariri and Lahoud (who supported Hizbollah's resistance project) was essentially the reflection of a recurrent divide in Lebanon, between a 'merchant republic' and a 'militant republic'.[29]

As this cleavage indicates, during part of his premiership, Hariri had to share power with a president opposed to his policies. In the case of the mosque, Hariri emerged victorious once he gained dominant control over the various stakeholders, thus allowing him to increase his visual presence in central Beirut. But as this last instance of negotiation also indicates, Hariri's projects at times generated fierce opposition.

Practices of Contestation

The dynamic of contestation is a third factor central to Hariri's symbolic legacy. Paradoxical as it may seem, such practices of contestation—even though enacted by opponents—eventually contribute to shape and legitimise the hagiography of Rafik Hariri to the same extent as the practices of appropriation and negotiation described above.

Contestation can be understood as an action which formally objects to something, be it tangible or not. A contestation entails an expression of disagreement, a challenging opinion or counter-claim on any given matter, by verbal or by other means. In this case, one form of opposition affects Hariri's mausoleum directly, while another one confronts his legacy from afar. Although the first one is situated after Hariri's death and the second one started before 2005, both practices of contestation have in common their use of urban space as a political instrument.

The first dynamic of contestation occurred in the wake of the July 2006 war, after Hizbollah and its allies within the 8 March coalition, which includes Michel Aoun's FPM since February 2006, mounted an increasingly harsh opposition campaign against the government led by Fuad Siniora (2005–9). Having blamed the cabinet for its poor handling of the 2006 war and accused some of its members of collaboration with Israeli attempts to crush the 'Islamic resistance in Lebanon' (the military branch of Hizbollah) during the hostilities, 8 March politicians launched a protest on 1 December 2006. They occupied Beirut's central squares and surrounded the *Grand Sérail*, the prime minister's official residence, in a bid to oust Siniora, a protagonist within Hariri's *Tayyar al-Mustaqbal* (Future Movement). The initially cheerful atmosphere of the sit-in had lost most of its vigour by the time the suffocating campaign ended its deadlock of Beirut Central District, some eighteen months later, as part of the Doha Agreement in May 2008.

The Doha Agreement followed a series of security breaches in which armed militants of Hizbollah assisted by gunmen affiliated with other former militias took control of several strategic positions of West Beirut. With remarkable ease, Hizbollah took control of predominantly Sunni neighbourhoods loyal to Hariri's *Mustaqbal*. Other parts of Lebanon (e.g. the Shouf Mountains, Jumblatt's Druze fiefdom) also came under attack from Hizbollah gunmen, with mixed results.[30]

The operations of early May 2008, which came in reaction to a government decision to dismantle parts of a Hizbollah-controlled parallel telecommunications network at the Rafic Hariri International Airport, claimed several lives and traumatised many Lebanese who felt the party had forsaken its promise never to turn its weapons against fellow citizens. Although further escalation was prevented through a much needed high-level reconciliation agreement brokered in Doha, Qatar, the months that followed failed to repair the gap of mistrust between the camps of 8 and 14 March. Most importantly, political disagreement had, at least initially, been expressed through spatial practices.

This evolution is among the more significant shifts to have occurred in Lebanon since Hariri's death. If the 'Independence Intifada' has been a pioneering experience in this respect, the year and a half long sit-in staged by the 8 March coalition in order to further its own political objectives and obstruct the 14 March agenda has taken this practice of contestation to new heights. The occupation of central urban space as an expression of societal disagreement has thus *de facto* been institutionalised in Lebanon.[31]

What is important here is that the dynamic of contestation instigated by the sit-in impacted on the commemorative space occupied by Hariri's mausoleum. The contestation led to a 'spatialisation of power', whereby urban space becomes an expression of political identity and confessional solidarity. This, in turn, resulted in the reinforcement of the space around the Muhammad al-Amin mosque and Hariri's gravesite as a sector under 14 March control.

This tangible visual and spatial opposition produced spectacular scenes on 14 February 2007, when the throngs of supporters who gathered on the lower part of Martyrs' Square on the occasion of the second annual commemoration of Hariri's assassination were separated by barbed wire from 8 March supporters (mainly Aounists) who had set up their tents on the upper part of the same square.

This spatialisation of political and communal power expressed through urban space is what Haugbolle, when discussing the 2005 events, has termed a 'geography of communitarian divisions'.[32] It is noteworthy that this dynamic, which became clearly visible in central Beirut after 2005, resembles to some extent the 'process of sanctifying sectarian lands', described by Khuri as a characteristic of sects in a multi-confessional context.[33] Furthermore, this spatialisation of power also extends into other neighbourhoods of Beirut, as shown by Harb when she describes the consolidation of a political territory by Hizbollah and Amal in the southern suburbs of Beirut.[34]

The transformations of downtown Beirut through interactions between 'spatial performances and symbolic actions' as described by Haugbolle, were the prelude to a dynamic that continues until today.[35] In fact, political mobilisation has not stopped. On the contrary, over the past few years, the Hariri complex has gradually taken over Beirut Central District by transforming it into a fiefdom.

This stronghold has been systematically fortified through physical interventions which partially echo Hizbollah's urban (re-)arrangements in the southern suburbs but which are at least as much the result of a sustained campaign implemented to pursue the (continuously redefined) battle of the 'martyr president'. While some spatial expressions of Hariri's power may have originated in the dialectics between protestation and reaffirmation, the same dialectics turned some practices of contestation into instruments of confirmation.

Instruments of Confirmation

This dynamic of confirmation is the fourth and final factor in this analysis of the elements constitutive of Hariri's symbolic legacy. Confirmation—literally to make firm—is understood as the action(s) or indication(s) showing, strengthening or reinforcing something that has been said or decided. The process of confirmation that reinforces Rafik Hariri's visibility is manifold and includes a number of practices—not all of them mutated practices of contestation—which may be seen as attributes of power, developing political significance and territorial exclusivity. It is impossible to cover all of these practices of confirmation, but two major tools of this confirmation process stand out. Though one may think of instruments of confirmation devised during Hariri's lifetime (e.g. his charitable foundation), most of the instruments analysed here were introduced after his assassination.

Apart from the annual 14 February commemorative events[36] and the 2005 renaming of the airport, the first important instrument of confirmation includes the installation of Rafik Hariri statues at two strategic locations in Beirut. The first, in the Ayn al-Mreisseh neighbourhood, stands amidst a roundabout in-between the Phoenicia and the St George hotels. This statue was unveiled on 14 February 2008, at the third annual commemoration of Hariri's assassination. At the same time, about a 100 metres further west, another sculpture was unveiled. Standing in the middle of the road, on the exact location of the assassination, this structure is supposed to light up daily at 12:55, the exact time of the blast that killed Hariri.

A second statue was unveiled on 31 March 2011 in front of the *Grand Sérail*, which Hariri had restored at his own expense. This impressive statue of Hariri now overlooks a multi-level water garden officially called the Hariri Memorial Garden, designed by Vladimir Djurovic who also conceived the award-winning Samir Kassir Square.

This recent evolution, besides being a practice confirming Hariri's personal legacy, is to be inscribed in a local tradition which has seen eminent politicians such as Emir Bashir, Riad al-Solh, Bishara al-Khoury and others honoured as distinguished Lebanese statesmen. However, as the projected Hariri Memorial Library in the vicinity of the mausoleum and the myriad banners and posters (almost invariably in Lebanese dialect)[37] suggest, this dynamic of installing Hariri-related artefacts is part of a wider tendency that consists of tagging urban space with a political identity. As indicated, these practices occur in relation and reaction to other political actors who engage in similar dynamics elsewhere in Beirut. This leads us to consider the second example of the confirmation dynamic which further explores the links between politics and built fabric.

The focal point of Sunni politics in Beirut is no longer Hariri's palatial residence in Qoraytem. Neither has the torch of symbolic leadership returned to Mussaytbeh, the communal stronghold during the heyday of the Salam family that preceded Hariri's gradual monopolisation of Sunni Beirut.[38] During the past few years, the confessional centre of gravitation has shifted to Centre House in the Beirut Central District where Saad Hariri has taken up residence. The move was not accidental, and underscores Saad Hariri's ambition to fulfil his father's political programme. The shift from Qoraytem to Centre House is therefore a highly important transition and epitomises the installation of what can be termed the 'Hariri dynasty', the emergence of which is among the most significant developments as we reflect on the 2005–12 period.[39]

After he was officially appointed as his father's political successor on 20 April 2005, Saad Hariri also inherited his father's office in Qoraytem, from where he initially operated. Later on, he moved his political and personal headquarters to downtown Beirut. This transfer was preceded by the installation of the state-of-the-art premises of Future News, a sister channel of the Hariri-controlled Future Television network, at the entrance of the Qantari neighbourhood. The television studios, which were attacked in May 2008, are located just opposite the former presidential palace which Hariri also refurbished at his own expense. The transition was further accompanied by the formal relocation of Saad Hariri and his family to Centre House in the Wadi Bou Jamil sector, where his residence is located just below the prime-ministerial offices of the *Grand Sérail* and next to the recently restored Magen Abraham Synagogue (possibly to emphasise Hariri's religious tolerance).

Crucial though these visual markers as practices of confirmation are to perpetuating Hariri's symbolic legacy, the unfolding cult is not limited to the elaboration of a sanctuary devoted to him. Neither is it spatially confined to Martyrs' Square and its surroundings. In fact, the dynamic goes both further geographically and deeper on a structural level. In this respect, the tribulations of the STL represent an interesting case in the series of events described here.

In fact, the STL is a fine example of how Hariri's legacy can serve as a basis for contestation and confirmation at the same time. While the STL's opponents denounce it as yet another Western interference in Lebanese affairs, the tribunal's supporters defend it as a historic occasion to end impunity. Moreover, the STL is not only a very convenient framework to seek attention for Hariri's legacy on the international public level, it is also a constant reminder of the 'injustice' done to Hariri and his allies. Given Volk's cogent observation that 'martyrs' narratives with their unambiguous assignment of right and wrong, provide their own form of justice and some consolation for mourning communities'[40] it should not be a surprise that the STL and the quest for (an ever more elusive and contested) 'truth' (*haqiqa*) has been at the core of the rhetoric developed around Hariri's martyrdom from 2005 onwards. In fact, every single procedural step in the work of the tribunal has been presented as a vindication of Hariri supporters. Significantly, even the STL was given spatial expressions since calls for 'the truth' appeared on digital counters and billboards throughout Beirut. As such, the STL clearly is an instrument of confirmation.

However, though it was initially an instrument of confirmation, over time, the STL also became a major object of contestation. Because the STL was reportedly targeting Syria, and later implicated members of Hizbollah, it gradually became the centre of controversy between Lebanese politicians and their regional allies. The result, and in contrast to its use in the hands of 14 March politicians, the STL has had a controversial impact on the local (and certainly the regional) level as a consequence of the systematic denunciations of 8 March representatives. The STL thus shows that practices of contestation do not systematically turn into instruments of confirmation but that opposite mutations exists as well and that some examples can actually be an expression of both dynamics.

Overall, the development of the STL as an instrument of confirmation owes much to the impetus of the Hariri family and to the advocacy of Rafik Hariri's political successor. The very appointment of Saad Hariri as political successor and the accompanying political dynasty have perhaps been the most effective ways to pursue Hariri's political project and can thus be seen as a third—or fourth, if we include the STL—instrument of confirmation.

Since he inherited his family's influence and patronage, Saad Hariri has been intensely involved in promoting his own position and his own turf in

Lebanese politics. Having led his coalition to victory in two successive elections (2005, 2009) and enjoying solid international backing, Saad Hariri became prime minister on 9 November 2009. His first official visit to Damascus in late December 2009 indicated a willingness to put national interest ahead of personal grievances but dismayed some of his followers.

However, mounting tensions within Lebanon about the status and the proceedings of the STL started to paralyse Saad Hariri's cabinet before it had completed its first year. On 12 January 2011, just as he was being received by US President Obama, news broke that eleven ministers had submitted their resignation, thus in effect toppling the Hariri-led government. The blow was all the more brutal since the Hizbollah-led opposition designated Tripoli-based Najib Mikati, a Syrian-backed wealthy Sunni politician who had formed an electoral alliance with Hariri in the 2009 elections, as its candidate to form a new cabinet. It looked as if Hariri, with his insistent support for the STL, had been outsmarted by political peers.[41] As the dynastic aspirations of the Hariri family suffered a severe blow, its members prepared for a long battle towards recovery.

Among Hariri's supporters, who denounced Mikati as a traitor, his 'coup' triggered a 'day of anger' with demonstrations degenerating into skirmishes in several Sunni neighbourhoods in Tripoli, Sidon and Beirut on 24 January 2011. A day later however, Saad Hariri, further handicapped by the tiresome cleavage between the 8 and 14 March camps, was confined to watch from abroad as President Michel Sleiman officially appointed Mikati as the prime minister-designate after a parliamentary vote gave the latter a majority of sixty-eight MPs, Walid Jumblatt's bloc having split over the issue.[42] Saad Hariri stayed on as caretaker prime minister until a new cabinet was confirmed by parliament in July 2011. By then, however, parts of the STL's indictment had been released and the political rhetoric had reached new heights.

Conclusion

The period that transformed former Lebanese Prime Minister Rafik Hariri (1944–2005) into a 'hero of liberation' and a worshipped 'martyr president' was not static and linear, but rather multi-faceted and heterogeneous. By adopting a technical and practical perspective that focuses on the micro level but does not ignore international ramifications, four key factors which contributed to the development of Hariri's political and symbolic legacy have been identified. These four dynamics include lifetime as well as post-humous practices of appropriation, negotiation, contestation and confirmation, most often displaying both political and religious characteristics, either of which may be emphasised depending on contextual imperatives.

While the glorification of Hariri had started before his violent death, due to his dramatic assassination his legacy took a decisive turn following the events that prevailed on the Lebanese political scene after February 2005. To start with, processes of appropriation and negotiation led to the installation of a semi-sacred commemorative space entirely dedicated to Hariri in one of Beirut's most prestigious locations. This mausoleum and the cult attached to it evolved considerably over time. Most significantly, his legacy has always been reformulated in interaction with the developments on the local and regional level. Thus, the shift from a national, inclusive memorial into a landmark bearing a more confessional connotation must be seen as an interesting indication that Hariri's legacy reflected a polarisation that was fostered, *inter alia* by the rise and fall of the 14 March coalition, thereby suggesting that it can serve as a useful socio-political prism to analyse Lebanese realities.

The importance of the STL and the meaningful transformations in the city's architectural environment in forging Hariri's political and symbolic legacy, on which his successor capitalises, can hardly be exaggerated. It is indeed crucial to understand the 'spatialisation of communal power' in and around the axis linking Ayn al-Mreisseh—Qantari—Solidere, as well as the gradual reconfiguration of the Martyrs' Square, as instruments confirming Hariri's heritage. Confronted with the slow (and sometimes erratic) proceedings of the STL, Hariri's political heir(s) and allies have not been idly awaiting the court's indictments, but seeking to complete the physical inscription of Hariri's legacy according to their own plans. While this occasionally sparked protests and riots, several of these practices of contestation eventually ended up redefining and reinforcing the objectives of Hariri's 'martyrdom'.

Inevitably, however, the political use of Hariri's legacy leads to ambiguities and contradictions in discourse. As the events of January 2011 and, to a lesser extent, the developments of the 'Arab Spring' have illustrated, Hariri's heritage is neither stable nor clear-cut, but rather a malleable narrative. For example, the political discourse following the ousting of Saad Hariri's cabinet included fear-mongering and the portrayal of Hizbollah as a state-within-the-state. This, in turn, led to Saad Hariri's positioning as a Lebanese politician defending a strong and democratic state, aiming to contain internal and external threats. That image, however, does not only contradict the political programme of his father who, during much of his years in office, tried to boost parallel bodies, such as the CDR, in order to circumvent bureaucratic obstacles while putting the country back on track. Saad Hariri's 2011 public profile as the guardian of potent state institutions also sounds somehow similar to the political programme of President Lahoud and his acolytes when they were denouncing the clientelist practices and mercantile policies operated by his father, the late Rafik Hariri.

As the Syrian crisis haunting the regime of Bashar al-Assad further polarised the Lebanese and put domestic politics on hold in late 2011–2012, one was left to conclude that transactions between Lebanese merchants and militants rarely result in peaceful prosperity.

PART IV

TRUTH, COEXISTENCE AND JUSTICE

10

'HISTORY' AND 'MEMORY' IN LEBANON SINCE 2005

BLIND SPOTS, EMOTIONAL ARCHIVES AND HISTORIOGRAPHIC CHALLENGES

Sune Haugbolle

Introduction

Since the end of the Lebanese civil war in 1990, much ink has been spilt on the various ways in which the war has been repressed, forgotten, remembered and represented by the Lebanese population, the Lebanese state and the creative classes of 'memory makers' who produce exhibitions, hearings, journalism and art relating to the war and—on a meta level—to the memory of the war. While much current academic work has thus been devoted to the making and unmaking of social memory, and to the politics surrounding attempts to administer and influence public forms of remembrance, the question could be asked whether academics' obsession with memory has not to some degree overshadowed a sustained historiographic debate over the actual events of the war. The same could be said about the situation on the ground in Lebanon, where the amount of resources and energy devoted to 'memory' events overshadows actual historical work on the war. There is of course a wealth of literature on the civil war, but much of it focuses on the political events, groups and actors. In comparison, social history has been subject to much less inquiry. Questions such as how ordinary people experienced the war, how urban spaces changed, how cultural life adapted and responded to mass violence, and other aspects of quotidian life during the war, have largely been dealt with under the category of 'memory' (*dhakira*), which refers at once to the legacy of the war and to a set of arguments about what has (not) been done with that legacy, and what should be done. 'Memory' has been the subject of art installations, books, films and other cultural representations. Put bluntly, the way in which the legacy of the war has been dealt with has produced a dichotomy where 'history' of the war has come to be equated with political events, whereas 'memory' has been construed as cultural production and representations of individual memories from the war period. This dichotomy raises a number of questions, which this chapter will address. How academically sound and useful for historiograhic debates is cultural memory work, and how can it contribute to filling the blind spots in our historical knowledge of the war? Is it possible to expand the realm of 'history' to also include elements of 'memory', and if so, how can such a process begin? Can scholars of Lebanese history and society learn from memory work? Through analyses of significant memory productions since 2005, I suggest new ways of approaching the topic of the civil war. I propose that, if approached with a healthy dose of scepticism regarding the kind of sources it presents, Lebanese memory work can provide a rich 'emotional archive' of quotidian war experiences for social history of the civil war. By emotional archive I mean that memory productions have stored and articulated various ways in which the war affected people, and that these representations can be systematised and hence be the object of historical work. Conversely, debates among professional historians about particular events in the war, the interpretations of which continue to divide social and political groups today, can, and should, form the basis for discussions in Lebanon about the war and its meaning today.

Memories of the Civil War and Production of History in Lebanon

Several scholars[1] have traced how Lebanese intellectuals, artists and activists since the mid-1990s have campaigned for a public process of memorialisation in protest against what they saw as amnesia perpetuated by the Lebanese state. Although an abundance of films, articles, books and events have been produced, it is an open question to what extent they succeeded in breaking the silence on a national level, or even more ambitiously, 'breaking the cycle of violence',[2] which is the purported end goal of such activities. In 2012, seven years after the Syrian army left Lebanon, the country has been through a series of dramatic events, from the killing of former Prime Minister Rafik Hariri, the ensuing 'Independence Intifada', the 2006 war between Israel and Hizbollah, prolonged government crises, Sunni-Shia tensions and a looming confrontation over the STL. Debates about the civil war have continued, but so have many of the fundamental problems which critics of state-sponsored amnesia pointed to in the 1990s. A crucial hindrance for free, public debate about the war is the fact that the vast majority of Lebanese continue to live within the confines of sectarian neighbourhoods, associations, schools and even media. Sectarian divisions and patterns of sociability in effect reproduce skewed historiographies of the war. In defiance of sectarian narratives about the war, civil society groups, media and, not least, artists have since 2005 continued to promote various forms of memory work aimed at countering what they see as misinformation and distorted interpretations of the past. As a result, despite much talk about collective amnesia, there is now not just a lively public (albeit rather elitist) debate about the war and about the difficulties of remembering and representing it, but also a considerable history of such a debate. This means that new participants in the debate perform on the basis of older argumentation in more or less conscious and critical ways. Most commonly this argumentation is not, it should be stressed, supported by academic studies of the war, but is based largely on particular narratives about the war and about memory. Debates about the war have changed since 2005 as a result of the changed political climate, but also in many ways remained within the same thematic frames that emerged in the 1990s—that the war had been repressed as a result of a concerted effort by political elites to impose a state-sanctioned amnesia, and that it was the role of civil society and cultural production to shake the population out of its lull and make it face up to the past, all for the sake of Lebanon's well-being.

The debate goes further back than the mid-1990s. In fact, civil war memorialisation begins during the war. Films by the likes of Maroun Baghdadi,[3] Jean Chamoun and Mai Masri, and novels by Elias Khoury, not to mention the rich but understudied genre of war-time songs, or the equally understudied Lebanese press during the war, all deal with the social and individual effects of war. After the war, other genres like the experimental video film, collective research projects, installations and web-based art, have added to the huge body of war-related work.[4] There is of course a fundamental difference between work produced during the civil war, the main function of which was to register the events and make sense of them as they unfolded, and post-war work that looks back and tries to come to terms with the war. At the same time, the different periods of memory productions are connected by the fact that contemporary artists are aware of former traditions and approaches to representation of war and memory, which makes it possible to view the corpus of works about the war as a totality. From this intertextuality follows also a keen awareness of competing discourses about the war and their political and ideological anchoring. On an institutional level, several generations of artists are bound together by influential artists' groups, most notably Ashkal Alwan (The Lebanese Association for Plastic Arts). Like any cultural field, Lebanon's art and culture scene is fraught with political and generational divisions, which mirror ideological schisms in society.[5] Some artists have even questioned whether the dominant position of civil war themes in Lebanese art can be justified. Still, the notion that an unresolved bundle of memories surround the civil war, and that it is the unique task of artists and intellectuals to enlighten the nation, continues to be the primary public script for the Lebanese intelligentsia's view of their society and its history—and of themselves.

Nancy

Since 2005, and not least during the height of sectarian tensions from 2006 to 2008, art projects have become expressively designed to warn of renewed sectarian conflict. A humorous example is Nada Sahnaoui's April 2008 installation *Haven't 15 Years of Hiding in the Toilets Been Enough?*, in which the artist—a veteran of war-related art—positioned rows of toilets in Martyr's Square, downtown Beirut, as a reminder of the absurdity of repeating something as devastating, and 'shitty', as a civil war.[6] Another significant cultural production about the civil war and memory that exemplifies the way in which the Lebanese cultural scene has dealt with the war in recent years, is Rabih Mroué's play *How Nancy Wished That Everything Was an April Fool's Joke*.[7] The play is of particular interest here because it treats the relation between memory and history. Originally scheduled to open in August 2007, this internationally acclaimed play was initially banned by an interior ministry censorship board for its treatment of delicate political issues, but eventually went ahead. For several participants in memory projects that I have spoken to the censorship incident confirmed that the Lebanese state, even in its post-Syrian version, continues to promote a politics of amnesia, ostensibly because it is essentially made up of the same political class as during the 1990–2005 period. While there may be some truth to this, it is worth noting that the play did eventually pass censorship, partly due to a public outcry, but also due to the intervention of Culture Minister Tarek Mitri.[8] In fact, very few cultural productions have been banned since 2005 because they broach 'public amnesia' regarding the war. The reason given by the censors in the case of *Nancy* related to its treatment of sectarianism. Reluctance to treat sectarianism has, in the past, been connected to the state's politics of amnesia by memory makers.[9] However, as already mentioned, the term amnesia is increasingly problematic in a post-2005 context given the proliferation of events and productions about the war. If there is indeed still such hardened amnesia in the larger population, it is a detriment to the penetration of the many projects and events about memory.

The set-up in the play is simple. On stage, four actors take turns in narrating personal stories starting with the outbreak of the civil war in 1975 and ending at the present time in Beirut. Through short intense monologues, they recount the history of the war. Curiously, although the characters are strangled, drowned, shot to pieces and left to rot for months on the battlefield, they always return to join new battles and new situations. In this way, their overlapping and interchanging stories combine to become a singular story about the civil war seen from the perspective of foot soldiers.

On this level of the play, which we could call the fictional level, the war is represented through four persons hailing from two Christian and two Muslim backgrounds. However, none of them stick to their original political line. The Shia goes from being a Communist, then Amal, then Hizbollah fighter; the Sunni joins various leftist groups, including the strictly Sunni Mourabitun, before becoming an international *jihadist* in Afghanistan and Bosnia; the Christian woman starts out a leftist in West Beirut but is drawn by opportunism to the Eastern sector and the Lebanese Forces; while the Christian man joins various Christian factions. The matter-of-factness with which people die and are resurrected produces roars of laughter in the audience throughout the play.[10] The impossibility of dying in a story that is all about death is the central joke, the dark humour that drives the action forwards. Militiamen and women are cannon fodder, but they keep bouncing back into action as if driven by a certain logic. This absurd logic is, of course, the logic of the war, which the play satirises. It could be seen as the logic of conflict as such, according to which battles do not finish the struggle but merely become the pretext for more battles, more heroism and yet more violence.

However, the play does not just employ satire and fiction to create a basis for reflection on the war amongst the audience. The background on the stage set represents a second level of the play, the documentary level. Throughout the play, a series of *shahid* (martyr) posters from the war appear on electronic screens over the head of each character, changing when he or she dies. The posters allude to the long line of actual destinies that lived and died in the war. In other words, they are artefacts of history, as opposed to the voices that recount memories of the war. By contrasting the real and the fictional representations of the war, the play achieves an eerie disjunction between the jolly, careless tone of the narration, accentuated by the localisms of their dialectical expressions, and the story of the war as archival history represented by the martyr posters. Moreover, it pits the bombastic, ideological visual language of martyr posters against individuals who change ideologies like they change underwear. History here is indeed very political and kept within the confines of ideological slogans, whereas the personal memories are confused, ironic and notoriously hard to pin down.

The aim of the play is both to comment on memory and to produce, or contribute to, the documentation of the civil war. On the fictional as well as the documentary level, *Nancy* confronts the audience with the archetypical 'little man' of the war, the many un-empowered individuals bouncing here and there at the will of their political masters. Towards the end of the play, the Christian man (played by Mroué himself) has become involved with the South Lebanese Army (SLA), the Israel-allied militia that fought in southern Lebanon until the liberation in 2000. When the Israeli occupation ends in May 2000, and the SLA leave for Israel overnight, he curses his luck: '*What* is wrong with me? The same bloody thing happens every time. They run away and I die'. The point is clear—the little man is a pawn in the game of militia leaders, who eventually abandon him. Political rhetoric is a charade.

The social critique of militia leaders and politicians is accentuated by the final scene. We are now in 2005. Hariri has been killed, and Lebanon is seized by new sectarian tensions. On the eve of 25 January 2007, a pivotal date in post-Syria Lebanon when Sunni-Shia clashes broke out in West

Beirut and the country appeared on the verge of sectarian conflict, all four protagonists head to Burj al-Murr, a huge, empty-shell tower in central Beirut which was a hotbed of snipers during the war and is one of the most poignant *lieux de mémoire* in Beirut. They head there because they know that 'whoever controls Burj al-Murr is likely to control the war', as one of the characters comments. The play ends when the lights go out and an army communiqué is read out, stating that four dead bodies were found on Burj al-Murr. They were questioned, but since their actions 'fell under the amnesty law, they were all free to go'. Mroué here lets the authorities carry through the absurd logic of the play, namely that fighters do not actually die. The state refuses to deal with an unbroken chain of personal tragedy going back to 1975. This could be interpreted as a critique of political discourses about violence that celebrates it but fails to reckon with its effects. The four soldiers, who are connected to a long line of (un)dead soldiers from 1975 to 2007, simply do not register as dead according to the state officials who find them. In this way, Mroué inscribes his work in a long tradition of artistic critique of the Lebanese state and its handling of the civil war legacies. The pacifist tone underlying this critique leaves no doubt that militarised sectarian identity is stupid, pointless and destructive, and that the best one can do is make fun of it.

Three crucial elements in Mroué's play stand out: satire, socio-political critique and truth-telling. All of these elements can be found in war-related cultural productions going back to the satirical plays of Ziad al-Rahbani in the late 1970s and early 1980s, the Lebanese cinematic tradition with its finger-pointing at sectarian leaders,[11] and the many happenings, hearings and exhibitions about the war in the 1990s and early 2000s that focused on telling a truth that politicians had kept hidden from the public. Of these three elements, truth-telling is perhaps the dominant in memory culture, also after 2005. In Lebanon, the logic of truth-telling as a path to national reckoning and ultimately reconciliation in Lebanon has been more or less consciously inspired by European debates after the Second World War, and later, by the wave of truth and reconciliation committees in various parts of the world from the 1980s onwards.[12] Other than truth, reconciliation and justice, Lebanese memory makers often invoke the notion of a national history, a singular truth which all Lebanese can attain knowledge of if they are correctly informed. In other words, the aim of memory work is not just therapeutic, but also a way of seeking or laying bare truth about the past. Memories of the war may be its material, but its ultimate goal is to create history, or rather, to expose history—not any history, but the True History. We can call this project a liberal memory project. By liberating the various memories about the war, the Nation will eventually arrive at a national history. As I point out in my book *War and Memory in Lebanon*, this logic ignores or glosses over the tensions between the many different historical narratives that coexist—to use a vexed term in a Lebanese context. The problem for Lebanon is exactly the multitude of divergent interpretations of the past and the way in which these narratives support particular forms of sectarian identity politics. Personal memories can in some cases subvert sectarian historiographies—for example by undermining the heroic charisma of dead leaders—but they can also be used to support them. Even within the group of memory makers, there are quite different ideas about what exactly the truth of the war is, and therefore also about what history would be. Memory makers rarely spell out how, in concrete terms, they view a process of unification, or even communication, between the many different voices that make up the 'memory-scapes' of Lebanon.[13] Simply having the voices heard in a public setting, it seems, is the end goal rather than the starting point for a much longer and much more complicated process. In theoretical terms, one could say that the liberal memory project rests on a very positivist notion of history, and that it ignores or is unaware of conceptions of history that view it as multi-vocal and, at least in parts, socially constructed.[14]

Emotional Archives and Structures of Feeling

The use of individual life stories in *Nancy* is typical of many productions about memory since 2005. The individual is at the centre of the project of memory making, and memory makers stress multivocality as a virtue in representations of memory. Yet, they rarely consider which implications the stress on individual memories may have for the possibility of a national history, which they also buttress. The audience (ostensibly the Lebanese writ large) needs to see the faces of the war, and needs to hear the actual (or, as in *Nancy*, fictional) voices relate their memories. By exposing them to these narratives, and to the performative effects of the narration, the memory makers hope that a national history will simply emerge on its own. Individual memories of the war have not been completely neglected by academics writing about the war. Although, as mentioned, far more research has been done on the political history of the war, some books like Miriam

Cooke's groundbreaking 1987 study of female authors of the 1980s, evocatively titled *War's Other Voices*, are preoccupied with the effect of war on persons rather than on political structures.[15] Cooke shows how a feminist alternative to masculine hegemony in Lebanese society emerged in women writers' work. Similar studies of cultural production during the war and about the war have paid attention to how 'voices of the war' participate in constructing and subverting nationalist and sectarian narratives.[16] The aim of installations, plays, films and other cultural representations dealing with the war is often the same—to show that individuals resisted the war, were victims of the war and that their personal stories in so many ways offer alternative narratives from the ones told by political history.

The personal focus on cultural production also has another, less-studied effect than negotiations of broad tropes like nationalism and sectarianism; it produces a vast repertoire of emotions connoted with the civil war. These emotions are inscribed in images, icons, sounds, familiar experiences, language and songs from the 1970s and 1980s, in the multiple sensuous experiences that make up what Raymond Williams[17] referred to as structures of feeling. I believe that memory culture can be seen as an archive for the representation of collective structures of feeling during the war. In Williams' work, the term describes the general organisation of emotion and experience in a given period, especially as developed along generational lines. It describes the ways in which common values or shared generational experiences shape subjective experience. For Williams, certain social practices, works of art and literature are the principle records of such structures. Today, one would have to include a range of new media. From a sociological perspective, if we want to understand how these various cultural constructions come into place, we must focus on the people who take on the task of reconstructing the structure of feeling of past periods. In Lebanon's case, these are the memory makers who consciously sought to produce historical memory of the civil war in Lebanon since 1990. Their motivations vary from very personal experiences of rupture, amnesia and nostalgia, to ideological vendetta against the militia warlords who, in many cases, became national leaders after the war. Some pertain to speak on behalf of the whole Lebanese people, while others reflect on their own (middle) class setting.[18] The point I want to make here is that these people, consciously or unconsciously, participate in the creation of emotional archives. By using the term archive I do not mean to imply that emotional archives are organised in any neat way, nor that they are necessarily conceptualised as such by their creators or by their audience. This, indeed, was also not Raymond Williams' point.[19] It is true that art, including cinema, is often conceptualised according to guiding principles and ideas about its possible impact on a receptive public. Indeed, many of Lebanon's memory makers have clear ideas about the kind of 'collective memory' (often no more than a euphemism for a particular historical narrative about villains and victims in the war) they would like to produce. But even if memory culture is designed to invoke ideological readings of history, it often does other things too. By default, reconstructions of the past draw on the sensuous experience of the period in question in order to establish authenticity of that past time. By doing so, artists—*independent of each other* (my emphasis)—approach the way in which the past was experienced by a group of people.[20] There is no way to prove or disprove the authenticity of these representations, other than perhaps their receptiveness among a given audience. Moreover, the accuracy of representations is besides the main point here, namely that memory culture can be analysed as a repertoire of emotions connected with the past.

Emotional archives may be a somewhat insubstantial concept and perhaps somewhat opposed to the historian's attempt at reaching solid knowledge about the past. As a theoretical and methodological tool, it is certainly closer to, for example, Hayden White's notion of narrative history than more empiricist schools of thought.[21] However, if we accept for a moment that memory culture does not produce a neatly organised archive, but a repository of narrative and emotional raw material for history writing, we may be able to glimpse its potential, particularly for social historians of the war. There are today thousands of films, novels, plays, songs and other cultural productions about the civil war. Some are quite famous and some have left a dent in the wider population's understanding of the war, while the majority exist in a subculture of cultural consumption. It is exactly the multiplicity of representations and the lack of a central locus where they are stored and examined that might make some argue that the archive is a badly chosen metaphor for the way in which public memory works. After all, memory culture is quite unstructured in the way it presents widely differing and often very subjective renditions of the past in the public sphere. The archive, on the other hand, is an ordered system of knowledge about the past, organised to preserve and facilitate access to the collective memory of nations or sometimes the human race. To this I would say that, as archival scholars also point out, all archives depend on interfaces (archivists or computer systems) to mediate between the past and the public.[22] Although we imagine the archive as a well-ordered system, it is only well-ordered to the extent that intermediaries guide the user effectively through the often colossal amount of source material that makes it possible to construct ideas about the past—and, as Jacques Derrida points out in his essay *Archive Fever*, these processes of intermediary representation are never devoid of power relations.[23] What may seem like neutral and objective processes are often revealed as places where archivists determine what constitutes legitimate evidence of the past and shape social memories. If we accept that memory culture is a form of emotional archive, we have to ask what kind of intermediary Lebanese memory makers are. Do their experiences represent the structures of feeling of the Lebanese population writ large (as most of them would like us to believe) or only, as Raymond Williams would perhaps have had it, a particular social class? Do they speak for anyone but themselves, or can their collective output really be seen as a national archive in the sense that all Lebanese will recognise bits and pieces of emotions, or that various emotions will be stoked by at least some of these cultural productions? How can this repository of emotions and experiences be operationalised in a way that is beneficial? In order to answer some of these questions, let us look at the institution that today most closely resembles an actual memory archive—UMAM Documentation & Research.

Commemorations and Urban Space

UMAM is the plural of *umma* (community) in Arabic and signals a plurality of voices which the organisation would like to set free by supporting various kinds of memory work.[24] By organising a continuous stream of exhibitions, hearings and other events related to the memory of the war, UMAM has, since 2005, established itself as the foremost institution for cultural events about the war. The institution is run by the couple Monika Borgman and Lokman Slim and is based in the southern suburbs of Beirut, a rather unique location for this kind of organisation, which would normally base itself in central and northern Beirut. UMAM's events range from traditional art exhibitions to interactive projects that aim at drawing in the audience. Some focus on Lebanon, others on similar post-conflict settings, which are meant to provoke comparisons and discussions about Lebanon's post-war period and issues related to remembering and forgetting. Several of UMAM's projects have been related to urban space and the way memories are inscribed in the texture of daily life in Beirut. One of UMAM's first events was a photo exhibition of graffiti in Beirut titled 'Masters of the walls—Beirut's graffiti revisited'.[25] Much of the graffiti referred to the war and in this way illustrated the way in which memories and slogans of the war are reproduced today in urban space.

The exhibition was one of several in the past six years to focus on how references to the war are lived and showcased on a daily basis in urban space. They refer to the problematic that graffiti, posters[26] and other material are used by political parties to mark off urban space into zones of identity and to commemorate particular events from the war. The tendency to stage war history goes all the way back to the 1980s, and has continued to develop, and in some cases increased in intensity, since 2005. For social scientists looking to explore the dynamics of urban commemorations in Beirut, mid-September is something of a high season, and a good time to observe how history is produced in urban space, and what war history means on a quotidian level. I have previously written about these September commemorations, based on fieldwork carried out in the early 2000s, before the Independence Intifada.[27] In September 2010, I returned to Beirut to observe how some of the commemorations had changed. The first and most prolific of the September commemorations takes place on September 14, when several groups and parties connected with the Christian Right—the Lebanese Forces, the Gemayel Foundation and the Kataeb Party—commemorate the death of the foremost Christian leader during the war, Bashir Gemayel, who was assassinated in East Beirut by a massive bomb. Two days later, on 16 September, the Lebanese Communist Party (LCP) and other groups commemorate the first martyrs of the *jabhat al-muqawama al-wataniya*, the Committee for National Liberation, a leftist coalition which launched its resistance activities against Israel on that day in 1982. On the same day, 16 September, there are several and changing commemorations of the Sabra and Shatila massacres, committed by Christian militiamen in direct response to the killing of Bashir Gemayel. Finally, on 25 September, the Christian parties have another commemoration, this time of all martyrs from the war. In short, a smorgasbord for the researcher!

The events commemorated all refer back to 1982, which was a crucial turning point in the civil war. For historians, the events are linked in crucial ways. Bashir Gemayel's death led to Sabra and Shatila—only a few much skewed historians would negate this (or actually just silence it). Partly as a result of numerous and very detailed accounts of participants in the Christian Right, from Joseph Abou Khalil to Robert Hatem,[28] as well as investigative journalists like Alain Ménargues,[29] we know who participated, what their motives were, and what they did—in the most disturbing detail. In fact, not a stone has been left unturned in the case of Sabra and Shatila.[30] One could even argue that it has become an iconic event that today overshadows other massacres such as those committed in Tell al-Zataar, Damour, Safra and Karantina. We know everything, perhaps save for the most damning of all details, namely whether or not Pierre Gemayel ordered the killings. However, the accumulation of historical details and academic knowledge has hardly left a single imprint on the lived memory of these events, and the way it is inscribed in urban space continues. In 2011, it continues to be deeply partisan and unreconciled.

The launch of the *jabhat al-muqawama al-wataniya* came in response to the presence of the Israeli occupying force in Lebanon from August 1982. In the years that followed, this secular resistance group was eventually superseded, partly through violence, by the Islamic resistance of Hizbollah. So, when the leftist parties commemorate the date today, they do it partly in response to a concerted campaign by Hizbollah since the war to 'own' the resistance. The conflict over the past between the left and Hizbollah flared up several times after the war, most notably in January 2004, when a large number of prisoners returned from Israel as a result of a prisoner swap negotiated by Hizbollah. Some had been held there since the war, and more than half of them belonged to leftist groups. However, the reception was monopolised by Hizbollah as a sign of their effort to overwrite the left's stake in the resistance history. As a result, many leading leftists spoke out openly against Hizbollah, and the episode was indeed referred to in the founding document of what later that year became the preparatory committee of the Democratic Left movement in 2004.[31]

This struggle over who owns the memory of the resistance struggle was directly related to the Syrian order in post-war Lebanon. As the document explains, there has been 'a decision to eliminate the left, on which all members of the alliance supporting the status quo agree'.[32] In other words, Hizbollah may have fought Israel during the war, but today (in 2004) it is part of the consensus to accept Syrian hegemony in Lebanon. The aim of the committee was to learn the mistakes from the past, unify and unite against the Syrian-sponsored order in Lebanon. This statement is even more remarkable when one considers that several of the founding members of the Democratic Left movement after the 2006 war wrote a public letter of support for Hizbollah, and that a large part of the left generally has sided with 8 March since then. It is remarkable to think how much of the Lebanese opposition in 2004, including Michel Aoun, revolved around confronting Syria and its role in Lebanese history, and it illustrates just how easily alliances change in the world of Lebanese politics.

The *jabhat al-muqawama al-wataniya* commemoration on 16 September was in 2004 couched mainly as an attempt to reclaim the resistance for the left, but given the tensions over the left's position vis-à-vis Hizbollah after 2006, it has today become more explicitly counterpoised against the Christian celebration of 'Shaykh Bashir' and the Christian Right's narrative of the events of 1982 more broadly. In 2010, tensions were particularly high after the LF had expanded their usual memorial campaign consisting of banners of Gemayel's face to also include the leader of the LCP, George Hawi, and writer Samir Qassir, both of whom were prominent members of the Democratic Left movement and both of whom were killed in June 2005 in car bombings that have been attributed to the Syrian security services. Now, in September 2010, roadside posters and signs in East Beirut declared these two prominent leftists and icons of the Lebanese secular resistance as martyrs for LF's cause. If one logged on to the LF's webpage in Arabic, a long list of martyrs appeared that included recently murdered Christians— Gibran Tueni, Samir Qassir and George Hawi—but also the Sunni leader Rafik Hariri. The LF's reasons for including these persons was to point out that they all died in defiance of the Syrian agenda to control Lebanon, a struggle for which Bashir Gemayel was presented as the 'crown' martyr, and hence also the precursor for the 14 March movement. Needless to say, the LCP was infuriated by this spectacular cooptation of leftists by a movement traditionally considered opposed to the left, and promised legal action.

My point with drawing attention to the contestations over September 1982 in Lebanon of 2010 is to show how civil war history is appropriated for political projects today with some remarkable disregard for the actual facts of history, and not least for the interconnectedness of those events. The fact that September 1982 is well-researched has hardly left a single mark on the interpretation and political usage that Lebanon's political parties continue to apply to these significant dates. However, even if the politics of commemoration depend on hardened discourses about the truth of the war, the appropriation of civil war history also changes according to the conflicts of the present day. Today's enemies can be made tomorrow's friends, and history bent accordingly, when political parties plan their yearly commemorations. During the civil war, George Hawi fought the LF and was, also after the war, its ideological opponent. However, for the LF in 2010, the master narrative about the war in which they couched their commemoration of Bashir Gemayel, had become that of Syrian hegemony and, more subtly, the perceived precariousness of the Christian population in Lebanon. The discourse of persecuted or existentially threatened Levantine Christians is by no means new, and was in fact central to the emergence of Bashir Gemayel as a saintly figure in the years preceding his death, and particularly in the years after.[33] But it is never constant and can be—has been—operationalised in various ways depending on the regional and national context. In 2010, the murder of Christians in Iraq and Egypt and the schism between 8 March and 14 March coalitions which was often phrased in sectarian terms (despite the obvious fact that Michel Aoun's FPM made up a sizeable part of the 8 March group), likely contributed to the Bashir ceremony being phrased in such terms.

The ceremonies are very emotive rituals that play on emotional memories of the war. However, in contrast to the cultural productions mentioned earlier, they do not focus on regular people or individual voices, but on iconic leaders and grand political narratives. They gloss over any causal link between the events. Sabra and Shatila are edited out of the Bashir ceremony—it is neither mentioned nor alluded to. Had it somehow been included, it would probably have been difficult to maintain the pomp and circumstance of the occasion, when thousands of supporters gathered at a church in East Beirut and marched to the place where Gemayel was assassinated. This is how political history is made in urban space—by a desire to wilfully edit out some and airbrush other perspectives, and not by a desire to understand history. The distortion of facts in the name of a political project constitutes a stumbling block for historians wishing to write the truth, because it constantly forces them to first challenge a living memory of events that promotes a future political agenda before even beginning to discuss what is historically salient and what is not.

'History' and 'Memory'—Never the Twain Shall Meet?

For memory makers like Monika Borgman and Lokman Slim, the Gemayel ceremony exemplifies everything that is problematic about the current politics of memory in Lebanon, and why it is necessary to push for alternative perspectives on the past. To them, the years since the death of Hariri have not improved the fundamental problem that political elites, who participated in the war and have no interest in supporting a national project of coming to terms with the past, continue to dominate political life. Moreover, increased sectarian tension has only exacerbated the tendency to seek shelter in one's own community and its myths. In reaction to this, they want to promote 'memory'—individual voices and alternative perspectives—in order to forge 'history', a national awareness of what happened during the war. As mentioned, Borgman and Slim launched the first activities of UMAM in 2005. Today, in 2012, they have established themselves as the most visible and well-funded 'memory mongers' in Lebanon. In addition to exhibitions, seminars and film screenings, UMAM is collecting a vast amount of material from the war, ranging from books, diaries, pamphlets and posters to personal items. At the time of writing, this material is still badly organised, but it is the ambition of UMAM to make it publicly available on the Internet. Borgman and Slim's impressive project is part of a larger memory project in Lebanese cultural life, as I have described it in this chapter, aimed at finding words and other expressions to describe the shape of history, that is, constructing salient narratives about the war. This project is meant as therapeutic, in that it allows traumatised individuals to speak out and other traumatised individuals to listen in and relive the past. But it also has a larger ambition of creating a new framework for a national history. Memory makers, as a social group, mostly live outside the logic of sectarianism and see themselves as part of a push to overcome the boundaries imposed by the sectarian system of governance. Their belief in the possibility of a liberal national history is related to this political position. For them, remembering is healthy, as it necessarily challenges the sectarian narratives of the war and makes visible the deeper human truth of a shared war experience in which victims suffered equally on both sides of the 'green line' separating East and West.

So far, the liberal memory project appears to have failed to impact or change the conditions for the constant reproduction of politicised myths that continue to dominate the politics of memory in Lebanon. Although it is hard to gauge what effect cultural events have on participants, only a handful of events, including some of UMAM's productions, have been able to transcend the inner-Beiruti scene of the educated middle classes where memory culture is made. Many memory events still have a feel of preaching to the choir, and the broader population has certainly not been 'enlightened' in the way that is often intended. However, the memory project could have objectives other than raising awareness in the public. If social historians of the war began to make use of the sources collected and created by memory makers, they could be of great use for an actual historiographic project. I have suggested that as a whole, memory culture constitutes emotional archives. Even if that may seem at first as a flimsy notion, it might be possible to systematise these archives. If so, we could gain great insight into some of the blind spots of the historiography of the war.

One place to start could be by addressing what the war felt like for civilians. This question is linked to fundamental sociological issues related to the war, the answer to which will have wide-ranging consequences for Lebanon. To take an example, the question of what motivated people to fight is central in understanding to what extent the civil war was imposed from the outside and to what extent it was based on local grievances. If we could gain a better understanding of the motivation of young men for joining the militias, we might be able to counter some of the myths surrounding the war. Why did the war continue for so long, and what motivated people to fight? The question has been raised by several historians and sociologists, including Samir Khalaf in his 2002 book *Civil and Uncivil Violence in Lebanon*. He sees violence as symptoms of deflected conflicts both in Lebanon and the region. In his variant of the inside-outside dialectic, civilians became 'proxy targets' of 'sanctified cruelty' perpetuated by hardened communitarian protagonists. Violence bred violence and became a self-reinforcing system.[34] Another academic, Michael Johnson, stresses that the tribal structures that dominated in village society were actually undone, more often than not, in the individualistic milieu of Beirut where migrants from the countryside settled from the 1950s onwards, creating the need for a surrogate nuclear family, which was in turn provided by sectarian movements like Kataeb and Amal.[35] The young man, in this framework, was the son, the (Christian, Muslim or Lebanese) nation was the mother and the sectarian leader was the father. Being soldiers for a cause, young men were given unrestricted power to demean the honour of the Other through violent acts. As Fawwaz Traboulsi also suggests, in his study of permutations of identity during the civil war, the construction of Others actually encapsulated disavowed aspects of the Self.[36] Not least, violence became an outlet for sexual frustration. The militias offered young men an opportunity to transgress restrictive boundaries of normal behaviour and release their tension through the barrel of a gun, often in spurts of extreme violence and violation of social norms. The resulting violence served to protect tribal or sectarian notions of *ird* (honour), and in turn the individualisation of modern society and of liberal nationalism—processes that had been under way in the 1950s and 1960s—was eroded. The notion of citizenship was replaced by factions, represented by individual fighters who attacked 'Others' seen to represent other factions. Territories were cleansed and Others shamed, all overseen by what many writers have called the war system.

These very valid perspectives on the question of motivation and participation in militias would have been vastly improved if the writers had had access to more life stories of militiamen (Johnson in particular is aware of personal narratives and tries to use them, but only in a limited and anecdotal way). Here, memory culture has in fact unearthed a wealth of material that is only waiting for social historians to systematise it and correlate it with existing theories, some of which I have sketched here. Historians should be invited to participate in work on these documents, so memory work is not just a 'cultural' practice. In short, memory culture should be married to civil war history writing.

The marriage between memory and history is not an easy one. As I conclude in my study of memory narratives from 1990 to 2005, memory culture is produced for particular reasons and often framed to fit a certain narrative of the war.[37] We must keep in mind, as Maurice Halbwachs noted already in the 1920s, that individual memory is constructed socially and subject to collective frameworks of memory.[38] It is always a challenge for the historian to gauge what is useful and accurate, and what is constructed to fit current situations, no matter which sources he or she works with. Having said that, memory culture is not just a collection of dubious sources. Constructions of memory also point to narratives about history. History is not just numbers, dates and facts, but equally the telling of stories, and the combination of events into salient narratives. In Lebanon, there are many different narratives, many different histories. Any attempt to write a history of the war must start by acknowledging the multiplicity of historical narratives. The next step must be a proper research agenda, by Lebanese or by foreign research institutions, to support collective research projects that include archival studies, ethnography, oral history and cultural studies. The French scholar Franck Mermier recently published the results of such a comprehensive research project.[39] Similar projects that actively involve Lebanese academics and memory makers in a creative collaboration could break new ground in the social history of the war by opening the door to the immense archive of sentiments, memories, impressions and expressions from and about the civil war and begin working on it in earnest.

11

SECTS AND THE CITY

SOCIO-SPATIAL PERCEPTIONS AND PRACTICES OF
YOUTH IN BEIRUT

Nasser Yassin

Introduction

It was an ordinary January morning in 2007 at the small campus of the
Beirut Arab University located in the western part of Beirut. Young men
and women from across Lebanon's sectarian fabric were strolling across the
campus or chatting in the university's canteen. An argument suddenly
broke out between a Shia student and a Sunni peer, most probably over the
Shia *Ashoura* rituals that are practiced yearly in commemoration of Imam
Hussein's martyrdom, one of the most sacred Shia Imams. What might have
been contained as an individual dispute escalated into a full-scale street
fight between Sunni and Shia students. The *shabab* (young men) of the
nearby neighbourhoods were called in and brewing political tension
between the 14 March and 8 March camps, the former supported by Sunnis and the latter by Shia, further fuelled the fight. Baseball bats, knives and
rifles were used, resulting in two students being killed and thirty injured,
before the Lebanese Army deployed its elite force, stopped the fighting and
declared a curfew.

The campus incident resembled other cases of street violence and particularly 'youth gang' violence in Beirut, but its significance lies in its sectarian context, especially in the aftermath of the assassination of former Prime Minister Rafik Hariri in February 2005. This, and similar incidents around the same time, posed a serious threat to the relative stability Lebanon experienced after 1991, illustrating the many challenges to post-conflict peace in the country.

This chapter examines the precariousness of the post-civil war era in Lebanon.[1] It aims to explore Lebanon's unsteady peace by untangling the complex nature of socio-spatial *perceptions* and *practices* among the youth residing in Beirut. It complements the work of Craig Larkin, which looks at the post-war memory of Lebanese youth, by focusing on the ways in which symbolic, social and spatial boundaries are perceived, constructed and experienced in the everyday lives of young Beiruti men and women.[2] In particular, this chapter examines how young women and men in post-civil war Beirut construct symbolic boundaries between themselves and others leading to compartmentalised forms of social relations. Moreover, it looks at how these young women and men distinguish between different types of spaces, depending on the utilisation of these spaces and places and the meaning they assign to them. Through the case of Beirut, the chapter contributes to the literature on post-war (a.k.a., 'post-conflict') cities, arguing for a more nuanced approach to socio-spatial practices that goes beyond the traditional dichotomies of either segregation *or* co-existence. It exposes the complex—and in many instances paradoxical—nature of social and spatial practices among the young Beirutis who co-exist within the spaces of their 'contested' city, albeit without empathy towards each other.

This research is based on focus group studies conducted with one hundred Lebanese youths aged between eighteen and twenty-five, both male and female, from various sectarian communities living and studying in the Greater Beirut area.[3] The focus group interviews were conducted in the winter of 2009, with participants recruited from public and private universities and technical colleges. They came from low- to middle-class socio-economic backgrounds and represented all sectarian communities, but the focus group interviews were conducted with homogenous youth groups belonging to the same sect. This was done to avoid the difficulty participants in mixed groups may have in providing their view of other sectarian communities. The focus group discussions were moderated by trained facilitators at a local research centre. The discussions were undertaken in the vernacular Arabic, recorded with the consent of the participants and finally transcribed in Arabic. To protect the identity of participants, verbatim statements exclude reference to personal names but includes, where necessary, sectarian affiliation. The questions used in the focus groups interviews were selected to help understand how youths perceive other sectarian communities, their interpretation of Beirut's city spaces and their everyday socio-spatial practices and mobility.

The Dynamics of Social and Spatial Divisions in Divided Cities

Almost all cities have divisions of certain sorts. Divisions can be based on class or race, ethnicity or sect. The latter forms can be referred to as 'cultural identity'-based divisions. It is the nature of the city that assumes heterogeneous and in some instances conflicting forms of social relations. Hence, creating physical, social or symbolic boundaries based on class or cultural identity is not an anomaly in urban societies. In contested cities, however, divisions between conflicting groups, be they racial, ethnic or sectarian, would strongly contribute to maintaining enmity and entrenching polarisation. Divisions would accentuate social distancing and become a source of contention, especially in cities emerging from civil strife and collective violence. The divisions tend to be substantiated, I contend, through two inter-related mechanisms—*territorialisation of city spaces* and *segregated living*.

In contested cities, conflicting groups seek to exert power and mark their identity on cityscapes. Controlling the spaces of a contested city becomes part and parcel of the assertiveness of collective identity. Through the alteration, transformation and control of spaces, sectarian groups engage in a process of constructing the boundaries of one's territory vis-à-vis the others. Anderson and Shuttleworth have described such dynamics as structured by *territoriality*, 'by the use of bordered spaces to include and exclude, to control, influence and express relationships of power'.[4] Territoriality becomes a means for reproducing sectarianism and group boundaries.[5] One contributing factor to the territorialisation of the city is collective fear. Fear is a mental construct involving different sets of emotions which are evoked through actual or perceived threats. As 'a social act which occurs within a cultural matrix', fear leads to combined physical and psychological survival-orientated reactions.[6] Fear generates mechanisms and motives for protection from a perceived threat.[7] According to Boal, conflicting groups would seek safety and security by living in homogenous spaces with co-sectarians, co-nationals or co-religious group members.[8] The desperate need for safety becomes self-defeating. Hamilton et al. have shown how segregation becomes 'an extreme way of avoiding forms of contact with the other, and which in turn reinforce[s] perceptions of hostility and otherness through a lack of contact or understanding of the other's interests and concerns'.[9]

Beyond the forms of physical segregation, members of groups and communities can create social segregation systems which are built on closed and dense intra-group networks of relations that transcend the spatial form. Here, inward socialising and communal networks between members of one group are not necessarily limited to a specific locality. Social boundaries will be formed and social interaction restricted to the same group, thus creating an intra-sectarian sphere. The end result of the dense and embedded social networks is a form of intra-group or intra-communal capital.[10] This form of 'collective capital' becomes closed, dense and homogenous, creating a sub-public sphere solely based on intra-group or intra-communal solidarity. Social clubs, places of worship, schools and civil society organisations become communally homogenous. Personal relations become embedded within a set of dense networks. Such networks create intra-group bonding which Portes and Sensenbrenner call 'bounded solidarity'.[11] Here, boundaries become less mundane and mostly symbolic. Symbolic boundaries are 'conceptual distinctions made by social actors to categorize objects, people, practices and even time and space'.[12] Through constructing symbolic boundaries, one would tend to 'separate people into groups or generate feelings of similarity and group membership'.[13] Territoriality and segregated living are inter-related and feed into the process of boundary construction between sectarian groups. In the city spaces, sectarian groups tend to assert themselves because it is on the walls, streets and neighbourhoods that the identity of groups is materialised. While the latter has been documented in contested cities, building symbolic walls can be even more divisive, as this chapter will show.

Construction of Symbolic Boundaries

Almost twenty years after the end of civil war in Lebanon, social interaction and relations among young Lebanese can, to the casual observer, appear to be convivial. Yet, an in-depth look will reveal the complex nature of social relations and uncover the paradox of social relations in Beirut. Young Beirutis socialise and interact with members of other sectarian groups, but they do not seem to trust each other to the level of forming friendships or other forms of 'deep' or intimate relations.

To a large degree, the composition and strength of these relationships depend on their context, as well as on the meaning given to them. Hence, at university campuses and institutions of higher education, students interact and socialise on a daily basis, regardless of their sectarian or political affiliation. Here, cordial relationships exist and even political discussions with conflicting points of view take place. Similarly, at the workplace and in business or trade contexts, mixed relationships are not seen as an anomaly. To a large degree, however, inter-sectarian relations between the youth appear to be *compartmentalised*. They come in various forms and are given different meanings. The compartmentalisation is part of the process of drawing symbolic boundaries between one group and the others. The compartmentalisation of social relations and boundary construction will be elaborated through the following analysis of the focus group discussions:

First, there is the level and quality of social trust. Social trust depends on a belief in the other's trustworthiness and is shaped by a complex web of personal, social, economic and political factors.[14] Trust among the Beiruti youth remains a private matter and limited to an intimate, inner circle. Most of the focus group participants declared that they did not trust colleagues or acquaintances, even those labelled as friends or casual friends (*ashab*) from other groups. When pressed to explain this feeling, participants could not clearly explain the reasons for this discomfort towards others. Some related this feeling to the education they received, others to the ideological differences and social customs that make the 'others not similar to what we are'.

One focus group with only Christian participants illustrates the precariousness of social trust among the youth of Lebanon, as shown in this excerpt from taped group discussions:

Facilitator (F): I would like to ask you why the Lebanese become complacent when they talk about other sectarian or religious communities in the presence of a member of these communities?

Participant (P) 1: Because of different customs and traditions. I mean, I have Sunni friends who were visiting me at home and they were surprised when they saw how I live [at] home, [dressed only] in my boxers, and exclaimed that I should not do this in front of my mom. This is what I mean with different customs and traditions.

Another experience happened to me when we were eating pizza and my [Sunni] friends would go mad if they found ham in the food. In these cases you feel there is distance between us and them. At the same time, I cannot be rude to them.

F: Do you not think you are applying double standards by showing 'fake' politeness?

P1: Not double standards at all. Look, Joe and I work in a restaurant where we have Sunni, Shia, Druze and Christian workmates. We respect their presence. But even if I hate Shias, when they are present I am obliged to respect [*ehterm*] them, even if I do not like them.

F: Even though you spend more time with your work mates than with your family.

P2: Yes, there is still a difference

F: Why?

P2: God knows.

P1: They have their own mentality, own religion and own customs which are different from ours.

F: But you almost live together.

P1: And we have fun together and joke together.

F: But do you trust them?

P1: No.

P2: No.

P3: In what sense?

F: To have them as your buddies?

P3: Maybe.

P4: I study in a university in which all sects and parties are represented and I think it is OK.

P2: I do not have a problem with them, but I do not trust them.

F: To what extent do you not trust them?

P2: [I do not trust them] involving themselves in my private life or entering into my home.

F: So the limit is your home?

P2: Yes.

P1: You are asking about the limits of trust. I will give you an example. I've known Sunnis and Shias for three years and we go out together and we drink together and they come visit me at home, but I cannot leave them at home alone with my mother and sister, this is my limit.

F: If your friend is Christian, would you leave him with your mother and sister?

P1: Yes, I know the way we are raised. They [Sunnis and Shias] have different ways of thinking—like in the story about wearing the boxers in front of my mom.

As shown in this example, the male participants draw symbolic boundaries between themselves as members of a homogenous 'group' and the 'others'. Such boundaries are primarily constructed to underpin the social distinction between sectarian groups, and include moral judgments of cultural or social beliefs and practices, as well as having different 'mentalities'. This type of value judgements are used to differentiate between the group's 'way of life' and feeds into the perceived 'untrustworthiness' of the other.

Trust is indeed founded on 'communitarian interdependencies', reciprocity and responsibility.[15] Hence, constructing boundaries would limit the very nature of interdependence and thus enhance suspicion and distrust. Again, the perception of the other 'not being like us' and 'having a different way of life' makes the other less trusted.

The low level of trust found in focus group discussions confirms the findings of quantitative studies, showing that inter-sectarian distrust is prevalent in post-conflict Lebanon. The study by Khawaja et al. shows that, among Lebanese adolescents in three disadvantaged Beirut neighbourhoods, 'only 6.3 per cent trusted most or many people'.[16] The study also reveals that the majority of adolescents 'did not engage in any form of instrumental exchange with neighbours, family, or friends during the month preceding the survey'.[17] Hanf's survey, conducted in 2006, shows that the level of distrust of one's social environment was as high as 84 per cent among survey respondents, up from 78 per cent in 2002.[18] The levels of distrust were similar across all communities, but were much higher in the districts of South Lebanon and to a lesser degree in the Christian neighbourhood of Ashrafieh, as well as in some quarters of Beirut's predominantly Shia suburbs.[19] Hanf's survey shows that Lebanese are turning to close circles of trusted friends and family members, as 94 per cent of the respondents declared that they only trust close relatives and 71 per cent only trust their closest friends.[20]

Second, the compartmentalised nature of inter-sectarian social relations is reflected at the discursive level through the use of labels that portray the negative-other and positive-self. These discourses appear to be collectively constructed out of the negative stereotyping of members of other groups. On many occasions, focus group participants did not shy away from deriding other sectarian groups, some describing the others as 'dirty' (*wisikheen*); 'sexually frustrated' (*mouhabteen jinsyaan*); 'having a distasteful lifestyle' (*bila zouk*); 'disgusting' (*mouqrayfeen*), 'fanatic' (*motassebeen*); 'full of hatred' (*hakoudeen*); 'terrorists'(*irhabyeen*); 'backstabbers'(*ghadarin*); 'having no God' (*Ma elon rab*); and 'self-centred' (*yehboun anfousahoum*). These powerful labels stem from, and in turn reinforce, narratives and myths that demonise and dehumanise the others.

Conversely, this inferior view of the others was often coupled with a superior view of the self. Many held very positive views about their own communities and this was reflected in how they described themselves. When one group was asked to describe their own community, almost all used positive attributes such as: 'generous'(*huramaa*); 'brave men' (*abadayet*); 'at the forefront of any battle'(*al jabha be kel el hroub*); 'united' (*mouwahadin*); 'zealous to their own religion' (*mokhlisin la mazhabon*); 'when needed [we] come together as one family' (*waet el daroura, mensir ayleh wehdeh*); and 'loyal' (*Awfiya*). In the same vein, others described their community either as 'clean' (*nedaf*); 'open-minded' (*minfiteheen*); 'educated' (*moutaalemeen*); 'well-bred' (*nassel mnih*) and 'civilised' (*moutahadereen*).

Again, we see continuity in constructing boundaries between one's own group and the others by the use of labels. Negative stereotypes and discourses of inferiority of the other, coupled with one's own group's superiority, are foundations in the process of boundary construction and maintenance. Such 'cognitive categorization' is commonplace in 'in-group/out-group' stereotyping and the process of constructing shared beliefs within any given collective.[21] In such a context, the construction of symbolic boundaries through negative stereotyping of other groups or communities is used to maintain and enforce social boundaries drawn between sectarian groups and communities, which are intrinsically 'accepted' in the current polity and in society.

Third, the prevailing view among the young participants in the focus groups was to reject the idea of mixed marriages, which is viewed as a 'headache' and the main cause of future marital problems. Many of the participants rejected marrying someone from a different religion or with other religious beliefs. This appeared vividly when discussing the idea of Christian and Muslim inter-marriage. It is also striking that among Muslim sects there is an emerging rejection of inter-sectarian marriages, with some participants adamantly rejecting mixed Sunni-Shia marriages. This was particularly striking when, on some occasions, it came from children of such mixed-marriages. One explanation can be that the current Sunni-Shia political schism has affected the attitude towards mixed marriages.

When asked why they rejected the idea of mixed marriages, the participants spoke of the difficulty of 'integrating' the other person into their own social and cultural realms—a view that was almost universally held across all sectarian and religious groups. In their elaboration, many of the youth juxtaposed socio-cultural aspects with religious beliefs or doctrines, such as lifestyle and dress code, insinuating the difficulty of marrying religious traditions and socio-cultural practices of one group with the others. Differences were highlighted, emphasising the way the others pray, practice rituals, commemorate religious figures or even celebrate religious events. In a question posed by the facilitator on mixed marriages, the response from one Shia participant illustrates how the participants juxtapose religion, culture and social practices in their rejection of mixed marriages:

… Islam forbids us to drink [alcohol] and I am not going to have a Christian girl [who drinks] and would be wearing a short skirt when I present her to my dad.

Asked by another participant if he can change her way of living, he continued:

She is used to such practices. She sits differently, showing her legs. I will be graduating soon, and I prefer to marry a respectable Muslim girl.

Reflecting on the prospects for children of mixed parents, one Christian girl described this 'complexity':

… a child will be torn between fasting during Ramadan or Easter, or celebrating Christmas; going to the church or the mosque. He or she will be really lost.

Another Christian girl was more categorical in rejecting mixed marriages when commenting on a mixed marriage between a Christian woman and a Shia man:

… why would someone want to marry a Shia man? I do not like this idea of mixed marriages. I mean, a [Christian] girl could find 1,000 Christian men who are nicer and more handsome. Perhaps that girl did it [married a Shia] for the money.

The religious practices of the 'others' were also characterised in derogatory terms. One Sunni participant described such differences:

My uncle is married to a Shia woman; during *Ashoura* she puts a black bandana on her head to commemorate the death of Hussein, which we Sunnis do not. We would tell him that he is not a 'man' as long as he permits his wife to do this, and he would get really angry and start quarrelling with her.

The shunning of mixed or inter-marriages by the Lebanese youth illustrates their failure to cross the imagined boundaries that exist between themselves and members of other sectarian groups. Their perception of mixed marriages as problematic is largely grounded in the difficulties they envisage in breaking down these boundaries, which are enforced through social, cultural and religious differences.

Socio-spatial boundaries: 'Banal' versus 'Exclusionary' Spaces

The compartmentalised nature of inter-sectarian social relations and the symbolic boundaries created out of this process are eventually translated onto the city's physical geography, influencing the ways in which young men and women perceive and use the spaces of their city. The focus group discussions show that they make a clear distinction between different types of spaces, depending on their utilisation. Some spaces were used for leisure, shopping, work and studying. These 'public' spaces allow for social mixing and are accepted as heterogeneous and viewed as neutral. In the schema of the young Lebanese, they are what I would call 'banal' spaces and places that carry little 'political' or 'communal/sectarian' meaning beyond their primary function of shopping, leisure or work. As such, choosing an area for shopping, a café or a night club, normally has no sectarian or political connotation. It stems in many cases from the logic of maximising utility. The southern suburbs of Beirut, for example, were visited for shopping by some participants regardless of their communal background, simply because goods and services there are cheaper. Similarly, spaces of leisure were sought after on the basis of their utility and for the services they offer. The predominantly Christian East Beirut and its suburbs were the preferred destination for fun and leisure activities among the youth, including the many Muslim (Sunni, Shia and Druze) participants. The preference for seeking out these places is that they are perceived as places for hanging out and having fun.

When it comes to choosing a place of residence, however, living in mixed neighbourhoods was neither common nor desirable to the participants. A relatively common answer across most of the groups was that: 'There is nothing that would oblige us to live in mixed areas'. In general, most of the participants preferred living in homogenous (same sect) neighbourhoods should they have the economic means. In one of the focus groups with Sunni participants, however, the respondents took a more eclectic view of the range of future places of residence:

F: I suppose most of you are living with your parents because you are still single, but when you get married or decide to raise a family, where would your choice of residence be?

P1: Wherever I find stability and safety.

P2: I would live in Christian areas so that my kids will become a bit more civilised.

P3: If the situation remains the same, travelling abroad is a better option than living in a Sunni area.

P4: I would definitely choose a Sunni area or neighbourhood.

P5: I would consider areas with mixed religious sects.

When the same issue was raised in a Shia group, some of the answers reflected the greater feeling of security by living in homogenous neighbourhoods:

F: If you were to choose a place of residence, what would be your favourite choice?

P1: Any area or neighbourhood in Beirut.

P2: Definitely not in Tarik al-Jdideh [a Sunni quarter], because it's a sensitive area; and neither in Ras al-Nabaa nor in al-Malla, because both are sensitive areas as well, and have witnessed Sunni-Shia clashes.

P3: I would rather live in areas where citizens of my own religious sect live.

P4: I would leave Beirut and live in Bchamoun; although it is mixed, it doesn't witness as much [sectarian] conflict as other quarters.

P5: I would live in Dahiyeh [southern suburbs which are predominantly Shia].

While the above perceptions and practices were seen by the participants as a 'logical' choice, the desire to live in homogenous places of residence is partly borne from feelings of insecurity. There were indeed security fears about living in areas where other communities were in the majority. As one participant put it: 'security means living with people from the same community'. Another participant applied the same logic: 'I don't live in areas where other communities are a majority; I prefer to live in a region where I have the full authority'. Moreover, a Christian male participant exposed his anxiety: 'If I go down to *Gharbiye* [West Beirut] I fear that they would know that I am Christian, especially if I was wearing my cross; I may be harassed, beaten or even get shot; that is why I prefer to stay in a Christian area'. Reasoning along the same lines, some Shia participants saw dangers in 'entering' [*doukhoul*] Sunni stronghold neighbourhoods: 'if you enter Tarik al-Jdideh [a Sunni quarter] and they know you are a Shia, you risk being beaten; better bid farewell to your family before entering there; ... even girls being fully veiled [*chador*] would be intimidated. That is why it is better to stay in Dahiyeh'. Many Sunnis felt the same anxiety towards the Shia areas; one girl argued: 'I don't dare to go Dahiyeh. I am afraid they will either insult me or kill me'.

The anxiety towards the spaces of the 'Other' also emerged in the discussions with Druze participants, when the facilitator asked about their favourite destination for shopping or social outing. They too were anxious of going to Dahiyeh, the Hizbollah-dominated southern suburbs of Beirut:

P1: To have fun, I prefer to go to Jounieh. It is more open there; I mean, you cannot go to Dahiyeh.

F: Why not?

P1: This is how I feel.

P2: We are not welcome down there [Southern Suburb].

P3: I feel the opposite.

P4: I do not have any problems with going to Dahiyeh.

P1: I may go there, but I would not feel at ease.

P2: There is always a feeling of fear [when you go there].

P5: In the end, you are a stranger.

P6: I would also go to Jounieh, or stay in my area.

P7: I was once shopping in Dahiyeh with my mom, who is a veiled *Sheikha* [observant Druze], and a Druze taxi driver approached us and asked us to leave the area immediately—implying that we could be harassed in Dahiyeh.

F: Where you in any way intimidated?

P7: No. As long as you do not voice your opinion in a provocative way, there would be no quarrels.

F: And what do you mean by 'provocative way'?

P7: For example by saying that 'your group did this to us' etc... It is better not to talk politics in order to avoid provoking others. I am zealous when it comes to my own community, but I have to be open-minded with the others.

F: And what are the things that provoke you?

P7: If anyone insults my sectarian community or if they intentionally badmouth a political leader whom I follow in front of me. I feel that these insults are directed at me and not at the politician or the *za'im* [communal leader].

Most of the above quotes exaggerate threats, sometimes to absurd levels and most originate from inflammatory media reports and unfounded popular stories of violence. This was accentuated following Rafik Hariri's assassination, especially after the violent incidents of January 2007 in the Beirut Arab University and later on 7 May 2008, when the 8 March group led by Hizbollah fighters stormed the offices belonging to their opponents in the 14 March group. The feeling of insecurity is telling, however, of the perceptions towards the 'Other' and the anxiety aroused from *trespassing* on their spaces. Fear is constructed and exaggerated by the media and through the rhetoric and discourse of political actors and political entrepreneurs.[22] Construction of fear involves a set of emotions that are evoked from the threats surrounding a person, which becomes part of the logic of mobilising against the other. Political actors would exaggerate the threat of the other to strengthen the inter-sectarian bonding of communities and group sentiments.

To alleviate fears of the other, exclusive spaces become a necessity and solidarities within one's community become imperative.[23] These spaces become laden with meanings. They are bounded settings where collective identity is constituted and where people who share the same beliefs and traditions congregate to make up one sectarian community. It is the place of the 'home' that needs to be homogenous and shared with people like 'us'. More importantly, it is a place that would distinguish 'us' from 'them'. Here, the territorialisation of collective identity is a foundation block in maintaining the identity of the collective—be it communal, tribal, ethnic etc.[24] As Doreen Massey argues, the constitution of any identity is a process that entails political, cultural as well as spatial articulations and manifestations.[25] She notes how it is 'important to begin by conceptualizing space in terms of a complexity of interacting social relations, it is also important to recognize that within that open complexity both individuals and social groups are constantly engaged in efforts to territorialize, to claim spaces, to include some and exclude others from particular areas'.[26] Hence, the building of religious sites, shrines, murals and display of political posters are indicators of the assertion of identity within the locality and in its space.

Consequently, the notion of 'entering' a locality where another group constitutes the majority has been expressed several times in the discussions of the focus groups. The use of the term *entering* is indicative of the boundaries inscribed onto the city. It connotes how the young men and women construct a mental map of the city drawing the boundaries between 'our area' and 'theirs'—'our city' and 'theirs'. Social relations are structured around the imagined spatial boundaries the youth draw in their city.

Conclusion: Co-existence Without Empathy

What transpires from discussions with young Lebanese is their ability to co-exist with members from other sectarian groups, although often without empathy. In their everyday lives, the youth mix and interact, share the same campuses, work together, go to the same shopping places and visit the same pubs and cafes, and yet, distrust and resentment powered by inter-sectarian stereotyping remain. The young Lebanese seem to live behind a facade of 'superficial normality',[27] confining their social trust to a small circle of relatives and close friends. At the spatial level, the youth confine their levels of social mixing with the 'other' to contexts and spaces which are perceived as *banal*. The banality of these spaces is derived from their apolitical and non-sectarian character. Conversely, the spaces of residence should ideally be homogenous. These are places that people with similar norms and common beliefs reside in, hence they have to be exclusive. More importantly, the spaces of residence have to be secure to live in. The perception of fear of the other has contributed considerably to the ways that young Beirutis perceive members of other sectarian communities. Fear erodes social trust and determines the ways in which youths perceive of their choice of permanent residence.

Therefore, the youth in post-civil war Beirut seem to be living in a paradox. They are torn between two worlds. On the one hand they mix with the 'Other' in their everyday lives and, in some instances, value being with the 'Other' as an experience of diversity that the city offers while on the other hand, and in equal strength, they tend to confine their social trust to a very small circle of friends and family members and to prefer living in communal enclaves, where parochialism is favoured through the juxtaposition of religion, culture and customs—often in the name of maintaining one's own collective identity. In the end, while the youth of post-civil war Beirut may appear cosmopolitan, they remain trapped by practices and beliefs that confine them within their own sectarian communities. They seem to have social and spatial perceptions and practices that maintain, and in many instances enforce, the symbolic and socio-spatial boundaries between them as members of sectarian groups and communities.

12

SPECIAL TRIBUNAL FOR LEBANON

HOMAGE TO HARIRI?

Are Knudsen

Introduction

In the short story *War Fever*, the British novelist J. G. Ballard portrays war-ravaged Beirut as the ultimate dystopia, where a sinister United Nations experiment propagates the most virulent viral strain known to man, the virus of war.[1] While the rest of the world is at peace, Beirut is at war and the inhabitants cynically manipulated by staged explosions, mock attacks and fake hate images that make militia violence and fighting flourish. 'We have to see what makes people kill', Dr Edwards, the UN-scientist in charge of the project, tells Ryan, an unwitting militia fighter taken hostage because his plan endangered the project. Ryan had stumbled upon the idea of donning a blue UN-peacekeeper helmet, thereby turning militiamen into peacekeepers, an idea that catches on until eventually fighting dies down for the first time in thirty years. But will the ceasefire last?

Ballard's *War Fever* was published just as the Lebanese civil war was coming to an end. At the time Lebanon had become synonymous with never-ending civil war, violence and mayhem giving rise to the noun 'Lebanonisation'. Yet, fifteen years and hundreds of ceasefires later, a seemingly unending civil war came to an end. But the country did not escape new outbreaks of violence. There were many assassinations and assassination attempts, a trend that continued throughout the post-civil war period and peaked after the killing of former Prime Minister Rafik Hariri, members of his staff, security detail and innocent bystanders on 14 February 2005 in downtown Beirut. The murder gave rise to the country's largest demonstrations ever, the Cedar Revolution, which meant that Hariri's murder could not be left unexamined. The demands for justice were local, regional and, importantly, international, supported by the USA, UK and France.

The UN criminal investigation into Hariri's murder was the largest and most sophisticated in the country's history and was followed by the establishment of an international tribunal, the Special Tribunal for Lebanon (STL), set up under UN auspices to try those involved in the murder. Could the Tribunal, as its supporters claim, be a first step in ending political violence and, more generally, promote a 'culture of accountability'? Or could the Tribunal, as its detractors claim, be a sinister plot, akin to Ballard's metaphorical *War Fever*, to drag Lebanon back into violent conflict? In order to answer these questions, this chapter examines the scale of human rights violations and impunity in Lebanon. This is followed by an analysis of the Tribunal's legal foundation, controversial ratification and domestic impact. The chapter argues that the Tribunal has entrenched political divisions, drummed up sectarian tensions and caused successive governance crises. The Tribunal's longer-term impact is dependent on the outcome of the Hariri trial, the Syrian revolt and the international community's willingness to pursue prosecution in a deeply divided country. Yet, the Tribunal's scope for solving the Hariri murder and preventing crimes of a similar nature is uncertain and could be limited to an 'in-and-out' injection of justice.

Impunity and Injustice

Lebanon has a long and troubled history of unsolved political assassinations. Since the 1950s, two presidents (Bashir Gemayel, René Moawad), three prime ministers (Riad al-Solh, Rashid Karami, Rafik Hariri), and several ministers, MPs, politicians, clerics, intellectuals and journalists have been assassinated. In post-civil war Lebanon there were at least thirty major assassinations and assassination attempts but only in a few isolated instances were formal investigations held. In those few that went on trial there was a miscarriage of justice, thus post-civil war justice was selective, politicised and limited to those who did not benefit from political immunity. The murder of Hariri in 2005 was followed by a string of high-level assassinations targeting MPs, journalists and intellectuals.[2] It proved a turning point. But why, against a background of widespread impunity, did the international community intervene to investigate and prosecute Hariri's murder? In this case, the identity of the victim was paramount, as was the potential Syrian involvement in his murder and the public demand for 'the truth' (al-haqiqa). Hariri was a statesman of international stature with strong personal connections to political leaders in the USA, UK and France.[3] Hariri was also an Arab leader with close ties to Saudi Arabia, a key ally of the USA. Hariri's international standing was the main reason why his murder brought the three permanent members of the UN Security Council— USA, UK and France—together in an alliance to investigate and later to prosecute his murder. At the time, there was also increasing weariness in the USA over Syria's role in the region with attempts to rein in a country on the 'wrong side' of the war on terror.[4]

In 2003 the US Congress passed a law aimed at curtailing Syria's hegemony in Lebanon.[5] A year later, the UN followed suit when the Security Council passed Resolution 1559 on 2 September 2004.[6] The resolution targeted two of the most critical and sensitive parts of Lebanon's post-war settlement—the incomplete demobilisation of militias, leaving Hizbollah out, and linked to this, the continued Syrian troop presence. Resolution 1559 called for an immediate end to Syrian troop deployment and the disarmament of Hizbollah and Palestinian militias. Additionally, it required the Lebanese army to deploy along the Israeli border, until then defended by Hizbollah and patrolled by UNIFIL. Each of these demands was a fundamental challenge to the post-war status quo and struck directly at the shaky foundations of Lebanon's post-war treaty, the Taif Agreement. At the time of Hariri's murder the international tribunals for Rwanda, the former Yugoslavia and Sierra Leone had proved their utility. Thus, by 2005, three criteria for international prosecution were fulfilled: a terror victim of international stature (Hariri); a suspect targeted by Western countries and the UN (Syria); and a legal precedence for international prosecution ('internationalised tribunals'). These factors were all necessary for the UN Security Council's approval of using Chapter VII, the UN Charter's strongest sanction, to intervene in a sovereign country such as Lebanon to investigate Hariri's murder and subsequently prosecute his assassins.

Unwilling and unable to prosecute war crimes, Lebanon has repeatedly turned to general amnesties to close troubling chapters in its history. The civil wars in 1958 and 1975–90 ended with a political stalemate, general amnesty and the proclamation; 'No victors, no vanquished'.[7] This comes at a cost. Post-war 'peace' is an interlude, a cold civil war, with grievances and grudges unresolved.[8] The most fateful of these amnesties was the General Amnesty Law (Law No. 84/91) giving amnesty for crimes committed before 28 March 1991. Despite an estimated 100,000–150,000 war-related deaths, savage murders and vengeance massacres the law effectively stopped legal action against war crimes and war criminals, enabled militia leaders to assume ministerial posts and for their militias to be turned into parties. The amnesty law enjoyed widespread political support but prevented the country from confronting its wartime record, punishing human rights violations and bringing those responsible to trial.[9]

Amnesty and amnesia share more than etymological roots;[10] since Lebanon did not prosecute war crimes, the memory of the war had to be subdued and subverted too. Lebanon applies strict censorship to all references to the civil war in what amounts to a state-sponsored amnesia.[11] The country emerged from the civil war without looking back. Typically Rafik Hariri coined his newspaper, radio, TV station and political movement *al-Mustaqbal*, the Future. Lebanon would disdain the past to embrace the future. There was no reason to dwell on the past, what was needed was to turn the page and to 'forgive and forget'. But many neither forgave nor forgot. The civil war demarcation line through central Beirut, the 'Green Line', disappeared but Beirut remained a divided city.[12] The post-war urban reconstruction of Beirut mimicked this amnesia, by tearing down remnants of the civil war as very few buildings were spared demolition and the most symbol-laden area, the Martyr's Square, remained an open void because the multiplicity of its meanings could not be reconciled.[13]

Victimhood and Martyrdom

During the civil war more than 17,000 people disappeared, the majority of them Christian civilians. Afraid that an impartial investigation into their disappearance could incriminate Syria, their fate was ignored or in some cases denied altogether. Unwilling to open war-related files, Prime Minister Hariri sought to close the chapter on the missing persons by naming them 'martyrs of Lebanon'.[14] Despite some recent progress towards uncovering the truth behind these disappearances, unearthing mass graves and recovering bodies, their fate remains unknown. The scores of people missing, murdered or presumed dead have made Lebanon a country of martyrs. The martyrs are remembered in anniversaries and memorials, revered in song and popular culture and, most visibly, reincarnated in larger-than-life posters lining highways, thoroughfares and popular neighbourhoods. All the Lebanese sects engage in the iconography memorialising slain leaders and yet none are bigger and more imposing than the images of the late Prime Minister Rafik Hariri. As time has passed since his murder the Hariri billboards have grown even bigger, bearing the inscription 'WE WILL NOT FORGET YOU'. Hariri also has a memorial statue in downtown Beirut in addition to his tomb next to the imposing al-Amin mosque he endowed. The iconography of slain martyrs is also used to bolster the credentials of present-day political leaders, hence posters show them hovering dreamlike behind their political heirs—a smiling Rafik Hariri pictured behind his son Saad(-eedin).[15] The posterising of slain leaders and cadre underlines that there is no tradition for solving and punishing political murders in Lebanon.[16] Instead, vigils, memorials and anniversaries are held to commemorate those dead who are commonly pronounced 'martyrs'. The absence of closure and justice is one reason why memorials and memorialising is so widespread—there will be neither truth nor justice. The bereaved families, followers and supporters are left to immortalise their slain leaders by seeking redemption rather than justice. So as to redeem their loss, victims are made martyrs. Hariri's death also made him a martyr but, crucially, his picture was displayed with the subtitle 'the truth', *al-haqiqa*, implying that an alternative way to redemption was through obtaining justice and uncovering the truth about his murder. For him there could not only be redemption through martyrdom, but, for the first time, justice and the truth about his murder.

Investigating a Terrorist Attack

The murder of Hariri created a political earthquake and was termed a 'terrorist bombing' by the President of the UN Security Council.[17] It was soon evident that Lebanon's law-enforcing agencies lacked the expertise, impartiality and, crucially, the desire to uncover the details of the attack. In order to investigate the murder, the UN stepped in and dispatched a fact-finding mission to Beirut. Despite the very short time at the mission's disposal, the investigation report documented the mechanics of the car bomb attack, concluded that Hariri was the victim of a terrorist plot and that the Lebanese judiciary lacked the capability to investigate and prosecute the murder.[18] The report recommended that the UN should establish an investigative commission that would lay the basis for prosecuting those responsible. On the basis of the recommendations, the United Nations International Independent Investigation Commission (UNIIIC) was established in April 2005 by Security Council Resolution 1595, reinforced by Chapter VII to ensure full cooperation from all member states.[19]

UNIIIC's first commissioner was the German prosecutor Detlev Mehlis. The first commission report, often referred to as the 'Mehlis Report', was issued on 20 October 2005.[20] It implicated Lebanese and Syrian military intelligence in the assassination and accused Syrian officials, including the Foreign Minister Walid Moallem, of misleading the investigation.[21] Mehlis oversaw one more report before resigning amidst rumours that he had received death threats. In January 2006 the Belgian lawyer Serge Brammertz replaced Mehlis. He supervised the next seven UNIIIC reports (3–9). The reports lacked the sensational details that were the hallmark of Mehlis' approach and Brammertz moved the inquiry away from relying on witness accounts to forensic evidence, an approach that depoliticised the investigation and increased Syrian co-operation with the commission.[22] In 2008 Brammertz resigned and was replaced by the Canadian prosecutor Daniel Bellemare who stewarded the two final UNIIIC reports before the unit closed operations and jurisdiction was transferred to the Tribunal. However, the domestic ratification of the Tribunal nearly ran aground, pitting political factions against each other and dividing the cabinet and the parliament.

The Politics of Prosecution

The murder of Hariri sharply increased political divisions and led to the formation of two opposing political blocs formed around Hariri's Future Movement (14 March) and Hizbollah's Loyalty to the Resistance (8 March). They took their names from the dates of the huge demonstrations following Hariri's murder. Hizbollah's show of force on 8 March was followed by the even bigger public protests on 14 March by pro-Hariri supporters. The divisions can be cast as one of contending visions for the country—the Riviera and the Citadel.[23] The 'riviera' model sees Lebanon as a haven for economic investment and entrepreneurial capitalism tied to the West and the wealthy Gulf states. Against this, the 'citadel' puts Lebanon as a bulwark against Western imperialism and Israeli aggression and with regional ties to an 'axis of resistance' (Iran, Syria). While the 2005 parliamentary elections temporarily glossed over these political divisions, the controversy over the Tribunal made them reappear. The 2005 parliamentary elections were a victory for Saad Hariri, Rafik Hariri's son and political heir, whose electoral alliance held an absolute majority in the parliament. By controlling the premiership, the cabinet and the parliament they would also be in a position to appoint the country's next president to replace Emile Lahoud. If they succeeded, the Future Movement and its 14 March allies would control the key posts of the state and overcome most of the checks and balances that prevent any party from controlling the state and ensure consociational power-sharing.[24]

With this in mind, one can understand why the ratification of the Hariri Tribunal led to a governance crisis when put before the 'unity cabinet' led by Prime Minister Fuad Siniora which (for the first time) included Hizbollah and Amal ministers. On 12 December 2005, the day after the second UNIIIC report was published, the prominent MP and Editor Gibran Tueni was killed by a car bomb. The Siniora cabinet responded by requesting that the UN extend the investigation accordingly and called for an international tribunal to prosecute those responsible. Shortly after, the request for a tribunal was narrowly approved by the cabinet, against the votes of the Hizbollah and Amal ministers who withdrew and later resigned from their posts. Undeterred, the Siniora cabinet continued the dialogue with the UN and in March 2006 a draft agreement between the UN and the government of Lebanon was prepared by the UN secretariat, approved by the Security Council and negotiated by the Secretary-General. When this draft agreement was put up for vote in the cabinet on 12 November 2006, another six ministers resigned. This nearly led to the cabinet's resignation as it was close to losing one-third of its twenty-four members. After another round of negotiations, the finalised agreement was signed by the cabinet on 23 January 2007 and a few days later by the UN.

In order to ratify the agreement, it had to be approved by the parliament. This proved impossible because the MPs loyal to Hizbollah stayed away from the parliament which, below the constitutional limit for representation, could not put the ratification for voting. The Siniora cabinet could not ratify the Tribunal, the president, Emile Lahoud was against ratifying it and the speaker of the parliament, Nabih Berri, was likewise opposed to it and did not adjourn the parliament to vote over it. This constitutional impasse prevented a ratification of the Tribunal. To end the deadlock, the Siniora cabinet petitioned the UN to ratify the Tribunal unilaterally and the petition was later seconded by seventy members of the parliament, many of them holed up for protection in the prime-ministerial offices, the *Grand Sérail*.[25] Since the government of Lebanon's ratification now was unlikely, the UN Security Council ratified the agreement unilaterally on 30 May 2007 with the adoption of Resolution 1757 which included the statutes of the Tribunal as an annex.[26] The resolution passed the Security Council with a very slight margin and with five member states abstaining (China, Indonesia, Qatar, Russia and South Africa).

Tribunal Mandate

In recent years war-crimes tribunals have been set up to try crimes that due to their gravity or magnitude ('genocide', 'massacres', 'ethnic cleansing', 'crimes against humanity') can be prosecuted under what is termed 'universal jurisdiction'. The tribunals have been either purely international (as in the case of the war-crimes tribunals in Yugoslavia and Rwanda) or hybrid courts (such as Sierra Leone). While the former takes place under international law, the latter mixes international and national law and are sometimes referred to as 'internationalized courts'.[27] The Tribunal is unique in that it is based only on Lebanese criminal law as well as the Lebanese definition of 'terrorism' as defined in Article 314 of the penal code.[28] Although established by a UN Security Council resolution (under Chapter VII), the STL is not a UN tribunal but set up under an agreement between the UN and the government of Lebanon. This means that only Lebanon is obliged to cooperate with it, as are the courts of Lebanon. Other states need not cooperate with the Tribunal but it can seek their cooperation on a voluntary basis. Put bluntly, the UN member states other than Lebanon can ignore the Tribunal at their will.[29] This means that a country like Syria need not co-operate with the Tribunal although it was obliged to co-operate with the UNIIIC investigation where the Security Council used Chapter VII, to make 'all States and all parties to cooperate fully with the Commission'. Syria opposes the Tribunal and will not extradite suspects. Should Syrian nationals be indicted, they would be prosecuted on the basis of domestic criminal law which includes the death penalty.[30] Due to the potential threat to the Tribunal, staff, plaintiffs and defendants, the Tribunal is located outside Lebanon, in Leidschendam, a suburb of The Hague in the Netherlands.

While this is a security measure, the distance from Lebanon is a problem both for the judicial process and its legitimacy at home in Lebanon. However, the Beirut Field Office runs an outreach programme and senior Tribunal staff have made several visits to Lebanon to meet with government officials, politicians and victims' family members.

The Tribunal's mandate is critical to the success of its mission and important enough to warrant a special issue of the *Journal of International Criminal Justice*.[31] The Tribunal's mandate is by far the narrowest of any international tribunal. It only seeks the perpetrators of Hariri's assassination, including those who planned it, those who knew about it and those who had the powers to stop it. Because of this limitation in its mandate, the Tribunal's jurisdiction is narrowly bracketed in time. It begins with the attack that nearly killed MP Marwan Hamade (1 October 2004) and ends in late 2005, a period that saw a surge of deadly attacks on politicians and journalists. Only if those murders and attacks can be linked to Hariri's assassination, is the Tribunal empowered to rule in the case.[32] As new attacks reverberated throughout Beirut, the Tribunal's jurisdiction was extended and ends in 2008.

The Tribunal's narrow mandate, purpose and time-frame underline that its objective is strictly limited to prosecuting Hariri's murder (and those found related to it). The aim is to provide a benchmark that will deter future attacks and strengthen the capability of the Lebanese judiciary to undertake robust prosecution on its own. Nonetheless, legal experts suspect that the provisions limiting the Tribunal's mandate are not the result of a judicial oversight but, quite the contrary, inscribed to cripple the Tribunal's effectiveness.[33] To give an example of these limitations, the early investigations into Hariri's murder claimed that the attack was either ordered or approved at the highest levels in Syria in collusion with officials in the Lebanese intelligence. However, unlike the other tribunals set up under international law, the mandate does not contain provisions that limit the immunity of heads of state. Unless there are sufficient grounds for lifting this immunity the Tribunal will not be able to try heads of state.[34]

The Tribunal will try suspects under Lebanese law but its chambers will be composed of four Lebanese and seven international judges selected after a nomination process. Probably because the Tribunal cannot demand cooperation from states other than Lebanon, the Tribunal allows trials *in absentia* in line with Lebanese law; in fact, no other international tribunal has allowed *in absentia* trials to the degree that this Tribunal does.[35] However, in order to increase the prospects of arresting and extraditing suspects, the Tribunal has sought co-operation with Interpol. The Tribunal is composed of four units headed by the president, the prosecutor general, the head of defence and the registrar.[36] During the Tribunal's first eighteen months' operation, three of the top officials resigned, in addition to six other senior staff, fuelling rumours that they quit over attempts to influence the Tribunal's work.[37] The long list of resignations weakened the Tribunal, raised doubts about its leadership and made analysts claim that the Tribunal was 'dying'.[38] Based on interviews with the first commissioner, Detlev Mehlis, Michael Young claimed that Mehlis' successor in this post, Serge Brammertz, was told by UN officials to delay investigations, water down findings and be reticent about the commission's progress. The reason for this, Young claimed, was the UN's policy of engagement vis-à-vis Syria, to which the Tribunal at the time was subservient. From 2009, Syria's emergence from international isolation had put the Tribunal on a track towards oblivion. The UNIIIC reports prepared under Brammertz seemed to support Young's claim as they were bland, repeated technical findings on leads being followed and included a reopening of the investigation into the explosion but without adding new evidence. This could have compromised the investigation and deprived Bellemare of the necessary evidence to prosecute suspects. The Tribunal's first official function on 1 March 2009 was to order the release of four Lebanese generals detained without trial since February 2005.[39] The chief prosecutor must have concluded that the evidence against the detainees would not stand up in a courtroom. In Lebanon too, there was a grudging consensus among the public, followers and especially within the late Hariri's Future Movement, that the Tribunal would not succeed in prosecuting those responsible.[40]

Politicisation of the Tribunal

Since its inception the Tribunal has been dogged by a bad reputation. First of all there is the claim that the Tribunal has been 'politicised'. This was inevitable as the Tribunal is seeking justice for one victim who was close to Western allies.[41] In this sense, both the Tribunal and the inquiry are political and have been politicised right from the start. To the Tribunal's critics, politicisation means that its ultimate purpose is not to prosecute Hariri's assassins but to pressurise Hizbollah, blackmail Syria and weaken Israel's enemies. Nonetheless, the Tribunal's first official function on 1 March 2009 was to order the release of the four generals detained without trial since 2005. To the Tribunal's supporters, the fact that the detainees were released proved that the Tribunal was not politicised. To the Tribunal's detractors, their detainment and eventual release was considered proof that the investigation was politicised right from the start. The problem for the Tribunal was that the more vehemently the charge of politicisation was refuted the more it seemed to be confirmed.

The claim to 'politicisation' brought the Tribunal into conflict with Lebanon's foremost politico-military movement, Hizbollah. In late May 2009 an article in the German magazine *Der Spiegel* claimed that Hizbollah was behind Hariri's murder.[42] The claim made international headlines but was not corroborated by other sources. Yet, the charge of involvement was rekindled during spring 2010 when eighteen Hizbollah members were summoned for questioning by Tribunal-investigators in Beirut. This provoked a strong response from Hizbollah's leader, Hassan Nasrallah, who criticised the politicisation of the Tribunal as well as the leaks in the investigation, but offered to cooperate with the inquiry as long as it remained impartial.[43] The Tribunal dismissed both claims to politicisation of the investigation and leaks during the inquiry,[44] but the leaks raised conflict levels and deepened the country's Sunni-Shia rift. While Hizbollah officials and clerics condemned the Tribunal, the (Sunni) Islamic Sharia Council voiced strong support for the Tribunal and the need to cooperate fully with the investigation.[45]

End Game?

The Hariri Tribunal has proved one of the stiffest challenges yet to international prosecution, due to the regional power-play, local tug-of-war and potential for political conflict in Lebanon. By 2010, it looked as if the Tribunal could be deterred from reaching its goals due to political divisions in Lebanon, the international community's rapprochement with Syria and the relentless attacks on the Tribunal's credibility. It is a measure of the regional changes that had taken place since 2005 that one of Saad Hariri's first official duties as prime minister was to travel to Damascus to greet President Bashar al-Assad. Soon after, Hariri announced that he regretted charging Syria with responsibility for his late father's murder, having been misled by 'false witnesses'.[46]

In July 2010, the Hizbollah leader Hassan Nasrallah announced that he had information that the Tribunal would indict 'rogue' Hizbollah members on involvement in Hariri's assassination.[47] The disclosure was critical enough to warrant a never-before-visit by the heads of state of Saudi Arabia and Syria to defuse tensions. Hizbollah upped the ante by terming the Tribunal an 'Israeli project', followed by video footage meant to corroborate Israeli involvement in Hariri's assassination and replace the Tribunal with a joint Arab-Lebanese commission.[48] At the same time, the Tribunal investigation was stepped up with 3D modelling of the crime scene in Beirut, a full-scale re-enactment of the underground explosion at a French army base and a request to Hizbollah to hand over all the evidence that could link Israel to Hariri's assassination.

The Tribunal was targeted as an 'Israeli project' relying on false witnesses and tampered evidence. Pressure also mounted on Prime Minister Hariri to charge Israel with responsibility for his father's assassination.[49] The many attacks on the Tribunal's credibility was followed by a spate of arrests of Israeli 'spies', some of them employed at the Alfa mobile network. This was particularly sensitive, because telephone logs from this company represent the key 'circumstantial evidence' on which the Tribunal prosecutor was expected to base his case.[50] Other lines of attack on the Tribunal targeted the controversial ratification process (by the Siniora cabinet) and aimed to stop the funding of the Tribunal, shared between Lebanon (49 per cent) and the UN (51 per cent). The Tribunal's budget for 2011 is about USD 66 million. Compared to the many political murders that have not been investigated, the costs for prosecuting Hariri's murder are staggering and could, some argue, be better spent on reforming the country's ailing justice sector.[51] There is also the risk that the Tribunal could be a costly 'in-and-out' injection of justice without a lasting impact on the justice sector.[52]

From late 2010, the growing pressure by the Hizbollah-led coalition to abolish the Tribunal raised fears that the announcement of indictments could lead to civil unrest. Moreover, there was damaging media reports detailing the execution of the attack on Hariri (using mobile phones), the suspects (Hizbollah members) and the circumstantial evidence (telephone logs) that will form the basis of the prosecutor's case.[53] Unauthorised media leaks also targeted Saad Hariri, when confidential audiotapes from his meetings with UNIIIC-investigators were aired on a local TV channel. In the leaked tapes Hariri named Syrian leaders and officials who masterminded his father's assassination. The media leaks were condemned by the Tribunal but added to the urgency of finalising the indictments.[54]

The looming Tribunal indictments put the country on edge as the political deadlock deepened. There were intense mediation efforts by Saudi Arabia and Syria seeking a compromise that would distance Lebanon from the Tribunal. The options tabled ranged from renouncing the Tribunal to outright rejection and non-cooperation. The latter was spelled out in Nasrallah's speech and included withdrawing the four Lebanese judges serving on the Tribunal, halting funding to the Tribunal and, by implication, annulling the controversial memorandum of understanding that ratified it.[55] This would free Lebanese institutions from any legal obligations, such as carrying out arrest warrants, leaving this to agencies such as Interpol. In the end, the Saudi-Syria deal faltered, a last-minute attempt at mediation by Turkey and Qatar failed too and the time for compromise ran out. Not only were the political and personal costs of a compromise over the Tribunal too high for Saad Hariri and the Future Movement but the USA also rejected it.

The failure of these initiatives led to the collapse of the Hariri cabinet on 12 January 2011, when eleven ministers submitted their resignation. The Hizbollah-led opposition later withdrew their support for Hariri and nominated the Tripoli ex-premier Najib Mikati for the post of prime minister.[56] On 25 January, a slim parliamentary majority elected Mikati as the new prime minister, followed soon after by street protests and road blocks by enraged Hariri supporters who saw this as a political coup. On 17 January, Bellemare handed the indictment over for review to the Tribunal's pre-trial judge. Five months later, on 28 June, the finalised indictment was made public and charged four Hizbollah members with responsibility for the attack on Hariri.[57] The publication of the indictment coincided with the Assad regime's brutal clampdown on civil unrest in Syria in the wake of the Arab Spring. The timing of the indictment could indicate that the Tribunal had been waiting for an opportune moment to publicise it, and charging Hizbollah members with responsibility heaped even more pressure on the beleaguered Syrian regime. In Lebanon, however, the indictment was received with a mixture of relief and indifference, neither giving rise to sectarian violence nor public protests. It is likely that Hizbollah's pre-emptive attack on the Tribunal and disclosure of the charges against four of its members had defused the indictment's explosive potential. Adding to this, none of the accused could be apprehended, forcing the Tribunal to begin preparations for trials *in absentia*. Finally, the new prime minister, Najib Mikati, had from the start reassured the UN that his cabinet would honour all of Lebanon's international commitments, including the Tribunal's funding. Following months of cabinet wrangling Mikati transferred Lebanon's share of the Tribunal's funding from the prime minister's own budget. Hizbollah opposed the transfer but did not stop it. It is likely that Syria agreed to the procedure to avoid the fall of the cabinet.[58]

Conclusion: Homage to Hariri?

The challenges before the Tribunal are an indication of the scale of Lebanon's security problems and the depths of its civil-war heritage, a reminder of J. G. Ballard's literary dystopia. Towards the end of Ballard's short story *War Fever* it becomes clear that Ryan's idea of turning militiamen into UN peacekeepers is a success and that the civil war could soon be over. This threatens the experiment and the callous UN plotters who fear this could spell the end to the experiment and, worse, eliminate the virus of war. Thus Ryan's initiative must be stopped and a few well-placed bombs and explosions end the eerie calm and sets the war in motion again. Beirut is again awash in violence and the virus of war is spreading, this time beyond its borders.

In an apparent allegory, the Tribunal is part of an UN-assisted plan to help Lebanon overcome impunity, end security breaches and pave the way to become a democracy based on a rule of law. However, the Tribunal can also be seen as an attack on the country's sovereignty that will multiply security problems and, like the apocalyptic ending to *War Fever*, bring more violence in its wake—which is exactly how its opponents interpret it. In this scenario the UN in present-day Lebanon is, like its fictitious counterpart in *War Fever*, seemingly helping out to relieve pain and suffering but in reality inflicting pain and suffering on the Lebanese by drumming up Sunni-Shia tensions and provoking internal strife. Thus, to the Tribunal's detractors, it is part of a sinister plot to dominate Lebanon, rewrite its history and compromise its sovereignty. The Tribunal has nothing to do with ending impunity and everything to do with inscribing a Sunni hagiography on Lebanon. This lament is echoed by legal experts who see the Tribunal's statutes as biased towards a specific version of the country's history.

Is the Tribunal mainly a tribute to Rafik Hariri, his political legacy and international standing? Should Hariri's murder be investigated even though it represents a singular attempt at seeking justice? To the Tribunal's proponents there are compelling reasons why Lebanon (with UN assistance) should prosecute those responsible for Rafik Hariri's murder. It would not only provide selective justice for Hariri, its main objective, but be a first step towards ending impunity, promote national security and strengthen the judiciary. However, the Tribunal's mandate prevents it from prosecuting heads of state and only obliges Lebanon to collaborate with it. These limitations, some argue, were included to limit the Tribunal's jurisdiction and could have been a result of politicisation of the inquiry. There is also speculation that UNIIIC's criminal investigation was made subservient to regional politics and the commissioner told to water down its findings. The Syrian crisis has since turned the tide in the Tribunal's favour but heralds a period of political instability, sectarian tensions and international mediation with the Tribunal in the shadow of Syria's internal revolt.

Could the Tribunal, if able to conclude its mission, prevent future terror attacks and deter would-be attackers? At the time of writing there has been no high-profile assassinations in Lebanon since late 2008,[59] but we do not know whether this can be credited to the Tribunal's deterrence or not. Indeed, the longer-term impact of the Tribunal on criminal prosecution and impunity is dependent on many factors, in particular the outcome of the Hariri trial. The stakes are high. Should the defendants be acquitted and the chief prosecutor unable to prove the charges, it would exonerate Hizbollah and tarnish the Tribunal. Should the accused be found guilty as charged, the Tribunal would be vindicated and Hizbollah disgraced. In both cases the verdict(s) will be disputed although the jury is not passing a verdict on the 'truth' but on the strength of the evidence at the court's disposal. The truth may never be known, especially if the Tribunal must conduct trials *in absentia*. Tellingly, some time ago the red ticker near the Future Movement's headquarters in Beirut counting the days since Rafik Hariri's murder stopped working. The text on the billboard next to the ticker claiming 'THE TRUTH FOR THE SAKE OF LEBANON' now rings hollow.

NOTES

1. INTRODUCTION: THE CEDAR REVOLUTION AND BEYOND

1. Young, Michael, *The Ghosts of Martyrs Square: An Eyewitness Account of Lebanon's Life Struggle*, New York: Simon & Schuster, 2010; Blanford, Nicholas, *Killing Mr Lebanon: The Assassination of Rafik Hariri and Its Impact on the Middle East*, London: I.B. Tauris, 2009.
2. Haugbolle, Sune, 'Spatial Transformations in the Lebanese "Independence Intifada"', *Arab Studies Journal*, Vol. 14, No. 2 (2006), pp. 60–77.
3. Cammett, Melani, and Sukriti Issar, 'Bricks and Mortar Clientelism: Sectarianism and the Logics of Welfare Allocation in Lebanon', *World Politics*, Vol. 62, No. 3 (2010), pp. 381–421.
4. A recent study suggests that the percentages of Maronites, Sunni and Shia Muslims in the population are roughly equal. Faour, Muhammad A., 'Religion, Demography, and Politics in Lebanon', *Middle Eastern Studies*, Vol. 43, No. 6 (2007), pp. 909–21.
5. Lebanon's election to one of the ten non-permanent seats in the UN Security Council in October 2009, the first time since 1952, can be seen as an attempt to draw Lebanon into the UN fold and insulate it from Syria's grip.
6. Baroudi, Sami E., and Imad Salamey, 'US-French Collaboration on Lebanon: How Syria's Role in Lebanon and the Middle East Contributed to a US-French Convergence', *The Middle East Journal*, Vol. 65, No. 3 (2011), pp. 398–425.
7. According to the Lebanese constitution, the cabinet (council of ministers) reaches its decisions by consensus. If there is no consensus, important national and constitutional issues may be put to a vote, needing two-thirds of the votes to be approved.
8. Seaver, Brenda M., 'The Regional Sources of Power-Sharing Failure: The Case of Lebanon', *Political Science Quarterly*, Vol. 115, No. 2 (2000), pp. 247–71.

9. Saouli, Adham, 'Stability under Late State Formation: The Case of Lebanon', *Cambridge Review of International Affairs*, Vol. 19, No. 4 (2006), pp. 701–17.

10. The Future Movement has the financial resources to arm itself, but until recently did not, although it did set up a private security firm, Future Security Plus (Élizabeth Picard, this volume).

11. Saouli, ibid., p. 714.

12. Norton, Augustus R., *Hezbollah: A Short History*, Princeton: Princeton University Press, 2007, p. 143.

13. U.S. Congress, Syria Accountability and Lebanese Sovereignty Restoration Act (Pl 108–175), Washington D.C.: 12 December 2003, www.lgic.org/en/help_act.php.

14. Knio, Karim, 'Lebanon: Cedar Revolution or Neo-Sectarian Partition?', *Mediterranean Politics*, Vol. 10, No. 2 (2005), pp. 225–32.

15. Makdisi, Karim, 'Constructing Security Council Resolution 1701 for Lebanon in the Shadow of the "War on Terror"', *International Peacekeeping*, Vol. 18, No. 1 (2011), pp. 4–20.

16. ICG, 'Lebanon's Politics: The Sunni Community and Hariri's Future Current', Beirut and Brussels: International Crisis Group, *Middle East Report*, No. 96, 26 May 2010.

17. This suggests that their roles, much like the Maronite Patriarchate in Bkirki, are not only religious but quasi-political, see Skovgaard-Petersen, Jakob, 'The Sunni Religious Scene in Beirut', *Mediterranean Politics*, Vol. 3, No. 1 (1998), pp. 69–80.

18. El-Khazen, Farid, 'Political Parties in Postwar Lebanon: Parties in Search of Partisans', *Middle East Journal*, Vol. 57, No. 4 (2003), pp. 605–24.

19. Issar, Cammett, 'Bricks and Mortar Clientelism'; The Future Movement also stands accused of extensive vote-buying and corruption, see Becherer, Richard, 'A Matter of Life and Debt: The Untold Costs of Rafiq Hariri's New Beirut', *The Journal of Architecture*, Vol. 10, No. 1 (2005), pp. 1–42.

20. Becherer, ibid.

21. Ghosn F., and A. Khoury 'Lebanon after the Civil War: Peace or the Illusion of Peace?' *The Middle East Journal*, Vol. 65, No. 3 (2011), pp. 381–97.

22. Ibid., pp. 386–7.

23. ICG, 'Trial by Fire: The Politics of the Special Tribunal for Lebanon', Beirut and Brussels: International Crisis Group, *Middle East Report*, No. 100, 2 December 2010.

24. Baroudi, ibid.

25. Seeberg, Peter, 'The EU as a Realist Actor in Normative Clothes: EU Democracy Promotion in Lebanon and the European Neighbourhood Policy', *Democratization*, Vol. 16, No. 1 (2009), pp. 81–99.

2. BEFORE THE REVOLUTION

1. O'Leary, Brendan, foreword in Kerr, Michael, *Imposing Power-Sharing: Conflict and Coexistence in Northern Ireland and Lebanon*, Dublin: Irish Academic Press, 2005, p. xxiv.
2. Jones, Clive, and Sergio Catignani (eds), *Israel and Hizbollah: an Interstate and Asymmetric War in Perspective*, London: Routledge, 2009.
3. Knudsen, Are, and Sari Hanafi (eds), *Palestinian Refugees: Identity, Space and Place in the Levant*, London: Routledge, 2011.
4. *The Daily Star*, 16 May 2008.
5. The Doha Agreement, http://www.nowlebanon.com/NewsArticleDetails.aspx?ID=44023&MID=115&PID=2.
6. *The New York Times*, 12 January 2011.
7. Choueiri, Youssef (ed.), *Breaking the Cycle: Civil Wars in Lebanon*, London: Stacey International, 2007.
8. *The Washington Post*, 3 March 2005.
9. Kerr, Michael, *Imposing Power-Sharing: Conflict and Coexistence in Northern Ireland and Lebanon*, Dublin: Irish Academic Press, 2005, Chapter 7.
10. *The New York Times*, 12 July 2006.
11. Hanf, Theodor, *Coexistence in Wartime Lebanon: Decline of a State and Rise of a Nation*, London: Centre for Lebanese Studies in association with I.B. Tauris, 1993.
12. Kaufman, Asher, 'Who Owns the Shebaa Farms? Chronicle of a Territorial Dispute', *Middle East Journal*, Vol. 56, No. 4 (2002), pp. 576–96.
13. *Daily Telegraph*, 31 July 2006.
14. *BBC News*, 1 August 2006, http://news.bbc.co.uk/1/hi/world/middle_east/5218210.stm.
15. Prime Minister Fuad Siniora's statement at the Islamic Summit held in Kuala Lumpur, 3 August 2006.
16. *Haaretz*, 30 August 2006.
17. Hanf, ibid.
18. El-Khazen, Farid, *The Communal Pact of National Identities: the Making and Politics of the 1943 National Pact*, Oxford: Centre for Lebanese Studies, 1991.
19. Maila, Joseph, *The Document of National Understanding: a Commentary*, Oxford: Centre for Lebanese Studies, 1992.
20. Hanf, *Coexistence in Wartime Lebanon*, p. 558.
21. El-Khazen, Farid, *The Breakdown of the State in Lebanon, 1967–1976*, Cambridge: Harvard University Press, 2000, pp. 140–75.
22. Seale, Patrick, *Assad: The Struggle for the Middle East*, Los Angeles: University of California Press, 1996, pp. 267–89.
23. The Ford Presidential Library: NSA Memos, Box 19, Memo of Conversation between Ford and Kissinger, The Cabinet Room, 18 June 1976.

24. Kerr, Michael, "'A positive aspect to the tragedy of Lebanon'": The Convergence of US, Syrian and Israeli Interests at the Outset of Lebanon's Civil War', *Israel Affairs*, Vol. 15, No. 4 (2009), pp. 355–71.
25. Interview with Vincent Battle, US Ambassador to Lebanon, Aoukar, 14 June 2002.
26. *The Independent*, 3 June 2005.
27. Al-Jazeera interview with Lakhdar Ibrahimi, War of Lebanon, Part 15. See also Baram, Amatzia, 'The Iraqi Invasion of Kuwait: Decision making in Baghdad' and Barry Rubin, 'The United States and Iraq: From Appeasement to War', in Baram, Amatzia, and Rubin, Barry (eds), *Iraq's Road to War*, Basingstoke: Palgrave, 1996, pp. 5–36 and 255–72.
28. Interview with Vincent Battle, US Ambassador to Lebanon, Aoukar, 14 June 2002.

3. THE LIMITS OF CORPORATE CONSOCIATION: TAIF AND THE CRISIS OF POWER-SHARING IN LEBANON SINCE 2005

1. Hudson, Michael, 'The Lebanese Crisis: The Limits of Consociational Democracy', *Journal of Palestine Studies*, Vol. 5, No. 3/4 (1976), pp. 109–22. See also Makdisi, Samir, and Marcus Marktanner, 'Trapped by Consociationalism: The Case of Lebanon', *Working Paper*, American University of Beirut, 2008, p. 12.
2. Horowitz, Donald L., *Ethnic Groups in Conflict*, Berkley: University of California Press, 2000, p. 568.
3. Hanf, Theodor, *Coexistence in Wartime Lebanon: Decline of a State and Rise of a Nation*, London: Centre for Lebanese Studies in association with I.B. Tauris, 1993, pp. 588–9.
4. This is clearly stated in the text: 'There shall be no legitimacy for any authority which opposes the pact of coexistence'. Taif Agreement, General Principles section, I. http://www.elections-lebanon.org/elections/docs_6_B_Ba_e.aspx.
5. Kerr, Michael, *Imposing Power-Sharing: Conflict and Coexistence in Northern Ireland and Lebanon*, Dublin: Irish Academic Press, 2005, p. 159.
6. Ibid.
7. Ibid., p. 174.
8. Interview with Farid El-Khazen, academic and Member of Parliament, Nakkash, 29 December 2010.
9. International Crisis Group, 'Lebanon: Hizbollah's Weapons Turn Inward', *Crisis Group Middle East Briefing*, 23, 2008, p. 2; see also International Crisis Group, 'Lebanon's Politics: The Sunni Community and Hariri's Future Current', *Middle East Report*, 96, (2010), p. i.
10. See also Interview with Nabih Berri, Parliament Speaker, Beirut, 31 December 2010; Interview with Nohad al-Machnouk, Future Movement Member of Parliament, Beirut, 30 December 2010.

11. It is worth noting Farid El-Khazen's assessment that consociationalism is not a 'switch-on, switch-off' system and that it was impossible to expect consociationalism to function immediately after Syria's withdrawal. Interview with El-Khazen, Nakkash, 29 December 2010.
12. Kerr, ibid., p. 167.
13. For evidence that Druze grievances stem from corporate consociatonalism, see El-Khazen, Farid, 'Kamal Jumblatt, The Uncrowned Druze Prince of the Left', *Middle East Studies*, Vol. 24, No. 2 (1988), p. 179. Jumblatt's vision to reform the political system indicates that corporate consociationalism historically created Druze resentment. See also p. 200: 'Jumblatt's boundless political ambitions could not be confined to Lebanon's politics of communal balancing and consensus… Jumblatt would not be satisfied by mere government service under a Maronite President and a Sunni Prime Minister'. His son Walid recalls that his father envisioned a non-confessional political system. Interview with Walid Jumblatt, Druze leader, Beirut, 3 January 2011.
14. Kerr, ibid., p. 176.
15. Lijphart, Arend, 'Constitutional Designs for Divided Societies', *Journal of Democracy*, Vol. 15, No. 2 (2004), p. 99. Initially the father of the consociational democratic theory stipulated four key requirements for a functional democracy but later revised his theory and identified two key requirements—power-sharing in the form of a grand coalition and group autonomy.
16. Cordell, Karl, and Stefan Wolff, 'Power-Sharing', in Cordell, Karl and Stefan Wolff (eds), *Routledge Handbook of Ethnic Conflict*, London: Routledge, 2011, p. 302.
17. O'Leary, Brendan, 'Debating Consociational Politics: Normative and Explanatory Arguments', in Noel, Sidney J. R. (ed.), *From Power-Sharing to Democracy: Post-Conflict Institutions in Ethnically Divided Societies*, Toronto: McGill-Queens University Press, 2005, p. 12.
18. Ibid.
19. Ibid., p. 13.
20. McGarry, John, and Brendan O'Leary, 'Iraq's Constitution of 2005: Liberal Consociation as Political Prescription', *International Journal of Constitutional Law*, Vol. 5, No. 4 (2007), p. 675.
21. http://www.stefanwolff.com/files/ConsociationalTheoryPaper.pdf.
22. McGarry et al., ibid., p. 675.
23. Ibid.
24. Nowhere is this written in the Taif Agreement but it was verbally agreed. See El-Khazen, Farid, 'The Postwar Political Process: Authoritarianism by Diffusion', in Hanf, Theordor, and Nawaf Salam, (eds), *Lebanon in Limbo: Postwar Society and State in an Uncertain Regional Environment*, Baden-Baden: Nomos Verlagsgesellschaft, 2003, p. 57.

25. McGarry et al., ibid., p. 691.
26. Ibid., p. 675 and p. 691.
27. Interview with Ali Hamdan, Senior Political and Media Advisor to House Speaker Nabih Berri, Beirut, 27 June 2011; Interview with Ali Fayyad, Hizbollah Member of Parliament, Beirut, 8 July 2011.
28. This does not overlook the war's external dimension. See Hanf, ibid., p. 175.
29. Ibid., p. 92.
30. El-Khazen, Farid, *The Communal Pact of National Identities: the Making and Politics of the 1943 National Pact*, Oxford: Centre for Lebanese Studies, 1991, p. 5.
31. Hanf, ibid., p. 72.
32. Henri Pharoun, quoted in Hanf, ibid.
33. Ibid. p. 587.
34. Hanf, ibid., p. 586.
35. Ibid., p. 91.
36. Ibid.
37. Ibid., p. 92.
38. El-Khazen, ibid., p. 178.
39. Kerr, ibid., p. 142.
40. Interview with al-Machnouk, 17 June 2011.
41. Hanf, ibid., p. 586.
42. Interview with Paul Salem, Director of the Carnegie Middle East Center, Beirut, 6 July 2011.
43. Maila, Joseph, *The Document of National Understanding: a Commentary*, Oxford: Centre for Lebanese Studies, 1992, p. 36.
44. Hanf, ibid., p. 587.
45. Traboulsi, Fawwaz, *A History of Modern Lebanon*, London: Pluto Press, 2007, p. 246.
46. Interview with Hamdan, 12 July 2011.
47. Hanf, ibid., p. 587.
48. Maila, ibid., p. 29.
49. Ibid., p. 42.
50. Hanf, ibid., p. 586.
51. Maila, ibid., p. 27.
52. Ibid., p. 45.
53. Kerr, ibid., p. 162.
54. Hanf, ibid., p. 586.
55. Norton, Augustus R., 'Lebanon After Taif: Is the Civil War Over?', *Middle East Journal*, Vol. 45, No. 3 (1991), p. 464.
56. Hudson, Michael, 'Lebanon after Ta'if: Another Reform Opportunity Lost', *Arab Studies Quarterly*, Vol. 21, No. 1 (1999), pp. 27–35.
57. Majed, Ziad, 'Hezbollah and the Shiite Community: From Political Confes-

sionalization to Confessional Specialization', *Briefing Paper*, The Aspen Institute, 2010, p. 7.

58. Document from Hizbollah Politburo, 'The Taif Accord: A Study of Content', Hizbollah Committee for Analysis and Studies (1989), p. 5. It criticises Maronite 'hegemony' through the presidential office—although it also acknowledges that in principle, executive authority was transferred from the president to the council of ministers.

59. Nasrallah television interview. See Saad-Ghorayeb, Amal, *Hizb'ullah: Politics and Religion*, London: Pluto Press, 2002, p. 26.

60. Interview with Hamdan, 27 June 2011.

61. Hizbollah maintain that the Taif Agreement awarded the Sunni community the highest authority. 'It is clear that the Sunni position generally leans more toward keeping the Ta'if Accord as is, in light of the special prerogatives it affords the Sunni Prime Minister... the Prime Minister plays, more than anyone else, a pivotal role within the power equilibrium'. See Fayyad, Ali, *Fragile States: Dilemmas of Stability in Lebanon and the Arab World*, Oxford: INTRAC, 2008, p. 61.

62. Interview with Fayyad, 8 July 2011.

63. Fayyad, *Fragile States*, p. 60.

64. Interviews with Berri, 31 December 2010; al-Machnouk, 30 December 2010.

65. Interview with al-Machnouk, 30 December 2010.

66. Maila foresaw the emergence of Maronite and Shia grievances of unequal participation in 1992. See Maila, ibid., p. 56.

67. Salem, Paul, 'Framing Post-War Lebanon: Perspectives on the Constitution and the Structure of Power', *Mediterranean Politics*, Vol. 3, No. 1 (1998), p. 15.

68. Interviews with Hamdan, 27 June 2011; Fayyad, Beirut, 8 July 2011.

69. O'Leary, ibid., p. 12.

70. Interview with Fayyad, Beirut, 13 July 2011.

71. Ibid.

72. Hamdan indicated that the Shia would never consider the presidency: 'There is a uniqueness to Lebanon that we respect... the president to always be a Maronite'. Interview with Hamdan, Beirut, 12 July 2011.

73. Interview with Fayyad, 8 July 2011.

74. Ibid.

75. Ibid.

76. For academic corroboration, see O'Leary, ibid., p. 23.

77. International Crisis Group', Managing the Gathering Storm', *Middle East Report*, 48 (2005), p. 1.

78. International Crisis Group', Lebanon's Politics: The Sunni Community and Hariri's Future Current', p.i.

79. Interview with al-Machnouk, 17 June 2011. See also Majed, ibid., p. 3.

80. Interviews with Berri, 31 December 2010; al-Machnouk, 17 June 2011; Fayyad, 8 July 2011.

81. Interviews with Hamdan, 27 June 2011; Fayyad, 8 July 2011.

82. Fayyad, *Fragile States*, p. 65. See also interview with Hamdan, 27 June 2011.

83. Interview with Hamdan, 12 July 2011.

84. Hariri served as prime minister in 1992–8; 1995; 1996; 2000–4.

85. Interview with Hamdan, 27 June 2011.

86. Ibid.; Hizbollah and Amal's Christian ally Michel Aoun agreed: 'Rafik Hariri took all the power and positions for himself'. Interview with Michel Aoun, head of the Free Patriotic Movement, Rabiyeh, 29 June 2011.

87. Interview with Fayyad, 13 July 2011.

88. Interview with al-Machnouk, 17 June 2011; Interview with Aref Abed, Senior Political and Media Advisor to Fuad Siniora, Beirut, 22 June 2011.

89. Interview with al-Machnouk, 17 June 2011.

90. Ibid.

91. Interview with Abed, 22 June 2011.

92. Maila, ibid., p. 42.

93. Interview with Salem, 6 July 2011.

94. Interview with Abed, 22 June 2011.

95. Interviews with Fayyad, 8 July 2011; Hamdan, 27 June 2011.

96. Interviews with al-Machnouk, 17 June 2011; Abed, 22 June 2011; Khaled Qabbani, a constitutional advisor at Taif. Interview, Beirut, 23 July 2011.

97. Interview with Salem, 6 July 2011.

98. Interview with Fayyad, 8 July 2011.

99. Ibid.

100. Interview with Hamdan, 27 June 2011; see also Fayyad, *Fragile States*, p. 66.

101. Interviews with Berri, 31 December 2010; al-Machnouk, 30 December 2010.

102. Previous interviews conducted with rival political actors and elites indicate an inherent willingness of segmental elites to uphold consociationalism. They recognise the necessity of sharing power to prevent conflict. See interviews with Berri, 31 December 2010; al-Machnouk, 30 December 2010; Jumblatt, 3 January 2011; El-Khazen, 29 December 2010; Fayyad, 5 January 2011.

103. Interview with al-Machnouk, 17 June 2011.

104. Interview with Fuad Siniora, 20 July 2011. See also El-Khazen, Farid, 'Lebanon—Independent No More: Disappearing Christians of the Middle East', *Middle East Quarterly*, Vol. 8, No. 1 (2001), pp. 43–50.

105. Hudson, ibid.

106. Taif Agreement, Political Reforms section. See http://www.elections-lebanon. org/elections/docs_6_B_Ba_e.aspx.

107. The Christian sects collectively comprise 39.9 per cent of the registered electorate—far less than the 50 per cent parity reserved for them in parliament. See Democracy Reporting International, 'Assessment of the Electoral Frame-

work: 'The Election Law of 2000 and the Draft Law by the Boutrous Commission', p. 16.

108. Interview with Siniora, 20 July 2011.

109. The Sunni and Shia communities are allocated twenty-seven seats each. The Sunni comprise 26.8 per cent of the registered electorate; and the Shia comprise 26.3 per cent. See DRI, 'Assessment of the Electoral Framework', p. 16.

110. Interview with Richard Chambers, Director of IFES Lebanon, Beirut, 12 July 2011.

111. Taif Agreement, 'Political Reforms', http://www.elections-lebanon.org/elections/docs_6_B_Ba_e.aspx.

112. Future and Amal attribute *qada* electoral districting as directly facilitating the outbreak of the 1975 conflict. See Interviews with Hamdan, 12 July 2011; Abed, 22 June 2011. Further, qada districting falls into O'Leary's framework of a corporate consociationalism as it obliged voters to elect candidates from their own confessions.

113. Interview with Qabbani, 23 July 2011.

114. Ibid.

115. Lijphart, 'Constitutional Design for Divided Societies', p. 100.

116. Ibid., p. 96.

117. Lijphart, Arend, and Bernard Grofman, 'Choosing an Electoral System', in Promper, Gerald M. (ed.), *Choosing an Electoral System: Issues and Alternatives*, New York: Praeger, 1984, p. 5.

118. Ibid.

119. This is a consequence of the *qada* and the so-called 'block vote' majoritarian system. See IFES, 'Electoral Systems and Lebanon', *IFES Introduction* (2009), p. 3 and p. 6.

120. Interview with Chambers, 12 July 2011.

121. Interview with al-Machnouk, 17 June 2011.

122. Ibid.

123. http://www.al-akhbar.com/node/13781.

124. Interview with al-Machnouk, 17 June 2011.

125. http://www.crisisgroup.org/en/regions/middle-east-north-africa/iraq-syria-lebanon/lebanon/087-lebanons-elections-avoiding-a-new-cycle-of-confrontation.aspx.

126. Interview with Jumblatt, 3 January 2011.

127. ICG, 'Lebanon: Hizbollah's Weapons Turn Inward', p. 1.

128. http://www.dailymotion.com/video/xrytt_hariri-interview-from-november-2001_news Rafik Hariri describing Hizbollah as a resistance organization.

129. Interview with Siniora, 20 July 2011.

130. Interview with Mohamamd Safadi, Finance Minister, Beirut, 21 July 2011.

131. ICG, 'Lebanon's Politics: The Sunni Community and Hariri's Future Current', p. 13.
132. Ibid., p. i.
133. http://www.carnegiemec.org/publications/?fa=20277&zoom_highlight=Doha+Accords+Lebanon.
134. See Interview with El-Khazen, 29 December 2010, for an assessment that converging Qatar-Saudi fears that a Sunni-Shia conflict would destabilise their own regimes, hastening external intervention. See also Jeffrey Feltman, Deputy Assistant Secretary, Near Eastern Affairs Bureau, House Foreign Affairs Committee, Subcommittee on Middle East and South Asia, 29 July 2008; http://www.csmonitor.com/World/Middle-East/2008/0522/p01s05-wome.html.
135. http://www.carnegiemec.org/publications/?fa=20277&zoom_highlight=Doha+Accords+Lebanon.
136. Interview with al-Machnouk, 30 December 2010.
137. Interview with Siniora, 20 July 2011.
138. Ibid.
139. Interview with Fayyad, 13 July 2011.
140. Nasrallah defended Hizbollah's actions as 'defending our weapons with our weapons'. See ICG, 'Lebanon: Hizbollah's Weapons Turn Inward', p. 4.
141. Nasrallah suggested the communications network is a cornerstone of their military operations. See ICG, ibid., p. 3.
142. Interview with Fayyad, 13 July 2011.
143. Interview with al-Machnouk, 30 December 2010.
144. Interview with Fayyad, 13 July 2011.
145. Ibid. He emphasised this analysis within his context as an academic and not a Hizbollah official.
146. Interview with Abed, 22 June 2011.
147. Interview with Siniora, 20 July 2011.
148. Interview with Fayyad, 13 July 2011.
149. Interview with Fayyad, 8 July 2011. He highlighted political confessionalism as one of the most 'threatening' issues and stipulated its abolishment along with implementing the Taif Agreement's electoral districts simultaneously as priorities.
150. Interview with Fayyad, 8 July 2011.
151. Interview with Hamdan, 12 July 2011.
152. Ibid.
153. Ibid.
154. IFES, *Lebanon Briefing Paper*, p. 1.
155. Interview with Chambers, 12 July 2011.
156. Interview with Fayyad, 8 July 2011. He described it as 'Shia silence'.

157. Interviews with Hamdan, 12 July 2011; Fayyad, 8 and 13 July 2011.
158. Interview with Fayyad, 13 July 2011.
159. http://www.nowlebanon.com/NewsArchiveDetails.aspx?ID=69858.
160. Interview with al-Machnouk, 17 June 2011.
161. Ibid.
162. Interview with Fayyad, 13 July 2011.
163. Interview with Abed, 22 June 2011.
164. Majed, 'Hezbollah and the Shiite Community', p. 5.
165. Ibid., p. 6.
166. Fayyad, *Fragile States*, p. 59.
167. Interview with Hamdan, 12 July 2011.
168. At the time of writing, Bashar al-Assad was still in power despite uprisings against his regime since March 2011.
169. Interview with unnamed Hizbollah-Amal official, Beirut, 2011.
170. Ibid.
171. Interview with al-Machnouk, 17 June 2011.
172. Such fears are not new. See Hanf, Ibid., p. 4.
173. Ibid.
174. Interview with Abed, 22 June 2011.
175. http://www.fpif.org/articles/iran-saudi_relations_rising_tensions_and_growing_rivalry.
176. Ibid.
177. Ibid.
178. International Crisis Group, 'Uncharted Waters: Thinking Through Syria's Dynamics', Policy Briefing, *Middle East Briefing*, 31, (2011), p. 4.
179. Hamdan did not deny that events in Syria were causing concern not only for Hizbollah but all political factions. Interview, 27 June 2011.
180. Interviews with Abed, 22 June 2011; al-Machnouk, 17 June 2011.
181. ICG, 'Syria After Lebanon, Lebanon After Syria', p. 19; Kerr, *Imposing Power-Sharing*, p. 161.
182. Term extended from Salibi, Kamal, *A House of Many Mansions: The History of Lebanon Reconsidered*, London: IB Tauris, 2003.
183. Interview with Abed, 22 June 2011.
184. Interview with al-Machnouk, 17 June 2011.
185. Hanf, ibid., p. 5.
186. Maila, ibid., p. 31.

4. FOREIGN INTERVENTIONS, POWER SHARING AND THE DYNAMICS OF CONFLICT AND COEXISTENCE IN LEBANON

1. See for example Lehmbruch, Gerhard, 'A Non-Competitive Pattern of Conflict Management in Liberal Democracies: The Case of Switzerland, Austria and Leb-

anon', in McRae, Kenneth D. (ed.), *Consociational Democracy*, Toronto: McClelland and Stewart, 1974, pp. 90–7; Lijphart, Arend, 'Consociational Democracy', *World Politics*, Vol. 21, No. 2 (1969), pp. 207–25.

2. See Tuéni, Ghassan, *Une guerre pour les autres*, Paris: Jean-Claude Lattès, 1985.
3. Brynen, Rex, 'Palestine and the Arab State System: Permeability, State Consolidation and the Intifada', *Canadian Journal of Political Science/Revue canadienne de science politique*, Vol. 24, No. 3 (1991), pp. 595–621.
4. See for example El-Khazen, Farid, *The Breakdown of the State in Lebanon, 1967–1976*, Cambridge: Harvard University Press, 2000; Tuéni, ibid.
5. Salloukh, Bassel F., 'The Art of the Impossible: The Foreign Policy of Lebanon', in Korany, Bahgat, and Ali Hillal Dessouki (eds), *The Foreign Policies of Arab States: The Challenge of Globalization*, Cairo: American University of Cairo Press, 2008, p. 284.
6. Makdissi, Ussama, *The Culture of Sectarianism: Community, History, and Violence in Nineteenth-Century Ottoman Lebanon*, Berkeley: University of California Press, 2000; Zamir, Meir, *Lebanon's Quest: The Road to Statehood, 1926–1939*, London: I.B. Tauris and Co., 2000.
7. See Kerr, Michael, *Imposing Power-Sharing: Conflict and Coexistence in Northern Ireland and Lebanon*, Dublin: Irish Academic Press, 2006; Seaver, Brenda, 'The Regional Sources of Power-Sharing Failure: The Case of Lebanon', *Political Science Quarterly*, Vol. 115, No. 2 (2000), pp. 247–72; Zahar, Marie-Joëlle, 'Power Sharing in Lebanon: Foreign Protectors, Domestic Peace, and Democratic Failure', in Rothchild, Donald, and Philip Roeder (eds), *Sustainable Peace: Power and Democracy after Civil Wars*, (Ithaca: Cornell University Press, 2005, pp. 219–40.
8. There are of course other important outside players in Lebanese politics. The Saudis, Iranians and Israelis come to mind. However, for the purposes of this chapter, I only focus on those players who were front and centre in the dynamics of Lebanese politics between 2004 and 2010.
9. The notion of mosaic also refers to lack of open dialogue and to the domination of private interests. Barakat, Halim, 'Social and Political Integration in Lebanon: A Case of Social Mosaic', *Middle East Journal*, Vol. 27, No. 3 (1973), pp. 301–18.
10. Raad, Ghassan, 'The Termination of Protracted Social Conflict in Lebanon: An Analytical Perspective', in Shehadi, Nadim, and Dana H. Mills (eds.), *Lebanon: A History of Conflict and Consensus*, London: I.B. Tauris and The Centre for Lebanese Studies, 1988, pp. 201–9.
11. Salibi, Kamal, *Crossroads to Civil War: Lebanon, 1958–1976*, New York: Delmar Books, 1976; Deeb, Marius, *The Lebanese Civil War*, New York: Praeger, 1980; Nasr, Salim, 'Backdrop to Civil War: The Crisis of Lebanese Capitalism', *MERIP Reports*, No. 73 (1978), pp. 3–13.

12. The National Pact attempted to reconcile two visions of Lebanon. Christians saw the country as a refuge for minorities and a bridge to the West whereas Muslims stressed Lebanon's Arab identity. The pact sought to strike a balance by advocating a neutral foreign policy.

13. El-Khazen, ibid.

14. See Zahar, ibid.

15. On the notion of permeability, see Noble, Paul, 'The Arab System: Pressures, Constraints, and Opportunities', in Korany, Bahgat, and Ali Hillal Dessouki (eds), *The Foreign Policies of Arab States: The Challenge of Globalization*, Cairo: American University of Cairo Press, 2008, pp. 41–77; Salloukh, Bassel F., and Rex Brynen (eds), *Persistent Permeability? Regionalism, Localism, and Globalization in the Middle East*, Burlington: Ashgate, 2004.

16. Salloukh, Bassel F., 'The Limits of Electoral Engineering in Divided Societies: Elections in Postwar Lebanon', *Canadian Journal of Political Science*, Vol. 39, No. 3 (2006), pp. 635–55.

17. Zahar, Marie-Joëlle, 'Peace by Unconventional Means: Evaluating Lebanon's Ta'if Accord', in Rothchild, Donald, Steve Stedman and Elizabeth Cousens (eds), *Ending Civil Wars: The Implementation of Peace Agreements*, Boulder: Lynne Rienner, 2002, fn. 20, p. 593.

18. El-Khazen, ibid.; Mackay, Sandra, *Mirror of the Arab World: Lebanon in Conflict*, New York: Norton and Norton, 2008, p. 186; Volker, Perthes, 'Myths and Money: Four Years of Hariri and Lebanon's Preparation for a New Middle East', *MERIP Middle East Report*, No. 203 (1997), p. 19; Tuéni, ibid.

19. El-Khazen, ibid., particularly pp. 125, 261, 327 and 342.

20. Zisser, Eyal, 'The Maronites, Lebanon and the State of Israel: Early Contacts', *Middle Eastern Studies*, Vol. 31, No. 4 (1995), pp. 889–918; Rabinovich, Itamar, *The War for Lebanon*, Ithaca: Cornell University Press, 1985, pp. 117, 162–3 and 168.

21. See for example Salloukh, ibid.; Posusney, Marsha P., 'Multi-Party Elections in the Arab World: Institutional Engineering and Oppositional Strategies', *Studies in Comparative International Development*, Vol. 36, No. 4 (2002), pp. 34–62; Gambill, Gary C., and Abou Aoun, Elie, 'Special Report: How Syria Orchestrates Lebanon's Elections', *Middle East Intelligence Bulletin*, Vol. 2, No. 7 (2000).

22. Zahar, Marie-Joëlle, 'Foreign Intervention and State Reconstruction: Bosnian Fragility in Comparative Perspective', in Bojicic-Dzelilovic, Vesna, and Denisa Kostovicova (eds), *State Weakness in the Balkans: Context, Comparison and Implications*, London: Ashgate, 2009, pp. 115–26. On Syria's role after Taif, see Perthes, Volker, 'Syrian Predominance in Lebanon', in Hollis, Rosemary, and Nadim Shehadi (eds), *Lebanon on Hold: Implications for Middle East Peace*, Oxford: Royal Institute of International Affairs and The Centre for Lebanese

Studies, 1996, pp. 31–4; Salem, Paul, 'The Wounded Republic: Lebanon's Struggle for Recovery', *Arab Studies Quarterly*, Vol. 16, No. 4 (1994), pp. 47–63; Mansour, Albert, *Al-inqilab 'ala al-Ta'if* (The Coup d'État against Ta'if), Beirut: Dar al-Jadid, 1993; Perthes, 'Myths and Money'; Harik, Judith P., 'Democracy (Again) Derailed: Lebanon's Ta'if Paradox', in Korany, Bahgat, Rex Brynen and Paul Noble (eds), *Political Liberalization and Democratization in the Arab World, Vol. 2: Comparative Experiences*, Boulder: Lynne Rienner, 1998, pp. 127–55; El-Khazen, Farid, *Lebanon's First Postwar Parliamentary Election, 1992: An Imposed Choice*, Oxford: Centre for Lebanese Studies, 1998; El-Khazen, Farid, *Intikhabat Lubnan ma Ba'd al-Harb 1992, 1996, 2000: Dimuqratiyya bila Khayar* (Lebanon's Postwar Elections 1992, 1996, 2000: Democracy without Choice), Beirut: Dar al-Nahar lil-Nashr, 2000; Nassif, Nicolas, and Boumonsef, Rosanna, *Al-Masrah wal-Kawalis: Intikhabat 96 fi Fusuliha* (The Stage and the Backstage: The Chapters of the 1996 Elections), Beirut: Dar al-Nahar lil-Nashr, 1996; Salam, Nawaf, 'Islah al-Nidham al-Intikhabi' (The Reform of the Electoral System), in Salam, Nawaf (ed.), *Khiyarat Lubnan* (Lebanon's Options), Beirut: Dar al-Nahar lil-Nashr, 2004, pp. 14–17.

23. Zahar, ibid., pp. 120–1.

24. Salloukh, Bassel F., 'Democracy in Lebanon: The Primacy of the Sectarian System', in Brown, Nathan J., and Emad el-Din Shahin (eds), *The Struggle over Democracy in the Middle East: Regional Politics and External Policies*, New York: Routledge, 2010, pp. 134–50. See also, Zahar, ibid.

25. Saideman, Stephen M., and Marie-Joëlle Zahar, 'Causing Security, Reducing Fear: Deterring Intra-State Violence and Assuring Government Restraint', in Saideman, Stephen M., and Marie-Joëlle Zahar (eds), *Intra-State Conflict, Governments and Security: Dilemmas of Deterrence and Assurance*, London: Routledge, 2008, pp. 1–19.

26. See for example Kostovicova, Denisa, and Vesna Bojicic-Dzelilovic (eds), *Persistent State Weakness in the Global Age*, London: Ashgate, 2009; Walter, Barbara F., 'Bargaining Failures and Civil War', *Annual Review of Political Science*, No. 12 (2009), pp. 243–61; Hironaka, Ann, *Neverending Wars: The International Community, Weak States, and the Perpetuation of Civil War*, Cambridge, MA: Harvard University Press, 2005.

27. Waltz, Kenneth N., *Theory of International Politics*, New York: McGraw Hill, 1979, pp. 102–28; Jervis, Robert, 'Cooperation under the Security Dilemma', *World Politics*, Vol. 30, No. 2 (1978), pp. 167–214; Walt, Stephen M., 'Alliance formation and the Balance of World Power', *International Security*, No. 9 (1985), pp. 2–43; Barnett, Michael N., 'Identity and Alliances in the Middle East', in Katzenstein, Peter (ed.), *The Culture of National Security: Norms and Identity in World Politics*, New York: Columbia, 1996, pp. 400–47; Doyle, Michael, 'Politics and Grand Strategy', in Rosecrance, Richard, and Arthur Stein (eds), *The*

Domestic Bases of Grand Strategy, Ithaca: Cornell University Press, 1993, pp. 22–47; Powell, Robert, *In The Shadow of Power*, Princeton: Princeton University Press, 1999, Chapter 5; Smith, Alastair, 'Alliance Formation and War', *International Studies Quarterly*, Vol. 39, No. 4 (1995), pp. 405–25; Sorokin, Gerald L., 'Alliance Formation and General Deterrence', *Journal of Conflict Resolution*, Vol. 38, No. 2 (1994), pp. 298–325.

28. For more details on the circumstances surrounding the granting of this exception and for a discussion of its consequences, see Zahar, 'Peace by Unconventional Means', pp. 577–9 and 588–90.

29. El-Hokayem, Emile, and Elena McGovern, *Towards a More Secure and Stable Lebanon: Prospects for Security Sector Reform*, Washington, D.C.: Henry L. Stimson Center, 2008, p. 3.

30. Over the period 1991–2004, the sectarian distribution of the officer corps shifted to one that was roughly 47 per cent Christian and 53 per cent Muslim. Salloukh, Bassel F., 'Syria and Lebanon: a Brotherhood Transformed', *MERIP Middle East Report*, No. 236 (2005), pp. 14–21.

31. Particularly through UNSC Resolution 1701 which required the demobilisation of all non-state armed forces in Lebanon by means of US support to the equipment and professionalisation of the LAF.

32. Oweis, Khaled Y., 'Lebanese Army Overturns Measures against Hezbollah', *Reuters*, 10 May 2008, available at http://www.reuters.com, cited in Nerguizian, Aram, and Anthony Cordesman, *The Lebanese Armed Forces: Challenges and Opportunities in Post-Syria Lebanon*, Washington, D.C.: Center for Strategic and International Studies, 2009, p. 19.

33. Initially meant to occur two years following the incorporation of reforms negotiated at Taif into the Lebanese Constitution, the withdrawal would ultimately be linked to the deconfessionalisation of politics. See Salloukh, ibid., p. 18.

34. Zahar, ibid.

35. See fn. 13 above for a complete list of references.

36. The National Pact gave the president extensive presidential prerogatives to 'safeguard Lebanon from being engulfed by its Muslim/Arab environment'. Christians, but more specifically the Maronites, came to see these prerogatives as a means to secure the physical security and the political survival of their communities. See Harik, Iliya, 'The Maronites and the Future of Lebanon: A Case of Communal Conflict', in Dorr, Steven, and Neysa Slater (eds), *Security Perspectives and Policies: Lebanon, Syria, Israel and the Palestinians*, Washington, D.C.: Defense Academic Research Support Program, 1991, pp. 45–55.

37. The 8 March supporters organised a sit-in at government buildings from November 2006 until May 2008.

38. Close to three million Americans have partial Lebanese ancestry. According to the Lebanese Information Center, 90 per cent are Christians and 80 per cent

of them vote. Lebanese Information Center, *Lebanon in US Foreign Policy*, 29 October 2008, available at http://www.licus.org. According to census data, Lebanese-Americans constitute over 30 per cent of Arab Americans, http://www.census.gov/acs/www/index.html.

39. Established in 1997, it boasts over three thousand paying members, over one hundred thousand constituents and has established twenty-five chapters all over the USA.

40. http://www.freelebanon.org/index.php?option=com_content&task=view&id=5&Itemid=38.

41. The ALC consists of four groups: the Lebanese Information Center, the American-Lebanese Coordination Council, the American Lebanese Alliance and the Assembly for Lebanon.

42. http://www.alcoalition.org/lib/ALC%20Mission%20Statement.pdf.

43. 'State Department welcomes Arab plan for Lebanon', *The Associated Press*, 23 October 1989.

44. The USA launched 'a diplomatic campaign to isolate the beleaguered Prime Minister, resulting in a December 27 UN Security Council statement calling for the implementation of the Taif agreement and expressing "deep concern" over Aoun's rejection of it'. Gambill, Gary C., 'US Mideast Policy and the Syrian Occupation of Lebanon', *Middle East Intelligence Bulletin*, Vol. 3, No. 3 (2001).

45. Gambill, ibid.

46. The USA needed Syria as a partner in the 'Desert Storm' coalition in the early 1990s, as a key player in bilateral peace talks with Israel throughout the decade and from 2000 onwards as a partner concerned with Iraq's weapons of mass destruction.

47. Murr Television (MTV-Beirut), 25 February 2001.

48. Pipes, Daniel, and Ziad Abdelnour, *Ending Syria's Occupation of Lebanon: The U.S. Role*, Washington, DC: The Lebanon Study Group/The Middle East Forum, May 2000, http://www.meforum.org/research/lsg.php.

49. http://www.alcc-research.com/main_pages/ALCC_WeAre.html.

50. Barry, Tom, 'On the Road to Damascus with the Neocons', *Asia Times*, 12 March 2004, http://www.atimes.com/atimes/Middle_East/FC12Ak04.html.

51. Ibid.

52. This would later be confirmed by Wikileaks. Lutz, Meris, 'Lebanon Wikileaks reveals cable saying defense minister gave Israel invasion advice [Updated]', *LA Times*, 2 December 2010, http://latimesblogs.latimes.com/babylonbeyond/2010/12/hezbollah-israel-murr-lebanon-united-states-war.html.

53. This section draws on Zahar, Marie-Joëlle, 'Liberal Interventions, Illiberal Outcomes: The UN, Western Powers and Lebanon', in Newman Edward, Paris, Roland, and Oliver P. Ritchmond (eds), *New Perspectives on Liberal Peacebuilding*, Tokyo: United Nations University Press, 2009, pp. 292–315.

54. Salloukh, 'The Limits of Electoral Engineering'.
55. The Lebanese system of Party Block Vote combines multimember districts with simple plurality rules. See Reynolds, Andrew and Ben Reilly, *The International IDEA Handbook of Electoral System Design*, Stockholm: International Institute for Democracy and Electoral Assistance, 2002. For a critique of the system, see Saad, Abdo, 'Le système électoral majoritaire freine l'avancée démocratique', *Confluences Méditerranée*, No. 56 (2006), pp. 109–14; Jaafar, Rudy, 'Democratic System Reform in Lebanon: An Electoral Approach', in Choueiri, Youssef M. (ed.), *Breaking the Cycle: Civil Wars in Lebanon*, London: Stacey International, 2007, pp. 285–305; Salloukh, ibid.
56. For example, in Mount Lebanon, a list with 53 per cent of the votes was elected while its competitor with 47 per cent of the votes did not win a single seat. Saad, ibid., p. 111.
57. Johnson, Michael, 'Managing Political Change in Lebanon: Challenges and Prospects', in Choueiri, Youssef M. (ed.), *Breaking the Cycle: Civil Wars in Lebanon*, London: Stacey International, 2007, p. 155.
58. European Union Observation Mission to Lebanon 2005, *Final Report on the Parliamentary Elections*, p. 38, http://www.eeas.europa.eu/human_rights/election_observation/lebanon/final_report_en.pdf.
59. Naïm, Mouna, 'Graves accusations réciproques entre personnalités druzes et Hezbollah', *Le Monde*, 3 January 2007.
60. Naïm, Mouna, 'Liban: Crise politique—Le projet de tribunal international continue d'opposer majorité et opposition libanaises', *Le Monde*, 6 February 2007.
61. Naïm, Mouna, 'Au Liban, l'ONU tente de résoudre la crise sur la création du "tribunal Hariri"', *Le Monde*, 18 April 2007. For an excellent analysis of the politicisation of the STL, see De Geouffre, Géraud, Antoine Korkmaz and Rafaëlle Maison, 'Qui va inculper les assassins du premier ministre Rafic Hariri? Douteuse instrumentalisation de la justice internationale au Liban', *Le Monde diplomatique*, April 2007, pp. 18–19.
62. 'Hariri Tribunal: UN Prosecutor Issues Sealed Indictment', *BBC News*, 17 January 2011, http://www.bbc.co.uk/news/world-middle-east-12209122.
63. See Khalaf, Samir, 'On Roots and Routes: The Reassertion of Primordial Loyalties', in Hanf, Theodor and Nawaf Salam (eds), *Lebanon in Limbo: Postwar Society and State in an Uncertain Regional Environment*, Baden-Baden: Nomos Verlagsgesellschaft, 2003, pp. 107–41. See also Zahar, 'Peace by Unconventional Means'.
64. '… while Ta'if preserved the custom of the Maronite presidency, the Shi'a speakership and the Sunni premiership, it greatly undermined the powers of the Maronite president while enhancing those of the Sunni prime minister, the council of ministers and the speaker'. Khalaf, ibid., p. 133.

65. Krayem, Hassan, 'The Lebanese Civil War and the Ta'if Agreement', in Salem, Paul (ed.), *Conflict Resolution in the Arab World*, Beirut: American University of Beirut Press, 1997, pp. 426–7.
66. Khalaf, ibid., pp. 133–5.
67. Sakr, Elias, 'Harb defends pitch to prohibit inter-religious land sale', *The Daily Star*, 5 January 2011, http://www.dailystar.com.lb/article.asp?edition_id= 1&categ_id=1&article_id=123262#ixzz1BSIVTymq.
68. Although Syria boasts a Sunni majority, the Assad regime is Alawite, an off-shoot of Shia Islam.
69. Zahar, 'Liberal Interventions, Illiberal Outcomes'. The argument that the Shia were once Lebanon's only true national community was made in Picard, Élizabeth, 'De la 'communauté-classe' à la 'Résistance Nationale': Pour une analyse du rôle des Chiites dans le système politique libanais (1970–1985)', *Revue française de science politique*, Vol. 35, No. 6 (1985), pp. 999–1027.
70. Khalaf, ibid., p. 113.

5. LEBANON IN SEARCH OF SOVEREIGNTY: POST-2005 SECURITY DILEMMAS

1. Tilly, Charles, 'War Making and State Making as Organized Crime', in Evans, Peter, Dietrich Rueschemeyer, and Theda Skocpol (eds), *Bringing the State Back In*, Cambridge: Cambridge University Press, 1985, pp. 169–87; Heydemann, Steven (ed.), *War, Institutions and Social Change in the Middle East*, Berkeley: University of California Press, 2000.
2. Adopted by the Lebanese deputies in order to end the civil war in November 1989 under Syrian and Saudi patronage.
3. UNSC resolution 1701 adopted on 11 August 2006, called for an 'end to hostilities between Hezbollah, Israel [and] permanent ceasefire to be based on creation of buffer zone free of armed personnel other than UN, Lebanese forces'.
4. Tawjihi, Kirras, chapters 1–2, http://www.lebarmy.gov.lb/English/Kirras.asp. This directorate under Armed Forces Command is in charge of political and ethical analyses published in its *Orientation Bulletin*.
5. UNSC resolution 1559 presented by France and the USA and adopted on 2 September 2004, called among other things upon withdrawal of all foreign forces from Lebanon.
6. The Lebanese army increased from 21,000 men in 1990 to 45,000 in 1995, and 72,000 in 2002, according to a CSIS working paper: Nerguizian, Aram, and Anthony Cordesman, *The Lebanese Armed Forces: Challenges and Opportunities in Post-Syria Lebanon*, Washington, D.C.: Center for Strategic and International Studies, 2009. It decreased to 56,000 in 2008 and 49,500 in 2010. With the *Quwwat al-Amn al-Dakhili* (Internal Security Forces), 13,000 men in 2001 and 14,600 in 2010, the total armed forces of Lebanon exceeded 70,000 to which one might add 25,000 retired personnel.

7. *L'Orient-Le Jour*, 14 April 1998.

8. Laws 12 and 17 (6 September 1990) reorganised the Internal Security Forces (ISF) and created the *Majlis al-amn al-markazi*, composed of the minister of interior, the state prosecutor, the Beirut governor, the army commander, the head of the ISF and the director of the internal security. See Hutayt, Amin, 'Al-amn wal-difa' fil-hala l-lubnaniyya' (Security and defense in the Lebanese context), *Working Paper*, Montreux, 10–20 April 2007, pp. 17–19.

9. According to Law 102 (1983). See Khalil, Ibrahim, 'Qanun al-difa'. Qiyada jam'iyya am shalal fil-qiyada? (The law of defense. Collective command or paralysis of command?), *Al-Difa' al-watani* (1990), pp. 17–45.

10. General Jamil al-Sayyed was a member of army intelligence from the late 1970s and became head of the B2 in the Beqaa upon his return from IMET formation in the USA in 1982. After the civil war he played a major role in restructuring army intelligence and became its deputy chief in 1992. President Emile Lahoud entrusted him with General Security in 1998, but he was jailed in Lebanon from August 2005 to April 2009 as part of the international inquiry into Hariri's assassination. He has, since being released, challenged his detention in court.

11. Law 97 of 21 September 1991 reinstated general draft.

12. *L'Orient-Le Jour*, 2 August 1997. Each draftee cost the state budget USD 1,000 a month according to *L'Orient-Le Jour*, 15 July 2003.

13. 'A Closer Look: Lebanon's military expenditure', *Information International Monthly*, No. 2, August 2002. Under PM Hariri, the government tried to limit the budget of the ministry of defence. In 1998, an unidentified military commando ransacked the office of the Minister of Finance, Fuad Siniora, who had attempted to scrutinise military expenses. 'Military Republic of Lebanon', *Information International Monthly*, No. 94, May 2010.

14. Minister of Defence Elias Murr to *al-Nahar*, 5 September 2007.

15. Nerguizian, ibid., p. 36.

16. 'U.S. studies Lebanon's military', *The Chicago Tribune*, 2 March 2006.

17. In May 2003 President Lahoud told US Secretary of State Colin Powell that he feared deployment of the Lebanese army to the south, along the Israeli border, would split the army along sectarian lines.

18. The United Nations interim force in Lebanon created by UNSC resolution 425 in April 1978 to supervise an expected Israeli retreat.

19. This chapter was documented through nine interviews with foreign military attachés in Beirut and five interviews with retired or acting LAF officers between February 2002 and July 2008.

20. Leenders, Reinoud, 'Regional Conflict Formations: is the Middle East next?', *Third World Quarterly*, Vol. 28, No. 5 (2007), pp. 959–82.

21. An assault against Islamist militants in Majdal Anjar in September 2004,

attempts at taking control of Taamir, an outlaw area in the neighbourhood of the Palestinian camp of Ayn al-Hilweh (Sidon) in 2005, 2006 and again in 2007, not to mention dozens of arrests, especially in Tripoli. Rougier, Bernard, *Everyday Jihad: The Rise of Militant Islam among Palestinians in Lebanon*, Cambridge, MA: Harvard University Press, 2007.

22. Interview with Admiral William Fallon, chief of US Central Command, Beirut, 29 August 2007.

23. *The Daily Star*, 22 March 2007; *al-Nahar*, 31 May 2007.

24. Fatah al-Islam, a *jihadist* off-shot of the pro-Syrian Palestinian group Fatah al-Intifada inspired by al-Qaida, first appeared in Lebanon in late 2006.

25. Schenker, David, 'Defending Lebanon or Israel', *Forbes.com*, 7 January 2010. http://www.forbes.com/2010/01/07/lebanon-israel-military-aid-opinions-columnists-david-schenker.html.

26. *Al-Safir*, 29 July 2010.

27. 170 military, some 220 insurgents and more than fifty civilians. The destruction of the refugee camp (95 per cent of the buildings and infrastructure were beyond repair) caused the displacement of some 27,000 people. See Knudsen, Are, '(In-)security in a Space of Exception. The Destruction of the Nahr el-Bared Refugee Camp in Lebanon', in MacNeish, John-Andrew, and J.H.S. Lie (eds), *Security and Development*, Oxford: Berghahn, 2010, pp. 99–112.

28. Nerguizian, ibid., pp. 13–18.

29. Secretary General Hassan Nasrallah quoted in *al-Manar*, 25 May 2007.

30. Defence Minister Elias Murr endorsed C-in-C General Sleiman's declaration that 'There is no possible link between the terrorist faction [Fatah al-Islam] and the Syrian SR', *Lebanese Press*, 5 September 2007.

31. According to several sources the Hariris had sought an electoral arrangement with Islamist groups in Sidon, Tripoli and Akkar during the May–June 2005 Legislative elections; and again to confront the demonstrations organised by Hezbollah in downtown Beirut since December 2006. Hersh, Seymour, 'The Redirection', *The New Yorker*, 3 March 2007.

32. Nerguizian, ibid., pp. 39–41; *L'Orient-Le Jour*, 29 May 2010.

33. The freeze on US military aid was lifted by US Congress in November 2010 after getting assurance 'that Lebanese troops would not use the equipment against Israel'. Majority change in the Lebanese government in February 2011 led to further US tergiversation.

34. The bombing of a bus in August 2008 created eighteen victims, ten of whom were soldiers. *The Guardian*, 13 August 2008.

35. Charara, Waddah, *Dawlat Hizb Allah. Lubnan mujtama'an islamiyyan* (The State of Hizbollah. Lebanon Islamic society), Beirut: Dar al-Nahar, 1998.

36. Hokayem, Emile, 'U.S. military assistance and the LAF', *Qifa Nabki*, 12 January 2010, available at http://qifanabki.com/2010/01/12/u-s-military-assistance-and-the-laf.

37. Nerguizian, ibid., p. 12. A total of forty-nine LAF officers, NCOs and soldiers died. Military installations, including bases and positions near Byblos, Batroun, Tripoli and a Brigade headquarters in the north were targeted by Israeli helicopters.
38. Young, Michael, 'What's Hizbullah's problem with the army?', *The Daily Star*, 25 May 2007.
39. Although advocated by Terje Roed Larsen, UN special envoy for the implementation of Security Council resolution 1559. See Report of the UNSG to the UNSC, 29 April 2005.
40. Atrissi, Talal, quoted in Wärn, Mats, 'The Voice of resistance: the point of view of Hizballah', May 1997, http://almashriq.hiof.no/lebanon/300/320/324/324.2/hizballah/warn/index.html.
41. Nasrallah, Hassan, quoted by *Agence France Presse*, 25 June 1998.
42. Iran offered to supply LAF with medium-range missiles as part of a five-year Iranian-Lebanese defence agreement. *The Daily Star*, 27 November 2008.
43. 'Hizbullah: UN troops welcome in South', *The Daily Star*, 30 March 2007; 'UNIFIL denies reports of weapons smuggling in South', *The Daily Star*, 4 May 2007.
44. At the time of the Paris III conference in January 2007, the national debt amounted to USD 41 billion, i.e. 180 per cent of the GDP.
45. McLaurin, Ronald, 'Lebanon and its army', in Azar, Edward E. (ed.), *The Emergence of a new Lebanon: Fantasy or reality?* New York: Praeger, 1984, pp. 79–114.
46. McLaurin, Ronald, 'From Professional to Political: The Redecline of the Lebanese Army', *Armed Forces & Society*, Vol. 17, No. 4 (1991), pp. 545–68.
47. The study by Barak, Oren, *The Lebanese Army: A National Institution in a Divided Society*, Albany: State University of New York Press, 2009, appears to overestimate the strength, autonomy and patriotism of the military, possibly in accordance with Barak's preference for having LAF rather than Hizbollah facing IDF.
48. Law 88 (13 June 1991). Picard, Élizabeth, *The Demobilization of the Lebanese Militias*, Oxford: Centre for Lebanese Studies, 1999.
49. Barak, Oren, 'Toward a Representative Military? The Transformation of the Lebanese Officer Corps since 1945', *Middle East Journal*, Vol. 60, No. 1 (2006), pp. 75–93.
50. According to official figures, voters included 1,558,000 Muslims (56.55 per cent) and 1,197,000 Christians (43.45 per cent) in 2000. The Muslim/Christian ratio for the total (resident and non resident) population was estimated around 60:40.
51. Dagher, Carole, *Le défi du Liban d'après guerre*, Paris: L'Harmattan, 2002.
52. According to unchecked sources, Elias Murr told the US embassy in 2008 that his recruitment efforts over the last two years had netted 20,000 new troops for LAF and brought the Christians to 25 per cent and the Sunni/Druze component to 50 per cent of the enlisted ranks.

53. The memorandum of understanding stated conditions for Hizbollah's disarmament: the return of Lebanese prisoners from Israeli jails and the elaboration of a defense strategy to protect Lebanon from the Israeli threat.

54. Samir Geagea quoted in *L'Orient-Le Jour*, 29 May 2010; Nerguizian, *The Lebanese Armed Forces*, pp. 39–41.

55. A Wikileaks cable, published by *al-Akhbar*, 2 December 2010, reported that Minister of Defense Elias Murr asked US Chargée d'Affaires Michele Sison on 11 March 2008 that an expected Israeli attack spare Christian areas and informed the USA that he instructed Sleiman that the LAF should not involve itself when Israel comes for Hizbollah. Full text on http://www.yalibnan.com/2010/12/03/wikileaks-secret-cable-memo-fuel-tensions-in-lebanon.

56. Adwan, Charles, 'Corruption in Reconstruction: the Cost of "National Consensus" in Post-war Lebanon', Lebanese Transparency Association, 2005, pp. 7–8. www.gdnet.org/fulltext/adwan.pdf; Dib, Kamal, 'A strategy to investigate Lebanese corruption and debt', *The Daily Star*, 14 June 2005.

57. United Nations Center for International Crime Prevention, Corruption assessment report on Lebanon, January 2001; *al-Nahar*, 30 May 2000.

58. *Fortune*, 15 May 2006; Mehlis Report I (S/2005/662, paragraph 217).

59. Denoeux, Guilain, and Robert Springborg, 'Hariri's Lebanon: Singapore of the Middle East or Sanaa of the Levant?', *Middle East Policy*, Vol. 6, No. 2 (1998), pp. 158–73.

60. Leenders, Reinoud, 'Public Means to Private Ends: State Building and Power in Post War Lebanon', in Kienle, Eberhard (ed.), *Politics from Above, Politics from Below*, London: Saqi Books, 2003, pp. 304–34.

61. *Al-Safir*, 4 February 2006.

62. *The Daily Star*, 11 August 2005, 25 August 2005, 5 October 2005; *al-Mustaqbal*, 6 November 2005; *al-Safir*, 17 January 2006; *L'Orient-Le Jour*, 3 October 2006; www.libnanews.com, 23 September 2006.

63. IIIC was established by UNSC resolution 1595, 7 April 2005.

64. For example, French gendarmes were unofficially in charge of the prime minister's security after Hariri's assassination. 'Beirutis turn to private security firms after wave of bombings', *The Daily Star*, 8 June 2007.

65. A Wikileaks cable reported the detailed description of the network, given by 14 March leader Marwan Hamadeh to the US Chargée d'Affaires on 16 April 2008. Full text on http://www.yalibnan.com/2010/12/07/wikileaks-cable-iran-telecom-is-taking-over-the-country.

66. See the minutes of the ministerial meeting called to discuss the rearmament of the paramilitary militias in *al-Akhbar*, 4 May 2007; Daragahi, Borzou and Raed Rafei, 'Private force no match for Hizbollah', *Los Angeles Times*, 12 May 2008.

67. Shehadi, Nadim, 'Riviera vs Citadel: the Battle for Lebanon', http://www.opendemocracy.net, 22 August 2006.

68. International Crisis Group, Lebanon: 'Hizbollah's Weapons Turn Inward', *Middle East Briefing*, No. 23, 15 May 2008.

69. *Magazine*, 21 April 2006; *al-Nahar*, 6 September 2010.

70. Commission of the European Union, Annex to European neighbourhood policy: country report Lebanon, Sec (2005) 289/3, Brussels, 2 March 2005; United States embassy in Lebanon, Press Release, 3 June 2010, 15 December 2010.

71. Army intervention to calm sectarian strife between Ayn al-Rummaneh and Shiyah in January 2008 resulted in six Shia victims. An officer was sentenced.

72. Negotiators in Doha agreed to overcome the constitutional rule imposing a six-month delay between General Sleiman's position as commander-in-chief and his election.

6. ENCLAVES AND FORTRESSED ARCHIPELAGO: VIOLENCE AND
GOVERNANCE IN LEBANON'S PALESTINIAN REFUGEE CAMPS

1. Arendt, Hannah, 'Reflections on Violence', *The New York Review of Books—Special Supplement*, 27 February 1969.

2. Agamben, Giorgio, *Homo Sacer. Sovereign Power and Bare Life*, Stanford: Stanford University Press, 1998; Arendt, Hannah, *The Origins of Totalitarianism*, San Diego: Harcourt Brace & Co., 1985. For more details, see Sari Hanafi, Sari, and Taylor Long, 'Governance, Governmentalities, and the State of Exception in the Palestinian Refugee Camps of Lebanon', *Journal of Refugee Studies*, Vol. 23, No. 2 (2010), pp. 34–60.

3. Petti, Alessandro, *Arcipelaghi e Enclave: Architettura dell'Ordinamento Spaziale Contemporaneo*, Milano: Bruno Mondadori, 2007.

4. Silverman, Stephanie, 'Redrawing the Lines of Control: Political Interventions by Refugees and the Sovereign State System', *conference paper* (Dead/Lines: Contemporary Issues in Legal and Political Theory, University of Edinburgh, 2008), p. 10.

5. Agamben, *Homo Sacer*, p. 121.

6. The five focus group sessions were held between March and July 2009 and lasted roughly four hours each. The focus groups consisted of 67 Palestinians (23 females and 44 males) in three camps: Nahr al-Bared (21 persons), Ayn al-Hilweh (28 and a youth group aged 18–24 from Nahr el-Bared and Beddawi (18 persons).

7. The International Information survey was conducted in 2009. It included face to face interviews with a sample of 1,047 young residents aged 18–24 years in four camps in Lebanon, including Ayn al-Hilweh (near Sidon, South Lebanon), Burj al-Barajneh (near Beirut), Burj al-Shemali (near Tyre, South Lebanon) and Beddawi (near Tripoli, North Lebanon).

8. Agamben, *Homo Sacer*.

9. Parts of this section builds on Hanafi and Long, *Governance, Governmentalities, and the State of Exception*.

10. Article 2 of section 1 of the agreement calls for a reorganisation of 'the Palestinian presence' in Lebanon through 'the foundation of local administrative committees in the refugee camps, composed of Palestinians, in order to defend the interests of the Palestinians residing in those camps, in collaboration with the local authorities and within the framework of Lebanese sovereignty'.

11. Peteet, Julie, 'Socio-Political Integration and Conflict Resolution in the Palestinian Camps in Lebanon', *Journal of Palestine Studies*, Vol. 16, No. 2 (1987), pp. 29–44.

12. Hanafi, Sari, 'Governance of the Palestinian Refugee Camps in the Arab East: Governmentalities in Quest of Legitimacy', *working paper*, Issam Fares Institute for Public Policy and International Affairs, 2010; Hanafi, *Governance, Governmentalities, and the State of Exception*.

13. UNRWA also maintains its own administrative apparatus in the camps. The highest-ranked UNRWA official wields significant power and influence. In at least one of the focus groups, this official referred to himself as '*mudir al-mukhayim*', meaning 'the camp director'. UNRWA typically appoints members of the new educated elite to leadership positions, such as engineers, teachers, and pharmacists, many of whom have a history of political activism and enjoy good relations with the camp populace.

14. Knudsen, Are, 'Islamism in the Diaspora: Palestinian Refugees in Lebanon', *Journal of Refugee Studies*, Vol. 18, No. 2 (2005), pp. 216–34.

15. Abboud, Samer, 'The Siege of Nahr al-Bared and the Palestinian Refugees in Lebanon', *Arab Studies Quarterly*, Vol. 31, No. 1–2 (2009), pp. 31–48.

16. According to the Lebanese Judiciary Council, Fatah al-Islam was composed of 69 Lebanese nationals, approximately 50 Palestinians (43 from Syria), 43 Saudis, 12 Syrians, one Tunisian, one Algerian, one Yemeni and one Iraqi. Hanafi, Sari, and Hassan, Sheikh I., 'Constructing and Governing Nahr al-Bared Camp. An "Ideal" Model of Exclusion [in Arabic]', *Majallat al-Dirasat al-Falastiniyya*, No. 78 (2009), pp. 39–52.

17. Agamben, *Homo Sacer*, p. 106.

18. Many interlocutors reported that some of the factions sought protection by recruiting '*zo'ran*' [gangs] and therefore could not be trusted.

19. International Information (2009). *Survey of Media and Communication Channels, Actors and Messages in Palestinian Camps*. Unpublished report.

20. For this project, see Nabulsi, Karma, *Palestinians Register: Laying Foundations and Setting Directions*, Oxford: Nuffield College, 2006.

21. Palestinian Human Rights Organisation. *Report on Violence. Jan.-May 2010*. Unpublished report, 2010. Palestinian Human Rights Organisation. *Report on the Lebanese Restrictions on Freedom of Movement: Case of Nahr El Bared*. November 2010.

22. Palestinian Association for Human Rights (Witness). *2009 Annual Report*. Unpublished report, 2009.

23. Najdeh Association. *Domestic Violence Program Annual Report January—December 2007*, 2007. http://association-najdeh.org/pdf/Domestic_Violence.pdf

24. See Kortam, Marie, *Jeune et violence dans le camp de Baddawi et le banlieu parisien*, PhD Thesis, Université de Paris VII, Paris, 2011.

25. Palestinian Human Rights Organisation, *Report on Violence. Jan.-May 2010.*

26. This category includes all forms of medical malpractice and refusal by UNRWA to subsidise medical treatment.

27. Palestinian Human Rights Organisation. *Report on the Lebanese Restrictions on Freedom of Movement: Case of Nahr al-Bared*, November 2010.

28. Zhang, Huafeng, and Tiltnes, Åge A., 'Socio-economic Assessment of Ein El-Hilweh Refugee Camp', *Tabulation report*, Fafo, December 2009.

29. This survey is based upon a sample of 904 households covering Ayn al-Hilweh and adjacent areas: 12 February-3 March, in-depth interviews with Ayn al-Hilweh inhabitants: 12 February-29 March 2008, and participant feedback and focus group discussions.

30. See for instance, the army declaration after the theft of a gun from a policeman, Samad, Abdel Khafi, 'Attack on a Security Officer', *al-Akhbar*, 2 September 2008.

31. Hanafi, 'Constructing and Governing Nahr al-Bared Camp'.

32. Buck-Morss, Susan, *Thinking Past Terror*, New York: Verso, 2003.

33. See the Palestinian Human Rights Organisation report at: http://www.palhumanrights.org/var/Urgent%20Appeal%20-%20PHRO%20Director%20faced%20a%20Military%20Intelligence%20Investigation%20-%20ARB.pdf.

34. Palestinian Human Rights Organisation, *Report on Violence. Jan.-May 2010.*

35. Najdeh Association, *Domestic Violence Program Annual Report January—December 2007.*

36. See http://www.nowlebanon.com/NewsArchiveDetails.aspx?ID=138168#ixzz 0yf5NiL00.

37. See 'Ayn al-Hilweh Killing Raises Fears of Deteriorating Security in Camp', *The Daily Star*, 15 September 2010.

38. Adra, Jawad, 'The Oppressive, The Marginalized and The Missing Third', *Information International Monthly*, No. 98, September 2010.

39. Kortam, *Jeune et violence dans le camp de Baddawi et le banlieu parisien.*

40. Information International, *Survey of Media and Communication Channels.*

41. Interview with Edward Kattoura, political consultant affiliated with Pursue Ltd., Beirut, April 2012.

42. Zhang and Tiltnes, 'Socio-economic Assessment of Ein Al-Hilweh.

43. The dispute started after an argument between Sheikh Hussein Qassem Maghreb, the imam of the mosque, who is loyal to Fatah, and members of the mosque committee, who are loyal to Hamas. 'Hamas, Fatah Clash in Refugee Camp after Prayer Dispute' *The Daily Star*, 24 August 2010.

44. Palestinian Human Rights Organisation, *A Case to Register in the Name of Humanity: Where are our Camps Going? Whom to Serve? And Until When?*, Unpublished document.
45. Agamben, *Homo Sacer*.
46. Khalili, Laleh, *Heroes and Martyrs of Palestine: The Politics of National* Commemoration, Cambridge: Cambridge University Press, 2007.
47. Information International, *Survey of Media and Communication Channels*.
48. The League of Partisans [*Usbat al-Ansar*] was founded in 1986 and boasts a strong presence in the Ayn al-Hilweh camp.
49. The Islamic Jihadist Movement [*al-Harakat al-Islamiyya al-Mujahida*] was very important in the 1980s, but lost influence after being banned in Lebanon in 1991.
50. Jund al-Sham is an Usbat al-Ansar splinter group. Its members were originally located in the Taamir neighbourhood adjoining Ayn al-Hilweh camp before moving to the Tawareh area in the camp.
51. A PLO official claimed that there were plans to transform the camp into a stronghold of al-Qaida, http://www.nowlebanon.com/NewsArchiveDetails. aspx?ID=138168#ixzz0yf5d6piM.
52. Al-Amin, Hazem, *The Lonely Salafist: A Palestinian Face of the Global Jihad and al-Qaida* [in Arabic], Beirut: Dar al-Saqi, 2009.
53. Rougier, Bernard, *Everyday Jihad: The Rise of Militant Islam among Palestinians in Lebanon*, Cambridge, MA: Harvard University Press, 2007.
54. Knudsen, 'Islamism in the Diaspora'.
55. Information International, *Survey of Media and Communication Channels*.

7. THE 'NEW CONTRACTOR BOURGEOISIE' IN LEBANESE POLITICS: HARIRI, MIKATI AND FARES

1. The research for this paper was made possible by a Leverhulme Trust 'Study Abroad Studentship' and a travel grant from the Council for British Research in the Levant (CBRL) and was conducted at the Centre for Arab and Middle East Studies (CAMES) at the American University Beirut (AUB).
2. See for example *New York Times*, 24 January 2011, http://www.nytimes. com/2011/01/25/world/middleeast/25lebanon.html?pagewanted=all; *The Guardian*, 24 January 2011, http://www.guardian.co.uk/world/2011/jan/24/hezbollah-backed-candidate-lebanon-pm.
3. Harvey, David, *A Brief History of Neoliberalism*, Oxford: Oxford University Press, 2005, p. 19.
4. Heydemann, Steven, *Networks of privilege in the Middle East: the Politics of Economic Reform Revisited*, New York: Palgrave Macmillan, 2004.
5. See Zahar's chapter in this volume.

NOTES pp. [127–130]

6. Johnson, Michael, *Class and Client in Beirut: The Sunni Muslim Community and the Lebanese State 1840–1985*, London: Ithaca Press, 1986, pp. 25–6.

7. Dekmejian, Hrair, *Patterns of Political Leadership: Egypt, Israel, Lebanon*, New York: State University of New York Press, 1975, pp. 22–3; Traboulsi, Fawwaz, *A History of Modern Lebanon*, London: Pluto Press, 2007, p. 115.

8. On the social crisis and its political effects see Nasr, Salim, 'Backdrop to Civil War: The Crisis of Lebanese Capitalism', *MERIP Middle East Report*, No. 73 (1978), pp. 3–13.

9. On the civil war economy, see Corm, George, 'The War System: Militia Hegemony and Reestablishment of the State', in Colling, D. (ed.), *Peace for Lebanon? From War to Reconstruction*, Boulder: Lynne Rienner, 1994, pp. 215–30; Picard, Élizabeth, 'The Political Economy of Civil War in Lebanon', in Heydemann, Steven (ed.), *War, Institutions, and Social Change in the Middle East*, Berkeley: University of California Press, 2000, pp. 292–322.

10. Nasr, Salim, 'The Political Economy of the Lebanese Conflict', in Shehadi, N., and Harney, Bridget (eds), *Politics and the Economy in Lebanon*, Oxford: Centre for Lebanese Studies, 1989, p. 44.

11. Sklair, Leslie, *The Transnational Capitalist Class*, Malden: Blackwell, 2000.

12. Hindess, Barry, *Politics and Class Analysis*, Oxford: Blackwell, 1987, p. 16.

13. Ibid., pp. 28–33; Scott, John, *The Sociology of Elites, Volume III: Interlocking Directorships and Corporate Networks*, Aldershott: Elgar, 1990.

14. In his study of Arab elites, Perthes uses the conventional definition of elites as decision-makers. Perthes, Volker, *Arab Elites: Negotiating the Politics of Change*, Boulder: Lynne Rienner, 2004. On Bourdieu's definition of elites see Hartmann, Michael, *The Sociology of Elites*, Oxford: Routledge, 2007.

15. Bourdieu, Pierre, *Language and Symbolic Power*, Cambridge: Polity, 1991, p. 170.

16. Unless indicated otherwise, this account of Hariri's business success is based on an interview with Robert Debbas, his long-time business partner and friend. Interview with Robert Debbas, Beirut, 27 February 2008.

17. The initial posters on Oger's trucks publicised the 'Project of Cleaning Beirut, courtesy of Rafik Hariri, Oger Liban 1982'. Once Fahd had been brought on board, they were replaced with posters advertising the clean-up as a donation by the Saudi King. Al-Fadl, Shalaq, *Tajrabatyy ma'a al-Hariri* (My Experience with Hariri), Beirut: Arab Scientific Publishers, 2006, p. 60.

18. Blanford, Nicholas, *Killing Mr Lebanon: the Assassination of Rafik Hariri and its Impact on the Middle East*, London: I.B. Tauris, 2006, pp. 25–6.

19. A good account of Hariri's involvement is provided in Kerr, Michael, *Imposing Power-Sharing: Conflict and Coexistence in Northern Ireland and Lebanon*, Dublin: Irish Academic Press, 2006 and Salem, Elie, *Violence and Diplomacy in Lebanon: The Troubled Years, 1982–1988*, London: IB Tauris, 1995.

261

20. Verdeil, Eric, 'Reconstruction manquée à Beyrouth, la poursuite de la guerre par le projet urbain', *Annales de la Recherche Urbaine*, No. 91 (2001), pp. 65–73.
21. Interview with Sabah al-Hajj, Beirut, 8 November 2008.
22. *Middle East Economic Digest*, 21 November 2008, p. 74.
23. *Al-Nahar Arab Report and Memo*, 4 June 1984, p. 6.
24. See the personal website of Najib Mikati, available at www.najib-mikati.net/EN/OurInterests/110/Philanthropy.
25. Unless indicated otherwise, the information on Fares is from *Middle East Intelligence Bulletin*, November 2003, pp. 12–17.
26. *Al-Nahar Arab Report and Memo*, 4 June 1984, p. 7.
27. See the website of the Issam Fares Foundation, available at http://www.fares.org.lb/main.asp.
28. Harvey, ibid., pp. 64–5.
29. Dumenil, Gerard, and Dominique Levy, 'The Neoliberal (Counter-)Revolution', in Saad-Filho, Alfredo, and Deborah Johnston (eds), *Neoliberalism: A Critical Reader*, London: Pluto Press, 2005, pp. 9–19.
30. See for example Heydemann, ibid.
31. Corm, George, 'Reconstructing Lebanon's Economy', in Shafik, N. (ed.), *Economic Challenges Facing Middle Eastern Countries: Alternative Futures*, Basingstoke: Macmillan, 1998, pp. 116–35; Denoeux, Guilain, and Robert Springborg, 'Hariri's Lebanon: Singapore of the Middle East or Sanaa of the Levant?', *Middle East Policy*, Vol. 6, No. 2 (1998), pp. 158–73; Gaspard, Toufic, *A Political Economy of Lebanon, 1948–2002: The Limits of Laissez-Faire*, Leiden: Brill, 2004.
32. Denoeux, ibid.
33. Kerr, ibid.
34. For an account of the rise and fall of Sunni militias in Beirut, see Johnson, ibid.
35. For a good account of the changes in Sunni politics in the early mid-1990s, see Skovgaard-Petersen, Jakob, 'The Sunni Religious Scene in Beirut', *Mediterranean Politics*, Vol. 3, No. 1 (1998), pp. 69–80.
36. The electoral process was tightly managed by two advisors to Rafik Hariri in order to produce the desired outcome. Skovgaard-Petersen, 'The Sunni Religious Scene in Beirut', pp. 78–9; Rougier, Bernard, *Everyday Jihad: The Rise of Militant Islam among Palestinians in Lebanon*, Cambridge, MA: Harvard University Press, 2007, pp. 130–1.
37. Managers and administrators in the Hariri Foundation health directorate stress that the health centres are open to all sects—Nur al-Din al-Kush, general manager of the directorate of health and social services of the Hariri Foundation, presentation at the American University Beirut on 6 February 2008. Interview with Suha al-Akkar, assistant to the general manager, directorate of health and social services, Hariri Foundation, Beirut, 29 January 2008.

38. On the political uses of the health centres and schools, as well as the struggle with Maqasid, see Cammett, Melani, and Sukriti Issar, 'Bricks and Mortar Clientelism: The Political Geography of Welfare in Lebanon', *World Politics*, Vol. 62, No. 3 (2010), pp. 381–421; Baumann, Hannes, 'The Ascent of Rafik Hariri and Philanthropic Practices in Beirut', in Mermier, F., and S. Mervin (eds), *Chefs Politiques et Sociabilités Partisanes au Liban*, Karthala: Paris, forthcoming. On the history of Maqasid, see Johnson, ibid.

39. Interview with Rania Zaatari al-Kush, manager of social health services at the directorate of health and social services of the Hariri Foundation, Beirut, 22 January 2008; Interview with Suha al-Akkar, assistant to the general manager, directorate of health and social services, Hariri Foundation, Beirut, 29 January 2008.

40. See Johnson, ibid.

41. For a comparison of how financing affects the politics of philanthropy, see Baumann, ibid.

42. Economist Intelligence Unit (EIU), Country Report: Lebanon, July 2002 (electronic version).

43. EIU, Country Report: Lebanon, 4. Quarter 1995, p. 14; EIU, Country Report: Lebanon, 1. Quarter 1996, p. 14; EIU, Country Report: Lebanon, October 2000 (electronic version).

44. International Telecommunications Union, *Arab States Telecommunications Indicators 1992–2001*, Geneva: ITU, 2002.

45. EIU, Country Report: Lebanon, July 2002 (electronic version); EIU, Country Report: Lebanon, January 2003 (electronic version).

46. According to *Forbes*, March 2011, http://www.forbes.com/profile/najib-mikati.

47. *Middle East International*, 18 August 2000, p. 13.

48. For information on the association, see http://www.fares.org.lb/profile.asp.

49. Unless indicated otherwise, the following section on Fares relies on *Middle East Intelligence Bulletin*, November 2003, pp. 12–17.

50. Ibid.

51. *Middle East International*, 23 March 2001, p. 13.

52. International Crisis Group, *Syria after Lebanon, Lebanon after Syria*, Brussels: ICG, 2005, p. 9.

53. Shehadi, Nadim, and Elizabeth Wilmshurst, *The Special Tribunal for Lebanon: The UN on Trial?*, London: Chatham House, 2007, p. 8.

54. Much of the analysis here is informed by International Crisis Group, *Lebanon's Politics: The Sunni Community and Hariri's Future Current*, Brussels: ICG, 2011.

55. Cammett, ibid.

56. *New York Times*, 22 April 2009. http://www.nytimes.com/2009/04/23/world/middleeast/23lebanon.html?pagewanted=2&_r=1&hp.

57. International Crisis Group, *Lebanon's Politics: The Sunni Community*, p. 22.

58. *Al-Akhbar*, 3 September 2011, English translation at www.mideastwire.com.
59. *Los Angeles Times*, 12 May 2008. http://articles.latimes.com/2008/may/12/world/fg-security12.
60. *The Daily Star*, 5 August 2008, http://www.dailystar.com.lb/article.asp?edition_id=1&categ_id=2&article_id=94793.
61. For instance the Lebanese branch of the Muslim Brotherhood, *Al-Akhbar*, 16 March 2011, English translation at www.mideastwire.com.
62. Lebanese Republic, 'Recovery, Reconstruction, Reform', paper presented at the International Conference for Support for Lebanon, Paris, 25 January 2007, http://www.rebuildlebanon.gov.lb/images_Gallery/Paris%20III%20document_Final_Eng%20Version.pdf.
63. *Naharnet*, 3 November 2008, http://www.naharnet.com/domino/tn/NewsDesk.nsf/getstory?openform&70D73D56458CEE7BC22574F60037F463.
64. *Al-Mustaqbal*, 25 January 2011, English translation at www.mideastwire.com.
65. *BBC News*, 24 January 2011, http://www.bbc.co.uk/news/world-middle-east-12272483.
66. An English translation is available from the 'Qifa Nabki' blog. http://qifanabki.com.
67. *New York Times*, 26 January 2011, http://www.nytimes.com/2011/01/27/world/middleeast/27lebanon.html.
68. Unless otherwise indicated, the following information on Safadi is from *The Guardian*, 7 June 2007. http://www.guardian.co.uk/world/2007/jun/07/bae6.
69. *Naharnet*, 26 February 2011, http://www.naharnet.com/stories/en/3449-Mikati-assures-of-his-ties-with-saudi-the-government-is-ready.
70. See the website of the Safadi Foundation, www.safadi-foundation.org.
71. The best account of government over-borrowing is presented by Gaspard, *A Political Economy of Lebanon*.
72. Fattouh, Bassam, 'A Political Analysis of Budget Deficits in Lebanon', *SOAS Economic Digest*, 2 June 1997.
73. Schimmelpfennig, Axel, and Edward Gardner, *Lebanon—Weathering the Perfect Storms*, Washington: IMF, 2008, p. 19.
74. *Middle East Economic Survey*, 8 July 2002, p. 3–4; EIU, Country Report: Lebanon, January 2002 (electronic version); EIU, Country Report: Lebanon, July 2002 (electronic version); Schimmelpfennig, Axel, and Edward Gardner, ibid., p. 5.
75. *Al-Nahar*, 25 November 2011, English translation at www.mideastwire.com.
76. International Crisis Group, *Lebanon's Politics: The Sunni Community*, p. 20.
77. *Naharnet*, 26 February 2011, http://www.naharnet.com/stories/en/3449-Mikati-assures-of-his-ties-with-saudi-the-government-is-ready.
78. *The Daily Star*, 29 November 2011, p. 2.

8. THE RECONSTRUCTION OF LEBANON OR THE RACKETEERING RULE

1. Yerly, René, 'Aux racines sociales des conflits interlibanais', *Développement et civilisation*, No. 365 (2008), pp. 1–6.
2. Yerly, René, 'Retour sur les années noires et perspectives', *Confluences Méditerranée*, No. 70 (2009), pp. 45–62.
3. Yerly, René, 'Repères Liban: Économie', *Moyen-Orient*, No. 2 (2009), pp. 39–41.
4. Rafik Hariri was prime minister from 1992 to 1998, and from 2000 to 2004. In July 2005 the Minister of Finance Fuad Siniora became prime minister, followed by Saad Hariri from September 2009 to January 2011.
5. From December 1998 to October 2000, Georges Corm served as minister of finance of the Lebanese Republic. See Corm, Georges, *Le Liban contemporain. Histoire et société*, Paris: La Découverte, 2005.
6. Verdeil, Eric, 'Reconstruction manquée à Beyrouth, la poursuite de la guerre par le projet urbain', *Annales de la Recherche Urbaine*, No. 91 (2001), pp. 65–73.
7. Raffestin, Claude, *Pour une géographie du pouvoir*, Paris: LITEC, 1980.
8. The spatial diversity was much stronger before the civil war and one could not really refer to a fragmentation of the territory at that time.
9. Corm, ibid., p. 101.
10. Balanche, Fabrice, 'Syrie-Liban: intégration régionale ou dilution?', *Mappemonde*, No. 79 (2005), http://mappemonde.mgm.fr/num7/articles/res05306.html.
11. Ibid.
12. Great Arab Free Trade Area: an Arab free trade zone which in January 2005 comprised seventeen Arab countries (members of the Arab League).
13. Bourgey, André, *Industrialisation et changements sociaux dans l'Orient arabe*, Beirut: CERMOC, 1982.
14. Kasparian, Robert, 'Mission des comptes économiques du Liban, Presidency of the Council of Ministers', October 2010, p. 78, www.economy.gov.lb/public/uploads/files/NA2009FR.pdf.
15. Verdeil, Eric, *Atlas du Liban*, Beirut: IFPO/CNRS, 2007, p. 127.
16. Interview with René Yerly, former Director of the Ministry of Finance (1998–2000), Beirut, 15 October 2005.
17. Owen, Roger, and Pamuk Sevket, *A History of the Middle East Economies in the Twentieth Century*, London: I.B. Tauris, 1998.
18. Kasparian, Choghig, *L'entrée des jeunes libanais dans la vie active et l'émigration*, Beirut: Presses de l'Université Saint-Joseph, 2003.
19. Société Libanaise de Développement et de Reconstruction, Lebanese Company for Development and Reconstruction in English.
20. Yerly, ibid.
21. Favier, Agnès, *Municipalités et pouvoirs locaux au Liban*, Beirut: CERMOC, 2001.

22. The National Pact confirmed the birth of an independent Lebanese state in 1943. It expressed a consensus between the new ruling elites (Maronites and Sunnis essentially). Christians gave up the protection of a foreign power (Western France in this case) and Muslims in return recognised the existence of an independent Greater Lebanon, thus abandoning their ambition to attach the country to a Syrian or Arabic entity. Traboulsi, Fawwaz, *A History of Modern Lebanon*, London: Pluto Press, 2007, p. 110.

23. Maktabi, Rania, 'The Lebanese Census of 1932 Revisited, Who are the Lebanese?', *British Journal of Middle Eastern Studies*, Vol. 26, No. 2 (1999), pp. 219–41.

24. Labaki, Boutros, *Bilan des guerres du Liban, 1975–1990*. Paris: L'Harmattan,1995.

25. The Shouf is a mixed region of Mount Lebanon where Druze and Christians live. During the war of the mountains in 1983–4, the Druze Progressive Socialist Party of Walid Jumblatt sought to displace the Christians.

26. Interview with Boutros Labaki, former vice-director of the Council for Development and Reconstruction, Beirut, 2006.

27. Fawaz, Mona, 'Neoliberal Urbanity and the Right to the City: A View from Beirut's Periphery', *Development and Change*, Vol. 40, No. 5 (2009), pp. 827–52.

28. Picard, Élizabeth, 'Élections libanaises: un peu d'air a circulé…', *Critique internationale*, No. 10 (2001), pp. 21–31.

29. To buy votes is a time-honoured tradition in Lebanon and has helped the Hariri family, supported by Saudi money, to prevail over the other parties. Worth, Robert, 'Foreign Money Seeks to Buy Lebanese Votes', *The New York Times*, 22 April 2009.

30. Having been accused of involvement in the assassination of Rafik Hariri on 14 February 2005, Syria was forced to withdraw its troops from Lebanon.

31. The parliamentary elections in June 2005 gave a majority of seats to the 'Future Movement' (the party of the Hariri family) and its anti-Syrian allies.

32. Guillaume, Boudisseau, 'Immobilier: en période de crise les gens investissent', *Le commerce du Levant*, No. 5578 (2008).

33. Interview with René Yerly, 14 February 2006.

34. Jihad Azour (2005–8) and Mohamad Chatah (2008–9).

35. *L'Orient-Le Jour*, 11 June 2011.

36. In Sidon, the hometown of the Hariri family, the city's rubbish has accumulated over forty years on the waterfront where it has formed a hill several hundred feet high. The cost of dealing with this waste mountain is prohibitive for the municipality of Sidon to the extent that no private company will intervene. Bonne, Emmanuel, *Vie publique, clientèle et patronage: Rafic Hariri à Saïda*, Aix-en-Provence: IREMAM, 1995.

37. Interview with Eric Verdeil, 20 November 2011.

38. Faour, Ghaleb, et al., 'Beyrouth: quarante ans de croissance urbaine', *Mappemonde*, No. 79 (2005). http://mappemonde.mgm.fr/num7/articles/art05305. html.

39. After the massacre of Christians in 1860, Western powers demanded the creation of an autonomous entity in Mount Lebanon designed to protect Christian populations.

40. Harb, Mona, *Le Hezbollah à Beyrouth: de la banlieue à la ville*, Paris: Karthala, 2010, p. 131.

41. Fawaz, Mona, 'Hezbollah as Urban Planner? Questions To and From Planning Theory', *Planning Theory*, Vol. 8, No. 4 (2009), pp. 323–34.

42. The LF is a Christian nationalist party that was created from a split within the Kataeb party in the 1980s. The party is led by Samir Geagea.

43. The FPM is headed by Michel Aoun, formed mainly of a Christian majority.

44. The Kataeb party has a minority of supporters in the Christian community today. The current leader, Amin Gemayyel was unable to maintain the seat held by his family in the Metn during the parliamentary elections of 2007.

45. Michel Murr was associated with Rafik Hariri in the LINOR project, a luxury gated community on the north Beirut seaside. Nabaa, René, *Rafic Hariri, un homme d'affaires Premier ministre*, Paris: L'Harmattan, 1998.

46. Neal, Mark W., and Richard Tansey, 'The Dynamics of Effective Corrupt Leadership: Lessons from Rafik Hariri's Political Career in Lebanon', *The Leadership Quarterly*, Vol. 21, No. 1 (2010), pp. 33–49.

47. The daily *al-Diyar* reported on 13 February 1997 about Rafik Hariri's pressure to appoint a new judge as chairman of the committee of Elyssar expropriations. The first judge estimated the price per square metre at USD 275. The second, favoured by Rafik Hariri, priced it at USD 50. Harb, *Le Hezbollah à Beyrouth*, p 216.

48. President from 1989 to 1998.

49. Khalil, Gebara, 'The Political Economy of Corruption in Post-War Lebanon, Reconstruction Survey', *Lebanese Transparency Association*, 2007, http://www.transparency-lebanon.org/index.php?option=com_content&view=article&id=34&Itemid=75&lang=en.

50. http://www.solidere.com/solidere.html.

51. *L'Orient-Le Jour*, 10 November 2005.

52. Wakim, Najah, Nasserist deputy of Beirut denounced early on the Hariri clientelist system of Solidere, *Les mains noires*, Beirut: All Print, 1998.

53. Interview with René Yerly, Beirut, 2005.

54. Beyhoum, Nabil, 'Reconstruire Beyrouth', *Etudes sur le Monde Arabe*, No. 5 (1992).

55. Interviews with numerous small shareholders of Solidere, Beirut, 2003–7.

56. Interview with the director of a foreign company in Beirut, Beirut, 2005.

57. Interview with René Yerly, 15 November 2005.

58. Harb, Mona, 'Transforming the Site of Dereliction into the Urban Culture of Modernity: Beirut's Southern Suburb and the Elyssar Project', in Rowe, Peter G., and Hashim Sarkis (eds), *Projecting Beirut: Episodes in the Construction and Reconstruction of a Modern City*, Munich: Prestel, 1998, pp. 173–81.

59. Clerc, Valérie, *Les quartiers irréguliers de Beyrouth*, Beirut: IFPO, 2008.

60. Deboulet, Agnès, 'Téhéran, Beyrouth, Le Caire: les citadins face aux projets autoroutiers', *Urbanisme*, No. 336 (2004), pp. 29–38.

61. Khayat, Tristan, 'La route de la discorde: construction du territoire municipal et aménagement métropolitain à Borj Hammoud', in Favier, Agnes (ed.), *Municipalités et pouvoirs locaux au Liban*, Beirut: CERMOC, 2001.

62. Yerly, ibid.

63. Lefebvre, Henri, *Le droit à la ville*, Paris: Anthropos, 1968.

64. *Le Commerce du Levant*, No. 5611 (2010).

65. Fawaz, Mona, 'The State and the Production of Illegal Housing: Public Practices in Hayy el Sellom, Beirut-Lebanon', in Rieker, Martina, and Kamran A. Ali (eds), *Comparing Cities: The Middle East and South Asia*, Oxford: Oxford University Press, 2009, pp. 197–220.

66. Seurat, Michel, 'Le quartier de Bab Tebbané à Tripoli (Liban): étude d'une "asabiyya urbaine"', in Zakaroya, Mona (ed.), *Mouvements communautaires et espace urbain au Machreq*, Beirut: CERMOC, 1985, pp. 45–86.

67. Minoui, Delphine, 'Au Liban, les clans chiites et sunnites se réarment', *Le Figaro*, 8 April 2008, http://www.lefigaro.fr/international/2008/04/09/01003–2008 0409ARTFIG00004-au-liban-les-clans-chiites-et-sunnites-se-rearment.php.

68. http://english.aljazeera.net/news/middleeast/2010/08/2010824181740529220. html.

69. The Association of Islamic Charitable Projects (*Jamiyyat al-Mashari al-Khayriyya al-Islamiyya*).

70. Balanche, Fabrice, 'Cessons la caricature: pro syriens et anti syriens au Liban', *La Presse*, 13 December 2006, http://www.cyberpresse.ca/article/20061213/ CPOPINIONS/61213039&SearchID=73275514690715.

71. Syrian Army departs from Lebanon.

72. Saad Hariri's coalition ('unity') cabinet fell after more than one-third of the ministers resigned.

73. PSP exited from the 14 March coalition officially at the end of 2010 and joined 8 March.

74. Najib Mikati is the new prime minister chosen by the 8 March coalition. He is a Sunni businessman from Tripoli with a close relationship with Syria and Saudi Arabia.

75. According to parliamentary elections in 2005 and 2009.

76. 31.5 per cent Shia, 29 per cent Sunni, 5.5 per cent Druze, 19.9 per cent

Maronite, 5 per cent Greek Orthodox, 4.2 per cent Greek Catholic, 3.6 per cent Armenian and 13 per cent other Christians. Courbage, Youssef, and Todd, Emmanuel, *Le rendez-vous des civilisations*, Paris: Seuil, 2008.

77. http://en.wikipedia.org/wiki/Free_Patriotic_Movement#Memorandum_of_ Understanding_between_the_FPM_and_Hezbollah.

78. Harb, *Le Hezbollah à Beyrouth*, p. 256: 'Downtown Beirut, now renamed Solidere, works well as an exclusive private club that is accessible and secure for the most affluent of the world'.

79. The Lebanese opposition decided to permanently occupy downtown Beirut, day and night. All parties installed tents for their supporters living on Martyr Square and the adjoining streets.

80. http://www.stl-tsl.org.

81. Nabaa, René, *Rafic Hariri, un homme d'affaires Premier ministre*, Paris: L'Harmattan, 1998.

82. Hamra is the main commercial area of West Beirut (the Muslim part of the city).

83. Gemmayzeh was a former harbour area. The development of recreational activities in this region (bars, restaurants and nightclubs) could be analysed as a revenge taken by civil society against Solidere, as this leisure area is developing in front of the Solidere zone without any plans or support from the authorities. Indeed, many Lebanese go to Gemmayzeh rather than Downtown as a political gesture.

84. At the heart of the Christian neighbourhood of Ashrafieh, Sassine Square is also the site of confrontations between the Communist party and the Lebanese Forces.

85. Minoui, ibid.

86. Gresh, Alain, 'Lebanon: Hizbullah's defeat', *Le Monde Diplomatique*, June 2009. http://mondediplo.com/blogs/lebanon-hizbullah-s-defeat.

87. Becherer, Richard, 'A Matter of Life and Debt: the Untold Costs of Rafiq Hariri's New Beirut', *The Journal of Architecture*, Vol. 10, No. 1 (2005), pp. 1–42.

88. Corm, ibid.

89. Lévy, Jacques, *L'espace légitime*, Paris: Presses de Sciences Po., 1994. p. 442.

90. Martinez-Garrido, Lourdez, 'Beirut Reconstruction. A Missed Opportunity for Conflict Resolution', *al-Nakhlah*, Autumn 2008, http://www.isn.ethz.ch/isn/ Digital-Library/Publications/Detail/?ots591=0c54e3b3–1e9c-be1e-2c24-a6a8c 7060233&lng=en&id=93647.

91. The term 'Dutch disease' originates from a crisis in the Netherlands in the 1960s that resulted from discoveries of vast natural gas deposits in the North Sea. The newfound wealth caused the Dutch guilder to rise, making exports of all non-oil products less competitive on the world market. Dutch disease is primarily associated with natural resource discovery, but it can result from any large increase in foreign currency, including foreign direct investment and high emigrant money transfer, as in Lebanon.

92. Harvey, David, *The New Imperialism*, Oxford: Oxford University Press, 2003.
93. Abdelnour, Ziad, 'The Three Faces of Corruption in Lebanon', *Middle East Intelligence Bulletin*, Vol. 3, No. 2 (2001), pp. 6–11.
94. Transparency International's corruption identification.
95. Kriegel, Annie, *Les communistes français*, Paris: le Seuil, 1968.

9. THE MAKING OF A MARTYR: FORGING RAFIK HARIRI'S SYMBOLIC LEGACY

1. Rafik Hariri in an interview with Ghassan Charbel, published by *al-Hayat* between 13 and 17 February 2006. Corm maintains that Hariri's private fleet consisted of at least four Boeings. By comparison, Lebanon's national carrier (MEA) counted only nine planes. Corm, Georges, *Le Liban contemporain. Histoire et société*, Paris: La Découverte, 2005, p. 269. Further details and images of Hariri's aircraft which include B777, B737 and B727 series can be found at specialist websites such as http://www.airliners.net/.
2. The theme of Lebanese martyrs is developed in Volk, Lucia, *Memorials and Martyrs in Modern Lebanon*, Bloomington: Indiana University Press, 2010; Chaib, Kinda, 'Le Hizbullah libanais à travers ses images: la représentation du martyr', in Mervin, Sabrina (ed.), *Les mondes chiites et l'Iran*, Paris: Karthala, 2007, pp. 113–31; Knudsen, Are, 'Acquiescence to Assassinations in Post-Civil War Lebanon?', *Mediterranean Politics*, Vol. 15, No. 1 (2010), pp. 1–23; Maasri, Zeina, *Off the Wall—Political Posters of the Lebanese Civil War*, London: I.B. Tauris, 2009; Schmitt, Paula, *Advertised to Death. Lebanese Poster Boys*, Beirut: Arab Printing Press, 2009.
3. Volk, ibid., p. 31.
4. For an illustrated account that captures the spirit, see for example: Tuéni, Ghassan, and Eli Khoury (eds), *Independence '05: The Beirut Spring*, Beirut: Dar an-Nahar & Quantum Communications, 2005 or Schiller, Norbert, *28 Days that Changed Lebanon 14/02/2005–14/03/2005*, Beirut: Focusmideast, 2006. Tellingly, Saad Hariri often appears with an image of the 'independence intifadah' in the background.
5. Haugbolle, Sune, 'Spatial Transformations in the Lebanese "Independence Intifada"', *The Arab Studies Journal*, Vol. 14, No. 2 (2006), pp. 60–77.
6. Volk, ibid., p. 189.
7. After his resignation as prime minister on 20 October 2004, Hariri grew ever closer to the political bloc opposed to the regime of President Lahoud and Syrian interference in Lebanese politics. Though Hariri did not join the group formally, members of his parliamentary bloc attended its meetings in the Bristol Hotel in a private capacity. The gatherings consisted of the mainly Christian politicians of the anti-Syrian Qornet Shehwan alliance as well as Druze politicians (Jumblatt's PSP) but excluded Michel Aoun's FPM. See Raad, Nada, 'Opposition demands total Syrian withdrawal from Lebanon' in *The Daily Star*, 3 February 2005.

8. Blanford, Nicholas, *Killing Mr Lebanon: the Assassination of Rafik Hariri and its Impact on the Middle East*, London: I.B. Tauris, 2006, p. 152; 'L'espoir en lettres de sang, 14 février 2005–14 février 2006, la Révolution du Cèdre en marche', *L'Orient-Le Jour* (Special supplement), 13 February 2006, p. 107.

9. 'Battle of the airwaves', *The Economist*, 17 March 2005.

10. Security Council Resolution 1559, which called for the withdrawal of all remaining foreign forces in Lebanon and the disarmament of the Lebanese and non-Lebanese militias, was adopted on 2 September 2004. This came less than a week after Lahoud's presidency had been extended—a move opposed by Hariri although in 1995 he had obtained a similar prorogation for Lahoud's predecessor. (NB: Hariri strongly opposed the extension, but eventually instructed his parliamentary bloc to vote in favour of it.)

11. '"Record" protest held in Beirut', *BBC News*, 14 March 2005, http://news.bbc.co.uk/2/hi/middle_east/4346613.stm. For a personal account, see Young, Michael, *The Ghosts of Martyrs Square. An Eyewitness Account of Lebanon's Life Struggle*, New York: Simon & Schuster, 2010.

12. Abdel-Latif, Omeyma, 'Lebanon's Sunni Islamists-A Growing Force', Carnegie Papers, No. 6 (2008). See also International Crisis Group, 'Lebanon's Politics: The Sunni Community and Hariri's Future Current', *Middle East Report*, No. 96, 26 May 2010.

13. See for example Shehadi, Nadim, and Elizabeth Wilmshurst, 'The Special Tribunal for Lebanon: The UN on Trial?', Chatham House International Law Briefing Paper, July 2007; International Crisis Group, 'Trial by Fire: The Politics of the Special Tribunal for Lebanon', *Middle East Report*, No. 100, 2 December 2010.

14. In another twist of irony, Hariri's assassination took place exactly in front of the iconic St George Hotel, whose owners (mainly Fadi Khoury) fought a long battle of symbolic and judicial resistance to Hariri and his reconstruction agency Solidere.

15. The cleavage over Lebanon's (Arab) identity in 1958 may seem like an obvious reference to point at, but some authors have suggested similarities that go back even further. For example, Gary Bass lucidly recounts how, in 1860, France lobbied European powers to intervene in the region. Although Bass guards himself from making explicit links between the 1860 massacres in Lebanon and Syria and the events unfolding nearly a century and a half later, he carefully documents how political calculations resulted in an 'international commission of inquiry' being sent to the Levant in an attempt 'to stop the killings'. See Bass, Gary J., *Freedom's Battle. The Origins of Humanitarian Intervention*, New York: Alfred A. Knopf, 2008. On the events of 1958, see Kerr, Malcolm, *The Arab Cold War: Gamal 'Abd al-Nasir and his Rivals: 1958–1970*, London: Oxford University Press, 1971.

16. Volk, ibid., p. 199.

17. For more details, see Vloeberghs, Ward, 'Worshipping the Martyr President: the *darîh* of Rafiq al-Hariri in Beirut', in Pierret, Thomas, Badouin Dupret, Paulo G. Pinto and Kathryn Spellman-Poots (eds), *Ethnographies of Islam*, (forthcoming).

18. In reference to the Syriac word *mār*, meaning saint, which is often used for Christian saints such as Mar Charbel, Mar Taqla, Mar Maroun etc.

19. The Société libanaise de développement et de reconstruction (SOLIDERE) is a privately owned real estate company set up in 1994 to oversee the recovery of Beirut's city centre. Rafik Hariri was among its most influential promoters and owned a substantial part of its shares, which are listed on the Beirut stock exchange. See Vloeberghs, Ward, 'The Genesis of a Mosque: Negotiating Sacred Space in Downtown Beirut', *Working Paper*, (European University Institute, RSCAS 2008/17), esp. pp. 5–10.

20. During a round-table discussion with the late Samir Kassir, there was even talk of a Lebanese national 'pantheon'. See 'Le kiosque arabe', *Radio France Internationale (RFI)*, 8 April 2005.

21. 'Hariri: See How Beirut Presents a Model for Coexistence Between Christianity and Islam', *al-Liwā*, 20 October 2008.

22. For details on this project and Hariri's involvement, see Vloeberghs, ibid., pp. 2–5.

23. See Vloeberghs, Ward, 'A Building of Might and Faith. Rafik al-Hariri and the Muhammad al-Amin Mosque. On the Political Dimensions of Religious Architecture in Contemporary Beirut', PhD thesis in political science, University of Louvain, Louvain-la-Neuve, 2010.

24. Interview with Saad Khaled, former Director General of Urbanism and mediator in Hariri's negotiations with the Muhammad al-Amin Association, Beirut, 16 April 2009.

25. It is important to observe that several cathedrals—and mosques—stand in the vicinity of the Muhammad al-Amin mosque. In fact, almost all communities (except the Shia) have built a monumental place of worship in central Beirut over the past few centuries.

26. See 'Architectural design for Muhammad al-Amin mosque... won't see the light. New original work from architect Rasem Badran', *al-Liwā*, 1 November 2002. Five days after this publication, a ceremony took place at the construction site with Rafik Hariri and Mufti Qabbani laying the first stone.

27. Khalaf, Samir, *Heart of Beirut. Reclaiming the Bourj*, London: Saqi, 2006, p. 31.

28. See Khan, Riz, *Alwaleed. Businessman, Billionaire, Prince*, New York: William Morrow, 2005, p. 318; Blanford, ibid., p. 85; Mermier, Franck, 'La mosquée Muhammad al-Amîn à Beyrouth: mausolée involontaire de Rafic Hariri', *Revue d'études des mondes méditerranéen et musulmans* (REMMM), No. 125 (2009), pp. 177–96. Since al-Walid was also a business partner to Hariri on other occa-

sions both before and after the former's contribution, the rivalry between both men should not be overstated. See: Vloeberghs, ibid., Chapter 4.

29. On these notions, see Traboulsi, Fawwaz, *A History of Modern Lebanon*, London: Pluto Press, 2007; El-Mufti, Karim, 'Reconstruction d'Etat dans les sociétés multicommunautaires: analyse comparative entre le Liban et la Bosnie-Herzégovine' (forthcoming). On Hariri's policies, see Denoeux, Guilain, and Robert Springborg, 'Hariri's Lebanon: Singapore of the Middle East or Sanaa of the Levant?', *Middle East Policy*, Vol. 6, No. 2 (1998), pp. 158–73. On Lahoud's role in the Lebanese Armed Forces, see Koekenbier, Pieter, 'A New Model Army? The Reconstruction of the Military in Post-war Lebanon', MA Thesis, University of Amsterdam, Amsterdam, 2005.

30. Dellerba, Isabelle, 'Les combats du Barouk', unpublished article prepared for *Libération* in May 2008.

31. One may wonder whether this contributed as a distant precursor for the dramatic change that swept Tunisia, Egypt and other Arab countries throughout 2011.

32. Haugbolle, ibid., p. 62.

33. Khuri, Fuad I., *Imams and Emirs. State, Religion and Sects in Islam*, London: Saqi, 2006, p. 76.

34. Harb, Mona, 'La Dâhiye de Beyrouth: parcours d'une stigmatisation urbaine, consolidation d'un territoire politique', *Genèses*, No. 51 (2003), pp. 70–91; Harb, Mona, *Le Hezbollah à Beyrouth: de la banlieue à la ville*, Paris: Karthala, 2010.

35. Haugbolle, ibid., p. 74.

36. In 2011, the gathering was held on Sunday 13 March rather than on Monday 14, in order to allow for more participants. See for example 'March 13 sun keeps March 14 crowd energized', *The Daily Star*, 14 March 2011.

37. Such as: 'he taught, he built, he liberated' or 'the hand that built a fatherland'. The remembrance dynamic also extends to the media. In 2005, al-Arabiya produced a documentary emphatically titled 'Shahīd ad-dawla…dawlat ash-shahīd', (Martyr of the nation, His Excellency the martyr). Lebanese media broadcast advertisements such as: 'dammak ghālī, sawtna 'ālī' (your blood is expensive, our voice is loud).

38. In particular Saib Salam (a four-time prime minister who died in 2000 and hailed from a notable family of Beirut) was an important competitor for Hariri during the beginning of his political career. See Saqr, Yusuf, 'A'ilat hakamat lubnan, (Families who governed Lebanon) Beirut: al-Markaz al-'Arabîlil-ma'alûmât, 2008; Johnson, Michael, *Class and Client in Beirut: The Sunni Muslim Community and the Lebanese State 1840–1985*, London: Ithaca Press, 1986.

39. It should be noted that Rafik Hariri's sister Bahia, who became minister of education in 2008, has two sons who occupy important political posts. As soon as

the political succession was settled, the inevitable support in terms of images and narratives appeared. See for example Al-Bqaily, Nabil, *The Golden Book. Saad Rafic Hariri*, (in Arabic) Beirut: Chemaly Printing Press, 2005.

40. Volk, ibid., p. 188.
41. It is illustrative of the volatile nature of Lebanese politics that Najib Mikati (b. 1955) has been both a political rival and a political partner to the Hariris. Before his 2009 electoral alliance with Saad Hariri, Mikati had served under Rafik Hariri. Between 2000 and 2004 he was minister of public works and transportation, a position he had inherited from his participation in the preceding, anti-Hariri cabinet led by Salim al-Hoss (1998–2000).
42. Though Jumblatt himself had announced his departure from the 14 March coalition on 2 August 2009 his support for the Mikati-led government angered members within his own parliamentary bloc. For an historic overview of Jumblatt's political positioning, see Rowayheb, Marwan, 'Walid Jumblatt and Political Alliances: The Politics of Adaptation', *Middle East Critique*, Vol. 20, No. 1 (2011), pp. 47–66.

10. 'HISTORY' AND 'MEMORY' IN LEBANON SINCE 2005: BLIND SPOTS, EMOTIONAL ARCHIVES AND HISTORIOGRAPHIC CHALLENGES

1. Khalaf, Samir, *Beirut Reclaimed: Reflections on Urban Design and the Restoration of Civility*, Beirut: Dar al-Nahar, 1993; Barak, Oren, "'Don't Mention the War?" The Politics of Remembrance and Forgetfulness in Postwar Lebanon', *Middle East Journal*, Vol. 61, No. 1 (2007), pp. 49–70; Choueiri, Youssef (ed.), *Breaking the Cycle: Civil Wars in Lebanon*, London: Stacey International, 2007; Volk, Lucia, *Memorials and Martyrs in Modern Lebanon*, Bloomington: Indiana University Press, 2010; Haugbolle, Sune, *War and Memory in Lebanon*, Cambridge: Cambridge University Press, 2010.
2. Choueiri, ibid.
3. Khatib, Lina, *Lebanese Cinema—Imagining the Civil War and Beyond*, London: I. B. Tauris, 2008.
4. Haugbolle, ibid., pp. 96–129.
5. Toukan, Hanan, 'On Being "The Other", in Post-Civil War Lebanon: Aid and the Politics of Art in Processes of Contemporary Cultural Production', *Arab Studies Journal*, Vol. 18, No. 1 (2010), pp. 118–62.
6. See http://www.nadasehnaoui.com/index.php.
7. Mroué, Rabih, *How Nancy Wished that it was all an April's Fool*, (DVD), Beirut: Ashkal Alwan, 2007.
8. See Quilty, Jim, 'Briefly banned play traces sects' political morphings', *The Daily Star*, 4 September 2007.
9. Haugbolle, ibid., pp. 79–82.

10. I refer to a DVD recording of a performance at the Monot Theatre in Beirut, October 2007. The DVD is produced for the Ashkal Alwan library.
11. Khatib, ibid.
12. Haugbolle, ibid., pp. 194–6.
13. Volk, ibid., pp. 154–88.
14. Lorenz, Chris, 'Can Histories Be True? Narrativism, Positivism, and the "Metaphorical Turn"', *History and Theory*, Vol. 37, No. 3 (1998), pp. 309–29.
15. Cooke, Miriam, *War's Other Voices: Women Writers in the Lebanese Civil War*, Cambridge: Cambridge University Press, 1987.
16. Saidawi, Rafif R., *Nadhra al-riwa'iya ila al-harb al-lubnaniya 1975–1995*, (The Narrative View on the Lebanese War 1975–1995) Beirut: Dar al-Farabi/Anep, 2003.
17. Williams, Raymond, *Politics and Letters—Interviews with New Left Review*, London: Verso, 1981.
18. Haugbolle, ibid., pp. 96–131.
19. Williams, ibid., p. 160.
20. Ibid., p. 159.
21. Lorenz, ibid.
22. Hedstrom, Margaret, 'Archives, Memory, and Interfaces with the Past', *Archival Science*, Vol. 2, No. 1–2 (2002), pp. 21–43.
23. Derrida, Jacques, *Archive Fever*, Chicago: University of Chicago Press, 1998.
24. http://www.umam-dr.org/aboutUs.php?location=aboutUs.
25. To which the author of this article contributed most of the photographs.
26. Maasri, Zeina, *Off the Wall—Political Posters of the Lebanese Civil War*, London: I.B. Tauris, 2009.
27. Haugbolle, ibid., pp. 194–227.
28. Eddé, Carla, 'Les mémoires des acteurs de la guerre: le conflit revisité par ses protagonistes', in Mermier, Franck, and Christophe Varin (eds), *Mémoires de guerres au Liban*, Paris: Sinbad, 2010, pp. 25–46.
29. Ménargues, Alain, *Les secrets de la guerre du Liban: du coup d'état de Béchir Gémayel aux massacres des camps palestiniens*, Paris: Albin Michel, 2004.
30. For a thorough overview of the historiography of Sabra and Shatila, see Signoles, Aude, 'Sabra and Chatila', *Online Encyclopedia of Mass Violence*, 2008, http://www.massviolence.org/Sabra-and-Chatila?artpage=6–8.
31. Haugbolle, ibid., pp. 208–11.
32. Ibid., p. 211.
33. Hage, Ghassan, 'Religious Fundamentalism as a Political Strategy—the evolution of the Lebanese Forces' religious discourse during the Lebanese Civil War', *Critique of Anthropology*, Vol. 12, No. 1 (1992), pp. 27–45.
34. Khalaf, Samir, *Civil and Uncivil Violence in Lebanon: A History of the Internationalization of Communal Conflict*, New York: Columbia University Press, 2002; pp. 1–22.

35. Johnson, Michael, *All Honourable Men: The Social Origins of War in Lebanon*, London: I. B. Tauris, 2001.

36. Traboulsi, Fawwaz, 'Identités et solidarités croisées dans les conflits du Liban contemporain', Phd thesis, Thèse de Doctorat d'Histoire, Département d'Histoire, Université de Paris VIII, Paris, 2003.

37. Haugbolle, ibid., pp. 228–37.

38. Halbwachs, Maurice, *On Collective Memory*, Chicago: University of Chicago Press, 1992.

39. Mermier, Franck (ed.), *Mémoires de guerres au Liban (1975–1990)*. Paris: Actes Sud, 2010.

11. SECTS AND THE CITY: UNDERSTANDING THE SOCIO-SPATIAL
     PERCEPTIONS AND PRACTICES OF YOUTH IN BEIRUT

1. Knudsen, Are, and Nasser Yassin, 'Political Violence in Post-Civil War Lebanon', in Suhrke, Astri, and Mats Berdal (eds), *The Peace In Between: Post-War Violence and Peacebuilding*, London: Routledge, 1997, pp. 117–31.

2. Larkin, Craig, 'Beyond the War? The Lebanese Postmemory Experience', *International Journal of Middle East Studies*, Vol. 42, No. 4 (2010), pp. 615–35.

3. I would like to thank the Heinrich Boell Foundation—Middle East for funding the focus group discussions, and Ms Riwa Jaber and Ms Reem Saad for translating the discussions.

4. Anderson, James, and Ian Shuttleworth, 'Spaces of Fear: Communal Violence and Spatial Behaviour', *Working Paper*, University of Cambridge Centre for Research in the Arts, Social Sciences and Humanities, 2003.

5. Anderson, James, and Shuttleworth, Ian, 'Sectarian Demography, Territoriality and Political Development in Northern Ireland', *Political Geography*, Vol. 17, No. 2 (1998), pp. 187–208.

6. Scruton, David, *Sociophobics: the Anthropology of Fear*, Boulder: Westview Press, 1986.

7. Bar-Tal, Daniel, 'Why Does Fear Override Hope in Societies Engulfed by Intractable Conflict, as It Does in the Israeli Society?' *Political Psychology*, Vol. 22, No. 3 (2001), pp. 601–27.

8. Boal, Frederick W., 'Belfast: Walls Within', *Political Geography*, Vol. 21, No. 5 (2002), pp. 687–94.

9. Hamilton, Jennifer, Ulf Hansson, John Bell and Sarah Toucas, *Segregated Lives: Social Division, Sectarianism and Everyday Life in Northern Ireland*, Belfast: Institute for Conflict Research, 2008.

10. Hardwick, Susan, 'Migration, Embedded Network and Social Capital: Towards Theorising North American Ethnic Geography', *International Journal of Population Geography*, Vol. 9, No. 2 (2003), pp. 163–79.

11. Portes, Alejandro, and Julia Sensenbrenner, 'Embeddedness and Immigration:

Notes on the Social Determinants of Economic Action', *American Journal of Sociology*, Vol. 98, No. 6 (1993), p. 1324.

12. Lamont, Michèle, and Virág Molnar, 'The Study of Boundaries in the Social Sciences', *Annual Review of Sociology*, Vol. 28 (2002), p. 168.

13. Ibid.

14. Leigh, Andrew, 'Trust, Inequality and Ethnic Heterogeneity', *The Economic Record*, Vol. 82, No. 258 (2006), pp. 268–80.

15. Hearn, Frank, *Moral Order and Social Disorder: The American Search for Civil Society*, New York: Aldine de Gruyter, 1997, p. 97.

16. Khawaja, Marwan, Sawsan Abdulrahim, Rima Soweid, and Dima Karam, 'Distrust, Social Fragmentation and Adolescent Health in the Outer City and Beyond', *Social Science and Medicine*, Vol. 63, No. 5 (2006), pp. 1304–15.

17. Ibid.

18. Hanf, Theodor, 'E Pluribus Unum? Lebanese Opinions and Attitudes on Coexistence', *Lettres de Byblos*, No. 14 (2007).

19. Ibid.

20. Ibid.

21. Lamont, ibid., p. 170.

22. Yassin, Nasser, 'Violent Urbanization and Homogenization of Space and Place: Reconstructing the Story of Sectarian Violence in Beirut', in Beall, Jo, Guha-Khasnobis, Basudeb, and Ravi Kanbur (eds.), *Urbanization and Development: Multidisciplinary Perspectives*, Oxford: Oxford University Press, 2010, pp. 205–18.

23. These findings confirm Hanf's survey which found that the proportion of Lebanese preferring to live with neighbours of the same background 'had risen enormously'. In 2006, he found that 'almost three fifths of the respondents would like to live among people with a similar background'. Strikingly, the rate in 2006 was even higher than during the civil war period (1975–1990). Hanf, ibid., pp. 18–9.

24. Tilley, Christopher, *A Phenomenology of Landscape*, London: Berg, 1994.

25. Massey, Doreen, 'The Spatial Construction of Youth Cultures', in Skelton, Tracey, and Gill Valentine (eds), *Cool Places: Geographies of Youth Culture*, London: Routledge, 1998, pp. 120–9.

26. Ibid., p. 126.

27. Halpern, Jodi, and Harvey Weinstein, 'Rehumanizing the Other: Empathy and Reconciliation', *Human Rights Quarterly*, Vol. 26, No. 3 (2004), pp. 561–83.

12. SPECIAL TRIBUNAL FOR LEBANON: HOMAGE TO HARIRI?

1. Ballard, James G., *War Fever*, New York: Farrar, Straus, Giroux, 1990.

2. Knudsen, Are, 'Acquiescence to Assassinations in Post-Civil War Lebanon?', *Mediterranean Politics*, Vol. 15, No. 1 (2010), pp. 1–23.

3. Blanford, Nicholas, *Killing Mr Lebanon: The Assassination of Rafik Hariri and Its Impact on the Middle East*, London: I.B. Tauris, 2009.

4. Strindberg, Anders, 'Syria under Pressure', *Journal of Palestine Studies*, Vol. 33, No. 4 (2004), pp. 53–69.

5. U.S. Congress, Syria Accountability and Lebanese Sovereignty Restoration Act (Pl 108–175), Washington D.C., 12 December 2003, www.lgic.org/en/help_act.php.

6. UNSCR, The Situation in the Middle East, New York: UN Security Council S/RES/1559, http://daccess-dds-ny.un.org/doc/UNDOC/GEN/N04/498/92/PDF/N0449892.pdf?OpenElement, 2004.

7. Mugraby, Muhamad, 'The Syndrome of One-Time Exceptions and the Drive to Establish the Proposed Hariri Court', *Mediterranean Politics*, Vol. 13, No. 2 (2008), pp. 171–94.

8. Knudsen, Are, and Nasser Yassin, 'Political Violence in Post-Civil War Lebanon', in Suhrke, Astri, and Mats Berdal (eds), *The Peace in Between: Post-War Violence and Peacebuilding*, London: Routledge, 2011, pp. 117–31.

9. However, the law (Article 3) does not provide amnesty for 'crimes of assassination or attempted assassination of religious figures, political leaders, and foreign or Arab diplomats', http://www.amnesty.org/en/library/asset/MDE18/003/2004/en/f4dbe07b-d585–11dd-bb24–1fb85fe8fa05/mde18003200 4en.pdf.

10. Sarkis, Hashim, 'A Vital Void: Reconstructions in Downtown Beirut', in Campanella, Thomas J., and Lawrence J. Vale (eds), *The Resilient City: How Modern Cities Recover from Disaster*, Oxford: Oxford University Press, 2005, pp. 281–97.

11. Haugbolle, Sune, *War and Memory in Lebanon*, Cambridge: Cambridge University Press, 2010.

12. Calame, Jon, and Esther Charlesworth (eds), *Divided Cities: Belfast, Beirut, Jerusalem, Mostar and Nicosia*, Philadelphia: University of Pennsylvania Press, 2009.

13. The Martyr's Square takes its name from Lebanese nationalists hanged in 1916 after revolting against Ottoman Turk rule.

14. Humphrey, Michael, and Maroun Kisirwan, 'Impunity, Nationalism and Transnationalism: The Recovery of the "Disappeared" of Lebanon', *Bulletin of the Royal Institute of Inter-Faith Studies*, Vol. 3, No. 2 (2001), pp. 113–40.

15. Martyrdom is not only an elite phenomenon but extends to militia members and soldiers. Volk, Lucia, 'Martyrs at the Margins: The Politics of Neglect in Lebanon's Borderlands', *Middle Eastern Studies*, Vol. 45, No. 2 (2009), pp. 263–82.

16. Schmitt, Paula, *Advertised to Death: Lebanese Poster Boys*, Beirut: Arab Printing Press, 2009.

17. UNSCR, The Situation in the Middle East, New York: UN Security Council, Meeting no. 5122, S/INF/60, 15 February 2005, http://unispal.un.org/UNISPAL.NSF/0/1293530F7CE7BF2A852570FB006E71A2.

18. FitzGerald Report, 'Report of the Fact-Finding Mission to Lebanon Inquiring

into the Causes, Circumstances and Consequences of the Assassination of Former Prime Minister Rafik Hariri', New York: Report submitted by Peter FitzGerald, Head of the United Nations Fact-Finding Mission in Lebanon, 24 March
2005 (S/2005/203), http://daccessdds.un.org/doc/UNDOC/GEN/N05/283/
96/PDF/N0528396.pdf?OpenElement.

19. UNSCR, The Situation in the Middle East, New York: UN Security Council
Resolution, S/RES/1595, http://daccess-dds-ny.un.org/doc/UNDOC/GEN/
N05/299/98/PDF/N0529998.pdf?OpenElement, 2005.

20. The UNIIIC reports (1–11) can be downloaded from the website of the Special Tribunal for Lebanon, http://www.stl-tsl.org/sid/49.

21. A leaked, unedited version of the Mehlis report named two Syrian officials as
being involved in Hariri's murder: Mahir al-Assad (Bashar al-Assad's brother),
head of Syria's Republican Guard, and Asef Shawkat (Bashar al-Assad's brother-
in-law), head of the Syrian military, http://www.nowlebanon.com/Library/Files/
EnglishDocumentation/Investigation%20Briefings/21%20October%202005.
pdf.

22. Wierda, Marieke, Habib Nassar and Lynn Maalouf, 'Early Reflections on Local
Perceptions, Legitimacy and Legacy of the Special Tribunal for Lebanon', *Journal of International Criminal Justice*, Vol. 5, No. 5 (2007), pp. 1065–81.

23. Shehadi, Nadim, 'Riviera Vs Citadel: The Battle for Lebanon', *OpenDemocracy.
net* (2007), http://www.opendemocracy.net/conflict-middle_east_politics/riv-
iera_citadel_3841.jsp.

24. Shehadi, Nadim and Elizabeth Wilmshurst, 'The Special Tribunal for Lebanon:
The UN on Trial?', London: Chatham House Middle East, *International Law
Briefing Paper* (2007), MEP/IL BP 07/01, www.chathamhouse.org.uk/publi-
cations/papers/download/-/id/512/file/10088_bp0707lebanon.pdf.

25. UNSCR, Letter Dated 29 January 2008 from the Prime Minister of Lebanon
Addressed to the Secretary-General, New York: United Nations Security Council, S/2008/60 (Annex), http://www.securitycouncilreport.org/atf/cf/%7B65
BFCF9B-6D27–4E9C-8CD3-CF6E4FF96FF9%7D/Lebanon%20S200860.
pdf.

26. UNSCR, The Situation in the Middle East, New York: United Nations Security Council, S/RES/1757 (2007), http://daccess-dds-ny.un.org/doc/UNDOC/
GEN/N07/363/57/PDF/N0736357.pdf?OpenElement; UNSCR, The Situation in the Middle East, New York: United Nations Security Council, S/
RES/1757 (2007), http://daccess-dds-ny.un.org/doc/UNDOC/GEN/N07/363/
57/PDF/N0736357.pdf?OpenElement; see also, Fassbender, Bardo, 'Reflections on the International Legality of the Special Tribunal for Lebanon', *Journal of International Criminal Justice*, Vol. 5, No. 5 (2007), pp. 1091–105.

27. Serra, Gianluca, 'Special Tribunal for Lebanon: A Commentary on Its Major
Legal Aspects', *International Criminal Justice Review*, Vol. 18, No. 3 (2008),
pp. 344–55.

28. The UN decided that the assassination of Hariri was a 'terrorist act' but did not qualify as a 'crime against humanity', hence could not be prosecuted by the International Criminal Court (ICC) in The Hague. El-Masri, Samar, 'The Hariri Tribunal: Politics and International Law', *Middle East Policy*, Vol. 15, No. 3 (2008), pp. 80–92.

29. However, the Tribunal could ask the UN Security Council to intervene and use Chapter VII to force a member state to co-operate with the Tribunal or extradite persons indicted by it.

30. Meeting with Walid Moallem, Syrian Foreign Minister, Oslo, 9 March 2010 (closed meeting with the Syrian Foreign Minister hosted by the Norwegian Ministry of Foreign Affairs).

31. Cockayne, James, 'Foreword', *Journal of International Criminal Justice*, Vol. 5, No. 5 (2007), pp. 1061–4.

32. If the Tribunal is able to solve a murder case but cannot establish a link to Hariri's murder, it can neither punish those responsible nor refer the case to Lebanese courts. Eberling, Björn, 'The Next Step in History-Writing through Criminal Law: Exactly How Tailor-Made Is the Special Tribunal for Lebanon?', *Leiden Journal of International Law*, Vol. 21, No. 2 (2008), pp. 529–38.

33. Other jurists argue that the mandate can be seen as an act of selective historiography that privileges a Sunni hagiography, ibid.

34. ICTJ, *Handbook on the Special Tribunal for Lebanon*, New York: The International Center for Transitional Justice (ICTJ), Prosecutions Program, 2008.

35. Gaeta, Paola, 'To Be (Present) or Not to Be (Present): Trials in Absentia before the Special Tribunal for Lebanon', *Journal of International Criminal Justice*, Vol. 5, No. 5 (2007), pp. 1165–74.

36. The office of the prosecutor is, along with the chambers, the registry and the defence office, one of the four organs of the STL. The registry coordinates the Tribunal's administration and operations and is led by the registrar functioning as its chief executive.

37. The first registrar, Robert Vincent, was appointed in March 2008 but resigned in late April 2009, well ahead of his three-year contract. His replacement, David Tolbert, took over as registrar in late August 2009, but filed his resignation on 12 January 2010. On 6 January 2010 the chief investigator Naguib (Nick) Kaldas resigned after only one year in this post.

38. Young, Michael, 'By the way, the Hariri tribunal is dying', *The Daily Star*, Beirut, 14 January 2010.

39. General Jamil al-Sayyed, the former head of the Lebanese general security directorate (Sûreté Générale), challenged his detention. Al-Sayyed was later granted a public hearing in Beirut and filed for the release of Tribunal documents related to his detention, http://www.stl-tsl.org/en/the-cases/in-the-matter-of-el-sayed.

40. 'Analysts say resignations show tribunal losing political support', *The Daily Star*, Beirut, 14 January 2010.

41. By comparison, Pakistan's appeal for an international probe to investigate the assassination of former Prime Minister Benazir Bhutto was turned down by the UN. 'Ban Rejects UN Hariri-Style Probe of Bhutto Assassination', *JURIST Legal News and Research Services*, 8 October 2008, http://jurist.law.pitt.edu/paperchase/2008/10/ban-rejects-un-hariri-style-probe-of.php.

42. Follath, Eric, 'Breakthrough in Tribunal Investigation: New Evidence Points to Hizbollah in Hariri Murder', *Spiegel Online International*, 23 May 2009, www.spiegel.de/international/world/0,1518,626412,00.html.

43. 'Leaders praise Nasrallah's "calm" response to STL questioning', *The Daily Star*, Beirut, 2 April 2010.

44. 'STL dismisses leaks by tribunal officials as false', *The Daily Star*, Beirut, 8 April 2010.

45. 'Islamic Sharia Council calls for STL cooperation', *The Daily Star*, Beirut, 6 April 2010.

46. 'Hizbullah, Syria welcome Hariri's change of heart on accusations', *The Daily Star*, Beirut, 8 September 2010.

47. 'Justice Minister stresses STL will not be politicized', *The Daily Star*, Beirut, 20 August 2010.

48. 'March 8 wants UN to abolish STL', *www.yalibnan.com*, 5 September 2010.

49. 'Hariri vows no turning back on support for Tribunal', *The Daily Star*, Beirut, 21 September 2010.

50. Macdonald, Neil, 'CBC Investigation: Who Killed Lebanon's Rafik Hariri?', *CBC Special Report*, 2010, http://www.cbc.ca/world/story/2010/11/19/f-rfa-macdonald-lebanon-hariri.html.

51. Interview with Muhamad Mugraby, lawyer, Beirut, 5 May 2010.

52. Chatham House, 'The Special Tribunal for Lebanon and the Quest for Truth, Justice and Stability', London: Chatham House, Meeting Report, http://www.chathamhouse.org/sites/default/files/public/Research/Middle%20East/1210_stl.pdf (2010).

53. Macdonald, ibid.

54. STL, Unlawful Broadcasts of Confidential Information under Investigation, The Hague: Special Tribunal for Lebanon, 18 January 2011, www.stl-tsl.org/sid/243.

55. Nasrallah, Hassan, Speech by Hezbollah Secretary General Sayyed Hassan Nasrallah 'on the Developments Following the Resignation of the Ministers and the Toppling of the Lebanese Government', Beirut: *Al Manar TV*, 16 January 2011, English transcript.

56. 'Bellemare sets Tribunal process in motion', *The Daily Star*, Beirut, 18 January 2011.

57. STL, Ayyash et al., (STL-11–01): Indictment (Public Redacted Version), The Hague: Special Tribunal for Lebanon, 2011, www.stl-tsl.org/en/the-cases/stl-11–01/main/filings/indictments/indictment-public-redacted-version.

58. In October 2011 the Tribunal's President, the late Antonio Cassese, resigned over health problems followed soon after by the announcement that Chief Prosecutor Daniel Bellemare would step down in 2012 for similar reasons.
59. The senior Druze politician Saleh Aridi was killed by a car bomb on 10 September 2008, http://news.bbc.co.uk/2/hi/7609412.stm.

BIBLIOGRAPHY

Abboud, Samer, 'The Siege of Nahr al-Bared and the Palestinian Refugees in Lebanon', *Arab Studies Quarterly*, Vol. 31, No. 1–2 (2009), pp. 31–48.

Abdel-Latif, Omeyma, 'Lebanon's Sunni Islamists—A Growing Force', *Carnegie Papers*, No. 6 (2008).

Abdelnour, Ziad, 'The Three Faces of Corruption in Lebanon', *Middle East Intelligence Bulletin*, Vol. 3, No. 2 (2001), pp. 6–11.

Agamben, Giorgio, *Homo Sacer. Sovereign Power and Bare Life*, Standford: Standford University Press, 1998.

Al-Amin, Hazem, *The Lonely Salafist: A Palestinian Face of the Global Jihad and al-Qaida*, (in Arabic), Beirut: Dar al-Saqi, 2009.

Al-Bqaily, Nabil, *The Golden Book. Saad Rafic Hariri*, (in Arabic), Beirut: Chemaly Printing Press, s.d. 2005.

Al-Fadl, Shalaq, *Tajrabatyy ma'a al-Hariri*, (My Experience with Hariri), Beirut: Arab Scientific Publishers, 2006.

Anderson, James and Ian Shuttleworth, 'Spaces of Fear: Communal Violence and Spatial Behaviour', *Working Paper*, University of Cambridge Centre for Research in the Arts, Social Sciences and Humanities, 2003.

———— 'Sectarian Demography, Territoriality and Political Development in Northern Ireland', *Political Geography*, Vol. 17, No. 2 (1998), pp. 187–208.

Arendt, Hannah, *The Origins of Totalitarianism*, San Diego: Harcourt Brace & Co., 1985.

———— 'Reflections on Violence', *The New York Review of Books—Special Supplement*, 27 February 1969.

Attié, Caroline, *Struggle in the Levant: Lebanon in the 1950s*, London: The Centre for Lebanese Studies in association with I.B. Tauris, 2003.

Ballard, James G., *War Fever*, New York: Farrar, Straus, Giroux, 1991.

Barak, Oren, *The Lebanese Army: A National Institution in a Divided Society*, Albany: State University of New York Press, 2009.

BIBLIOGRAPHY

——— '"Don't Mention the War?" The Politics of Remembrance and Forgetfulness in Postwar Lebanon', *Middle East Journal*, Vol. 61, No. 1 (2007), pp. 49–70.

——— 'Toward a Representative Military? The Transformation of the Lebanese Officer Corps since 1945', *Middle East Journal*, Vol. 60, No. 1 (2006), pp. 75–93.

Barakat, Halim, 'Social and Political Integration in Lebanon: A Case of Social Mosaic', *Middle East Journal*, Vol. 27, No. 3 (1973), pp. 301–18.

Baram, Amatzia, 'The Iraqi Invasion of Kuwait: Decision making in Baghdad', in Amatzia Baram and Barry Rubin, (eds), *Iraq's Road to War*, Basingstoke: Palgrave, 1996, pp. 5–36.

——— and Barry Rubin, (eds), *Iraq's Road to War*, Basingstoke: Palgrave, 1996.

Barnett, Michael N., 'Identity and Alliances in the Middle East', in Peter Katzenstein (ed.), *The Culture of National Security: Norms and Identity in World Politics*, New York: Columbia, 1996, pp. 400–47.

Baroudi, Sami E., and Imad Salamey, 'US-French Collaboration on Lebanon: How Syria's Role in Lebanon and the Middle East Contributed to a US-French Convergence', *The Middle East Journal*, Vol. 65, No. 3 (2011), pp. 398–425.

Bar-Tal, Daniel, 'Why Does Fear Override Hope in Societies Engulfed by Intractable Conflict, as It Does in the Israeli Society?', *Political Psychology*, Vol. 22, No. 3 (2001), pp. 601–27.

Bass, Gary J., *Freedom's Battle. The Origins of Humanitarian Intervention*, New York: Alfred A. Knopf, 2008.

Baumann, Hannes, 'The Ascent of Rafiq Hariri and Philanthropic Practices in Beirut', in Mermier, F., and S. Mervin (eds), *Chefs Politiques et Sociabilités Partisanes au Liban*, Karthala: Paris, forthcoming.

Becherer, Richard, 'A Matter of Life and Debt: the Untold Costs of Rafiq Hariri's New Beirut', *The Journal of Architecture*, Vol. 10, No. 1 (2005), pp. 1–42.

Berger, Peter, and Thomas Luckmann, *La construction sociale de la réalité*, Paris: Méridien Klincksieck, 1986.

Beshara, Adel, *Outright Assassination: The Trial and Execution of Antun Sa'adeh, 1949*, Reading: Itacha Press, 2010.

——— *Lebanon: Politics of Frustration—the Failed Coup of 1961*, London: RoutledgeCurzon, 2005.

Beyhoum, Nabil, 'Reconstruire Beyrouth', *Etudes sur le Monde Arabe*, No. 5 (1992).

Blanford, Nicholas, *Killing Mr Lebanon: the Assassination of Rafik Hariri and its Impact on the Middle East*, London: I.B. Tauris, 2006.

Boal, Frederick W., 'Belfast: Walls Within', *Political Geography*, Vol. 21, No. 5 (2002), pp. 687–94.

Bonne, Emmanuel, *Vie publique, clientèle et patronage: Rafic Hariri à Saïda*, Aix-en-Provence: Institut de recherches et d'études sur le monde arabe et musulman, 1995.

Bourdieu, Pierre, *Language and Symbolic Power*, Cambridge: Polity, 1991.

BIBLIOGRAPHY

Bourgey, André, *Industrialisation et changements sociaux dans l'Orient arabe*, Beirut: Centre d'études et de recherches sur le Moyen-Orient contemporain, 1982.

Brynen, Rex, 'Palestine and the Arab State System: Permeability, State Consolidation and the Intifada', *Canadian Journal of Political Science/Revue canadienne de science politique*, Vol. 24, No. 3 (1991), pp. 595–621.

Buck-Morss, Susan, *Thinking Past Terror*, New York: Verso, 2003.

Calame, Jon, and Esther Charlesworth (eds), *Divided Cities: Belfast, Beirut, Jerusalem, Mostar and Nicosia*, Philadelphia: University of Pennsylvania Press, 2009.

Cammett, Melani, and Sukriti Issar, 'Bricks and Mortar Clientelism: The Political Geography of Welfare in Lebanon', *World Politics*, Vol. 62, No. 3 (2010), pp. 381–421.

Chaib, Kinda, 'Le Hizbullah libanais à travers ses images: la représentation du martyr', in Mervin S. (ed.), *Les mondes chiites et l'Iran*, Paris: Karthala, 2007, pp. 113–31.

Charara, Waddah, *Dawlat Hizb Allah. Lubnan mujtama'an islamiyyan*, (The State of Hizbollah. Lebanon Islamic society), Beirut: Dar al-Nahar, 1998.

Choueiri, Youssef (ed.), *Breaking the Cycle: Civil Wars in Lebanon*, London: Stacey International, 2007.

Clark, Janine, 'Islamic Associations and the Middle Class', *ISIM Newsletter*, No. 14 (2004), p. 51.

——— 'Social Movement Theory and Patron-Clientelism: Islamic Social Institutions and the Middle Class in Egypt, Jordan, and Yemen', *Comparative Political Studies*, Vol. 37, No. 8 (2004), pp. 941–68.

Clerc, Valérie, *Les quartiers irréguliers de Beyrouth*, Beirut: IFPO, 2008.

Cockayne, James, 'Foreword', *Journal of International Criminal Justice*, Vol. 5, No. 5 (2007), pp. 1061–4.

Cooke, Miriam, *War's Other Voices: Women Writers in the Lebanese Civil War*, Cambridge: Cambridge University Press, 1987.

Cordell, Karl, and Stefan Wolff (eds), *Routledge Handbook of Ethnic Conflict*, London: Routledge, 2011.

——— 'Power-Sharing', in Cordell, Karl, and Stefan Wolff (eds), *Routledge Handbook of Ethnic Conflict*, London: Routledge, 2011.

Corm, George, *Le Liban contemporain. Histoire et société*, Paris: La Découverte, 2005.

——— 'Reconstructing Lebanon's Economy', in Shafik, N. (ed.), *Economic Challenges Facing Middle Eastern Countries: Alternative Futures*, Basingstoke: Macmillan, 1998, pp. 116–35.

——— 'The War System: Militia Hegemony and Reestablishment of the State', in Colling, D. (ed.), *Peace for Lebanon? From War to Reconstruction*, Boulder: Lynne Rienner, 1994, pp. 215–30.

Courbage, Youssef, and Emmanuel Todd, *Le rendez-vous des civilisations*, Paris: le Seuil, 2007.

BIBLIOGRAPHY

Dagher, Carole, *Le défi du Liban d'après guerre*, Paris: L'Harmattan, 2002.

Deboulet, Agnès, 'Téhéran, Beyrouth, Le Caire: les citadins face aux projets auto-routiers', *Urbanisme*, No. 336 (2004), pp. 29–38.

Deeb, Marius, *The Lebanese Civil War*, New York: Praeger, 1980.

Dekmejian, Hrair, *Patterns of Political Leadership: Egypt, Israel, Lebanon*, New York: State University of New York Press, 1975.

Denoeux, Guilain, and Robert Springborg, 'Hariri's Lebanon: Singapore of the Middle East or Sanaa of the Levant?', *Middle East Policy*, Vol. 6, No. 2 (1998), pp. 158–73.

Derrida, Jacques, *Archive Fever*, Chicago: University of Chicago Press, 1998.

Doyle, Michael, 'Politics and Grand Strategy', in Rosecrance, Richard, and Arthur Stein (eds), *The Domestic Bases of Grand Strategy*, Ithaca: Cornell University Press, 1993, pp. 22–47.

Dumenil, Gerard, and Dominique Levy, 'The Neoliberal (Counter-)Revolution', in Saad-Filho, Alfredo, and Deborah Johnston (eds), *Neoliberalism: A Critical Reader*, London: Pluto Press, 2005, pp. 9–19.

Eberling, Björn, 'The Next Step in History-Writing through Criminal Law: Exactly How Tailor-Made Is the Special Tribunal for Lebanon?', *Leiden Journal of International Law*, Vol. 21, No. 2 (2008), pp. 529–38.

Eddé, Carla, 'Les mémoires des acteurs de la guerre: le conflit revisité par ses protagonistes', in Mermier, Franck, and Christophe Varin (eds), *Mémoires de guerres au Liban*, Paris: Sinbad, 2010, pp. 25–46.

Eddé, Henri, *Le Liban d'où je viens*, Paris: Buchet-Chastel, 1997.

El-Hokayem, Emile, and Elena McGovern, *Towards a More Secure and Stable Lebanon: Prospects for Security Sector Reform*, Washington, D.C.: Henry L. Stimson Center, 2008.

El-Khazen, Farid, 'The Postwar Political Process: Authoritarianism by Diffusion', in Hanf, Theodor, and Nawaf Salam (eds), *Lebanon in Limbo: Postwar Society and State in an Uncertain Regional Environment*, Baden-Baden: Nomos Verlagsgesellschaft, 2003, pp. 53–74.

———— 'Political Parties in Postwar Lebanon: Parties in Search of Partisans', *Middle East Journal*, Vol. 57, No. 4 (2003), pp. 605–24.

———— 'Lebanon—Independent No More: Disappearing Christians of the Middle East', *Middle East Quarterly*, Vol. 8, No. 1 (2001), pp. 43–50.

———— *Intikhabat Lubnan ma Ba'd al-Harb 1992, 1996, 2000: Dimuqratiyya bila Khayar*, (Lebanon's Postwar Elections 1992, 1996, 2000: Democracy without Choice), Beirut: Dar al-Nahar lil-Nashr, 2000.

———— *The Breakdown of the State in Lebanon, 1967–1976*, Cambridge: Harvard University Press, 2000.

———— *Lebanon's First Postwar Parliamentary Election, 1992: An Imposed Choice*, Oxford: Centre for Lebanese Studies, 1998.

BIBLIOGRAPHY

——— *The Communal Pact of National Identities: the Making and Politics of the 1943 National Pact*, Oxford: Centre for Lebanese Studies, 1991.

——— 'Kamal Jumblatt, The Uncrowned Druze Prince of the Left', *Middle East Studies*, Vol. 24, No. 2 (1988), pp. 178–205.

El-Masri, Samar, 'The Hariri Tribunal: Politics and International Law', *Middle East Policy*, Vol. 15, No. 3 (2008), pp. 80–92.

El-Mufti, Karim, *Reconstruction d'Etat dans les sociétés multicommunautaires: analyse comparative entre le Liban et la Bosnie-Herzégovine*, forthcoming.

Faour, Muhammad A., 'Religion, Demography, and Politics in Lebanon', *Middle Eastern Studies*, Vol. 43, No. 6 (2007), pp. 909–21.

Fassbender, Bardo, 'Reflections on the International Legality of the Special Tribunal for Lebanon', *Journal of International Criminal Justice*, Vol. 5, No. 5 (2007), pp. 1091–105.

Favier, Agnès, *Municipalités et pouvoirs locaux au Liban*, Beirut: Centre d'études et de recherches sur le Moyen-Orient contemporain, 2001.

Fawaz, Mona, 'The State and the Production of Illegal Housing: Public Practices in Hayy el Sellom, Beirut-Lebanon', in Rieker, M., and K. Ali (eds), *Comparing Cities: The Middle East and South Asia*, Oxford: Oxford University Press, 2009, pp. 197–220.

——— 'Hezbollah as Urban Planner? Questions To and From Planning Theory', *Planning Theory*, Vol. 8, No. 4 (2009), pp. 323–34.

——— 'Neoliberal Urbanity and the Right to the City: A View from Beirut's Periphery', *Development and Change*, Vol. 40, No. 5 (2009), pp. 827–52.

Fayyad, Ali, *Fragile States: Dilemmas of Stability in Lebanon and the Arab World*, Oxford: INTRAC, 2008.

Gaeta, Paola, 'To Be (Present) or Not to Be (Present): Trials in Absentia before the Special Tribunal for Lebanon', *Journal of International Criminal Justice*, Vol. 5, No. 5 (2007), pp. 1165–74.

Gambill, Gary C., 'US Mideast Policy and the Syrian Occupation of Lebanon', *Middle East Intelligence Bulletin*, Vol. 3, No. 3 (2001).

——— and Aoun, Elie Abou, 'Special Report: How Syria Orchestrates Lebanon's Elections', *Middle East Intelligence Bulletin*, Vol. 2, No. 7 (2000).

Gaspard, Toufic, *A Political Economy of Lebanon, 1948–2002: The Limits of Laissez-Faire*, Leiden: Brill, 2004.

Ghosn, Faten, and Amal Khoury, 'Lebanon after the Civil War: Peace or the Illusion of Peace?', *The Middle East Journal*, Vol. 65, No. 3 (2011), pp. 381–97.

Hage, Ghassan, 'Religious Fundamentalism as a Political Strategy—the evolution of the Lebanese Forces' religious discourse during the Lebanese Civil War', *Critique of Anthropology*, Vol. 12, No. 1 (1992), pp. 27–45.

Halbwachs, Maurice, *On Collective Memory*, Chicago: University of Chicago Press, 1992.

BIBLIOGRAPHY

Halpern, Jodi, and Harvey Weinstein, 'Rehumanizing the Other: Empathy and Reconciliation', *Human Rights Quarterly*, Vol. 26, No. 3 (2004), pp. 561–83.

Hamilton, Jennifer, Ulf Hansson, John Bell, and Sarah Toucas, *Segregated Lives: Social Division, Sectarianism and Everyday Life in Northern Ireland*, Belfast: Institute for Conflict Research, 2008.

Hanafi, Sari, 'Governance of the Palestinian Refugee Camps in the Arab East: Governmentalities in Quest of Legitimacy', *Working Paper*, Issam Fares Institute for Public Policy and International Affairs, 2010.

————— and Taylor Long, 'Governance, Governmentalities, and the State of Exception in the Palestinian Refugee Camps of Lebanon', *Journal of Refugee Studies*, Vol. 23, No. 2 (2010), pp. 34–60.

————— and I. Sheikh Hassan, 'Constructing and Governing Nahr al-Bared Camp. An "Ideal" Model of Exclusion', *Majallat al-Dirasat al-Falastiniyya*, No. 78 (2009), pp. 39–52.

Hanf, Theodor, 'E Pluribus Unum? Lebanese Opinions and Attitudes on Coexistence', *Lettres de Byblos*, No. 14 (2007).

————— *Coexistence in Wartime Lebanon: Decline of a State and Rise of a Nation*, London: Centre for Lebanese Studies in association with I.B. Tauris, 1993.

————— and Nawaf Salam (eds), *Lebanon in Limbo: Postwar Society and State in an Uncertain Regional Environment*, Baden-Baden: Nomos Verlagsgesellschaft, 2003.

Harb, Mona, *Le Hezbollah à Beyrouth: de la banlieue à la ville*, Paris: Karthala, 2010.

————— 'La *Dâhiye* de Beyrouth: parcours d'une stigmatisation urbaine, consolidation d'un territoire politique', *Genèses*, No. 51 (2003), pp. 70–91.

————— 'Transforming the Site of Dereliction into the Urban Culture of Modernity: Beirut's Southern Suburb and the Elyssar Project', in Rowe, Peter G., and Hashim Sarkis (eds), *Projecting Beirut: Episodes in the Construction and Reconstruction of a Modern City*, Munich: Prestel, 1998, pp. 173–81.

Hardwick, Susan, 'Migration, Embedded Network and Social Capital: Towards Theorising North American Ethnic Geography', *International Journal of Population Geography*, Vol. 9, No. 2 (2003), pp. 163–79.

Harik, Iliya, 'The Maronites and the Future of Lebanon: A Case of Communal Conflict', in Dorr, Steven, and Neysa Slater (eds), *Security Perspectives and Policies: Lebanon, Syria, Israel and the Palestinians*, Washington, D.C.: Defense Academic Research Support Program, 1991, pp. 45–55.

Harik, Judith P., 'Democracy (Again) Derailed: Lebanon's Ta'if Paradox', in Korany, Bahgat, Rex Brynen and Paul Noble (eds), *Political Liberalization and Democratization in the Arab World, Vol. 2: Comparative Experiences*, Boulder: Lynne Rienner, 1998, pp. 127–55.

Hartmann, Michael, *The Sociology of Elites*, Oxford: Routledge, 2007.

Harvey, David, *A Brief History of Neoliberalism*, Oxford: Oxford University Press, 2005.

BIBLIOGRAPHY

——— *The New Imperialism*, Oxford: Oxford University Press, 2003.

Hatem, Robert, *From Israel to Damascus: The Painful Road of Blood, Betrayal and Deception*, La Masa, CA: Vanderblumen Publications, 1999.

Haugbolle, Sune, *War and Memory in Lebanon*, Cambridge: Cambridge University Press, 2010.

——— 'Spatial Transformations in the Lebanese "Independence Intifada"', *The Arab Studies Journal*, Vol. 14, No. 2 (2006), pp. 60–77.

Hearn, Frank, *Moral Order and Social Disorder: The American Search for Civil Society*, New York: Aldine de Gruyter, 1997.

Hedstrom, Margaret, 'Archives, Memory, and Interfaces with the Past', *Archival Science*, Vol. 2, No. 1–2 (2002), pp. 21–43.

Heydemann, Steven, *Networks of privilege in the Middle East: the Politics of Economic Reform Revisited*, New York: Palgrave Macmillan, 2004.

——— (ed.), *War, Institutions and Social Change in the Middle East*, Berkeley: University of California Press, 2000.

Hindess, Barry, *Politics and Class Analysis*, Oxford: Blackwell, 1987.

Hironaka, Ann, *Neverending Wars: The International Community, Weak States, and the Perpetuation of Civil War*, Cambridge, MA: Harvard University Press, 2005.

Horowitz, Donald L, *Ethnic Groups in Conflict*, Berkeley: University of California Press, 2000.

Hudson, Michael, 'Lebanon after Ta'if: Another Reform Opportunity Lost', *Arab Studies Quarterly*, Vol. 21, No. 1 (1999), pp. 27–35.

——— 'The Lebanese Crisis: The Limits of Consociational Democracy', *Journal of Palestine Studies*, Vol. 5, No. 3/4 (1976), pp. 109–22.

Humphrey, Michael, and Maroun Kisirwan, 'Impunity, Nationalism and Transnationalism: The Recovery of the "Disappeared" of Lebanon', *Bulletin of the Royal Institute of Inter-Faith Studies*, Vol. 3, No. 2 (2001), pp. 113–40.

Hutson, Royce, Taylor Long and Michael Page, 'Pathways to Violent Radicalisation in the Middle East: A Model for Future Studies of Transnational Jihad', *The RUSI Journal*, Vol. 154, No. 2 (2009), pp. 18–26.

ICTJ, *Handbook on the Special Tribunal for Lebanon*, New York: The International Center for Transitional Justice (ICTJ), Prosecutions Program, 2008.

Itani, Fida, *Al-jihadiyyun fi lubnan: min quwwat al-fajr ila fath al-islam* (Jihadism in Lebanon: From the Forces of Dawn to Fatah al-Islam) Beirut: Dar al-Saqi, 2008.

Jaafar, Rudy, 'Democratic System Reform in Lebanon: An Electoral Approach', in Choueiri, Youssef M. (ed.), *Breaking the Cycle: Civil Wars in Lebanon*, London: Stacey International, 2007, pp. 285–305.

Jervis, Robert, 'Cooperation under the Security Dilemma', *World Politics*, Vol. 30, No. 2 (1978), pp. 167–214.

Johnson, Michael, 'Managing Political Change in Lebanon: Challenges and Prospects', in Choueiri, Youssef M. (ed.), *Breaking the Cycle: Civil Wars in Lebanon*, London: Stacey International, 2007, pp. 137–65.

———— *All Honorable Men: The Social Origins of War in Lebanon*, London: I. B. Tauris, 2001.

———— *Class and Client in Beirut: The Sunni Muslim Community and the Lebanese State 1840–1985*, London: Ithaca Press, 1986.

Jones, Clive, and Sergio Catignani (eds), *Israel and Hizbollah: an Interstate and Asymmetric War in Perspective*, London: Routledge, 2009.

Nidal Nabil, Jurdi, 'The Subject-Matter Jurisdiction of the Special Tribunal for Lebanon', *Journal of International Criminal Justice*, Vol. 5, No. 5 (2007), pp. 1125–38.

Kanaan, Claude Boueiz, *Lebanon 1860–1960: A Century of Myth and Politics*, London: Saqi Books, 2005.

Kasparian, Choghig, *L'entrée des jeunes libanais dans la vie active et l'émigration*, Beirut: Presses de l'Université Saint-Joseph, 2003.

Kaufman, Asher, 'Who Owns the Shebaa Farms? Chronicle of a Territorial Dispute', *Middle East Journal*, Vol. 56, No. 4 (2002), pp. 576–96.

Kerr, Malcolm, *The Arab Cold War: Gamal 'Abd al-Nasir and his Rivals: 1958–1970*, London: Oxford University Press, 1971.

Kerr, Michael, '"A positive aspect to the tragedy of Lebanon": The convergence of US, Syrian and Israeli interests at the outset of Lebanon's civil war', *Israel Affairs*, Vol. 15, No. 4 (2009), pp. 355–71.

———— *Imposing Power-Sharing: Conflict and Coexistence in Northern Ireland and Lebanon*, Dublin: Irish Academic Press, 2006.

Khalaf, Samir, *Heart of Beirut. Reclaiming the Bourj*, London: Saqi, 2006.

———— 'On Roots and Routes: The Reassertion of Primordial Loyalties', in Hanf, Theodor, and Nawaf Salam (eds), *Lebanon in Limbo: Postwar Society and State in an Uncertain Regional Environment*, Baden-Baden: Nomos Verlagsgesellschaft, 2003, pp. 107–41.

———— *Civil and Uncivil Violence in Lebanon: A History of the Internationalization of Communal Conflict*, New York: Columbia University Press, 2002.

———— *Beirut Reclaimed: Reflections on Urban Design and the Restoration of Civility*, Beirut: Dar al-Nahar, 1993.

Khalil, Ibrahim, 'Qanun al-difa'. Qiyada jam'iyya am shalal fil-qiyada?' (The law of defense. Collective command or paralysis of command?), *Al-Difa' al-watani* (1990), pp. 17–45.

Khalili, Laleh, *Heroes and Martyrs of Palestine: The Politics of National Commemoration*, Cambridge: Cambridge University Press, 2007.

Khan, Riz, *Alwaleed. Businessman, Billionaire, Prince*, New York: William Morrow, 2005.

Khatib, Lina, *Lebanese Cinema—Imagining the Civil War and Beyond*, London: I.B. Tauris, 2008.

BIBLIOGRAPHY

Khawaja, Marwan, Sawsan Abdulrahim, Rima Soweid and Dima Karam, 'Distrust, Social Fragmentation and Adolescent Health in the Outer City and Beyond', *Social Science and Medicine*, Vol. 63, No. 5 (2006), pp. 1304–15.

Khayat, Tristan, 'La route de la discorde: construction du territoire municipal et aménagement métropolitain à Borj Hammoud', in Favier, Agnes (ed.), *Municipalités et pouvoirs locaux au Liban*, Beirut: Centre d'Etudes et de Recherches sur le Moyen-Orient Contemporain, 2001.

Khuri, Fuad I., *Imams and Emirs. State, Religion and Sects in Islam*, London: Saqi, 2006.

Knio, Karim, 'Lebanon: Cedar Revolution or Neo-Sectarian Partition?', *Mediterranean Politics*, Vol. 10, No. 2 (2005), pp. 225–32.

Knudsen, Are, '(In-)security in a Space of Exception. The Destruction of the Nahr el-Bared Refugee Camp in Lebanon', in MacNeish, John-Andrew, and Lie, J.H.S. (eds), *Security and Development*, Oxford: Berghahn, 2010, pp. 99–112.

———— 'Acquiescence to Assassinations in Post-Civil War Lebanon?', *Mediterranean Politics*, Vol. 15, No. 1 (2010), pp. 1–23.

———— 'Islamism in the Diaspora: Palestinian Refugees in Lebanon', *Journal of Refugee Studies*, Vol. 18, No. 2 (2005), pp. 216–34.

———— and Sari Hanafi (eds), *Palestinian Refugees: Identity, Space and Place in the Levant*, London: Routledge, 2011.

———— and Nasser Yassin, 'Political Violence in Post-Civil War Lebanon', in Suhrke, Astri, and Berdal, Mats (eds.), *The Peace In Between: Post-War Violence and Peacebuilding*, London: Routledge, 1997, pp. 117–31.

Koekenbier, Pieter, *A New Model Army? The Reconstruction of the Military in Postwar Lebanon*, MA Thesis, University of Amsterdam, Amsterdam, 2005.

Kortam, Marie, *Jeune et violence dans le camp de Baddawi et le banlieu parisien*, PhD thesis, Université de Paris VII, Paris, 2011.

Kostovicova, Denisa, and Vesna Bojicic-Dzelilovic (eds), *Persistent State Weakness in the Global Age*, London: Ashgate, 2009.

Krayem, Hassan, 'The Lebanese Civil War and the Ta'if Agreement', in Salem, Paul, (ed.), *Conflict Resolution in the Arab World*, Beirut: American University of Beirut Press, 1997, pp. 426–7.

Kriegel, Annie, *Les communistes français*, Paris: le Seuil, 1968.

Labaki, Boutros, *Bilan des guerres du Liban, 1975–1990*, Paris: L'Harmattan,1995.

Lamont, Michèle, and Molnar, Virág, 'The Study of Boundaries in the Social Sciences', *Annual Review of Sociology*, Vol. 28 (2002), pp. 167–95.

Larkin, Craig, 'Beyond the War? The Lebanese Postmemory Experience', *International Journal of Middle East Studies*, Vol. 42, No. 4 (2010), pp. 615–35.

Leenders, Reinoud, 'Regional Conflict Formations: is the Middle East next?', *Third World Quarterly*, Vol. 28, No. 5 (2007), pp. 959–82.

———— 'Public Means to Private Ends: State Building and Power in Post War Lebanon', in Kienle, Eberhard (ed.), *Politics from Above, Politics from Below*, London: Saqi Books, 2003, pp. 304–34.

Lefebvre, Henri, *Le droit à la ville*, Paris: Anthropos, 1968.

Lehmbruch, Gerhard, 'A Non-Competitive Pattern of Conflict Management in Liberal Democracies: The Case of Switzerland, Austria and Lebanon', in McRae, Kenneth D. (ed.), *Consociational Democracy*, Toronto: McClelland and Stewart, 1974, pp. 90–7.

Leigh, Andrew, 'Trust, Inequality and Ethnic Heterogeneity', *The Economic Record*, Vol. 82, No. 258 (2006), pp. 268–80.

Lévy, Jacques, *L'espace légitime*, Paris: Presses de Sciences Po., 1994.

Lijphart, Arend, 'Constitutional Designs for Divided Societies', *Journal of Democracy*, Vol. 15, No. 2 (2004), pp. 96–109.

———— 'Consociational Democracy', *World Politics*, Vol. 21, No. 2 (1969), pp. 207–25.

———— and Grofman, Bernard, 'Choosing an Electoral System', in Promper, Gerald M. (ed.), *Choosing an Electoral System: Issues and Alternatives*, New York: Praeger, 1984, pp. 3–12.

Lorenz, Chris, 'Can Histories Be True? Narrativism, Positivism, and the "Metaphorical Turn"', *History and Theory*, Vol. 37, No. 3 (1998), pp. 309–29.

Maasri, Zeina, *Off the Wall—Political Posters of the Lebanese Civil War*, London: I.B. Tauris, 2009.

Mackay, Sandra, *Mirror of the Arab World: Lebanon in Conflict*, New York: Norton and Norton, 2008.

Maila, Joseph, *The Document of National Understanding: a Commentary*, Oxford: Centre for Lebanese Studies, 1992.

Majed, Ziad, 'Hezbollah and the Shiite Community: From Political Confessionalization to Confessional Specialization', *Briefing Paper*, The Aspen Institute, 2010.

Makdisi, Karim, 'Constructing Security Council Resolution 1701 for Lebanon in the Shadow of the "War on Terror"', *International Peacekeeping*, Vol. 18, No. 1 (2011), pp. 4–20.

Makdisi, Samir, and Marcus Marktanner, 'Trapped by Consociationalism: The Case of Lebanon', *Working Paper*, American University of Beirut, 2008.

Makdissi, Ussama, *The Culture of Sectarianism: Community, History, and Violence in Nineteenth-Century Ottoman Lebanon*, Berkeley: University of California Press, 2000.

Maktabi, Rania, 'The Lebanese Census of 1932 Revisited. Who are the Lebanese?', *British Journal of Middle Eastern Studies*, Vol. 26, No. 2 (1999), pp. 219–41.

Mansour, Albert, *Al-inqilab 'ala al-Ta'if* (The Coup d'État against Ta'if), Beirut: Dar al-Jadid, 1993.

Massey, Doreen, 'The Spatial Construction of Youth Cultures', in Skelton, Tracey, and Gill Valentine (eds.), *Cool Places: Geographies of Youth Culture*, London: Routledge, 1998, pp. 120–9.

McGarry, John, and Brendan O'Leary, 'Iraq's Constitution of 2005: Liberal Consociation as Political Prescription', *International Journal of Constitutional Law*, Vol. 5, No. 4 (2007), pp. 670–98.

McLaurin, Ronald, 'From Professional to Political: The Redecline of the Lebanese Army', *Armed Forces & Society*, Vol. 17, No. 4 (1991), pp. 545–68.

——— 'Lebanon and its army', in Azar, Edward E. (ed.), *The Emergence of a new Lebanon: Fantasy or reality?*, New York: Praeger, 1984, pp. 79–114.

Ménargues, Alain, *Les secrets de la guerre du Liban: du coup d'état de Béchir Gémayel aux massacres des camps palestiniens*, Paris: Albin Michel, 2004.

Mermier, Franck (ed.), *Mémoires de guerres au Liban (1975–1990)*, Paris: Actes Sud, 2010.

——— 'La mosquée Muhammad al-Amîn à Beyrouth: mausolée involontaire de Rafic Hariri', *Revue d'études des mondes méditerranéen et musulmans (REMMM)*, No. 125 (2009), pp. 177–96.

Mroué, Rabih, *How Nancy Wished that it was all an April's Fool*, (DVD), Beirut: Ashkal Alwan, 2007.

Mugraby, Muhamad, 'The Syndrome of One-Time Exceptions and the Drive to Establish the Proposed Hariri Court', *Mediterranean Politics*, Vol. 13, No. 2 (2008), pp. 171–94.

Nabaa, René, *Rafic Hariri, un homme d'affaires Premier ministre*, Paris: L'Harmattan, 1998.

Nabulsi, Karma, *Palestinians Register: Laying Foundations and Setting Directions*, Oxford: Nuffield College, 2006.

Nagel, Caroline R., 'Reconstructing Space, Re-Creating Memory: Sectarian Politics and Urban Development in Post-War Beirut', *Political Geography*, Vol. 21, No. 5 (2002), pp. 717–25.

Najah, Wakim, *Les mains noires*, Beirut: All Print, 1998.

Nasr, Salim, 'The Political Economy of the Lebanese Conflict', in Shehadi, Nadim, and Bridget Harney (eds), *Politics and the Economy in Lebanon*, Oxford: Centre for Lebanese Studies, 1989, pp. 42–50.

——— 'Backdrop to Civil War: The Crisis of Lebanese Capitalism', *MERIP Middle East Report*, No. 73 (1978), pp. 3–13.

Nassif, Nicolas, and Rosanna Boumonsef, *Al-Masrah wal-Kawalis: Intikhabat 96 fi Fusuliha* (The Stage and the Backstage: The Chapters of the 1996 Elections), Beirut: Dar al-Nahar lil-Nashr, 1996.

Neal, Mark W., and Richard Tansey, 'The Dynamics of Effective Corrupt Leadership: Lessons from Rafik Hariri's Political Career in Lebanon', *The Leadership Quarterly*, Vol. 21, No. 1 (2010), pp. 33–49.

Nerguizian, Aram, and Anthony Cordesman, *The Lebanese Armed Forces: Challenges and Opportunities in Post-Syria Lebanon*, Washington, D.C.: Center for Strategic and International Studies, 2009.

BIBLIOGRAPHY

Noble, Paul, 'The Arab System: Pressures, Constraints, and Opportunities', in Korany, Bahgat, and Ali Hillal Dessouki (eds), *The Foreign Policies of Arab States: The Challenge of Globalization*, Cairo: American University of Cairo Press, 2008, pp. 41–77.

Norton, Augustus R., *Hezbollah: A Short History*, Princeton: Princeton University Press, 2007.

———— 'Lebanon After Taif: Is the Civil War Over?', *Middle East Journal*, Vol. 45, No. 3 (1991), pp. 457–73.

O'Leary, Brendan, 'Debating Consociational Politics: Normative and Explanatory Arguments', in Noel, Sidney J. R. (ed.), *From Power-Sharing to Democracy: Post-Conflict Institutions in Ethnically Divided Societies*, Toronto: McGill-Queens University Press, 2005, pp. 3–44.

Owen, Roger, and Pamuk Sevket, *A History of the Middle East Economies in the Twentieth Century*, London: I.B. Tauris, 1998.

Perthes, Volker, *Arab Elites: Negotiating the Politics of Change*, Boulder: Lynne Rienner, 2004.

———— 'Myths and Money: Four Years of Hariri and Lebanon's Preparation for a New Middle East', *MERIP Middle East Report*, No. 203 (1997), pp. 16–21.

———— 'Syrian Predominance in Lebanon', in Hollis, Rosemary, and Nadim Shehadi (eds), *Lebanon on Hold: Implications for Middle East Peace*, Oxford: Royal Institute of International Affairs and The Centre for Lebanese Studies, 1996, pp. 31–4.

Peteet, Julie, 'Socio-Political Integration and Conflict Resolution in the Palestinian Camps in Lebanon', *Journal of Palestine Studies*, Vol. 16, No. 2 (1987), pp. 29–44.

Petti, Alessandro, *Arcipelaghi e Enclave: Architettura dell'Ordinamento Spaziale Contemporaneo*, Milano: Bruno Mondadori, 2007.

Picard, Élizabeth, 'Élections libanaises: un peu d'air a circulé…', *Critique internationale*, No. 10 (2001), pp. 21–31.

———— 'The Political Economy of Civil War in Lebanon', in Heydemann, Steven (ed.), *War, Institutions, and Social Change in the Middle East*, Berkeley: University of California Press, 2000, pp. 292–322.

———— *The Demobilization of the Lebanese Militias*, Oxford: Centre for Lebanese Studies, 1999.

———— 'De la 'communauté-classe' à la 'Résistance Nationale': Pour une analyse du rôle des Chiites dans le système politique libanais (1970–1985)', *Revue française de science politique*, Vol. 35, No. 6 (1985), pp. 999–1027.

Portes, Alejandro, and Julia Sensenbrenner, 'Embeddedness and Immigration: Notes on the Social Determinants of Economic Action', *American Journal of Sociology*, Vol. 98, No. 6 (1993), pp. 1320–50.

Posusney, Marsha P., 'Multi-Party Elections in the Arab World: Institutional Engineering and Oppositional Strategies', *Studies in Comparative International Development*, Vol. 36, No. 4 (2002), pp. 34–62.

BIBLIOGRAPHY

Pouillard, Nicolas, *Utopies, tiers-mondismes et théologie du non-renoncement: islamismes, mouvements de gauche et nationalismes de "libération" entre attractions, répulsions et affinités électives, de la révolution iranienne à nos jours. Les cas libanais et palestiniens*, PhD thesis, Ecole des Hautes Etudes en Sciences Sociales, Paris, 2009.

Powell, Robert, *In The Shadow of Power*, Princeton: Princeton University Press, 1999.

Raad, Ghassan, 'The Termination of Protracted Social Conflict in Lebanon: An Analytical Perspective', in Shehadi, Nadim, and Dana H. Mills (eds), *Lebanon: A History of Conflict and Consensus*, London: I.B. Tauris and The Centre for Lebanese Studies, 1988, pp. 201–9.

Rabinovich, Itamar, *The War for Lebanon*, Ithaca: Cornell University Press, 1985.

Raffestin, Claude, *Pour une géographie du pouvoir*, Paris: LITEC, 1980.

Reynolds, Andrew, and Ben Reilly, *The International IDEA Handbook of Electoral System Design*, Stockholm: International Institute for Democracy and Electoral Assistance, 2002.

Rougier, Bernard, 'Fatah al-Islam: un réseau jihadiste au coeur des contradictions libanaises', *Qu'est ce que le Salafisme*, Paris: Presses Universitaires de France, 2008.

————— *Everyday Jihad: The Rise of Militant Islam among Palestinians in Lebanon*, Cambridge, MA: Harvard University Press, 2007.

Rowayheb, Marwan, 'Walid Jumblat and Political Alliances: The Politics of Adaptation', *Middle East Critique*, Vol. 20, No. 1 (2011), pp. 47–66.

Rubin, Barry, 'The United States and Iraq: From Appeasement to War', in Baram, Amatzia, and Barry Rubin (eds), *Iraq's Road to War*, Basingstoke: Palgrave, 1996, pp. 255–72.

Saad, Abdo, 'Le système électoral majoritaire freine l'avancée démocratique', *Confluences Méditerranée*, No. 56 (2006), pp. 109–14.

Saad-Ghorayeb, Amal, *Hizb'ullah: Politics and Religion*, London: Pluto Press, 2002.

Saidawi, Rafif R., *Nadhra al-riwa'iya ila al-harb al-lubnaniya 1975–1995* (The Narrative View on the Lebanese War 1975–1995), Beirut: Dar al-Farabi/Anep, 2003.

Saideman, Stephen M., and Marie-Joëlle Zahar, 'Causing Security, Reducing Fear: Deterring Intra-State Violence and Assuring Government Restraint', in Saideman, Stephen M., and Marie-Joëlle Zahar (eds), *Intra-State Conflict, Governments and Security: Dilemmas of Deterrence and Assurance*, London: Routledge, 2008, pp. 1–19.

Salam, Nawaf, 'Islah al-Nidham al-Intikhabi' (The Reform of the Electoral System), in Salam, Nawaf (ed.), *Khiyarat Lubnan* (Lebanon's Options), Beirut: Dar al-Nahar lil-Nashr, 2004, pp. 14–17.

Salem, Elie, *Violence and Diplomacy in Lebanon: The Troubled Years, 1982–1988*, London: IB Tauris, 1995.

Salem, Paul, 'Framing Post-War Lebanon: Perspectives on the Constitution and the Structure of Power', *Mediterranean Politics*, Vol. 3, No. 1 (1998), pp. 13–26.

BIBLIOGRAPHY

——— 'The Wounded Republic: Lebanon's Struggle for Recovery', *Arab Studies Quarterly*, Vol. 16, No. 4 (1994), pp. 47–63.

Salibi, Kamal, *A House of Many Mansions: The History of Lebanon Reconsidered*, London: IB Tauris, 2003.

——— *Crossroads to Civil War: Lebanon, 1958–1976*, New York: Delmar Books, 1976.

Salloukh, Bassel F., 'Democracy in Lebanon: The Primacy of the Sectarian System', in Brown, Nathan J., and Emad el Din Shahin (eds), *The Struggle over Democracy in the Middle East: Regional Politics and External Policies*, New York: Routledge, 2010, pp. 134–50.

——— 'The Art of the Impossible: The Foreign Policy of Lebanon', in Korany, Bahgat, and Ali Hillal Dessouki (eds), *The Foreign Policies of Arab States: The Challenge of Globalization*, Cairo: American University of Cairo Press, 2008, pp. 283–318.

——— 'The Limits of Electoral Engineering in Divided Societies: Elections in Postwar Lebanon', *Canadian Journal of Political Science*, Vol. 39, No. 3 (2006), pp. 635–55.

——— 'Syria and Lebanon: a Brotherhood Transformed', *MERIP Middle East Report*, No. 236 (2005), pp. 14–21.

——— and Rex Brynen (eds), *Persistent Permeability? Regionalism, Localism, and Globalization in the Middle East*, Burlington: Ashgate, 2004.

Saouli, Adham, 'Stability under Late State Formation: The Case of Lebanon', *Cambridge Review of International Affairs*, Vol. 19, No. 4 (2006), pp. 701–17.

Saqr, Yusuf, *A'ilat hakamat lubnan* (Families who governed Lebanon), Beirut: al-Markaz al-'Arabîlil-ma'alûmât, 2008.

Sarkis, Hashim, 'A Vital Void: Reconstructions in Downtown Beirut', In Campanella, Thomas J., and Lawrence J. Vale (eds), *The Resilient City: How Modern Cities Recover from Disaster*, Oxford: Oxford University Press, 2005, pp. 281–97.

Schiller, Norbert, *28 Days that Changed Lebanon 14/02/2005–14/03/2005*, Beirut: Focusmideast, 2006.

Schimmelpfennig, Axel, and Edward Gardner, *Lebanon—Weathering the Perfect Storms*, Washington: IMF, 2008.

Schmitt, Paula, *Advertised to Death. Lebanese Poster Boys*, Beirut: Arab Printing Press, 2009.

Scott, John, *The Sociology of Elites, Volume III: Interlocking Directorships and Corporate Networks*, Aldershot: Elgar, 1990.

Scruton, David, *Sociophobics: the Anthropology of Fear*, Boulder: Westview Press, 1986.

Seale, Patrick, *The Struggle for Arab Independence: Riad Al-Solh and the Makers of the Modern Middle East*, Cambridge: Cambridge University Press, 2010.

——— *Asad: The Struggle for the Middle East*. Los Angeles: University of California Press, 1996.

BIBLIOGRAPHY

Seaver, Brenda, 'The Regional Sources of Power-Sharing Failure: The Case of Lebanon', *Political Science Quarterly*, Vol. 115, No. 2 (2000), pp. 247–72.

Seeberg, Peter, 'The EU as a Realist Actor in Normative Clothes: EU Democracy Promotion in Lebanon and the European Neighbourhood Policy', *Democratization*, Vol. 16, No. 1 (2009), pp. 81–99.

Serra, Gianluca, 'Special Tribunal for Lebanon: A Commentary on Its Major Legal Aspects', *International Criminal Justice Review*, Vol. 18, No. 3 (2008), pp. 344–55.

Seurat, Michel, 'Le quartier de Bab Tebbané à Tripoli (Liban): étude d'une "asabiyya urbaine"', in Zakaroya, Mona (ed.), *Mouvements communautaires et espace urbain au Machreq*, Beirut: Centre d'Etudes et de Recherches sur le Moyen-Orient Contemporain, 1985, pp. 45–86.

Silverman, Stephanie, 'Redrawing the Lines of Control: Political Interventions by Refugees and the Sovereign State System', *conference paper*, Dead/Lines: Contemporary Issues in Legal and Political Theory, University of Edinburgh, 2008.

Silverstein, Paul A., and Ussama Samir Makdisi, 'Introduction: Memory and Violence in the Middle East and North Africa', in Silverstein, Paul A., and Makdisi, Ussama Samir, (eds.), *Memory and Violence in the Middle East and North Africa*, Bloomington: Indiana University Press, 2006, pp. 1–24.

Sklair, Leslie, *The Transnational Capitalist Class*, Malden: Blackwell, 2000.

Skovgaard-Petersen, Jakob, 'The Sunni Religious Scene in Beirut', *Mediterranean Politics*, Vol. 3, No. 1 (1998), pp. 69–80.

Smith, Alastair, 'Alliance Formation and War', *International Studies Quarterly*, Vol. 39, No. 4 (1995), pp. 405–25.

Sorokin, Gerald L., 'Alliance Formation and General Deterrence', *Journal of Conflict Resolution*, Vol. 38, No. 2 (1994), pp. 298–325.

Strindberg, Anders, 'Syria under Pressure', *Journal of Palestine Studies*, Vol. 33, No. 4 (2004), pp. 53–69.

Suhrke, Astri, and Berdal, Mats (eds.), *The Peace In Between: Post-War Violence and Peacebuilding*, London: Routledge, 1997, pp. 117–31.

Tilley, Christopher, *A Phenomenology of Landscape*, London: Berg, 1994.

Tilly, Charles, 'War Making and State Making as Organized Crime', in Evans, P., Rueschemeyer, D., and T. Skocpol (eds), *Bringing the State Back In*, Cambridge: Cambridge University Press, 1985, pp. 169–87.

Toukan, Hanan, 'On Being "The Other", in Post-Civil War Lebanon: Aid and the Politics of Art in Processes of Contemporary Cultural Production', *Arab Studies Journal*, Vol. 18, No. 1 (2010), pp. 118–62.

Traboulsi, Fawwaz, *A History of Modern Lebanon*, London: Pluto Press, 2007.

——— *Identités et Solidarités Croisées dans les Conflits du Liban Contemporain*, PhD thesis, Département d'Histoire, Université de Paris VIII, Paris, 2003.

Tuéni, Ghassan, *Une guerre pour les autres*, Paris: Jean-Claude Lattès, 1985.

────── and Eli Khoury (eds), *Independence '05: The Beirut Spring*, Beirut: Dar an-Nahar and Quantum Communications, 2005.

Verdeil, Eric, *Atlas du Liban*, Beirut: IFPO/CNRS, 2007.

────── 'Reconstruction manquée à Beyrouth, la poursuite de la guerre par le projet urbain', *Annales de la Recherche Urbaine*, No. 91 (2001), pp. 65–73.

Vloeberghs, Ward, 'Worshipping the Martyr President: the *darîh* of Rafiq al-Hariri in Beirut', in Pierret, Thomas, Badouin Dupret, Paulo G. Pinto and Kathryn Spellman-Poots (eds), *Ethnographies of Islam*, forthcoming.

────── *A Building of Might and Faith. Rafiq al-Hariri and the Muhammad al-Amin Mosque. On the Political Dimensions of Religious Architecture in Contemporary Beirut*, PhD thesis in political science, University of Louvain, Louvain-la-Neuve, 2010.

────── 'The Genesis of a Mosque: Negotiating Sacred Space in Downtown Beirut', *working paper*, European University Institute, RSCAS 2008.

Volk, Lucia, *Memorials and Martyrs in Modern Lebanon*, Bloomington: Indiana University Press, 2010.

Walt, Stephen M., 'Alliance formation and the Balance of World Power', *International Security*, No. 9 (1985), pp. 2–43.

Walter, Barbara F., 'Bargaining Failures and Civil War', *Annual Review of Political Science*, No. 12 (2009), pp. 243–61.

Waltz, Kenneth N., *Theory of International Politics*, New York: McGraw Hill, 1979.

Weber, Max, *The Theory of Social and Economic Organization*, New York: The Free Press of Glencoe, 1964.

Wierda, Marieke, Habib Nassar and Lynn Maalouf, 'Early Reflections on Local Perceptions, Legitimacy and Legacy of the Special Tribunal for Lebanon', *Journal of International Criminal Justice*, Vol. 5, No. 5 (2007), pp. 1065–81.

Williams, Raymond, *Politics and Letters—Interviews with New Left Review*, London: Verso, 1981.

Yassin, Nasser, 'Violent Urbanization and Homogenization of Space and Place: Reconstructing the Story of Sectarian Violence in Beirut', in Beall, Jo, Basudeb Guha-Khasnobis and Ravi Kanbur (eds), *Urbanization and Development: Multidisciplinary Perspectives*, Oxford: Oxford University Press, 2010, pp. 205–18.

Yerly, René, 'Repères Liban: Économie', *Moyen-Orient*, No. 2 (2009), pp. 39–41.

────── 'Retour sur les années noires et perspectives', *Confluences Méditerranée*, No. 70 (2009), pp. 45–62.

────── 'Aux racines sociales des conflits interlibanais', *Développement et civilisation*, No. 365 (2008), pp. 1–6.

Young, Michael, *The Ghosts of Martyrs Square. An Eyewitness Account of Lebanon's Life Struggle*, New York: Simon & Schuster, 2010.

Zahar, Marie-Joëlle, 'Foreign Intervention and State Reconstruction: Bosnian Fragility in Comparative Perspective', in Bojicic-Dzelilovic, Vesna, Denisa Kostovicova (eds), *State Weakness in the Balkans: Context, Comparison and Implications*, London: Ashgate, 2009, pp. 115–26.

———— 'Liberal Interventions, Illiberal Outcomes: The UN, Western Powers and Lebanon', in Newman, Edward, Roland Paris and Oliver Richmond (eds), *New Perspectives on Liberal Peacebuilding*, Tokyo: United Nations University Press, 2009, pp. 292–315.

———— 'Power Sharing in Lebanon: Foreign Protectors, Domestic Peace, and Democratic Failure', in Rothchild, Donald, and Philip Roeder (eds), *Sustainable Peace: Power and Democracy after Civil Wars*, Ithaca: Cornell University Press, 2005, pp. 219–40.

———— 'Peace by Unconventional Means: Evaluating Lebanon's Ta'if Accord', in Rothchild, Donald, Steve Stedman and Elizabeth Cousens (eds), *Ending Civil Wars: The Implementation of Peace Agreements*, Boulder: Lynne Rienner, 2002, pp. 567–97.

Zamir, Meir, *Lebanon's Quest: The Road to Statehood, 1926–1939*, London: I.B. Tauris and Co., 2000.

Zhang, Huafeng, and Åge A. Tiltnes, 'Socio-economic Assessment of Ein El-Hilweh Refugee Camp', *Tabulation report*, Fafo, December 2009.

Zisser, Eyal, 'The Maronites, Lebanon and the State of Israel: Early Contacts', *Middle Eastern Studies*, Vol. 31, No. 4 (1995), pp. 889–918.

INDEX

INDEX

Chamoun, Jean, 187
Chamseddine, Sheikh Mohammad
 Mahdi, 78
Chehab, Faud, 11, 32, 86, 128,
 146–7, 160, 162
Chirac, Jacques, 138, 165, 167
Christian community, 30, 85, 138,
 158, 160, 169
 '14 March' coalition and, 27, 30,
  71, 85, 96–7, 100, 138, 157,
  198, 199
 1992 elections, 71, 72, 76, 78
 2000 Election Law and, 75
 '8 March' bloc and, 30, 85, 96–7,
  100, 138, 157–8, 199
 al-ihbat almassihi (hopelessness and
  discontent), 70, 77
 army and security forces and, 94,
  95, 96–7
 in Beirut, 151, 152
Christian Lebanese lobbies in USA,
 71–3
civil war commemorations, 196,
 198–9
civil war disappearances, 222–3
 Free Patriotic Movement, 91
 Rafik Hariri's economic policy and,
  147–8
 intra-Maronite splits (late 1980s),
  96
 Israel and, 66
 militias, 30, 95, 96, 100, 128, 157,
  196–7, 198, 199
 see also Lebanese Forces (LF)
  (Christian militia)
 Taif Agreement (1989) and, 51, 56,
  65, 71, 76, 97
 see also Maronite community
Christian Right, 196–7, 198
citizenship, xvi–xvii, 83, 85, 202
civil war (1958), 65, 66, 86, 89, 222
civil war (1975–90)

1976 Constitutional Document, 33
8 March/14 March blocs and, 30–1
army and security forces and, 94–5
artistic works and projects on,
 187–93, 194, 195–6
Ballard's War Fever and, 219, 220,
 232
commemorations in urban spaces,
 195–6, 197, 199
contractor bourgeoisie and, 128–31
corporate consociationalism and,
 42–4
disappearances during, 222–3
displacement of population, 149
foreign intervention and, 32, 34–6,
 66
general amnesty after, 222
Geneva meetings (1983), 130
Theodor Hanf's work on, 31, 57,
 59
historiographic analysis of, 20,
 185–6, 187, 190–3, 199, 200,
 201
'history'-'memory' dichotomy, 20,
 185–95, 196–202
identity-forming narratives and,
 31–2
Lausanne meeting (1984), 130
massacres during, 196–7, 199
memory projects, 20, 185, 186,
 187–96, 199–202
militia agreement (1985), 130
militias and, 84, 94–5, 128, 133,
 156, 201–2, 222
motivations for fighting, 201–2
Multilateral Force (1982–3), 89
ownership of resistance struggle,
 196–200
pre-war political system and, 66
remembrance of, 13, 20, 185, 186,
 187–202
sectarian divide and, xvii, 5, 16, 29,
 30–1, 38, 65

304

INDEX

Saudi-Syria mediation efforts, 79,
230–1
sovereignty and, 10–11, 21, 31, 232
street protests against, 155, 158
Syria and, 15, 21, 178–9, 226, 227,
228, 229, 230–1, 232
strikes, 5, 101
Sukleen, 150, 151
Sunni community
'14 March' coalition, 27–8, 30, 85,
101, 138, 139–41, 157, 159,
167, 179
army and security forces and, 94,
101
in Beirut, 100, 133–5, 149, 150,
151, 155–6, 159, 168–73, 174,
177, 203–4, 212
break with Damascus (from 2005),
11
Cedar Revolution and, 166–7
conservative Islamic ideology, 117
contractor bourgeoisie and, 19,
127, 132–5, 138–43
corporate consociational framework
and, 5, 17, 40–1, 42, 43–53, 59,
65, 149
Future Movement and, 11–12, 17,
41, 43, 47, 51, 54, 56, 57, 58–9,
100, 139–40, 151, 156, 157
Hariri assassination and, 166–7,
169
Hariri family and, 11, 100, 126,
133–4, 136, 137–41, 144,
147–8, 151, 155–6, 159, 170–1,
177, 179
'Higher Islamic Council', 11
Hizbollah and, 53, 54–5, 117, 139,
141
insurgency in Syria and, 58–9
Islamist movements, 133, 140, 156
Jihadist militants and, 90, 91, 119
National Pact and, 32, 42–3,
127–8

numerical size of, 5
Palestinian refugee camps and, 91,
117, 118, 119
politics of the troika and, 42, 78,
91
pre-war bourgeoisie and, 127–8,
132–3, 140
regional power struggle with Shias,
66, 78–9, 100–1, 139, 144, 167
Saudi Arabia and, xviii, 35, 58, 78,
79, 137, 139, 140, 143, 167
Special Tribunal and, 21, 143, 229
Taif Agreement (1989) and, 16–17,
40–1, 43, 44–53, 56, 59, 65
turmoil in Arab world and, 57–8
see also sectarian divide, Sunni-Shia
Sûreté Générale, 98, 100
Syria
'14 March' coalition opposes, 27–8,
138, 139
Baathist political culture, 85, 86,
97–9, 160
'common destiny' (talazum al-
masarayn), 87
Damascus-Tehran alliance, 16, 26,
27, 35, 73, 77, 167, 225
demobilisation of militias and, 7,
68, 92, 95–6
exploitation of Lebanese economy,
95, 97–9
Issam Fares and, 130–1, 144
Gulf War and, 33, 36, 37
Rafik Hariri and, 3, 10, 132, 134,
138, 144, 147, 157, 165, 167
Hariri assassination and, 4, 10,
221, 224, 227, 229
hegemonic control of Lebanon
(1990–2005), 3–5, 16, 30,
32–40, 66–7, 72–4, 85–9, 95–9,
102, 132, 136–7, 146, 197–8
see also Taif Agreement (1989)
Hizbollah and, xviii, 4, 7, 11, 26,

36, 57, 58, 85, 92, 93, 94, 98,
139, 166, 197–8, 231
insurgency (from 2011), xv, xviii, 7,
15, 16, 21, 57, 58–9, 120, 181,
231, 233
international community's rapprochement with, 6, 228, 229
Iran-Syria-Hizbollah axis, 5, 25,
27, 35, 68, 72, 73, 79, 94, 96
Jihadist militants and, 90
Lebanese civil war and, 32, 34–6,
66
Lebanese security services and,
86–9, 95–6, 97–9, 102
Mikati family and, 130, 135, 144
Nahr al-Bared conflict and, 9
rapprochement with Saudi Arabia,
140
Saad Hariri and, 6, 138, 140, 160,
229
Security Council resolution 1559 and,
16, 221
Special Tribunal for Lebanon and, 15,
21, 178–9, 226, 227, 228, 229,
230–1, 232
as Sunni Arab homeland, 11
Taif Agreement (1989) and, 4, 10,
16, 26, 33, 34–6, 37, 39–40, 58,
69–70, 72, 73, 74, 77–8, 86,
132, 136
Treaty of Brotherhood (May 1991),
86–7
in US sphere of influence, 34–6,
37, 72
withdrawal from Lebanon (April
2005), 4, 6, 24, 25, 26, 27, 31,
56, 68, 73, 85, 138–9, 165, 166
see also al-Assad, Bashar; al-Assad,
Hafez
Syrian Social National Party (SSNP),
100, 101

Taif Agreement (1989)

allocation of the state's highest offices, 40, 44–5, 46, 47–50
Amal Movement and, 16–17,
40–1, 44, 45, 46–51, 55–7, 58
Christian community and, 51, 56,
65, 71, 76, 97
corporate consociational framework, 16–17, 31, 33, 35, 39–41,
42, 43, 44–56, 58, 59, 65–6
demobilisation of all non-state
armed groups, 7, 68, 92
distribution of parliamentary seats,
51, 55, 65
electoral districting system, 52
finance ministry post and, 44, 47
Future Movement and, 17, 40, 41,
43, 44, 46, 47, 48, 49, 50–3, 55,
56, 57–8
Rafik Hariri and, 35, 45, 47–8, 50
Hizbollah and, 16–17, 27, 35,
40–1, 44, 45, 46, 47–8, 49–51,
53, 55–7, 58, 68, 73–4, 75–6
implementation of, 10, 31, 33, 37,
50–5, 73
Maronite community and, 40, 41,
44, 45, 48, 49, 50, 59, 65, 77
military and police institutions,
84–5
National Pact (1943) and, 32–3,
65, 66
opposition veto power and, 71, 76,
77, 79
proper political representation
(sihat al-tamthil al-siyasi), 71,
75, 76, 80
proportional representation (PR)
and, 52
provision to abolish political confessionalism, 50, 51, 55
remembrance of civil war and, 13
Shia community and, 16–17, 40–1,
43, 44–51, 53, 55–6, 58, 59,
73–4, 75–6